D1598611

Discard

Gadamer's Repercussions

Gadamer's Repercussions

Reconsidering Philosophical Hermeneutics

EDITED BY

Bruce Krajewski

UNIVERSITY OF CALIFORNIA PRESS

Berkeley   Los Angeles   London

University of California Press
Berkeley and Los Angeles, California

University of California Press, Ltd.
London, England

© 2004 by the Regents of the University of California

Library of Congress Cataloging-in-Publication Data

Gadamer's repercussions : reconsidering philosophical
hermeneutics/edited by Bruce Krajewski.
    p.   cm.
  Includes bibliographical references and index.
  ISBN 0-520-23186-4 (cloth : alk. paper)
    1. Gadamer, Hans Georg, 1900–.   I. Krajewski, Bruce, 1959–
II. Title.
B3248.G34G37   2003
193—dc22

                                            2003017218

Manufactured in the United States of America
13   12   11   10   09   08   07   06   05   04
10   9   8   7   6   5   4   3   2   1

The paper used in this publication is both acid-free and totally
chlorine-free (TCF). It meets the minimum requirements of
ANSI/NISO Z39.48–1992 (R 1997) *(Permanence of Paper).* ∞

CONTENTS

ACKNOWLEDGMENTS / *vii*
PREFACE / *ix*
LIST OF ABBREVIATIONS / *xiii*

Introduction. From Word to Concept:
The Task of Hermeneutics as Philosophy / *1*
Hans-Georg Gadamer, translated by Richard E. Palmer

I. GADAMER'S INFLUENCE

1. After Historicism, Is Metaphysics Still Possible?
   On Hans-Georg Gadamer's 100th Birthday / *15*
   Jürgen Habermas, translated by Paul Malone

2. Being That Can Be Understood Is Language / *21*
   Richard Rorty

3. On the Coherence of Hermeneutics and Ethics:
   An Essay on Gadamer and Levinas / *30*
   Gerald L. Bruns

4. Gadamer and Romanticism / *55*
   Andrew Bowie

5. Literature, Law, and Morality / *82*
   Georgia Warnke

6. A Critique of Gadamer's Aesthetics / *103*
   Michael Kelly

II. GADAMER AND DIALOGUE

7. On Dialogue: To Its Cultured Despisers / *123*
   Donald G. Marshall

8. Gadamer's Philosophy of Dialogue and Its Relation to the
   Postmodernism of Nietzsche, Heidegger, Derrida, and Strauss / *145*
   Ronald Beiner

9. Meaningless Hermeneutics? / *158*
   Joel Weinsheimer

III. GADAMER IN QUESTION

10. Radio Nietzsche, or, How to Fall Short of Philosophy / *169*
    Geoff Waite

11. The Art of Allusion: Hans-Georg Gadamer's
    Philosophical Interventions under National Socialism / *212*
    Teresa Orozco, translated by Jason Gaiger

12. On the Politics of Gadamerian Hermeneutics:
    A Response to Orozco and Waite / *229*
    Catherine H. Zuckert

13. The Protection of the Philosophical Form:
    A Response to Zuckert / *244*
    Teresa Orozco, translated by Paul Malone

14. Salutations: A Response to Zuckert / *256*
    Geoff Waite

CONTRIBUTORS / *307*
INDEX / *311*

ACKNOWLEDGMENTS

I am indebted to the committee responsible for the Laurentian University Research Fund for its financial assistance in the production of this book and to the contributors for their edifying work. Gaby Miller kept finding ways to support my work. I am grateful to Diane Tessier, Interlibrary Loan Department, Laurentian University; to the Interlibrary Loan Department at Georgia Southern University; to Ed Dimendberg, who shepherded the book through its early stages at the University of California Press; to his successor, Laura Pasquale; to Kelly Smith, Pat Seguin, Doug Parker, Jesse Brady, Laura Duhan Kaplan, Mark Hochstrasser, David Darby, Tommy Armstrong; and to Don Marshall, who provided sagacious advice. Monika Beer helped to provide clues for making my way to publishers in Germany. Geoff Waite guided me toward understanding the larger picture. The translators who helped with this volume—Jason Gaiger, Paul Malone, Richard Palmer—deserve special mention for their scholarly labors. At a crucial point, Howard Kaplan in the Office for Research Services and Sponsored Programs at Georgia Southern contributed a significant sum to pay the permissions fee for the photograph on the cover. Eric Smoodin, Kate Toll, Cindy Fulton, Hillary Hansen, Randy Heyman, Sharron Wood, and the staff at University of California Press deserve thanks as well for their invaluable assistance.

This book is dedicated to my parents, George and Cathryn Krajewski, who encourage my efforts.

B. K.

PREFACE

This volume brings together some of the leading scholars in philosophical hermeneutics, as well as a few outsiders. Many of the contributors agreed to participate in this collection on the basis of their admiration for the work of Hans-Georg Gadamer, certainly one of the key German philosophers of the twentieth century, whose work has influenced not only philosophy but also the study of literature, art, music, sacred and legal texts, and medicine. The occasion for this collection was Gadamer's centenary in 2000. However, from the beginning, this collection was not intended as a festschrift, despite natural associations some have made when hearing about the catalyst for its production, nor did I set out to be disrespectful of Gadamer.

Some anticipated a celebratory volume, with the accompanying festive atmosphere. Others feared something like a replay of what has taken place with Ezra Pound, E. M. Cioran, Paul de Man, Martin Heidegger, Maurice Blanchot,[1] and others regarding those individuals' activities during the National Socialist period. This anxiety surfaced prior to Richard Wolin's "Untruth and Method: Nazism and the Complicities of Hans-Georg Gadamer,"[2] a triumphant piece of oddness (as noted by, among others, Richard Palmer) that, in part, tries to translate Gadamer's own statements about his political life into shocking discoveries. This is not to say that *res ipsa loquitur,* or that Gadamer revealed all that might seem relevant about *that* matter. As a former student of Heidegger, Gadamer might have anticipated that the interrogation lamp on Heidegger would be directed eventually at Heidegger's family, friends, acquaintances, and students as well. We cannot distance ourselves in our study of Heidegger from the judgment that condemns Heidegger for his political action and inaction. Substitute "Gadamer" for every instance of "Heidegger" in that last sentence, and one begins to sense a problem with Wolin's position, one that wants to come to grips with an intellectual stain that spreads across a number of figures, while simultaneously acting as if that gripping leaves Wolin's (or my own) hands unstained. Some of Gadamer's well-intentioned guardians, already on heightened alert after the appearance of Teresa Orozco's book about Gadamer,[3] want to protect him posthumously from an interrogation, as if wanting to avert a trauma, which seems, in my view, to run counter to the consensus among Gadamerian scholars about the importance of *openess,* of encounters with *otherness,* of *tradition,* and of *dialogue,* all terms requiring more, not less, attention in the context of a philosophy (philosophical hermeneutics) embedded in a tradition prone to concealment (see Gadamer on Plato's *Seventh Letter*) and explicitly linked to the figure Hermes, hardly a model of *Unverborgenheit.* Gadamer was well aware of the pertinence of Stanley Rosen's (Platonic) question, "To what extent, if any, can philosophy exist in public?"[4]

The energies that Gadamerian insiders devote to anxieties about the possibility of a more thorough accounting of Gadamer's life during National Socialism are misplaced.[5] As Geoff Waite put it in this volume, "neither Gadamer's acts of collaboration and opportunism nor their admission has proven 'devastating'" (265). Perhaps those energies can be redirected toward what James Risser claims is Gadamer's (and repeatedly his followers') interest in putting claims and judgments "to the test in shared inquiry so that what is is raised up in partial aspect and placed 'in the light of unconcealment' *[ins Licht Unverborgenheit].*"[6]

Unlike Wolin, Waite addresses Gadamer's life and writings during the National Socialist period as matters that *remain* pertinent. Waite is not looking back from a superior ethical position but is asking, among other things, how he himself is called into question by the circumstances that Gadamer faced. "Waite stresses that he does not really know what he would have done in circumstances the same as faced by Gadamer in the Third Reich" (281). No such self-examination is to be found in Wolin's article.

At least equally important in considering "why we should care"[7] about what went on with Gadamer in the Third Reich is linked to the complex relationship that philosophical hermeneutics has with the history of philosophy itself. While the information about Gadamer's "acts of collaboration and opportunism" has not been devastating, it has also not led to a reconsideration of the tradition that is philosophical hermeneutics, a tradition that ought to trouble those of us who study it. As Gerald Bruns explains, using the story of Oedipus as one of his examples, "the hermeneutical experience of what comes down to us from the past is structurally tragic rather than comic. It is an event that exposes us to our own blindness or the limits of our historicality and extracts from us an acknowledgment of our belongingness to something different, reversing what we had thought. It's just the sort of event that might drive us to put out our eyes."[8]

Gadamer's eyes, my own, and presumably yours are at stake. Working on this collection has reversed some things I had thought about philosophical hermeneutics. I see some things differently at this point. I have more work to do, more things for which to answer. Gadamer thought about his own eyes as well. In a telling passage that has relevance to the "Radio Nietzsche" chapter, Gadamer writes about the significance of the year 1900, "the year Nietzsche's eyes closed, and [Gadamer's] opened to—or beheld—the light of the world" *[in dem Nietzsche die Augen schloss und ich das Licht der Welt er-blickte].*[9] Implicit in this image is a continuation of sorts. One philosopher dies and another is born, one set of eyes closes while another set opens. What does Gadamer's late, disquieting ocular image suggest about his own view of his role as a philosopher immediately after Nietzsche?

My aims for the book were numerous. It seemed important to attend to some of Gadamer's writings that have received little or no attention in either English or German. Also, I wanted to invite people to rethink some of Gadamer's work, especially texts like *Truth and Method,* the book published in 1960 that in at least one sense put Gadamer on the intellectual map. For a work like *Truth and Method,* a number of people know already what they think about it, or what they are supposed to think, and I wanted contributors to consider whether that work—or others—might warrant revisiting, an attention to repercussions.

In some cases, contributors set out on their own, journeying through territory I had not imagined, resulting in some edifying surprises. From my view, one that not everyone will share of course, the best result of this set of essays is its provocation. This collection will call on readers and scholars of Gadamer to acknowledge that more is at stake with Gadamer's work than might be immediately apparent, stakes and repercussions that bind contributors and readers, and that call for something other than defensiveness and/or dismissal, and something other than celebration.

NOTES

1. See, for example, Paul Morrison, *The Poetics of Fascism: Ezra Pound, T. S. Eliot, Paul de Man* (New York: Oxford University Press, 1996); Adam Gopnik, "The Get-Ready Man [on Cioran]," *The New Yorker* (June 19 and 26, 2000), 172–80; Tom Rockmore and Joseph Margolis, eds., *The Heidegger Case: On Philosophy and Politics* (Philadelphia, Penn.: Temple University Press, 1992); and Steven Ungar, *Scandal and Aftereffect: Blanchot and France since 1930* (Minneapolis: University of Minnesota Press, 1995).

North American analytic philosophy has not been immune to similar scrutiny. See John McCumber's *Time in the Ditch: American Philosophy and the McCarthy Era* (Evanston, Ill.: Northwestern University Press, 2001).

2. Richard Wolin, "Untruth and Method: Nazism and the Complicities of Hans-Georg Gadamer," *The New Republic* (May 15, 2000): 36–45. See also the *International-ale Zeitschrift für Philosophie* 1 (2001), which is entitled *Schwerpunktthema: Hermeneutik*

und Politik in Deutschland vor und nach 1933. For some helpful corrections to Wolin's article, see Richard E. Palmer, "A Response to Richard Wolin on Gadamer and the Nazis," *International Journal of Philosophical Studies* 10.4 (2002): 467–82. See also "The real Nazis had no interest at all in us . . . ," an interview with Doerte von Westernhagen in *Gadamer in Conversation,* ed. and trans. Richard E. Palmer (New Haven, Conn.: Yale University Press, 2001), 115–32.

3. Teresa Orozco, *Platonische Gewalt: Gadamers politische Hermeneutik der NS-Zeit* (Berlin: Argument Verlag, 1995).

4. Stanley Rosen, "Man's Hope," *The Public Realm: Essays on Discursive Types in Political Philosophy,* ed. Reiner Schürmann (Albany: State University of New York Press, 1989), 44

5. An unfortunately typical but concise example of the ways in which scholars of philosphical hermeneutics treat the issue can be found on the dust jacket of the English translation of Jean Grondin's *Hans-Georg Gadamer: A Biography* (New Haven, Conn.: Yale University Press, 2003): "[Gadamer] chose to remain in his native Germany in the 1930s, neither supporting Hitler nor actively opposing him, but negotiating instead an unpolitical position that allowed him to continue his philosophical work." The section of this collection called "Gadamer in Question" asks of such scholars of philosophical hermeneutics how *they* continue to negotiate an unpolitical position that allows them to continue their philosophical work.

6. James Risser, *Hermeneutics and the Voice of the Other: Re-Reading Gadamer's Philosophical Hermeneutics* (Albany: State University of New York Press, 1997), 241.

7. Georgie Warnke, "Pace Wolin," *International Zeitschrift für Philosophie* 1 (2001): 77.

8. Gerald L. Bruns, *Hermeneutics Ancient and Modern* (New Haven, Conn.: Yale University Press, 1992), 204.

9. Hans-Georg Gadamer, Hermeneutische Entwürfe. Vorträge und Aufsäfe (Tübingen: Mohr Siebeck, 2000), 134.

ABBREVIATIONS

GADAMER

AP   *Ästhetik und Poetik I: Kunst als Aussage*. Tubingen: J.C.B. Mohr, 1993.

DD   "Destruktion and Deconstruction," in *Dialogue and Deconstruction: The Gadamer-Derrida Encounter,* ed. Diane Michelfelder and Richard Palmer. Albany, NY: SUNY Press, 1989.

EH   *The Enigma of Health: The Art of Healing in a Scientific Age.* Stanford: Stanford University Press, 1996.

GW   *Gesammelte Werke.* Tübingen: J. C. B. Mohr (Paul Siebeck) 1986 –.

IG   *The Idea of the Good in Platonic-Aristotelian Philosophy.* Trans. P. Christopher Smith. New Haven, Conn.: Yale University Press, 1986.

PA   *Philosophical Apprenticeships.* Trans. Robert R. Sullivan. Cambridge, MA: MIT Press, 1985.

PH   *Philosophical Hermeneutics.* Trans. David E. Linge. Berkeley: University of California Press, 1976.

PL   *Philosophische Lehrjahre: Eine Rückschau.* Frankfurt: Klostermann, 1977.

RAS   *Reason in the Age of Science.* Trans. Frederick G. Lawrence. Cambridge, MA: MIT Press, 1981.

RB   *The Relevance of the Beautiful and Other Essays.* Ed. Robert Bernasconi. Trans. Nicholas Walker. Cambridge: Cambridge University Press, 1986.

TM   *Truth and Method.* 2d revised ed. Trans. Joel Weinsheimer and Donald G. Marshall. New York: Crossroad, 1989.

VG   *Über die Verborgenheit der Gesundheit.* Frankfurt: Suhrkamp, 1993.

WM   *Wahrheit und Methode: Grundzüge einer philosophischen Hermeneutik.* 4th ed. Tübingen: J. C. B. Mohr (Paul Siebeck), 1975.

LEVINAS

AE   *Autrement qu'être ou au-delá l'essence.* The Hague: Martinus Nijhoff, 1974.

BPW   *Emmanuel Levinas: Basic Philosophical Writings.* Ed. Adriaan T. Pepezak, Simon Critchley, and Robert Bernasconi. Bloomington: Indiana University Press, 1996.

CPP   *Collected Philosophical Papers.* Transl. Alphonso Lingis. The Hague: Martinus Nijhoff, 1987.

DEHH   *En déouvrant l'existence avec Husserl et Heidegger.* 3d ed. Paris: Vrin, 1974.

EN   *Entre Nous: Essais sur le penser-à-l'autre.* Paris: Editions Grasset & Fasquelle, 1991.

HAH   *Humanisme de l'autre homme.* Montpellier: Fata Morgana, 1976.

LR   *The Levinas Reader.* Ed. Sean Hand. Oxford: Basil Blackwell, 1989.

NTR   *Nine Talmudic Readings.* Trans. Annette Aronowicz. Bloomington: Indiana University Press, 1990.

OTB   *Otherwise than Being or Beyond Essence.* Trans. Alphonso Lingis. The Hague: Martinus Nijhoff, 1981.

QL   *Quatre lectures talmudiques.* Paris: Editions de Minuit, 1968.

SS   *Du sacré au saint.* Paris: Editions de Minuit, 1977.

TeI   *Totalité et infini. Essai sur l'extériorité.* The Hague: Martinus Nijhoff, 1961.

TI   *Totality and Infinity: An Essay on Exteriority.* Trans. Alphonso Lingis. Pittsburgh, Penn.: Duquesne University Press, 1969.

TTO   "The Trace of the Other," in *Deconstruction in Context.* Ed. Mark Taylor. Chicago: University of Chicago Press, 1986.

OTHER

BT   Martin Heidegger. *Being and Time.* Trans. John Macquarrie and Edward Robinson. New York: Harper & Row, 1962.

Dde   *Dialogue and Deconstruction: The Gadamer-Derrida Encounter.* Ed. and trans. Diane P. Michelfelder and Richard E. Palmer. Albany, NY: State Univeristy of New York Press, 1989.

EPH   *Hans-Georg Gadamer on Education, Poetry, and History: Applied Hermeneutics.* Ed. Dieter Misgeld and Graeme Nicholson. Trans. Lawrence Schmidt and Monica Reuss. Albany, NY: State University of New York Press, 1992.

PHGG   *The Philosophy of Hans-Georg Gadamer.* Ed. Lewis Edwin Hahn. Chicago: Open Court, 1997.

SR   *The Specter of Relativism: Truth, Dialogue, and "Phronesis" in Philosophical Hermeneutics.* Ed. Lawrence K. Schmidt. Evanston, IL: Northwestern University Press, 1995.

SZ   Martin Heidegger. *Sein und Zeit.* Tübingen: Max Neimeyer, 1984.

Introduction

From Word to Concept

The Task of Hermeneutics as Philosophy

HANS-GEORG GADAMER, *translated by Richard E. Palmer*

I would first like briefly to justify the theme I have chosen, namely: "from word to concept." The subject matter is a topic belonging both to philosophy and to hermeneutics. In truth, concepts are really one of the distinguishing marks of philosophy. Indeed, philosophy first entered Western culture in this form. For this reason the concept is the first thing I would like to discuss. Of one thing I am sure: the concept, which very often presents itself as something strange and demanding, must begin to speak if it is to be really grasped. For this reason I would first like to revise my topic a little to read: "*Not only from word to concept but likewise from concept to word.*"

Let's think back to the beginning for a moment. The point we must start out from is the fact that conceptual thinking is a basic characteristic of the Occident. But even the word "Occident" [*Abendland,* land of the evening] is no longer so current as it was in my youth, when Oswald Spengler announced its decline.[1] Today, we would prefer to speak of "Europe," but again nobody really knows what Europe will be; at most we know what we would like it to be one day. For this reason I believe my topic is not so very far removed from the most pressing questions of today. Nor do I think I have simply chosen to speak again about one of my favorite topics to express my thanks for this festive occasion. Rather, because these are questions I am continuously at work on, I want to confront them here once again.

How did it really come about in human history, that in the very dire historical situation in which the Greek city-state culture found itself (i.e., under pressure from the Persian, the Asiatic, and later the Punic African spirit) at exactly this time conceptual thinking, the enduring intellectual creation whose bright rays have streamed out over the globe right down to the present day, arose in Greek culture? You all know, of course, what I am referring to. I am speaking about *science*—obviously about that science we all learn in school, Euclidean geometry first and foremost. What wonderful precision it displayed in logically proving things that nobody doubted, yet which nevertheless required the very highest intellectual effort for their proof! This success in proving represents an intellectual heroic deed that moved human thought for the first time beyond all knowledge based on experience *[Erfahrungswissen]* and founded what is now called "science" *[Wissenschaft]*.

I can speak only with greatest admiration about what this powerful capacity of reason truly is: the miracle of numbers and geometry that grounds the enormous edifice of mathematics. If I begin with this basic assumption that science had its birth in Greece and it was from the Greeks that we inherited our thinking and reflection about the possibility of knowledge as such, then I would go on to pose the further question: What does knowing *[Wissen]* signify for us?

You know the answer. It appears in the form in which Socrates received his reply from the Delphic oracle: *that no human being then living was wiser than he.* His great admirer and disciple, Plato, has shown us what this wisdom consists of, namely knowing about not knowing. It is the uncompromising and incorruptible manner by which we humans seek, during the short span of life that ends in death, to comprehend the other person, the unknown, the *ignoramus* and *ignorabimus,* the not-knowing of our true place in the world.

If I begin to ponder the matter in this way, then the following question presses itself on me: How has this mathematizing capacity of the Greeks, this logical power, this taking shape of the most speakable of all languages—as Nietzsche called Greek (but in truth all languages are speakable for those who understand how to think)—how did it manage to gain prominence throughout the world? If we pose the question in this way, I think we come somewhat nearer the theme, *"word and concept,"* and therewith closer to what I have in mind when I focus on the situation of the world today and on our conception of the world, a conception that must no longer be purely Eurocentric.

There can be no uncertainty any more that the effects of our science-based civilization, with its unbelievable capacity to alter the givens of nature for our own use, life, and survival, have become a tremendous, worldwide problem. There is no doubt that all this has become an important question that is addressed to us, not least because science itself has taught us more and more about what a very short episode humanity represents within the evolution of the universe.

Along with the privilege of our present power to transform the given, have we not received one last great gift? Also along with this power, have we perhaps been presented with a task that completely exceeds the powers of our understanding? When one looks beyond what we regard as the "civilized motherland" of European and Anglo-Saxon cultural traditions, when one looks around the world today—at Japan, China, India, South Africa, or South America—one finds that in all these cultures the same mathematized and formalized thinking is gaining the upper hand. How will these two factors go together? Or will one dominate the other? Somehow, a global transformation is emerging. I don't want to argue here that the international adoption of the British bathroom betokens a revolution, or that the adoption of the European business suit in offices from Japan to China to India is deeply significant, but rather that at least in certain realms of life a unitary cultural model is emerging, which, like a revolution, is turning everything upside down.

In all this there is a fact worth considering: whole blocks of humanity that are quite different from each other in terms of cult, religion, and honoring their ancestors—in short, that have different collective ways of living together in conformity with their social rules—these cultures are now confronted by the resplendent methodological mastery represented by science. Indeed, we can measure our fate by how, either harmonizing or clashing, this fusing of cultures takes place, perhaps even shaping our own future. Or better: *by how that future will be determined by us.* Our fate will be decided by how well the world that bears the stamp of science, and that was philosophically expressed through the world of concepts, will be able to bring itself into harmony with the equally deep insights into the destiny of humanity that have come to expression, for example, in a dialogue of a Chinese master with his disciple, or in other kinds of testimony from religiously founded cultures that are completely strange to us.

How have we gotten ourselves into this situation? Not completely without poetry, and this holds true for the Greek world as well. The oldest written evidence of Greek conceptual thinking comes in the form of Homeric poetry—testimonies sung in Homeric verse. Not philosophy but the epic stands at the beginning of our written heritage. And we experience this when we see how *the concept suddenly began to speak*—spreading suddenly from Greek city-state cultures to the whole Mediterranean world—when, embedded in the lines of a verse text, it uttered the question, *ti to on*—What is being? What is it we call nothingness?

I could continue and show how Plato's question actually developed out of this one question and led to the establishing of metaphysics, which through Aristotle finally came to be accepted throughout the world and left its imprint on two thousand years of Western thought, until from out of it in the seventeenth century modern science emerged, as well as the modern sciences of experience and mathematics. But at the moment, it is perhaps more appropriate for us to remember that we are in a room dedicated to Hegel. So we have good reason to recall that it was Hegel who saw himself faced with the philosophical task of gathering together the new "sciences" and everything else that did not merge with science, such as metaphysics and religion, and thereby to raise them up into a the unitary whole of an encompassing concept.

The modern sciences of experience, on the one hand, with their mathematical instrumentalization, and the Socratic thinking that constantly questions things, on the other, seeking the Good with an attitude of not-knowing—these are two ways of experiencing reality that do not seem to go together. Perhaps for a moment we should venture the leap of laying out before ourselves how this great cultural epoch of modern Europe had reached a certain fulfillment when Hegel sought to make persuasive a reconciliation between the truth of the sciences, the truth of metaphysics, and that of the Christian religion.

Hegel did not bring this about through the mad delusion that science is the unconditional master of cultivating certainty through method. No, one should not forget that as Hegel strove for his great synthesis between the absolute knowledge of metaphysics and the exact knowledge of the methodical sciences, he also always envisioned within this synthesis the message of art and of religion. For Hegel, this synthesis was not just a matter of mastering certain areas of knowledge with the help of abstraction and measurement; it involved those forms of knowing or forms of questioning that *do not let go of us,* such as when we stand before works of art or when we are touched by poetic creations. Also, works that invite theological reflection or fulfill the pious requirement for human beings to consider their finitude reach a very moving intensity.

There was a time when one was well aware that this kind of knowing was quite different from that of mathematics and logic. At that time, for example, one called the study of law "juris*prudence*"—that is, a kind of intelligence or wisdom in judging. Law students were to develop in themselves a power of making distinctions so that they could judge what was right in a balanced, differentiated, and "objective" way.

In the meantime, however, the "scientific" ideal been so able to absolutize itself today that [in German] one now terms the study of law the *science* of law *[Rechtswissenschaft]* and the study of art the *science* of art *[Kunstwissenschaft]*. Earlier, the study of art was called the history of art *[Kunstgeschichte]*. And in Germany today, the discipline of studying literature is called the *science* of literature *[Literaturwissenschaft]*, when earlier it was called the history of literature. What the earlier term signified was that from the beginning one assumed that one cannot "know" literature in the same sense that one obtains "knowledge" through measurement and mathematics following the model of the natural sciences. A quite different capacity was required for this kind of knowledge.

When I have the honor, as now, of speaking at an institution oriented to

the "sciences" of the human spirit [*Geisteswissenschaften,* meaning the humanities and also the social sciences, sometimes translated as the "human
sciences"], I do this well aware that these "sciences" *[Wissenschaften]* are
not sciences in the rigorous mathematical and natural scientific sense. Although the social sciences have certainly applied mathematical methods in
their historically developed forms of methodical-critical research, I believe
they are nevertheless also guided and determined by other things: historical models *[Vorbilder],* experience, strokes of fate, and in any case by a different kind of exactness from that in mathematical physics.

In the natural sciences one speaks of the "precision" of mathematizing.
But is the precision attained by the application of mathematics to living
situations ever as great as the precision attained by the ear of the musician
who in tuning his or her instrument finally reaches a point of satisfaction?
Are there not quite different forms of precision, forms that do not consist
in the application of rules or in the use of an apparatus, but rather in a grasp
of what is right that goes far beyond this? I could go into endless examples
to make plausible what I mean when I say that hermeneutics is not a doctrine of methods for the humanities and social sciences *[Geisteswissen-
schaften]* but rather a basic insight into what thinking and knowing mean
for human beings in their practical life, even if one makes use of scientific
methods.

A distinctive capacity is required in human beings in order for them to make
the right use of human knowledge. Plato once posed the question—and
not in some context distant from my point: What really constitutes the true
statesman? I venture to say that for Plato such a statesman was not just thinking of how to win the next election. Rather, Plato had something essentially
different in mind, a quite specific talent: a certain instinctive feeling for balance, an instinct for creating situations of balance and for sensing the many
possibilities of how to create and manage situations so as to maintain balance. In his dialogue about the true statesman *[The Statesman],* Plato at one
point speaks at some length about this ability. He starts out by presupposing
that there are two different possible ways of measuring, and both appear to
be indispensable. In the first form of measuring one goes after things with
a ruler in order to make them available and controllable, like the meter-
ruler in Paris that all other metric measurements must follow. Here one is
clearly concerned with what the Greeks called *poson,* quantity.

The second kind of measuring consists of striking the "right measure,"
finding what is appropriate. We experience this, for example, in the wonder
of harmonious tones sounding together, or in the harmonious feeling of
well-being that we call "health." This concerns what the Greeks called *poion,*
quality.

I was able to elucidate this distinction not so long ago in my book *The Enigma of Health* (VG, EH), dealing specifically with illness as the object of medical science. Illness in itself is certainly a threat that one has to be on guard against. When one becomes ill, a doctor with knowledge and skill is needed, and one hopes that the doctor can "bring it under control" *[beherrschen]*. Health, on the other hand, is clearly something quite different, something we do not observe or control in the same way. Rather, it is something we follow—like a path, for example. When we are on this path we have the feeling that "now we are headed in the right direction." The path under our feet becomes a way. There are, of course, many other instances in addition to becoming physically healthy that I register as a clear contrast to the ideal of scientific governance and control.

We understand the term "scientific rigor" *[Wissenschaftlichkeit]* to mean objectivity, and it is surely a good thing for us to bring under critical control the subjective presuppositions that are in play when one observes anything. Scientific results must in principle be clearly understandable and repeatable by anyone. This is what makes the idea of objective knowledge possible. All this is fully in order. But one should also not forget what the word "object" in German means. It mean "standing-against" *[Gegenstand]*, that is, *resisting* *[Widerstand]*. In the sphere of illness and health, however, we are dealing with a knowing *[Wissen]* that does not simply rule over and control objects. For with regard to health, we cannot simply reconstruct the ways of Nature. Rather, we must be content to break the resistance of the illness and to help Nature prevail using her own secret ways. To do this requires the *art* of the doctor to find the "right measure." This is not just science *[Wissenschaft]* but rather a different kind of knowing that with its own fulfillment withdraws, one might say. Certainly this concept of art as something that basically only helps nature prevail is something different from what "art" is in the creative and formative arts and also the literary arts. But even here one finds something akin to it in how these arts are carried out, and this marks a kind of boundary between it and what one associates with the objectivity of science. In medicine as in other arts one is concerned with much more than the mere application of rules.

In my book *Truth and Method,* I began my considerations first of all with art, and not with "science" or even with the human sciences *[die Geisteswissenschaften]*. Even within the human sciences it is *art* that brings the basic questions of human being to our awareness in such a unique way—indeed, in such a way that no resistance or objection against it arises. An artwork is like a model *[ein Vorbild]*.

By this I mean that an artwork is, so to speak, irrefutable *[unwiderleglich]*. For example, one calls poetry irrefutable. Consider what the German word *"Gedicht"* [poem] means. Here, once again, it helps to know a bit of Latin. *Gedicht* comes from the Latin *dicere* [to say] and also *dictare* [to dictate]. This mean a poem is a *Diktat* [something dictated, as in taking dictation, or more strongly, a command]. The poem compels through the way it says what it says. Indeed, this holds for all rhetorical uses of language. But the poem compels over and over, and the better one knows it, the more compelling it is. Nobody would ever object to listening to a recitation by saying that he or she already knew the poem.

In disciplines like art history, literature, and music [*Musikwissenschaft*, the "science" of music], and likewise in the classical studies of philology and archaeology, one who never really opens him- or herself up to a work of art but still claims to be an expert in the field, who always knows it better, is really a "philistine." In all the sciences that I understand a bit about, there comes a moment in which something is *there*, something one should not forget and cannot forget. This is not a matter of mastering an area of study. Take, for example, the discipline of art history. In art history the requirements of science, as such, appear to be satisfied in all areas where we can successfully apply historical methods. This is the reason, I think, that iconography has become so popular in the modern science of art [*Kunstwissenschaft*]. But is scientific knowing what art has in mind? In iconography whether the object of questioning is a work of art or not does not matter. Hence, for iconography, kitsch is really far more interesting.

I am not saying that this is the case for the genuine historian of art; but for understandable reasons, the scientized historical method of understanding works of pictorial art continues to gain importance in academic circles. This should not, however, be the only permissible approach. I fully believe and hope that here, and everywhere, a balance between both forms of knowledge is attainable, a balance that accepts both the scientific and the artistic sides. In the passage from Plato's *Statesman* that we mentioned earlier, you will recall that Plato, too, expressly states that both kinds of measuring are required—the measuring that measures, and the "right measure," the appropriate [*das Angemessene*], that one tries to find. There are other cases of this kind that I would claim have an equal right to stand alongside the scientific ideal. In science, as I have said, one is generally concerned with a knowing that breaks down resistance, and only in the end does it require art [rather than science], an aptitude for art [*Kunstfertigkeit*] that I illustrated with the example of the physician. This second sort of knowing supports itself, carries within itself a capacity of its own that involves itself [*sich einsetzt*]. This is the reason I have focused on these forms of knowledge, and not just because I have a special preference for the arts. I think it is not permissible that one form should try to be the whole answer: one form of measuring is not more important than the other. Rather, both forms are important.

There is something we also can learn from the German word for measure: we say in German, for instance, "He has a measured nature [*hat ein gemessenes Wesen],* always appropriate."[2] What is expressed in these words is something like the security of a balance between open-mindedness *[Aufgeschlossenheit]* and peace within oneself. Now, in these observations I do not presume to situate myself within the social sciences. Indeed, I have no competence to talk about the social sciences in the way that, for example, a political scientist can. Nevertheless, we can consider what "politics" is in relation to the miracle of balance. What is this, really? Let me give you an example of this miracle that I myself experienced as a youth, when I learned to ride a bicycle. I had a somewhat lonely youth and received a bicycle to keep me occupied. I had to learn to ride it all by myself. There was a little hill in our back yard, and there I tried to teach myself how to ride it. I climbed up the hill and after a few failed attempts made a great discovery: as long as I held onto the handlebars as tight as I could, I always tipped over! But suddenly I stopped this and it happened as if by itself. Today, I see in this example what the politicians have learned and what their task is: they must above all create a balance if they want to steer toward and reach their goal.

If a politician wants to realize future possibilities at all, he or she must be persuasive, and this is not easy. Here, the decisive point is the same as in our example. It is virtually unbelievable that a little less pressure in holding onto the handlebars, even just a little bit less, enables one to hold the bicycle in balance and to steer it. But if you exert just a little too much pressure, then suddenly nothing goes right. I apply this experience not just to politics, however, but to all our behavior, conditioned as it is by modern forms of life where we are governed by rules, prescriptions, and orders. Yet a proper conformity to such an order is not a matter of blindly and angrily applying rules. What I am talking about here is first of all simply the consequence that follows from a well-regulated conformity to the proper rules of behavior. The reshaping of reality by modern technology now poses new tasks for us all. We must make justice our starting point and central concern, and in particular we must make right use of our knowledge and ability to do things.

Environmental problems force themselves on us here. Nature, too, is a reality that one cannot protect solely by means of measuring and calculating. Rather, it is something with which and in which one must learn to live, so that one may breathe more freely. It is essential, then, that we behave more appropriately. We all feel this in ourselves, I think, when we observe animals in their ways of life. We should hold them in respect in the same way that one holds in respect other human beings with their varied beliefs and ways of life.

These are relevant questions that we are all struggling with today, for now we see what depends on them: movements to settle inequities, to create balance, and for exchange. It is essential, therefore, to recognize all the varied forms of human life and the expressions of their particular worldviews. In doing so, we find ourselves in the realm of hermeneutics. This I call the art of understanding. But what is understanding, really? Understanding, whatever else it may mean, does not entail that one agrees with whatever or whomever one "understands." Such a meeting of the minds in understanding would be utopian. Understanding means that I am able to weigh and consider fairly *what the other person thinks!* One recognizes that the other person could be right in what he or she says or actually wants to say. Understanding, therefore, is not simply mastering something that stands opposite you *[das Gegenüber]*, whether it is the other person or the whole objective *[gegenständliche]* world in general. Certainly understanding can be this, so that one understands in order to master or control. Indeed, man's will to rule over nature is natural and it makes our survival possible. Even the story of creation in the Old Testament speaks of this order of the world and of humans reigning over all of nature. And yet it still remains true that ruling and the will to power are not everything.

Indeed, it is important that the extent of this ruling over nature be kept within limits by other powers, especially those of commonality—in the family, in comradeship, in human solidarity—so that one understands and is understood. Understanding always means first of all: oh, now I understand what you want! In saying this, I have not said that you are right or that you will be judged to be correct. But only if we get to the point that we *understand* another human being, either in a political situation or in a text, will we be able to communicate with one another at all. Only when we consider seriously the enormous tasks that await humanity in the future, only then, I think, will we also come to appreciate the world-political significance of *understanding*. You will recall how I pictured the world at the beginning of this lecture. A cadre of highly educated East Asians is attending German and European universities. Very often they astonish us with the tremendous discipline with which they work, and the rapidity with which they are able to produce perfectly written texts, even though oral expression is sometimes almost impossible. It is just unbelievable that many of these people speak almost unintelligibly but are able to write error-free texts! These are differences in communicative behavior that we must become aware of in their broad significance if we are to encounter other cultures. All this goes both ways, of course. The Japanese student coming here probably also finds at first that we do not speak intelligibly but only squawk and sputter.

This will be a task of the future world, of that I am sure. Just as we must realize that people speaking other languages do not just babble but are really speaking, so too they, for their part, will need at least to become familiar with our world if they want to speak and understand German and not just hear it as some kind of squawking and sputtering.

This venturesome elite of East Asian scholars is already doing a lot in this regard, and it should be self-evident to us that their efforts do not entail giving up their own inherited ways of life and their own basic religious ideas. Of course, we do not know anything about what the great conversations of the future between members of different religions may hold in store. And while our young people today in their own stressful years of development find a guru from India fascinating, it is still essential that they should learn to understand the other ways of life as wholes, that they understand all that comprises the basis of these cultures: the view of the family, of ancestors, death, and the living on of ancestors within us, and also such a decisive concept in these cultures as their evaluation of human life. In part, all of these are controlled by forms of lawfulness quite different from those that have become natural to us through our long history of Christian education and culture. And when we define philosophy as hermeneutics, we cannot be satisfied just to repeat the same thing as existed before, as if what hermeneutics basically wanted were simply to put forward a conservative view of the world that merely extended Christian values. Perhaps, but only perhaps, this might suffice as a standard for arriving at an understanding of understanding in Europe. But such a standard is far too narrow.

I do not know what answers humanity will one day finally arrive at concerning how people will live together, either in relation to the rights of the individual versus the rights of the collective, or in relation to the violence that comes from the family or from the state. Consider just the almost unbelievable miracle that the communist revolution in China, which surely has not dealt gently with the elders, was, even with its almost unlimited power, unable to destroy the family order. So clearly there are everywhere in the world individualities and customs of irreconcilable otherness. I do venture to say, however, that if we do not learn hermeneutic virtue—that is, if we do not realize that it is essential first of all to *understand* the other person if we are ever to see whether in the end perhaps something like the solidarity of humanity as a whole may be possible, especially in relation to our living together and surviving together—if we do not, we will never be able to accomplish the essential tasks of humanity, whether on a small scale or large.

It is easy to claim that humankind today is in a desperate situation. For we have finally reached the point where human beings threaten to destroy themselves, and everyone can become aware of this. Doesn't this pose for everyone today a genuine task of thinking: to be very clear about the fact that human solidarity must be the basic presupposition under which we can work together to develop, even if only slowly, a set of common convictions *[gemeinsame Überzeugungen]*? It seems to me that while European civilization has admirably brought to full development the culture of science with its technical and organizational applications, it has for the past three centuries neglected the law of balance.

It has come into possession of deadly weapons of mass destruction, but has it developed a level of maturity high enough to realize what responsibility our culture now bears for humanity as a whole? Is it not the case that in all such questions, we are faced with tasks that require a consciousness possessed of far-sightedness and carefulness *[Weitsicht und Vorsicht]*, and also an openness to each other, if we are to carry out the tasks that will shape our future, tasks whose accomplishment is necessary for peace and reconciliation?

I am of the opinion that with all our technical and scientific progress we still have not learned well enough how to live with each other and with our own progress. I would like to close with the following remark: What I have tried to make clear to you today is that hermeneutics as philosophy is not some kind of methodological dispute with other sciences, epistemologies, or such things. No, hermeneutics asserts something nobody today can deny: we occupy a moment in history in which we must strenuously use the full powers of our *reason,* and not just keep doing science only.

Without our bringing concepts to speak and without a common language, we will not be able to find the words that will reach other persons. It is true that the way goes "from word to concept," but we must also be able to move "from concept to word," if we wish to reach the other person. Only if we accomplish both will we gain a reasonable understanding of each other. Only in this way, too, will we possess the possibility of so holding ourselves back that we can allow the other person's views to be recognized. I believe it is important to become so absorbed in something that one forgets oneself in it—and this is one of the great blessings of the experience of art, as well as one of the great promises of religion. Indeed, in the end this is one of the basic conditions for human beings to be able to live together at all in a human way.

NOTES

"Vom Wort zum Begriff. Der Aufgabe der Hermeneutik als Philosophie" by Hans-Georg Gadamer first appeared in a volume in the Bamberger Hegelwoche series, *Menschliche Endlichkeit und Kompensation,* ed. Odo Marquard (Bamberg: Verlag Fränkischer Tag, 1995), 111–24, and is reprinted with permission of Universitäts Verlag Bamberg © 1995. The text dates back to an address given in the Bamberger Hegelwochen of 1994, an occasion on which Gadamer received an honorary doctorate. Subsequently, in 1996, the essay appeared in a handsome limited-edition volume by Hans-Georg Gadamer, *Die Modern und die Grenze der Vergegenständlichung,* edited by Bernd Klüser with contributions by Hans Belting, Gottfried Boehm, and Walther Ch. Zimmerli, and with five plates of modern art by Sean Scully (Munich: Bernd Klüser, 1996), 19–40. In 1997 it was included in the *Gadamer Lesebuch,* edited by Jean Grondin (Tübingen: Mohr Siebeck, 1997), 100–110. The present translation is from the original Bamberg publication, but the two later texts have been consulted, and the slight changes and corrections introduced by Gadamer in the later editions have been incorporated into this translation. One of these changes is the omission of Gadamer's opening words of greeting to the Bamberg audience, which were also omitted from the *Gadamer Lesebuch*. Professor Gadamer, when consulted by the translator, felt that these words of greeting need not be included in the present publication of the essay. The translator wants to thank Lawrence K. Schmidt for his careful review of this translation and Meredith Cargill for many helpful comments.

1. Oswald Spengler, *Der Untergang des Abendlandes: Umrisse einer Morphologie der Weltgeschichte*, vol. 1, *Gestalt und Wirklichkeit* (Vienna: Wilhelm Braumüller, 1918); vol. 2, *Welthistorische Perspektiven* (Munich: Oscar Beck, 1922). There are innumerable editions by Beck, and the work has been translated into English and six other languages. The English translation is *The Decline of the West,* vol. 1, *Form and Actuality;* vol. 2, *Perspectives of World History* (New York: Alfred Knopf, 1926 and 1928, then in one volume in 1932).

2. *"Steckt in Angemessenheit"* in the Bamberger text, corrected to *"stets in Angemessenheit"* in the *Gadamer Lesebuch,* 106.

PART ONE

Gadamer's Influence

Chapter 1

After Historicism, Is Metaphysics Still Possible?

On Hans-Georg Gadamer's 100th Birthday

JÜRGEN HABERMAS, *translated by Paul Malone*

Understanding and Event [Verstehen und Geschehen] was to be the title of *Truth and Method* after the publisher expressed his dissatisfaction with the dry suggestion *Principles of a Philosophical Hermeneutics* and the pioneering title *Truth and Method* had not yet been hit upon. Over the decades, this book has stimulated philosophical discussion in Germany as no other. Its career is not so much owing to its manifestly hostile stance toward the human sciences, which misunderstand their "understanding" as method; rather, its success can be explained by the relevance of one basic question that Gadamer's hermeneutics seeks to answer. The original title, *Understanding and Event*, well expresses this thought: the interpreter's understanding "belongs to" an event produced by the text itself, which is in need of interpretation.

THE CHALLENGE

Philosophical hermeneutics seeks to lead the way out of a dilemma that the young Gadamer saw himself faced with when he took up his studies in Breslau and continued them in Marburg. The rise of the historical human sciences in the nineteenth century had shattered philosophy's confidence in an overarching reason through the course of history. "Time," as it was soon afterward thematized in Heidegger's *Being and Time,* and which inexorably transformed all theories into historical constructs, had affected the core of reason.

The historicizing intellectual movement could no longer be tamed by conventional conceptual means. The return to a transcendental critique of science in the style of neo-Kantianism failed, as did the epistemological realist break from the transcendental prison in the style of a Nicolai Hartmann, whose stratified ontology Gadamer became acquainted with first-

hand. If the unity of reason disintegrates into the multiplicity of its historical voices, however, the truth must relinquish its claim to universal validity.
What, then, safeguards the binding force of our judgments, of our very ori-
entations in life?

This question became charged with existential significance, taking on
a completely new dimension when Gadamer attended the lectures of the
Privatdozent Heidegger in the summer semester of 1923 in Freiburg. The
answer that the mature Gadamer would ultimately find, of course, distances
him further from Heidegger than he himself would care to acknowledge.

From the observer's standpoint, Gadamer concedes that historicism is
correct. He is convinced that "the legacy of the classical-Christian tradition,
common to us all, no longer bears our weight." In the philosophically relevant sense of metaphysical interpretations of reason, too, this tradition is no
longer "weight-bearing." The fact that the binding force of our vital orien-
tations has been dependent on the persuasiveness of such a tradition steers
Gadamer's thought along the hermeneutic perspective. How does the living acquisition of authoritative traditions appear from the perspective of
the participants themselves? We too, the historically disillusioned contemporaries, are indeed participants. We become entangled in formative processes so long as we grow up with identity-forming traditions.

Our historically enlightened culture, of course, poses itself the question
whether, in the reflexively fractured attitude of the now widespread historical consciousness, we can find our way back to a means of taking up traditions that leaves the binding force of persuasive traditions undamaged.
Philosophical hermeneutics seeks an answer by means of a critique of the
false methodological self-conception of the human sciences. It is to be a
liberal-conservative answer, not the conservative-revolutionary answer of
Heidegger.

Heidegger directs his eschatological glance forward. After 1945 his ex-
pectant gaze, converted to apocalyptic ideas, is fixed on the withdrawal
symptoms of a destitute present that seem to herald the approach of something wholly other, of the absent God. Gadamer looks in the opposite direction. He casts his rescuing eye back toward the endangered substance to be
hermeneutically won from a bountiful tradition. After Hegel and after historicism, he discovers the source of the authority of a historically affected
fluid reason in the civilizing power of tradition.

THE CONTINUITY OF A LONG LIFE

A tradition can be convincing only, of course, if it remains current due to
the influence of "classic" works. On the basis of works that themselves make
repeated claims to topicality, new criteria are continually formed. It is the

great works, or the "eminent texts," that establish the connection of "understanding and event." With every new interpretation by a successive generation, of course, the criteria of judgment change. That which stays constant through this change, that which promises unity, universality, and generality, is solely the standard-setting power of the classic itself. The general becomes a constant in the medium of the effective history of authentic works.

Gadamer enjoys the rare privilege of a long life, spanning the century. He can thus check his hermeneutic insights against a contemporary context that now reaches into the fourth generation. The organic soundness of a constitution that was by no means robust from birth may have confirmed him in his experience of the continuity of a "weight-bearing" event. (As an adult, Gadamer was stricken with infantile paralysis.) No less endangered than the health of the body, indeed, is the continuity of the selfhood that we ascribe to ourselves. Gadamer seems, through all the historic crises of the century, to have remained himself. Kant lived to be eighty, Schelling almost eighty. Those too, taking into account the change in life expectancy, were long life spans. The sheer length, however, of Gadamer's experienced period of ruptures and accelerations through this entire catastrophe-ridden century—this is indeed unprecedented.

The thorough biography of Gadamer by Jean Grondin is essentially free of hagiographic tendencies. All the more convincingly, it draws the portrait of an intellect at first hesitant and uncertain, unpolitical and adaptable, but always liberal and self-critical; provided with shrewdness, sensitivity, and a sure eye by his good middle-class background; classically educated and independent of judgment. Gadamer holds with great energy to his early acquired basic philosophical themes and insights.

The student assimilated the end of the First World War with Spengler and Theodor Lessing, in the style of the then widespread middle-class intellectual quietism and cultural pessimism. The lecturer in Marburg experienced the end of the Weimar Republic with concern, but from a distance; and he maneuvered himself with caution, diplomatic skill, and a little luck through the 1930s, without breaking off amicable contacts with Löwith and other emigrants. The professor in Leipzig avoided the political involvement in which many of his contemporaries, out of opportunism or conviction, became entangled during the Nazi period.

The rector, appointed by the authorities of the Soviet occupation, made an astonishingly aggressive speech, marked by the consciousness that the corrupted German university was not in need of "self-assertion" but rather of renewal. To the trinity of a certain other rectoral address, to Heidegger's 1933 expressed recommendation of "labor service, military service, and service to knowledge," Gadamer replies by invoking the hermeneutic virtues of objectivity, honesty with oneself, and tolerance of others.

THE LATE COMING TO INFLUENCE

The successor to Jaspers's chair gained public stature in West Germany—and an outstanding influence in his discipline. Gadamer, together with Helmuth Kuhn, made the *Philosophische Rundschau* the leading journal in the field. And Heidelberg would not have become the philosophical center of West Germany for two or three decades had he not brought Löwith back from emigration and, with such colleagues as Henrich, Spaemann, Theunissen, and Tugendhat, gathered round himself the best of the succeeding generation as well. At the end of his active, extremely successful teaching career, the now-famous philosophical teacher reacted to the student protests certainly not with sympathy, but without widespread hostility. Open as ever, he became involved with Karl-Otto Apel and others in debates on hermeneutics and ideological critique. He faced up, in his way, to the *Zeitgeist* that had been set in motion.

A remarkable aspect of Gadamer's fitful intellectual life journey is his late coming to influence. Not until the 1950s did he force himself—or allow himself to be moved by the words of his clear-sighted wife—to work his course lectures on the "Introduction to the Human Sciences" and on "Art and History," polished over the decades, into a book. It was completed in his sixtieth year. His peers of the 1950s and 1960s—Popper, Adorno, and Gehlen—although they were two, three, and four years younger than Gadamer, published the works with which they established their philosophical positions considerably earlier: already in 1934 *Logic of Scientific Discovery* had appeared, in 1940 *Man, His Nature and Position in the World,* and in 1944 the *Dialectic of Enlightenment*. Nonetheless, *Truth and Method* casts a long shadow.

The stars were auspicious. In the human sciences a hermeneutic trend began to develop. Above all, Gadamer's "ontological shift of hermeneutics guided by language" offered a movable viewpoint from which others could perceive the convergence of the later philosophies of Heidegger and Wittgenstein. As Karl-Otto Apel long ago demonstrated, the semantics of world disclosure and the pragmatics of language games meet on the field of a dialogic hermeneutics.

The American philosopher Richard F. Bernstein has even placed Gadamer at the point of convergence of neopragmatism, Critical Theory, and deconstructionism. The mediating temperament of an author intent on connection and not on segregation, who prefers accepting ambiguities to singling out alternatives, corresponds to the broad international effective history of *Truth and Method*.

This weekend, when guests from all over the world rush to the celebratory lectures of Richard Rorty and Michael Theunissen in Heidelberg, when almost the entirety of German philosophy gathers there around the master, the reasons for this are not exclusively to be found in their respect for his work, nor in the anticipated affability of a doyen in his dotage. He is, in fact, still quite capable of passing judgments with a sharp tongue. Their respect is also devoted to the person, and to his role as mediator between two generations of philosophy.

Gadamer occupies an intermediary position in the philosophy of the Federal Republic of Germany. With his gesture of reverence for his teacher Heidegger, on the one hand, he keeps alive something of the spirit of the German mandarins. On the other hand, he passes on the claim of metaphysical thought and an elitist self-conception of philosophy, rather than plausible quotations. Gadamer did, indeed, still travel through the Latin countries of Europe like a phenomenological governor; in Germany, however, he refused to play the role of the last mandarin. The trace of academic arrogance, rather, refers to the achievement of the classical philologist who "only reads books more than two thousand years old."

Gadamer was never tempted to claim for himself a privileged access to truth. He put aside the pretension of the initiated herald and seer, and with his austere bearing fit in with the postwar generation on its path to desublimate the embarrassing German-Greek pathos.

The admonition to hermeneutic "modesty" warns of the high-handedness of a subjectivity that blinds itself to the context-dependency of its utterances. A congenial sort of modesty, however, also characterizes the personality and the self-conception of a philosopher who initially felt himself so rejected by Heidegger that he first decided to take his finals as a teacher of Greek. This early insecurity may have kept Gadamer from following his master along treacherous paths. His difference from Heidegger, of course, is not merely a question of style.

THE RELATIONSHIP TO HEIDEGGER

Of Heidegger's three prominent Marburg pupils, Gadamer is the most devoted. Although Karl Löwith and Gerhard Krüger distanced themselves quite early from the positions of their common teacher, Gadamer avoided any public word of criticism. After the war, it was he who made a determined effort to rehabilitate Heidegger. Gadamer overcame a great deal of opposition to produce a festschrift for Heidegger's sixtieth birthday in 1949. He pushed through Heidegger's acceptance as a member of the Heidelberg Academy of Science. He demanded that Heidegger receive the newly instituted Hegel Prize of the city of Stuttgart. At the ceremony commemorating his late teacher, Gadamer spoke of "Heidegger's lifelong search for God."

His biographer declares that *Heidegger's Ways* is the book "that Gadamer never stopped writing." Rightly, however, Jean Grondin immediately adds: "While Heidegger, faced with the acute oblivion of being in the technological age, no longer expected anything but a radical new beginning of the history of being, Gadamer appealed to the classical values, never totally forgotten, of dialogue, practical reason, and power of judgment." Here Gadamer's allegiance had reached its limits.

For the religiously unmusical Gadamer, it is not a dressed-up search for God that serves as an organum of philosophy, but rather art. While the concept of the history of being lives off religious intuitions that Heidegger, under Nietzsche's influence, recoined in the 1930s into a new paganism, the idea of effective history is developed on the basis of aesthetic experiences. Gadamer holds to the profane model of art. The temporalized *Sein* that always remains "itself" does not make itself perceptible as the occurrence of an overpowering force of destiny, but rather occurs as the fundamental "*Sein* of the work of art," which in ever-new readings "makes itself valid as truth."

Art seems to solve the riddle of the "temporal core of truth" (Adorno). A work that proves itself as "classic" through the ages and remains constant in its effect remains binding, no matter how the interpretations and the criteria of evaluation change in the course of time.

To be sure, Gadamer purchases the assimilation of philosophical statements to the "poetic word" at a high price. He thereby assimilates the validity of truth to the authenticity of literature and the plastic arts. Gadamer sees very well that in aestheticizing philosophy, what is at stake is nothing less than truth: "What does 'truth' mean, when a linguistic construct has cut off all reference to an authoritative reality and comes true in itself?" But he does not shrink from the consequence that has brought many critics into the arena.

In his view, philosophical statements, in a non-metaphorical sense, can as little be "true" or "false" as poetic utterances. Philosophical texts and theories are understood by Gadamer as self-referential constructs that "miss" not the facts, but rather "themselves" alone; that is, they can become powerless or "fall into empty sophistry." Thus an image of "genuine" philosophizing arises, according to which the rhetorical power of linguistic disclosure of the world has always already outstripped the revisionist power of the better argument.

Must the truth not be given the latitude to make an appeal, if we are to be able to learn something in our dealings with it? When the serpent of philosophy narcissistically rolls itself up for an eternal heart-to-heart dialogue with itself, the world's instructive refutation dies away unheard. However, we critics of Gadamer can remain at ease. The best refutation of his own view is provided us by the paradigm-shifting argumentative strategies of the guest of honor himself—who has remained young and eager for discussion.

NOTE

This essay first appeared in the *Neue Zürcher Zeitung*, Feb. 12, 2000. It is reprinted here with the permission of Dr. Uwe Justus Wenzel.

Chapter 2

Being That Can Be Understood Is Language

RICHARD RORTY

In a book called *Reason in the Age of Science,* Hans-Georg Gadamer asked the question: Can "philosophy" refer to anything nowadays except the theory of science?[1] His own answer to this question is affirmative. It may seem that the so-called "analytic" tradition in philosophy—the tradition that goes back to Frege and Russell and whose most prominent living representatives are Quine, Davidson, Dummett, and Putnam—must return a negative answer. For that tradition is often thought of as a sort of public relations agency for the natural sciences.

Those who think of analytic philosophy in this way often describe Gadamer's own work as a sort of apologia for the humanities. In this view of the matter, each of what C. P. Snow called "the two cultures" has its own philosophical claque. Those who accept Snow's picture of the intellectual scene think of the quarrel over science versus religion that divided the intellectuals of the nineteenth century as having evolved into the contemporary quarrel between the kinds of people whom we Californians call the "techies" and the "fuzzies."

This crude and oversimplified picture of the tension within contemporary philosophy is not altogether wrong. But a more detailed account of the history of philosophy in the twentieth century would distinguish between a first, scientistic phase of analytic philosophy and a second, anti-scientistic phase. Between 1900 and 1960 most admirers of Frege would have agreed with Quine's dictum that "philosophy of science is philosophy enough." But a change came over analytic philosophy around the time that philosophers began reading Wittgenstein's *Philosophical Investigations* side by side with Kuhn's *Structure of Scientific Revolutions.* Since then, more and more analytic philosophers have come to agree with Putnam that part of the problem with present-day philosophy is a scientism inherited from the nineteenth century.

Putnam urges us to give up the idea that natural science has a distinctive "method," one that makes physics a better paradigm of rationality than, for example, historiography or jurisprudence. He is joined in this appeal by philosophers of physics like Arthur Fine, who asks us to abandon the assumption that natural science "is special, and that scientific thinking is unlike any other."[2] Putnam and Fine both ridicule the idea that the discourse of physics is somehow more in touch with reality than any other portion of culture. Post-Wittgensteinian Anglophone philosophy of language, of the sort found in Putnam, Davidson, and Brandom, has collaborated with post-Kuhnian philosophy of science, of the sort found in Latour, Hacking, and Fine. The result of this collaboration has been a blurring of the lines between the sciences and the humanities, and an attempt to make Snow's techie-fuzzie controversy seem as quaint as the nineteenth-century debate over the age of the earth.

This is not to say that scientism is dead. There are many distinguished analytic philosophers, particularly admirers of Kripke like David Lewis and Frank Jackson, who are unabashed physicalist metaphysicians. They think of themselves as continuing the struggle against mystificatory nonsense that Thomas Huxley waged against Bishop Wilberforce, Russell against Bergson, and Carnap against Heidegger. These philosophers still award a special ontological status ("fundamental reality") to the elementary particles discovered by the physicists. They believe that natural science gives us essences and necessities. They think that Wittgensteinian philosophers of language are dangerously irrationalist in saying that all distinctions between essences and accidents, or between necessities and contingencies, are artifacts that change as our choice of description changes. They think that Kuhnian philosophers of science are equally misguided in refusing to grant natural science any metaphysical or epistemological privileges.

This quarrel over whether natural science is special presently dominates analytic philosophy. I want to suggest that a much-quoted sentence from Gadamer might serve as a slogan for those philosophers of language and science who follow Putnam and Fine rather than Kripke and Lewis. The sentence is: "Being that can be understood is language" ("Sein, das verstanden werden kann, ist Sprache"). That claim encapsulates, I shall argue, both what was true in nominalism and what was true in idealism.

Let me define "nominalism" as the claim that all essences are nominal and all necessities *de dicto*. This amounts to saying that no description of an object is more true to the nature of that object than any other. Nominalists think that Plato's metaphor of cutting nature at the joints should be abandoned once and for all. Proponents of nominalism are often described as "linguistic idealists" by the materialist metaphysicians. For the latter believe that Dalton and Mendeleev did indeed cut nature at the joints. From this Kripkean perspective, Wittgensteinians are so infatuated with words that they lose touch with the real world, the world modern science has opened up to us. Philosophers of this sort accept the account of the history of philosophy that Gadamer summed up when he wrote that "the rapid downfall of the Hegelian empire of the Absolute Spirit brought us to the end of metaphysics, and thereby to the promotion of the empirical sciences to the topmost position in the kingdom of the thinking mind."

Nominalism, however, is a protest against any sort of metaphysics. To be sure, it was misleadingly associated with materialism by Hobbes and other early modern philosophers, and is still so associated by Quine. But these thinkers are inconsistent in holding that words denoting the smallest bits of matter cut nature at the joints in a way that other words did not. A consistent nominalist will insist that the predictive and explanatory success of a corpuscularian vocabulary has no bearing on its ontological status, and that the very idea of "ontological status" should be dropped.

This means that a consistent nominalist cannot countenance a hierarchical organization of the kingdom of the thinking mind that corresponds, as Plato's organizational charts did, to an ontological hierarchy. So struggles for priority between metaphysics and physics, or between techies and fuzzies, look ludicrous from a nominalist perspective. So does Heidegger's distinction between metaphysics and Thinking, as well as his claim that "in the end, philosophy's business is to safeguard the power of the most elementary words." For a nominalist, Heidegger's favorite words such as *phusis* (Greek for "nature") or *Wesen* (German for "essence") are no more "elementary" or "primordial" than words such as "aubergine" and "baseball." The more resonant words have no philosophical privilege over the rawest neologisms any more than the elementary particles over the latest human artifacts.

To defend my suggestion that nominalism can best be summarized in Gadamer's doctrine that only language can be understood, I shall take up the obvious objection to that claim. Techies are quick to expostulate that the paradigm of achieving greater understanding is modern science's increasing grasp of the nature of the physical universe—a universe that is not language. The nominalist riposte to this objection is: we never understand anything except under a description, and there are no privileged descriptions. There is no way of getting behind our descriptive language to the object as it is in itself—not because our faculties are limited but because the distinction between "for us" and "in itself" is a relic of a descriptive vocabulary, that of metaphysics, which has outlived its usefulness. We should interpret the term "understanding an object" as a slightly misleading way of describing our ability to connect old descriptions with new. It is misleading because it suggests, as does the correspondence theory of truth, that words can be checked against nonwords in order to find out which words are adequate to the world.

In a nominalist account, the progress made by modern science consists in formulating novel descriptions of the physical universe, and then fusing the horizons of these new discourses with those of common sense and of older scientific theories. More generally, to understand something better is to have more to say about it—to be able to tie together the various things previously said in a new and perspicuous way. What metaphysicians call moving closer to the true nature of an object nominalists call inventing a discourse in which new predicates are attributed to the thing previously identified by old predicates, and then making these new attributions cohere with the older ones in ways that save the phenomena. To put the point in Robert Brandom's Hegelian way: to understand the nature of an object is to be able to recapitulate the history of the concept of that object. That history, in turn, is simply the history of the uses of the various words used to describe the object. As Jonathan Rée has suggested in his recent *I See a Voice,* objects are like onions: lots of layers made up of descriptions (the further into the onion, the earlier the description), but without a nonlinguistic core that will be revealed once those layers have been stripped off.

The central thesis of idealism is that truth is determined by coherence among beliefs rather than correspondence to the intrinsic nature of the object. This doctrine suggests, though it does not entail, the central thesis of nominalism: that we should replace the notion of "intrinsic nature" with that of "identifying description." For the notions of real essence and of truth-as-correspondence stand or fall together. Gadamer's slogan gives us a way of sweeping both aside. For it is not an announcement of a metaphysical discovery about the intrinsic nature of being. It is a suggestion about how to redescribe the process we call "increasing our understanding."

From the Greeks to the present, this process has usually been described with the help of phallogocentric metaphors of depth. The deeper and more penetrating our understanding of something, so the story goes, the further we are from appearance and the closer to reality. The effect of adopting Gadamer's slogan is to replace these metaphors of depth with metaphors of breadth: the more integration between these descriptions, the better is our understanding of the object identified by any of those descriptions.

In the natural sciences, the obvious example of such better understanding is the integration of a macroscopic with a microscopic vocabulary. But the difference between these two sets of descriptions is of no more ontological or epistemological significance than the difference between a description of the Mass in the terms of orthodox Catholic theology and a description in the terms of comparative anthropology. In neither case is there greater depth, nor a closer approach to reality. But in both there is increased understanding. We understand matter better after Hobbes's corpuscles are supplemented by Dalton's atoms, and then by Bohr's. We understand the Mass better after Fraser, and better still after Freud. But if we follow out the implications of Gadamer's slogan, we shall resist the temptation to say that we now understand what either matter or the Mass really is. We shall be careful not to explicate the distinction between lesser and greater understanding with the help of a distinction between appearance and reality.

The latter distinction has legitimate, unphilosophical uses in describing perceptual illusions, financial chicanery, government propaganda, misleading advertising, and so on. But intellectual progress is only occasionally and incidentally a matter of detecting illusions or lies. The appearance-reality distinction is no more appropriate for describing the advances made between Priestley and Bohr than the advances made in our understanding of the *Iliad*. We pride ourselves on our ability to fuse Homer's own descriptions of his poems with those used by Plato, by Virgil, by Pope, by nineteenth-century philologists, and by twentieth-century feminist scholars. But we do not, and should not, say that we have penetrated the veil of appearances that originally separated us from the poem's intrinsic nature. The poem has no such nature any more than matter does.

The fuzzie-techie debate, like the religion-science debate of the nineteenth century, is a quarrel about which area of culture gets us closer to the way things "really" are. But as the twentieth century wore on, proposals for the peaceful coexistence of religion and science proliferated. Debate about the respective merits of the two has come to seem jejune. With luck, the quarrel between the techies and the fuzzies will, in the course of the next century or two, gradually dissipate in the same way. For the attempt to find a philosophically interesting difference between techies and fuzzies was a symptom of the attempt to preserve a certain picture of the relation between language and nonhuman entities. This is the picture that Wittgensteinian nominalists and Kuhnian philosophers of science are helping us to give up. If they succeed, we shall no longer find it paradoxical to assert that being that can be understood is language. This slogan will be taken as a commonsensical account of what understanding is, rather than as a contrived attempt to improve the image of the humanities.

Gadamer has often been accused of inventing a linguistic variety of idealism. But, as I suggested earlier, we should instead think of him as keeping the gold in idealism and throwing out the metaphysical dross. Idealism only acquired a bad name because it was slow to abandon the appearance-reality distinction. Once this distinction is set aside, idealism and nominalism become two names for the same philosophical position. The ill effects of that distinction can be seen in Berkeley. Having said that "nothing can be like an idea except an idea," Berkeley went on to infer that only ideas and minds are real. What he should have said was that only a sentence can be relevant to the truth of another sentence, a nominalist claim that is devoid of metaphysical implications.

Berkeley's metaphysics is a typical result of the idea that thoughts or sentences lie on one side of an abyss, and are true only if they connect with something that is on the other side of the abyss. This picture held Berkeley captive, and led him to conclude that there was no abyss: that reality was somehow mental or spiritual in nature. Later idealists, such as Hegel and Royce, repeated his mistake when they defined reality as perfect knowledge or perfect self-consciousness. This, too, was an attempt to get rid of an abyss, this time by making our present epistemic situation continuous with the ideal epistemic situation—making our own network of mental states continuous with that of the Absolute. But this sort of pantheistic speculation left idealism vulnerable to scientism—to the justified contempt of those who heard the claim that only the mental is real as *reductio ad absurdum* of metaphysics. So it is, but no more so than the claim that only the material is real. To get beyond metaphysics would be to stop asking the question of what is or is not real.

Our ability to shrug off this question increased when we took what Gustav Bergman called "the linguistic turn"—a turn taken more or less simultaneously by Frege and by Peirce. For that turn eventually made it possible for logical positivists like Ayer to de-metaphysicize a coherence theory of truth. They urged us to stop talking about how to cross the abyss that separates subject from object and to talk instead about how assertions are justified. The positivists saw that once we substitute language for "experience" or "ideas" or "consciousness," we can no longer reconstruct Locke's claim that ideas of primary qualities have some sort of closer relation to reality than ideas of secondary qualities. But it was precisely this claim that the Kripkean revolt against Wittgenstein resurrected. In doing so, the Kripkeans were proclaiming that the linguistic turn had been a bad, idealistic idea.

The current quarrel between the Kripkeans and their fellow analytic philosophers is one way of continuing the old debate about what, if anything, was true in idealism. But a more fruitful way to approach this quarrel may be to take up a suggestion of Heidegger's. Heidegger viewed the series of great metaphysicians from Plato to Nietzsche as control freaks: people who thought that thinking would let us achieve mastery. In a Heideggerian account, the metaphysicians' phallogocentric metaphors of depth and penetration are expressions of the will to take possession of the inner citadel of the universe. The idea of becoming identical with the object of knowledge, like that of representing it as it really is in itself, expresses the desire to acquire the object's power.

The scientism of the nineteenth century mocked both religion and idealist philosophy, because natural science offered a kind of control that its rivals could not. This movement saw religion as a failed attempt to achieve control. It saw Absolute Idealism as an escapist, self-deceptive attempt to deny the need for control. The ability of natural science to predict phenomena, and to provide technology for producing desired phenomena, showed that only this area of culture offered true understanding, because it alone offered effective control.

The strong point of this scientistic line of thought is that although understanding is always of objects under a description, the causal powers of objects to hurt or help us are unaffected by the way they are described. We shall get sick and die, no matter how we describe disease and death. The Christian Scientists are, alas, wrong. The weak point of scientism is the inference from the fact that a certain descriptive vocabulary enables us to predict and utilize the causal powers of objects to the claim that this vocabulary offers a better understanding of those objects than any other. That non sequitur is still put forward by the Kripkeans. Whether or not one sees it as a non sequitur depends on whether one is willing to redescribe understanding in the way that Gadamer has suggested.

To follow up on Gadamer's redescription, we should have to give up the idea of a natural terminus to the process of understanding either matter, or the Mass, or the *Iliad,* or anything else—a level at which we have dug down so deep that our spade is turned. For there is no limit to the human imagination—to our ability to redescribe an object, and thereby recontextualize it. A descriptive vocabulary is a way of relating an object to other objects—putting it in a new context. There is no limit to the number of relations language can capture, nor of contexts that descriptive vocabularies can create. Whereas the metaphysician will ask whether the relations expressed in a new vocabulary are really there, the Gadamerian will ask only whether they can be woven together with the relations captured by previous vocabularies in a helpful way.

As soon as one uses a term like "helpful," however, those who believe in real essences and in truth as correspondence will ask "helpful by what criterion?" To think that such a demand for criteria is always reasonable is to imagine that the language of the future should be a tool in the hands of the language of the present. It is to become a control freak—someone who thinks that we can short-circuit history by finding something that lies behind it. It is to believe that we can now, in the present, construct a filing system that will have an appropriate pigeonhole for anything that might possibly turn up in the future. Those who still hope for such a filing system will typically select some single area of culture—philosophy, science, religion, art—and assign it "the first rank in the kingdom of the thinking mind." But those who follow Gadamer, like those who follow Habermas, will drop this project of ranking. They will substitute the idea of what Habermas calls a "domination-free" *(herrschaftsfrei)* conversation that can never come to an end, and in which the barriers between academic disciplines are as permeable as those between historical epochs.

Such people hope for a culture in which struggles for power between bishops and biologists, or poets and philosophers, or fuzzies and techies, are treated simply as power struggles. Rivalries such as these will doubtless always exist, simply because Hegel was right that only a dialectical *agon* will produce intellectual novelty. But in a culture that took Gadamer's slogan to heart, such rivalries would not be thought of as controversies about who is in touch with reality and who is still behind the veil of appearances. They would be struggles to capture the imagination, to get other people to use one's vocabulary.

A culture of this sort will seem to materialist metaphysicians like one in which the fuzzies have won—a culture in which poetry and imagination have finally gained the victory over philosophy and reason. So my little sermon on a Gadamerian text will probably look to them like one more public relations exercise on behalf of the humanities. I shall end by saying why I think that this is not the right way to look at the matter.

In the first place, a Gadamerian culture would have no use for faculties called "reason" or "imagination"—faculties that are conceived as having some special relation to truth or reality. When I speak of "capturing the imagination," I mean nothing more than "being picked up and used." In the second place, a Gadamerian culture would recognize that everybody's filing system will need to have pigeonholes into which to fit everybody else's filing system. Every area of culture would be expected to have its own parochial description of every other area of culture, but nobody will ask which of these descriptions gets that area right. The important thing is that it will be *herrschaftsfrei;* there will be no one, overarching filing system into which everybody is expected to fit.

My sermon on the text "Sein, das verstanden werden kann, ist Sprache" obviously has not been offered as an account of the real essence of Gadamer's thought. Rather, it is offered as a suggestion about how a few more horizons might be fused. I have tried to suggest how Gadamer's own description of the movement of recent philosophical thought can be integrated with some alternative descriptions currently coming into use among analytic philosophers.

I suspect and hope, however, that once another century has passed, the distinction I have just employed—the distinction between analytic and non-analytic philosophy—will strike intellectual historians as unimportant. Philosophers in the year 2100, I suspect, will read Gadamer and Putnam, Kuhn and Heidegger, Davidson and Derrida, Habermas and Vattimo, Theunissen and Brandom, side by side. If they do, it will be because they have at last abandoned the scientistic problem-solving model of philosophical activity with which Kant burdened our discipline. They will have substituted a conversational model, one in which philosophical success is measured by horizons fused rather than problems solved, or even by problems dissolved. In this philosophical utopia, the historian of philosophy will not choose her descriptive vocabulary with an eye to distinguishing the real and permanent problems of philosophy from the transient pseudo-problems. Rather, she will choose the vocabulary that enables her to describe as many past figures as possible as taking part in a single, coherent conversation.

Gadamer once described the process of *Horizontverschmelzung* as what happens when "the interpreter's own horizon is decisive, not as the standpoint of which he is convinced or which he insists on, but rather as a possible opinion he puts into play and at risk." He went on to describe this process as "the consummatory moment of conversation *[Vollzugsform des Gesprächs]* in which something is expressed *[eine Sache zum Ausdruck kommt]* that is neither my property nor that of the author of the text I am interpreting, but is shared" (TM388). To replace the appearance-reality distinction with the distinction between a limited and a more extensive range of descriptions would be to abandon the idea of the text or thing we are discussing (the *Sache*) as something separated from us by an abyss. It would be replaced by a Gadamerian conception of the *Sache* as something forever up for grabs, forever to be reimagined and redescribed in the course of an endless conversation. This replacement would mean the end of the quest for power, and for finality, that Heidegger called "the history of metaphysics."

That tradition was dominated by the thought that there is something nonhuman that human beings should try to live up to, a thought that today finds its most plausible expression in the scientistic conception of culture. In a future Gadamerian culture, human beings would wish only to live up to one another, in the sense in which Galileo lived up to Aristotle, Blake to Milton, Dalton to Lucretius, and Nietzsche to Socrates. The relationship between predecessor and successor would be conceived, as Gianni Vattimo has emphasized, not as the power-laden relation of overcoming *(Überwindung),* but as the gentler relation of turning to new purposes *(Verwindung).* In such a culture, Gadamer would be seen as one of the figures who helped give a new, more literal sense to Hölderlin's line, "Ever since we are a conversation . . . " *(Seit wir ein Gespräch sind . . .).*

NOTES

This essay first appeared in the *London Review of Books* 22, no. 6, Mar. 16, 2000, and is reprinted here with permission. It was given as an address at the University of Heidelberg on the occasion of Gadamer's hundredth birthday.

1. "Philosophy or Theory of Science?" in *Reason in the Age of Science* (Cambridge, Mass.: MIT Press, 1983), 151.

2. Fine, "The Viewpoint of No-one in Particular," *Proceedings and Addresses of the American Philosophical Association,* vol. 72 (Nov. 1998), 19.

Chapter 3

On the Coherence of Hermeneutics and Ethics

An Essay on Gadamer and Levinas

GERALD L. BRUNS

Does not philosophy consist in treating mad ideas with wisdom?
EMMANUEL LEVINAS

HABITATION

My purpose in what follows is to take up the relation of hermeneutics and ethics as it emerges in a post-Heideggerian philosophical context. In terms of proper names this means giving an account of the conceptual symmetries and differences between Gadamer's philosophical hermeneutics and Emmanuel Levinas's ethical theory, which is sometimes called an ethics of alterity or of responsibility, in order to contrast it with subject-centered theories that emphasize thinking and acting in accord with rules, principles, duties, codes, beliefs, teachings, communities, theories of the right and the good, and so on, where to be in accord with such things, however we figure them, is what justifies us, or anyhow puts us above reproach. Levinasian ethics is concerned with the claims other people have on us in advance of how right we are with respect to rules and beliefs or how in tune we are with a just and rational order of things. For Levinas, ethics is not possible from a starting point of self-interest.[1]

Being under claims of history and tradition rather than claims of concepts and rules is central to Gadamer's thinking, which is critical of subjectivist accounts of human understanding in ways that coincide with Levinas's project. As Gadamer puts it, understanding is so permeated by "the historicity of existence" that it is "not suitably conceived as a consciousness of something" (GW3:18/PH125). Better to say: understanding something comes from dwelling with it. Likewise Levinas: "Humanity . . . must not be first understood as consciousness" (AE132/OTB83). Consciousness is always separate from its objects, impervious and indifferent to them (which is all that objectivity means). "What affects a consciousness," Levinas says, "presents itself at a distance" (AE161/OTB101). My neighbor, by contrast, is closer to me than any object of consciousness; indeed, the other is closer to me than I am to myself (AE137–38/OTB86–87). As Levinas puts it, human subjectivity "is structured as the other in the same" (AE46/OTB25).

Foundational for both Gadamer and Levinas is Heidegger's "hermeneutics of facticity," with its characterization of our relation to the world (and to others in it) in terms of habitation rather than intuition or representation. In *Being and Time* Heidegger regards our practical involvement with the things of everyday life as ontologically prior to the theoretical attitude that determines the formation of concepts and propositions (SZ149/BT189). How the world touches us matters as much as how we grasp it conceptually. Heidegger's idea is that the theoretical attitude, whatever its philosophical importance with respect to how knowledge is possible, is oblivious to the world we inhabit. Theory is indifferent to what is singular and irreplaceable. Whereas by contrast our being-in-the-world is a relation of concern or care *(Sorge)* rather than one of disinterested regard (SZ191–96/BT235–41). It is an (arguably ethical) relation of being-with and attunement rather than a logical relation highlighted by the propositional attitude. "The world of Dasein," Heidegger says, "is a *with-world [Mitwelt]*. Being-in is Being-with Others" (SZ118/BT155). However we describe it, our relation to the world and to others is closer and more intimate than is suggested by any philosophical culture whose ideal is the self-certainty of an objectifying consciousness (SZ158/BT200–201).

This proximity of the world and of others in it is a matter of central importance to both Gadamer and Levinas—but each thinks through this issue much differently from the way Heidegger introduced it. Levinas, for example, sharply criticizes Heidegger for repressing the ethical dimension of our being-in-the-world in favor of ontology, where ontology means a concern with the unity of being or totality of all that is.[2] If Heidegger situates us in the world as inhabitants rather than disengaged punctual observers, he is nevertheless still asking the disengaged subject's question: What is our relation to the *being* (that is, the totality) of things? If the answer is "care," Heidegger's interest is nevertheless in the ontological rather than ethical meaning of care, and Dasein's care is always ultimately for itself, not for others (SZ317–23/BT364–70: "Care and Selfhood"). In his analysis of dwelling and habitation in *Totality and Infinity* Levinas points out that "In *Being and Time* the home does not appear apart from a system of implements," and there is no one in the house but me (TeI184/TI170). I dwell among implements designed to domesticate the world for me, and it is one from which others have to be excluded if I am to come into my own, working out my ownmost possibilities or my destiny. To be sure, as Heidegger says, "As being-with, Dasein 'is' essentially for the sake of Others" (SZ123/BT160), but it is just this condition of being-for-others that must be overcome if the existence of Dasein is to be authentic. Inauthenticity simply means: "Dasein stands in *subjection* [*Botmässigkeit,* subservience] to the others. It itself *is* not; its being has been taken away by the Others. The everyday possibilities of being of Dasein are at the disposal of the whims of the Others." Moreover, these Others "are not *definite* Others. On the contrary, any Other can represent them": they are faceless in the manner of an urban crowd. The question of who they are invites a shrug: "The 'who' is not this one and not that one, not oneself and not some and not the sum of them all. The 'who' is the neuter, the *they [das Man]*" (SZ126/BT164).

Levinas reverses completely this interpretation of being-for-the-sake-of-others in order to replace fundamental ontology with a fundamental ethics, where the relation of one-for-the-other is no longer an ontological defect. For Levinas, it is not that I am a self aiming for freedom and authenticity but tragically find myself blocked and absorbed by a faceless otherness. On the contrary, it is the face of the other that singles me out and makes me what I am (defines what it is to be human). For Levinas, being human starts out from a position of responsibility to and for others rather than from one of consciousness and self-reflexive freedom. Being-for-others is the adventure—"the fine risk to be run" (AE191/OTB120)—that gives human existence its meaning and transcendence (or, more exactly, as we shall see, its meaning *as* transcendence).

Meanwhile Gadamer's hermeneutics starts out from section 32 of *Being and Time,* with its idea that interpretation is never a presuppositionless grasping of something given but always proceeds according to a forestructure of prejudices (SZ150/BT191–92). The question for Gadamer is what happens to these prejudices in our encounter with whatever calls for understanding. Gadamer follows Heidegger's insistence on historicity: our understanding of texts (or of tradition, or of other people) is always local and contingent; it is always an event circumscribed and conditioned by the historical and cultural situation in which it occurs. In a word, understanding is always finite. However, this finitude entails the fact that what we try to understand is irreducible to the concepts and categories that our situation makes available to us. Tradition, for example, is always in excess of our capacity to appropriate it. So we can never understand the other purely and simply in terms of ourselves or by remaining fixed in what seem to us self-evident determinations of how things are (WM265–69/TM281–85). The example of the classical text shows that understanding the other always entails a critical demand for a change (in us), whether in terms of a revision of prior understanding (prejudices) or, more radically, in terms of a conversion of our habitual modes of thought and feeling to other ways of being that are opened up to us in our encounter with others (WM273–75/TM289–90). This means (whatever else it means) that our relation to the other is not simply one of cognition, nor is it even simply a relation of being-with or cohabitation (sharing beliefs and whatnot). Nor, indeed, is it a reciprocal interaction along a logically level plane, because we are always in a condition of exposure to what we want to understand; that is, in the understanding of anything—whether of a text or the world or of other people—we always find ourselves under a claim. In Gadamer's language, in the understanding of anything we are always in the position of being addressed (WM283/TM299). So understanding is not just an executive project. It is an event in which we always find ourselves situated in the accusative mode or mode of responsibility. Hence understanding always entails a call for action.

The symmetry between Gadamerian hermeneutics and Levinasian ethics begins with the recognition of human finitude clarified in the accusative case rather than in terms of whatever might limit the nominative, declarative, or imperative sovereignty of a consciousness presiding over a domain of objects. Levinas expresses this by remarking how philosophical modernity is structured on the model of Homer's *Odyssey* (DEHH191/TTO348). That is, its hero is a consciousness capable of self-reflection, a movement of departure and return that defines subjectivity as knowledge and action against opposing forces. I go out into the world in order to take it in, and if I suffer, it is in a struggle for self-possession and possession of the world as if it were my household.[3] Likewise my every action presupposes a redemptive economy of commensurate rewards and punishments. Even gift giving is structured on the model of eventual return. Against Odysseus, however, Levinas places the figure of Abraham, who is called out of his homeland by an absolute other for the sake of a time and a world to come that he will never experience; and there is no turning back (HAH46/CPP93). It is this "departure without return" and without reward that defines the ethical subject (DEHH191/TTO349). On the model of Abraham, the "I" is for-the-other: a pure gift outside every possibility of exchange or compensation. As Levinas puts it, "the *for* of the-one-for-the-other . . . is a *for* of total gratuity, breaking with interest" (AE154/OTB96). Levinasian ethics is an ethics of "radical generosity" (DEHH191/TTO349).

For example, what happens when I encounter another person? Sartre in his famous account of the look treats this encounter as an event of cognition in which, being seen, I become another's representation, a piece of furniture in another's world of intentional objects.[4] Levinas maps onto this encounter another model—not the Greek or philosophical model of knowing and being known but the Jewish or Biblical model of election, of being summoned out of one's house or place of security and comfort. This is the prophetic experience of being called into the wilderness, of being inspired, exposed to the world, offered as a sacrifice, turned inside out like a cloak and put under a claim that cannot be redeemed. For Levinas, the ethical subject is defined by a responsibility that is prior to any rational deliberation and executive decision; it is an anarchic responsibility prior to the kind of commitments that rational subjects (as Kant envisioned them) know how to contract or refuse or hedge with loopholes and provisos. The Kantian subject can always find the freedom to go back on its word. In the Levinasian encounter with the other, I can no longer comport myself as a cogito, a self-contained rational subject, a Hegelian consciousness conceived as a *pour soi,* that is, a power of representation or intentionality in pursuit of its own sovereignty. I now exist in the accusative, no longer an "I" but a "me," someone now at the disposal of—answerable to and for—another. I *am* my responsibility prior to any freedom of choice. As Levinas likes to express it, the good "has chosen me before I have chosen it. No one is good voluntarily" (AE25/OTB11). (In the last section of this essay I will return to the question of the good in Levinas and Gadamer, for both of whom the good is internal to proximity. Briefly, for Levinas, the good is simply "a non-allergic relation with alterity" [TeI38/TI47]; and likewise Gadamer's concern is not with the good in its purity but with "the good in human life" [GW7:144/IG30].)

TOWARD THE STRANGER

It follows that neither hermeneutical understanding nor the ethical relation of myself and another is an action or movement capable of being brought under the description of rules or principles. On the contrary, openness or responsiveness to one's situation and to others in it replaces the figure of an autonomous agent acting upon what is given from a position justified in advance. Unlike Habermas, for example, neither Gadamer nor Levinas conceives the ethical in terms of the justification of norms.[5] Gadamer, for example, thinks of understanding on the model of Aristotle's concept of φρόνησις, or practical wisdom, which is a ground-level or dialectical mode of thinking different both from theoretical consciousness (ἐπιστήμη), or knowing what things are, and from technical know-how (τεχνή), or knowing how things are made or how they work. φρόνησις involves responsiveness to what particular situations call for in the way of action, where knowing how to act cannot be determined in advance by an appeal to rules, principles, or general theories (WM304–5/TM321–22). Knowledge here cannot be conceptualized or codified in general terms because it has to do with singular and unprecedented states of affairs, particularly as these involve us with other people (φρόνησις" is in fact the name of "the arete proper to human dealings") (GW7:148/IG37).[6] At the level of everyday life we are beneath the reach of universals. The classic example is knowing what friendship calls for in our being with others.[7] Knowledge in this event cannot be separated out from experience; it is, so to speak, embedded in situations that we live through and which shape us in very particular ways. It can be learned but cannot be taught. So stories are better than theories. Hence Aristotle's remark that "while young men become geometricians and mathematicians and wise in matters like these, it is thought that a young man of practical wisdom cannot be found. The cause is that such wisdom is concerned not with universals but with particulars, which become familiar from experience, but a young man has no experience, for it is length of time that gives experience" (*Nicomachean Ethics*, 1142a).

Indeed, φρόνησις" (and Aristotelian ethics generally) presupposes the condition of familiarity that comes with being with others and learning one's way around in a shared and settled environment, and the same can be said of hermeneutics, where understanding is never a process that starts from scratch but, as in Heidegger's analysis, is a condition of belonging to the world, a mode of being that one enlarges by integrating what is alien into what is at hand. Thus to understand is to contextualize, to arrange and assemble into a unity in which nothing is foreign or out of place. Levinasian ethics, however, takes us onto radically different ground. In his "Philosophy and the Idea of Infinity" (1957), Levinas distinguishes between two kinds of truth. On the one hand, there is the truth of identity that characterizes propositions (*s* is *p*). Truth here is the truth of representation and cognition. It is what governs the integration of differences into an order of things, as when one makes sense of what is strange by finding a place for it within one's conceptual scheme, a movement that Levinas calls "the reduction of the other to the same" (DEHH165–66/CPP48). Here everything follows the logic of identity. On the other hand, however, there is the truth of experience that is essentially a reversal of this reduction to identity:

> For experience deserves its name only if it transports us beyond what constitutes our nature. Genuine experience must even lead us beyond the nature that surrounds us. . . . Truth would thus designate the outcome of a movement that leaves a world that is intimate and familiar, even if we have not yet explored it completely, and goes toward the stranger, toward a *beyond,* as Plato puts it. Truth would imply more than exteriority: transcendence. (DEHH165/CPP47)

For Levinas, transcendence means departure from "the immanence of the known," that is, from a world defined by consciousness and its representations.[8] The ethical relation—the encounter with another—is a movement toward the stranger, that is, toward the nonidentical, rather than a movement of recognition in which I take the other into my world, gathering up the other as a component of my self-possession or as part of my domestication or familiarization of my world. Indeed, it is not too much to say that for Levinas the dispossession of the self is the condition of the ethical as such.

This comes out very starkly in an essay on "Substitution" (1968), which Levinas calls the "germ" of *Otherwise than Being* (1974), of which it forms the central chapter.[9] The essay begins with a sharp contrast between *consciousness* as the grasping of objects through the mediation of concepts, and *sensibility* as the unmediated condition of being touched. The adventure of consciousness, Levinas says, is in reality "no adventure. It is never dangerous; it is self-possession, sovereignty, ἀρχή. Anything unknown that can occur to it is in advance disclosed, open, manifest, is cast in the mould of the known, and cannot be a complete surprise" (AE157/OTB99). Sensibility, by contrast, is "a relation not of knowing but of proximity" (AE157/OTB100), where proximity is defined as an "*anarchic* relationship with a singularity without the mediation of any principle, any ideality" (AE158/OTB100). Singularity means: the other—the human being—is refractory to categoies, not any *kind* of anything and just to that extent not belonging to any conceptual order. The other is outside every form of mediation or reference.[10] However, the anarchy of this relationship is the crucial note. Like Plato's desire for the good, responsibility is "without why." The Levinasian world is not a Leibnizian world in which nothing is without reason. Quite the contrary, it is a world in which before anything else I am someone to whom things happen, that is, someone to whom *others* happen, and these happenings cannot be traced back to any order of causes, reasons, or explanations. My relation to the other is not one that I enter into as into a contract; it is "a responsibility that is justified by no prior commitment" (AE162/OTB102).[11] It is not a movement of consciousness but a reversal of consciousness that Levinas characterizes with a vocabulary that is perpendicular to the philosophical tradition that comes down to us from Descartes and Kant, Hobbes and Hegel. Ethical responsibility, he says, is "an *assignation* by others I do not even know" (AE159/OTB100); it is an *obsession* that "traverses consciousness countercurrentwise, is inscribed in consciousness as something foreign, a disequilibrium, a delirium" (AE159/OTB101); it is a *persecution,* "where the persecution does not make up the content of a consciousness gone mad; it designates the form in which the ego is effected, a form which is a defecting from consciousness. This inversion of consciousness is . . . a passivity beneath all passivity. It cannot be defined in terms of intentionality, where undergoing is always also an assuming, that is, an experience always anticipated and consented to, an origin and ἀρχή (AE160/OTB101).[12] So responsibility cannot mean moral responsibility in any traditional philosophical sense. "The ethical situation of responsibility is not comprehensible on the basis of an ethics" (*La situation éthique de la responsabilité ne se comprehend pas àpartir de l'éthique:* Levinas distinguishes *l'éthique,* a moral system, from *éthique,* the ethical) (AE191/OTB120). On the contrary, as Levinas says, "[responsibility] means concretely: accused of what others do or suffer, or responsible for what others do or suffer. The uniqueness of the self is the very fact of bearing the fault of another" (AE177/ OTB112). The ethical subject bears all the marks of the scapegoat.

As if the ethical were, philosophically, a world upside-down—as, in crucial ways, it is—Levinasian ethics derives from a historical world in which the Holocaust is not unthinkable but is, in fact, a premise that cannot be evaded, part of an ineradicable background memory that must inform all future reflection on what it is to be human. Indeed, Levinas is deeply critical of a philosophical anthropology that starts out with—in order to justify—an autonomous ego acting in its own interests. Such an idea presupposes a Hobbesian/Hegelian world in which my relationship with others is always a struggle for domination in which I either subsume or eliminate what is not myself. In such a world the Holocaust is horrifying but not surprising. By contrast Levinas proposes a world in which being human means being a gift or offering for others. Since our imaginations and, indeed, our historical experiences are Hobbesian/Hegelian, such an anthropology is more than a little frightening—and Levinas's language makes no attempt to disguise the extremity of his thought, where persecution, for example, is not a metaphor but defines ethical responsibility as existence despite oneself.[13] Not surprisingly, it is in his commentaries on the Talmud that Levinas is most explicit on this point: "To bear responsibility for everything and everyone is to be responsible despite oneself. To be responsible despite oneself is to be persecuted. Only the persecuted must answer for everyone, even for his persecutor" (SS46/NTR114–15). As Robert Bernasconi says in glossing this line, Levinasian ethics is not derived from the philosophical tradition. "Levinas's achievement is that he has developed a philosophy that arises from the non-philosophical experience of being persecuted."[14] It is a philosophy marked by historical realism rather than by the formal realism of a thinking that aims at the logical justification of its concepts and assertions.

Persecution defines a condition of radical passivity in which I am no longer an "I" but a who or a me. The who or the me, Levinas says, is a "term in recurrence," a *oneself (soi)* who exists "on the hither side of consciousness and its play, beyond or on the hither side of being which it thematizes, outside of being, and thus in itself in exile" (AE163/OTB103). Levinas characterizes this condition as a *hypostasis*, that is, a condition of exposure in which I no longer exist as a for-oneself *(pour soi)* according to the traditional philosophical definition but am entirely for-another—no longer the autonomous agent of Kantian ethics but instead one who exists in the accusative. This is how I am constituted as an ethical subject.[15] "In obsession," Levinas says, "the accusation effected by [grammatical] categories turns into an absolute accusative in which the ego proper to free consciousness is caught up. It is an accusation without foundation, prior to any movement of the will, an obsessional and persecuting accusation. It strips the ego of its pride and the dominating imperialism characteristic of it" (AE174–75/OTB110). It is worth repeating that this being-for-another "is subjectivity itself" (AE175/OTB111). It is not part of any economy of salvation in which I play out a redemptive role of suffering. Justice (justification) is always for others, not for myself (AE32–33/OTB16).

> "To give his cheek to the smiter and to be filled with insults" [Lamentations 3:30], to demand suffering in the suffering undergone . . . is not to draw from suffering some kind of magical redemptive virtue. In the trauma of persecution it is to pass from the outrage undergone to the responsibility for the persecutor, and, in this sense, from suffering to expiation for the other. Persecution is not something added to the subjectivity of the subject and his vulnerability; it is . . . subjectivity as *the other in the same.* (AE176/OTB111)

As Levinas likes to say, the other "slips into me like a thief" (Job 4:12).

Subjectivity structured as "the other in the same" is what Levinas means by "substitution": "The word *I* means *here I am* [*me voici:* literally, see me here], answering for everything and for everyone" (AE180–81/OTB114). I am no longer self-identical but am one-for-the-other. It is important to stress, however, that Levinas does not regard this as a condition of alienation. On the contrary, the other is now internal to my identity, "because the other in the same is my substitution for the other through responsibility, for which I am summoned as someone irreplaceable. I exist through the other and for the other, but without this being alienation: I am inspired. This inspiration is the psyche. The psyche can signify this alterity in the same without alienation in the form of incarnation, as being-in-one's-skin, having-the-other-in-one's-skin" (AE181/OTB114). If my relation to the other is a movement outside self-possession toward the stranger, it is nevertheless not a pathological event. For Levinas, the ethical relation of one-for-the-other is what makes being human possible. It is why a humanism that simply emphasizes the autonomy and self-transparency of the ego is, as Levinas says, "not sufficiently human" (AE203/OTB129). For Levinas, as Adriaan Peperzak says, "the self in the accusative *[se, soi-même]* is the core of human significance."[16]

ETHICS AS HERMENEUTICAL EXPERIENCE

Levinasian ethics is not easily translatable into Gadamer's language, but it is not outside his philosophical horizon. On the contrary, philosophical hermeneutics presupposes something like an ethics of alterity and responsibility just to the extent that it characterizes the hermeneutical situation on the model of dialogue in which I am not a subject surveying a field but am caught up in a ground-level movement of question and answer that alters me as it unfolds. My openness to this event is the condition of its possibility, and the condition is as much ethical as it is logical precisely because what is called for is my capacity for listening to what is said (WM343/TM361). The dialogical subject is porous and exposed to what is said in the nature of the case; this is what it means to be historical or, more exactly, this is what human historicity means. To be sure, the ethical relation for Levinas is a relation of face-to-face in which the other (not what the other says) addresses me.[17] Moreover, being face-to-face is not a reciprocal relation, that is, in the ethical relation I am responsible for everything and everyone but no one is responsible for me. I am irreplaceable; the burden of the other's distress is mine and cannot be shifted elsewhere. This is what responsibility means: "No one can substitute himself for me, who substitutes myself for all" (AE200/OTB126). In the ethical relation, I am unique, and my uniqueness means that "no one else could be substituted [for me] without transforming responsibility into a theatrical role" (AE214/OTB136). Responsibility is not an office or a function. The face of the other faces me with an exigency that cannot be worked off like a debt. The face of the other in this respect is transcendent, outside every system of exchange including the give-and-take of dialogue (it faces me, Levinas likes to say, from a "height").[18] "Responsibility is prior to dialogue, to the exchange of question and answer, the thematization of [what is] said" (AE176/OTB111).

Of course, this looks very much like what Gadamer means when he insists upon openness as a condition that makes not only dialogue but all human relations possible (WM343–44/TM361–64). The difference is perhaps that Gadamer runs together openness to tradition, openness to the claim of truth in what is said, openness as the "logical structure" of the question, and openness to other persons, whereas a Levinasian would insist on discriminating between openness in these various senses, including the sense of Heidegger's "Gelassenheit" (openness to things, or to the "mystery"), and the more radical openness of hypostasis, "the risky uncovering of oneself . . . abandoning all shelter, exposure to traumas, vulnerability" (AE82/OTB48). The point of such discrimination would be to underscore a subtle but fundamental difference between hermeneutical and ethical conceptions of subjectivity. However, it is possible to think through these different conceptions in ways that intertwine them.[19]

For example, a useful distinction can be drawn between being-with (or being-alongside-of) and being face-to-face as alternative modes of relationship with the other. The first is predominantly hermeneutical, as Gadamer clarifies this term; that is, it implies a relationship of mutual understanding, participation, attunement, being on the same track, being in the swing of the game, having words and interests (not to say a world) in common.[20] Ethically it is a relation whose culmination is friendship or at least solidarity. My relation to the other in any case aims at a "we" and implies the possibility of community. The face-to-face relation as Levinas understands it is different from this. It is not an I-Thou relation but a relation to a "he," that is, an *illeity (il, elle)* who is outside every horizon and who calls me into question, that is, summons me out of my house, situating me in my ethical condition as hostage (being one-for-the-other) (AE174–75/OTB110). This is very close to what Gadamer describes as a hermeneutical experience, which is an encounter with what cannot be contained within my conceptual capacity to make sense of things.[21] Experience, as Hegel said, is a "reversal of consciousness *[Umkehrung des Bewußtein]*" (WM357/TM354). Experience has the structure of a question, that is, it is an event that calls consciousness into question as an agent that presides over its knowledge and holds reality in its grasp. In experience truth is not our correspondence to reality but our exposure to it as to a fate or a nemesis. Reality here is not an object but a limit and a magnitude beyond cognition (WM338–44/TM354–59).

Similarly, Levinas calls the face-to-face encounter "an experience in the strongest sense of the term: a contact with a reality that does not fit into any a priori idea, which overflows all of them. . . . A face is pure experience, conceptless experience" (DEHH177/CPP59): it is *conceptless* because experience is not a mode of cognition but the opening up of subjectivity, exposing it to alterity. "Consciousness," Levinas says, "is called into question by a face. . . . A face confounds the intentionality that aims at it. . . . The I loses its sovereign self-coincidence, its identification, in which consciousness returns triumphantly to itself to rest on itself. Before the exigency of the other the I is expelled from this rest" (HAH53/CPP97). Experience is "a reversal of subjectivity" (DEHH225/CP116), so that now subjectivity is that of

> a man of flesh and blood, more passive in its extradition to the other than the passivity of effects in a causal chain, for it is beyond the unity of apperception of the *I think,* which is actuality itself. It is a being torn up from oneself for another in the giving to the other of the bread out of one's own mouth. This is not an anodyne formal relation, but all the gravity of the body extirpated from its *conatus essendi* in the possibility of giving. The identity of the subject is brought out, not by a rest on itself, but by a restlessness that drives me outside of the nucleus of my substantiality. (AE222/OTB142)[22]

Still, the crucial difference between Gadamer and Levinas is that ultimately Gadamer will want to understand this event as redounding to oneself in the way of self-knowledge. "In the last analysis," he says, "all understanding is self-understanding" (GW2:130/PH55).[23] To be sure, for Gadamer hermeneutical experience is not just an experience of limits or an "experience of one's own historicity" (WM340/TM357). "Hermeneutical experience is concerned with *tradition,*" where tradition is not simply an archive or treasure-house of culture; rather, "it is *language*—it expresses itself like a Thou" (WM340/TM358). This means that tradition can never be reduced to an object of cognition, no more than a person can (WM340–

41/TM358–59). But this also means that my relation to tradition is not a Hobbesian-Hegelian relation of struggle for ownership or mastery (WM341–42/TM359). It is a human relation that calls upon me to respond otherwise than through the exercise of conceptualization and control.

> In human relations the important thing is . . . to experience the Thou truly as a Thou—i.e., not to overlook his claim but to let him really say something to us. Here is where openness belongs. But ultimately this openness does not exist only for the person who speaks; rather, anyone who listens is fundamentally open. Without such openness to one another there is no genuine human bond. Belonging together always also means being able to listen to one another. (WM343/TM361)

But for Gadamer *listening-to* is always ultimately a *listening-for:* our relation to the other or to tradition is always a relation to what is said, that is, to a *Sache:* the claim of the other is a truth claim as well as an ethical claim, and our responsibility takes the form of understanding and acknowledgment rather than the radical form of generosity envisaged by Levinas as substitution or being "one-for-the-other" to the point of being "a hostage" (AE186/OTB117). Moreover, truth here is not simply *adequatio in re;* it is rather that what is said bears upon me in my situation with the force of law, and my task is to see and understand myself in the light of what is said. My understanding of the other is *for me;* its goal is, among other things, the enlargement of my horizon. From a Levinasian point of view, hermeneutics is thus faithful to a philosophical tradition that remains recognizably Greek in its fundamental outlook. Departure is balanced by return. Gadamer would not disagree. The first hermeneut was Odysseus, who turned himself into the other—and back again.[24]

LEVINASIAN HERMENEUTICS

Indeed the relation between Gadamer and Levinas is not so much one of disagreement as one of mutually illuminating differences—differences that are paradoxically coherent with one another. This is the more true since Levinas does not oppose Jewish and Greek traditions in any exclusionary way but seeks something very like a fusion of prophetic and Platonic horizons. For example, from a Gadamerian standpoint what is remarkable and instructive about Levinasian ethics is its constant recourse to hermeneutical categories of speaking and signifying, expression and communication, enigma and sense, as a way of clarifying the ethical relation of responsibility. Thus the face for Levinas is not a phenomenon—not something given to perception like a mask; rather, the face is a language without words, a primordial language that signifies of itself. "The face speaks" (TeI61/TI166), but not in the sense that discourse emanates from its mouth. "The primor-

dial essence of language is to be sought not in the corporeal operation that
discloses it to me and to others and, in the recourse to language, builds up
a thought, but in the presentation of meaning." The question is how this
"presentation of meaning" is to be understood. It is important to mark that
Levinas's word for meaning here is *sens*—in contrast to *signification* (the distinction is not always preserved in the English translations of Levinas).
Meaning as *signification* is the product of discourse, where discourse is simply conceptual determination, intentionality, the predication of *this as that*.
But the presentation of meaning as *sens* is not a function of semantics or of
discursive reason. "Meaning *[sens]* is the face of the Other, and all recourse
to words takes place already within the primordial face to face of language"
(TeI226–27/TI206). The face "is the meaning *[sens]* of language before
language scatters into words" (AE236/OTB151), as if the face were foundational for language and reason.

As Levinas elucidates it, the distinction between *signification* and *sens* entails a corresponding distinction between different dimensions of hermeneutics, an exegetical or historical-cultural dimension and a dimension of
transcendence, that is, an ethical dimension that cuts across the limits of
historical and cultural significations and therefore stands apart from the
vast heterogeneous array of moral systems, each with its own logic and capacity for self-justification. Exactly how the difference between historical
and ethical dimensions of hermeneutics is to be understood is perhaps most
fully articulated in Levinas's 1964 essay "Meaning and Sense" *(Signification
et sens)*. Like Gadamer's hermeneutics, "Meaning and Sense" starts out from
section 32 of Heidegger's *Being and Time,* with its idea that the intelligibility
of things is not a given but is essentially a hermeneutical construction:
namely, taking *"something as something,"* that is, understanding things in the
context of our involvement with them or in our belonging-together within
the world (SZ149/BT189). So Levinas: "There is no given already possessing identity. . . . To be given to consciousness [is to] be placed in an illuminated horizon—like a word, which gets the gift of being understood from
the context to which it refers. The meaning *[signification]* would be the very
illumination of this horizon" (HAH20/CPP77). That is, the *signification* of a
thing—and, ultimately, of being—is a relation of part and whole, a movement within a hermeneutical circle whose circumference is at once ontological and linguistic (or at all events semantic).

> The given is present from the first *qua* this or that, that is, as a meaning
> *[signification]*. Experience is a reading, the understanding of meaning an ex-
> egesis, a hermeneutics, and not an intuition. *This taken qua that*—meaning is
> not a modification that effects a content existing outside of all language.
> Everything remains in a language or in a world, for the structure of the world
> resembles the order of language, with possibilities no dictionary can arrest.
> (HAH22/CPP78) [25]

This is roughly what Gadamer means by saying, "Being that can be understood is language" (WM450/TM474). "In the *this qua that,*" Levinas says, "neither the *this* nor the *that* are first given outside of discourse. . . . There never was a moment meaning came to birth out of a meaningless being, outside of a historical position where language is spoken. And that is doubtless what is meant when we were taught that language is the house of being" (HAH23/CPP78–79).

This is to say (with Heidegger) that being is internal to time and history and so is distributed across multiple and heterogeneous cultures as a plurality of meanings. Being is epochal. Accordingly, as Levinas says, "Culture and artistic creation are part of the ontological order itself. They are ontological par excellence: they make the understanding of being possible" (HAH28/CPP82). Hence the universal—but also endlessly historical—scope of hermeneutics. "There exists no *meaning in itself [signification en soi],* which a thought would have been able to reach by jumping over the deforming or faithful but sensory reflections that lead to it. One has to traverse history or relive duration or start from concrete perception and the language established in it in order to arrive at the intelligible" (HAH31/CPP83). In other words, being—"the intelligible"—is given in tradition: "All the picturesqueness of history, all cultures, are no longer obstacles separating us from the essential and the intelligible but ways that give us access to it. Even more! They are the only ways, the only possible ways, irreplaceable, and consequently implicated in the intelligible itself" (HAH31/CPP83–84).

Unlike Gadamer, however, Levinas is no historicist. He is a moral realist for whom the absence of a *meaning in itself*—"the pure indifference of a multiplicity" distributed along a horizontal plane of historical and cultural differences (HAH40/CPP89)—is an absurdity, a reduction of the ethical to the anthropological. To be sure, there is nothing outside of time and history, but for Levinas there is more to time and history than the epochal history of being. Granted that human cultures are multiple, heterogeneous, and entirely relative to one another (the others of each other but not of any One). What matters is that these cultures are porous and penetrable, thus allowing "the possibility of a Frenchman learning Chinese and passing from one culture into another." But what about this passage? It is not just a lateral movement that would eventually assemble human cultures into an anthropological totality of cultural differences; rather, it discloses a deeper orientation. What is it, after all, that leads "a Frenchman to take up learning Chinese instead of declaring it to be barbarian (that is, bereft of the real virtues of language), to prefer speech to war?" (HAH39/CPP88). What is it to translate oneself into the other? Levinas sees in this translation the ethical movement of substitution or generosity, the essential movement of the one-for-the-other that gives the multiplicity of cultural meanings "a unique sense *[sens]*" (HAH39/CPP88)—an intelligibility that, like Plato's One (like the other, like *me* as an ethical subject), is "beyond being." The movement of the one-for-the-other is a movement toward transcendence, but a transcendence that cannot be conceptualized in the language of ontology. Its temporality is older than the history of being, as if belonging to "a past that was never present" (HAH64–65/CPP103; DEHH198/TTO355).[26] This is the temporality in which the other confronts me; it is the temporality in which I am exposed to the other, without the shelter of cultural mediations that enable me to cope with the other and its claim on me. Put it that traditional hermeneutics (which is as old as philology itself) construes understanding as contextualization, where meaning is a two-way relation between part and whole, and where parts are infinitely portable from one whole to another. Here, as Levinas says, the other "is present in a cultural whole and is illuminated by this whole, as a text by its context. The manifestation of the whole ensures his presence; it is illuminated by the light of the world. The understanding of the other is thus a hermeneutics, an exegesis" (HAH50/CPP95). In addition, Gadamer's hermeneutics emphasizes understanding as participation and praxis, the solidarity of belonging-together in work and play, the collaboration of one with the other in a dialogue on what matters to both. Here, as Levinas puts it, the other is "the collaborator and the neighbor of our cultural work of expression" (HAH50/CPP95). For Gadamer, hermeneutics embraces the whole of the human life-world as its practical understanding of itself in all of its dimensions (art, scientific reason, the ethical, law, philosophy, the social and political relations of everyday life). But beyond the hermeneutical life-world there is for Levinas the relation to the other as such, without reference to anything else, outside of every context of signification (the other is, in Maurice Blanchot's stark phrase, "man without horizon").[27] Here is Levinas's ethical hermeneutics of *sens:* "The other who faces me is not included in the totality of being expressed. He arises behind every assembling of being as he to whom I express what I express. I find myself again facing another. He is neither a cultural signification nor a simple given. He is *sense [sens]* primordially" (HAH50/CPP95). And here "primordially" simply means: prior to (beyond or, better, on the hither side of or otherwise than) any epoch of meaning or of being. Imagine this as a Levinasian extension of the universal scope of hermeneutics to include what we might think of as a transcendence of tradition.

One is reminded of the prophets who addressed the world from outside the city and its priestly codes. The other's address to me occupies this kind of transcendental position (exteriority with respect to the world as so many cultural structures): "the epiphany of the other involves a signifyingness *[significance]* of its own independent of [any] meaning received from the world. The other comes to us not only out of a context, but also without mediation; he signifies by himself" (HAH50–51/CPP95). Indeed, the idiom of prophecy in Levinas's articulation of transcendence is explicit: "the epiphany of the face is a *visitation*" (HAH51/CPP95). It is not an appearance or phenomenon whose expression discloses an order of intentions; it is an intervention from the outside, an interruption of every context: "The face *enters* into our world from an absolutely foreign sphere, that is, precisely from an absolute, that which in fact is the very name for ultimate strangeness. The signifyingness of a face *[la signifiance du visage]* in its abstractness is in the literal sense of the term extraordinary, outside of every order, every world" (HAH52/CPP96). The abstractness of the face means precisely that the face is not any sort of medium, that is, it is not the face of this or that, not a face intimating this or that. It is a face stripped bare of every signification but what it signifies of itself: "Stripped of every form, a face is paralyzed in its nudity. It is a distress. The denuding of a face is a denuding and already a supplication in the straightforwardness that aims at me" (HAH52/CPP96). In its distress, it is a face that occupies me like an obsession, which is to say it is not before me like an image or phenomenon but is under my skin like a demonic invasion. So there is no chance I can shake it.

However, there is more: the epiphany of the face has a Platonic as well as a prophetic character. If "the ethical situation of responsibility is not comprehensible on the basis of an ethics" in the sense of moral system (*l'éthique:* AE191/OTB120), that is because the "unique sense" of the face is itself the basis of ethics; it is a transcendental condition of ethical judgment:

> The saraband of innumerable and equivalent cultures, each justifying itself in its own context, creates a world which is, to be sure, de-occidentalized, but also disoriented. To catch sight, in meaning *[signification]*, of a situation that precedes culture, to envision language out of the revelation of the other (which is at the same time the birth of morality) in the gaze of a man aiming at a man precisely as abstract man, disengaged from all culture, in the nakedness of his face, is to return to Platonism in a new way. It is also to find oneself able to judge civilizations in a new way. Meaning *[signification]*, the intelligible, consists in a being showing itself in its nonhistorical simplicity, in its absolutely unqualifiable and irreducible nakedness, existing "prior to" history and culture. (HAH60/CPP101)

A "return to Platonism in a new way"? The point is that the face of the other is a supplication aimed at me (and no one else); it "imposes itself upon me without my being able to be deaf to its call or to forget it, that is, without my being able to stop holding myself responsible for its distress" (AE52–53 /OTB96–97). It is, Levinas says, "as though the whole edification of creation rested on my shoulders" (AE53/OTB97). However, this burden also has a foundational meaning. If my responsibility disengages me "from all culture," it also (and therefore) enables me "to judge civilizations" from a nonrelativist position, the way Levinas himself judges Kantian and utilitar-

ian ethics—indeed, all modern and contemporary moral philosophy—as
indifferent to the other and, therefore, as failed philosophy. The good is not
relative to civilizations and their theories. It is

> otherwise than being. It no longer keeps accounts. . . . It destroys without leav-
> ing souvenirs, without transporting into museums the altars raised to the idols
> of the past for blood sacrifices, it burns the sacred groves in which the echoes
> of the past reverberate. The exceptional, extra-ordinary, transcendent char-
> acter of the good is due to just this break with being and history. To reduce
> the good to being, to its calculations and its history, is to nullify goodness.
> (AE35–36/OTB18)

As if what Levinas were proposing were a hermeneutics beyond tradition.

For Gadamer, of course, breaking with "being and history"—breaking
with tradition—cannot be made intelligible and defensible for the very reason of human finitude. Grant all that Levinas says, my encounter with the
other will always be within the horizon I inhabit; otherwise it will simply be
unreal. The point is that my horizon is not a conceptual order in which the
other would merely appear as an intelligible component. I do not inhabit
my horizon simply as a cognitive agent grasping whatever is placed before
me. Horizons are not reducible to perspectives or worldviews, which are essentially overdrawn metaphors of spectatorship. Neither are they totalities
in the way Levinas imagines totality, namely as the world objectified by consciousness, a world whose components are integrated one with another according to a logic of identity or "the reduction of the other to the same." For
Gadamer, horizon is a concept of finitude, not of totality.

Part of what needs to be sorted out here is the difference between the
ways Levinas and Gadamer think of history. In "Philosophy and the Idea of
Infinity," Levinas speaks of "the conquest of being by man over the course
of history" as if history were the history of consciousness expressing itself
in ever-widening processes of rationalization and control (DEHH166/
CPP48). Not that this idea doesn't capture something, as readers of Max
Weber and Adorno will quickly recognize. But for Gadamer history is incompatible with totality. History is precisely what resists rational ordering of
every sort. This resistance, moreover, is not a defect to be overcome but a
limit of reason, a fact of human finitude that exposes the (by turns comic
and tragic) absurdity of modernity's ideal of "smooth functioning as a good
in itself."[28] This conception of the historicity of history explains why Gadamer's famous notion of the "fusion of horizons," contrary to many quick
summaries of it, has nothing to do with any logic of integration or unification of perspectives, but rather presupposes the ethical character of existence in which one's horizon—one's finitude—is defined by the proximity
of others whose presence cannot be objectified: this is what the dialogical

character of the life-world comes down to.[29] This conception of finitude is not incompatible with Levinas's notion of transcendence, else how could Levinas say that "it is only man who could be absolutely foreign to me — refractory to every typology, to every genus, to every characterology, to every classification" (TeI71/TI73)? Why is the other not more infinitely alien still, otherwise than human?[30] Moreover, in my encounter with the other it is not just me who is called into question; my whole world is touched and altered (indeed, made what it is) by this encounter, precisely because I am not detachable from my horizon but am a portion of its reality. I would be unreal otherwise: this is what historicity means. Finally, there is ample space for Gadamer to agree that "the good is not relative to civilizations and their theories," because for Gadamer the good is not an idea. On the contrary, it is part of the definition of our finitude.

ON THE PROXIMITY OF THE GOOD

Gadamer is a classicist who follows Plato in conceiving the ethical as the desire for the good, but his classicism is (like Levinas's) a return to Plato rather than a continuation of a certain reception of Plato within the history of philosophy. (Tradition is not repetition.) Thus in *The Idea of the Good in Platonic-Aristotelian Philosophy* Gadamer reads Plato against Aristotle's charge that Plato's conception of the good is a supreme but empty θέωρια divorced from human life. It is true that in the *Republic* (508e) the good is the sun that radiates throughout the world but is inaccessible in itself. But in the later dialogues Plato's concern shifts away from the good as such. What matters to Plato in the *Philebus,* Gadamer says, "is not the idea of the good but the good in human life" (GW7:144/IG30). The desire for the good is not meant to take us out of the world but to enable us to inhabit it in the right way. The good is not a "supreme mathema" indifferent to human concerns; on the contrary, it is the human "turning away from the realm of the ideal to what is best in reality" (GW7:144/IG30). The good is thus not an object of μάθεμα. "In the *Philebus,*" Gadamer says, "the good has precisely the function of providing practical orientation for the right and just life as this life is a mixture of pleasure and knowing" (GW7:145/IG31). "Knowledge of the good," Gadamer says, "is always with us in our practical life" (GW7:159/IG57). In this respect the good as Plato (and Gadamer with him) conceives it is very close to Levinas's notion of a *sens* beyond being, which is likewise an orientation or movement rather than an idea.

For Levinas the good is also always with us, but it is so specifically and exclusively in the face of the other, which inspires in us the movement of one-for-the-other, that Levinas, citing the *Philebus* (50e), characterizes as a desire "that is conditioned by no prior lack" (HAH48/CPP95). In other

words, Levinas translates Plato's ethical desire for the good into the gratuitous desire for the other—gratuitous because it is *not* an expression of
need but a transcendence of self-interest, a disinterestedness, a generosity,
and, pointedly, not an appetite (HAH49/CPP94/TeI21–23/TI32–35).
For Levinas, as for Gadamer, the good is not inhuman; on the contrary, to
be human, says Levinas, is to be "elected by the good," that is, summoned to
a responsibility beyond being, that is, a responsibility prior to (and foundational for) every norm of conduct (AE194–95/OTB122). Levinas thus
thinks of himself as reversing the "antiplatonism"—that is, the historicism—of Heideggerian phenomenology and of much of poststructuralist
thinking, with its Nietzschean emphasis on the social construction of the
subject and the corresponding discovery of local interests underlying objective norms. Ethics as "non-indifference to the other" (AE142/OTB89),
Levinas says, "marks a return to Greek wisdom" (AE60/OTB101). The
other who confronts me is "beyond being" (επεχεινα τεζ ουσιας), that is,
irreducible to representation, on the hither side of the history of being and
the dissemination of moralities: "the *beyond [au-delà]* . . . is not 'another
world' behind the world. . . . The *beyond* is precisely beyond the 'world,' that
is, beyond every disclosure, like the One of the first hypothesis of the *Parmenides,* transcending all cognition, be it symbolic or signified" (HAH62/
CPP102). But now the One is no longer remote, supersensible, or inaccessible to the human; on the contrary, the One—the Good—is that which
touches me at the level of sensibility, that is, as "an event of proximity rather
than of knowledge" (DEHH225/CPP116). The "beyond" is, for Levinas, *beneath* or on the "hither side" of the world as a theme of disclosure. This is
what the phrase "otherwise than being" means.

Would Gadamer think this good? I think in the end he might fault Levinas for setting the ethical relation too sharply against hermeneutics—
for having, finally, too abstract a conception of the ethical or, indeed, what
amounts to the same thing, for having an impoverished conception of hermeneutics, reducing hermeneutics to the purely logical procedure of contextualization. For Gadamer, understanding constitutes the historical and
practical condition for all human relations, social and political as well as
ethical. The universal scope of hermeneutics moves from the ground up
(rather the way, for Levinas, the ethical relation of proximity and singularity constitutes "the condition for all solidarity" and provides, moreover, for
the possibility of justice that makes human life livable after all, even in the
aftermath of the Holocaust and in the midst of modernity as "the era of
"man-made mass death" (AE186/OTB117).[31] However, an account that
would clarify the ethical as the condition of solidarity would, a Gadamerian
might argue, require something very like a detour into hermeneutics.

For example, one might say that from Gadamer's perspective Levinas's
conception of the ethical is too purely ethical, not sufficiently social (not

sufficiently historicized)—a possibility, in fact, to which Levinas himself is clearly responding in those sections of his work where he emphasizes that the ethical relation of one-for-another is not an exclusive or exclusionary "I-Thou" relation (a relation of love, for example). Rather, in the face of the other I always encounter what Levinas calls "the third party," that is, all the others in the world whose nakedness and destitution constitute a call for justice:

> Language as the presence of the face does not invite complicity with the pre-ferred being, the self-sufficient 'I-Thou' forgetful of the universe; in its frank-ness it refuses the clandestinity of love, where it loses its frankness and mean-ing and turns into laughter and cooing. The third party looks at me in the eyes of the Other—language is justice. It is not that there first would be the face, and then the being it manifests or expresses would concern himself with justice; the epiphany of the face qua face opens humanity." (TeI234/ TI213)[32]

So (this would be Gadamer's point) the ethical does not and cannot stand by itself, outside of every context, because my responsibility to and for the other cannot stop with the other but opens onto (among other things) pol-itics, where responsibility entails responsiveness to the here-and-now exi-gencies of social action.

At all events Gadamer glosses the formula "beyond being" (επεχεινα τεζ ουσιας) by locating it precisely within the here and now. For Gadamer (in contrast to Levinas), *"The good is no longer the one"* (GW7:192/IG115). The good belongs to the hermeneutical domain of the "between" where ethics and aesthetics (or, for all of that, cognition and action, theory and practice, the transcendent and the everyday, and so on through whatever list of op-positions one might devise) constitute a mixture that cannot be distilled into distinct orders of reality, much less into separate categories of experi-ence. Here is where Gadamer differs most completely from Habermas, who divides the human life-world into separate cultural districts of science, so-cial practice, and art, over which philosophy is then installed as a quasi-transcendental "guardian of rationality."[33] In the context of the *Philebus*, Gadamer says, "'the good,' which is at the same time 'the beautiful,' does not exist somewhere apart for itself and in itself, somewhere 'beyond.' Rather, it exists in everything that we recognize as a beautiful mixture. What is viewed from the perspective of the *Republic* (or the *Symposium*) is here de-termined to be the structure of the 'mixed' itself. In each case it would seem to be found only in what is concretely good and beautiful" (GW7:192–93/ IG115). This means that the good cannot be conceptualized apart from the question of how one should live within the contingencies in which one finds oneself. Or, in other words, at the end of the day, the question of the good is the question of φρόνησις".

NOTES

1. For example, self-respect and the need to be free of self-reproach (the goals of "a rational plan of life") are the main features of John Rawls's ethical theory. See *A Theory of Justice* (Cambridge, Mass.: Harvard University Press, 1971), esp. 433–46. Much of contemporary moral philosophy sees ethics as a function of rational choice, where my concern is always with what will help me to achieve my goals, which comes down to the question of what comes back to me in the way of profit for my right conduct. In the long run decency toward others pays. The writings of Martin Hollis on this matter are very instructive. See, for example, *The Cunning of Reason* (Cambridge: Cambridge University Press, 1987). Levinas's philosophy can be read as a thoroughgoing critique of rational-choice theory.

2. See Adriaan T. Peperzak, "On Levinas's Criticism of Heidegger," in *Beyond: The Philosophy of Emmanuel Levinas* (Evanston, Ill.: Northwestern University Press, 1997), 204–17. For a discussion of the ethical in Heidegger's thinking—where the ethical includes the relation to a nonhuman as well as human alterity—see Joanna Hodge, *Heidegger and Ethics* (London: Routledge, 1995).

3. In "Philosophy and the Idea of Infinity," Levinas writes: "Cognition consists in grasping the individual, which alone exists, not in its singularity . . . but in its generality, of which alone there is science." To which he adds:

> And here every power begins. The surrender of exterior things to human freedom through their generality does not only mean . . . their comprehension, but also their being taken in hand, their domestication, their possession. Only in possession does the I complete the identification of the diverse. To possess is, to be sure, to maintain the reality of the one possessed, but to do so while suspending its independence. In a civilization which the philosophy of the same reflects, freedom is realized as a wealth. Reason, which reduces the other [to the same], is appropriation and power. (DEHH168/CPP50)

Likewise in "Ethics as First Philosophy," Levinas writes:

> In knowledge there . . . appears the notion of an intellectual activity or of a reasoning will—a way of doing something which consists . . . of seizing something and making it one's own, of reducing to presence and representing the difference of being, an activity which *appropriates* and *grasps* the otherness of the known. A certain grasp: as an entity, being becomes the characteristic property of thought, as it is grasped by it and becomes known. Knowledge as perception, concept [*Begriff*, from *greifen*, to grasp], comprehension, refers back to an act of grasping. The metaphor should be taken literally: even before any technical application of knowledge, it expresses the principle rather than the result of the future technological and industrial order of which every civilisation bears the seed. The immanence of the known to the act of knowing is already the embodiment of seizure. (LR76)

4. *Being and Nothingness,* trans. Hazel E. Barnes (New York: Philosophical Library, 1956), 344–58.

5. See Habermas, "Discourse Ethics: Notes on a Program of Philosophical Justification," in *Moral Consciousness and Communicative Action,* trans. Christian Lenhardt and Shierry Weber Nicholsen (Cambridge, Mass.: MIT Press, 1990), 43–115.

6. On the social character of φρόνησις" see P. Christopher Smith, "The I-Thou Encounter *(Begegnung)* in Gadamer's Reception of Heidegger" (PHGG514–19). See also Joseph Dunne, *Back to the Rough Ground: 'Phronesis' and 'Techne' in Modern Phil-*

osophy and Aristotle (Notre Dame, Ind.: University of Notre Dame Press, 1993), esp. 104–67 (on Gadamer). It is worth contrasting Gadamer's notion of fronesi" with the concept of communicative praxis in Habermas's "discourse ethics." Discourse ethics does not concern human beings in concrete situations where action is required; rather it concerns "participants" in "moral argumentation" about the ethical norms of a particular human life-world—or, in other words, people who are no longer participants in a life-world but have become moral spectators, under whose "unrelenting moralizing gaze" the life-world has lost the normative power it has for its inhabitants. See Habermas, "Discourse Ethics: Notes on a Program of Philosophical Justification," 107–8. See Dunne, *Back to the Rough Ground,* 193–226, on the shift from "praxis" to "technique" in Habermas's thought.

7. See Gadamer, "Freundschaft und Selbsterkenntnis Zur Rolle der Freundschaft in der grieschen Ethik" (GW7:396–406).

8. See Adriaan Peperzak, "Transcendence," in *Beyond: The Philosophy of Emmanuel Levinas,* 162–70. For Levinas, ontology and epistemology run together, so that "transcendence," "beyond," and "otherwise than being" refer to a dimension of existence outside the grasp of cognition, or beyond subjectivity conceived as spirit, consciousness, intentionality, or conceptual determination. This dimension of exteriority (on the hither side of being) is the dimension of ethical reality.

9. A translation of the 1968 version of "Substitution" appears in *Emmanuel Levinas: Basic Philosophical Writings,* ed. Adriaan T. Peperzak, Simon Critchley, and Robert Bernasconi (Bloomington: Indiana University Press, 1996), 79–95.

10. The singular is, in other words, outside the relation of universal and particular, that is, it is an infinity outside every totality. As Plato puts it in the *Parmenides* (164c), we are the others of each other, not of any one, "for there is no one." See *Totality and Infinity* (TeI21–45/TI33–52), and "Transcendence and Height," in *Emmanuel Levinas: Basic Philosophical Writings,* 10–31, esp. 12: "The Other *[l'Autre]* thus presents itself as human Other *[Autrui];* it shows a face and opens the dimension of *height,* that is to say, it *infinitely* overflows the bounds of knowledge."

11. That is—against Kant—responsibility is prior to freedom; it is not an exercise of autonomy. Levinas writes, "To be without a choice can seem to be violence only to an abusive or hasty and imprudent reflection, for it precedes the freedom non-freedom couple, but thereby sets up a vocation that goes beyond the limited and egoist fate of him who is only for-himself, and washes his hands of the faults and misfortunes that do not begin in his own freedom or in his present" (AE183–84/OTB116).

12. Levinas scholars have still not come to terms with these concepts of obsession, persecution, and hostage as descriptions of the structure and condition of the ethical subject. What seems generally recognized is that these terms are meant to define the radical character of a passivity that situates the subject outside the alternatives of the active or passive voice. Passivity, as Levinas understands it, is absolute, that is, outside (for example) the master-slave relation, where submission is still a position that one occupies as a consequence of one's decision (not to risk death, for example), whereas "the passivity more passive than all passivity" refers to a passion in which one is gripped or possessed before one realizes it. Passivity means being porous, subject to the passage whereby the other is inside my skin.

13. In *Otherwise than Being* Levinas characterizes the condition of *despite oneself* in

terms of patience and aging "The *despite* is here not opposed to a wish, a will, a nature, a subsistence in a subject, which a foreign power would contrary. The passivity of the 'for-another' expresses a sense in it in which no reference, positive or negative, to a prior will enters. It is the living human corporeality, as a possibility of pain, a sensibility which of itself is the susceptibility to being hurt, a self-uncovered, exposed and suffering in its skin" (AE86/OTB51). In this condition of corporeality one belongs to a different temporality from that of the active agent of intentionality, representation, objectification, and freedom of the will. Here "what is a subject is the inverse of a thematizing subject: a subjectivity in aging [whose] effort is an undergoing, a passive form of the self in 'that comes to pass' *[cela se passe]*" (AE90/OTB53). In the temporality of patience, the self is "a goodness despite oneself" (AE92/OTB54).

14. See Bernasconi, "'Only the Persecuted': Language of the Oppressor, Language of the Oppressed," in *Ethics as First Philosophy: The Significance of Emmanuel Levinas for Philosophy, Literature and Religion*, ed. Adriaan T. Peperzak (London: Routledge, 1995), 85.

15. In an essay "Response and Responsibility in Levinas" in *Ethics as First Philosophy*, Bernhard Waldenfels emphasizes the face-to-face relation of responsibility as constitutive of human subjectivity:

> Behind somebody who "gives himself" when giving an answer, there is no person in the form of the nominative. There is neither a sovereign speaker or actor preceding the responding nor a judge considering both sides; the respondent who does not merely transform existing sense becomes what he is by and in the very process of responding. He or she is not a subject in the traditional sense, "underlying" certain acts, but a respondent through and through, who in a certain sense remains unknown to him- or herself. If we want to continue calling him a "subject," then we do so in the sense of his "subjection" to the demands of the Other. (42)

16. Peperzak, *Beyond: The Philosophy of Emmanuel Levinas*, 104.

17. Levinas distinguishes between Saying *(le Dire)* and the Said *(le Dit)*, where Saying is a movement toward the other, "the risky uncovering of oneself, in sincerity, the breaking up of inwardness and the abandon of all shelter, exposure to traumas, vulnerability" (AE82/OTB48), whereas the Said is the product of a logical movement in which I take a position toward something, thematize it propositionally, fix it as an object (AE65/OTB37).

18. The "height" of the Other is not a position of strength but, paradoxically, one of destitution and weakness. In *Totality and Infinity* Levinas writes: "The being that presents himself in the face comes from a dimension of height, a dimension of transcendence whereby he can present himself as a stranger without opposing me as an obstacle or enemy. More, for my position as *I [moi]* consists in being able to respond to the essential destitution of the Other, finding resources for myself. The Other who dominates me in his transcendence is thus the stranger, the widow, the orphan, to whom I am obligated" (TeI237/TI215).

19. See James Risser, *Hermeneutics and the Voice of the Other: Re-reading Gadamer's Philosophical Hermeneutics* (Albany, NY: SUNY Press, 1997), 172–82. Risser points out that, in contrast to Paul Ricoeur's "hermeneutics of the text," Gadamer's is "a hermeneutics of the voice," and that the concept of voice entails conditions of proximity, even intimacy, such that I am never in a position in which I can simply take over

or appropriate what the other says but am exposed to the other in my ownmost be-ing. Risser does not hesitate to characterize this exposure by reconceptualizing Gadamer's notion of good will as desire, where "desire is the condition of dialogue," meaning that "dialogue is dependent upon being able to turn toward the other and to be open in order to be addressed by the other." Desire as a turn toward the other clearly matches the Levinasian structure of generosity. As Risser says:

> every speaking is a speaking to the other as a desire for the other. There is always in the communicative situation the voice of the other as the desired voice. In this context it is difficult to understand how the event of understanding can be construed as appropria-tion, as making something one's own, turning the event of understanding into a unity of understanding . . . . [For] Gadamer it is precisely the voice of the other that breaks open what is one's own, and remains there—a desired voice that cannot be sus-pended—as the partner in every conversation. (181)

20. See Gadamer's remarks on participation in "The Hermeneutics of Suspi-cion," in *Hermeneutics: Questions and Prospects* (Amherst: University of Massachusetts Press, 1984), 64. In *Truth and Method* Gadamer writes, "Understanding is to be thought of less as a subjective act than as participating in an event of tradition" (WM274–75/TM290).

21. See Gerald L. Bruns, "On the Tragedy of Hermeneutical Experience," in *Hermeneutics Ancient and Modern* (New Haven, Conn.: Yale University Press, 1992), 179–94, esp. 183–84.

22. The section "Substitution" in *Otherwise than Being* puts it more extravagantly: the encounter with the other "is an accusation without foundation, prior to any movement of the will, an obsessional and persecuting accusation. It strips the ego of its pride and the dominating imperialism characteristic of it. The subject is in the ac-cusative, without recourse in being, expelled from being, outside of being, like the one in the first hypothesis of *Parmenides,* without a foundation, reduced to itself, and thus without condition. In its own skin" (AE174–75/OTB110).

23. It should be noticed, however, that Gadamer goes on to say that self-understanding should not be construed as self-possession *[Selbstbesitzes]:* "For the self-understanding only realizes itself in the understanding of a subject-matter and does not have the character of a free self-realization The self that we are does not possess itself; one could say that it 'happens'" (GW2:130/PH55). Here Gadamer and Levinas are very close. Self-understanding is an event in which the self journeys out of itself. Gadamer cites the example of Augustine, for whom the self is inacces-sible except in its exposure to God.

24. Speaking of Gadamer's hermeneutics in terms of a desire for the other, James Risser writes, "The voice of the other, as desired, draws one beyond oneself, to think with the other, 'and to come back to oneself as if to another'" (*Hermeneutics and the Voice of the Other,* 182). See Gadamer's essay "*Destruktion* and Deconstruction" [DD110/GW2:269]).

25. Possibly Levinas blurs Heidegger's distinction between the "hermeneutical 'as,'" in which the structure of *something-as-something* concerns whatever is ready-at-hand within our everyday practical concern, and the "apophantical 'as,'" in which something is objectified by means of an assertion and so stands before us "*as a* 'what'" (SZ158/BT200).

26. A "past that was never present" is Levinas's way of figuring the concept of the

trace, which is a non-phenomenological event, a passing that leaves traces but not anything like evidence on which a reconstruction could be raised. See Adriaan Peperzak, *Beyond,* 105–6.

27. One of Blanchot's essays on Levinas is entitled "The Relation of the Third Kind: Man without Horizon," in *The Infinite Conversation,* trans. Susan Hanson (Minneapolis: University of Minnesota Press, 1993), 66–74. For Blanchot the other is outside every world; he (if he is the word) belongs to the outside as such, which one might describe in terms of space as surface rather than as volume, so that the other is always in a condition of exile, traversing the surface of the earth in endless restlessness since he is incapable of experiencing space except as radical exteriority.

28. See "Notes on Planning for the Future" (EPH169).

29. See Gerald L. Bruns, "What is Tradition?" in *Hermeneutics Ancient and Modern,* 208–11.

30. Maurice Blanchot poses just this question in "The Relation of the Third Kind." Blanchot's argument is that if one is to pursue Levinas's own thought rigorously, and to situate the other in an absolute transcendence, radical alterity must be thought of as neutral, that is, neither human nor nonhuman but in excess of every category or name, even beyond the unnameable name of negative theology (God): "*autrui* [Blanchot insists on the lower case] is a name that is essentially neutral and that, far from relieving us of all responsibility of attending to the neutral, it reminds us that we must, in the presence of the other who comes to us as *Autrui,* respond to the depth of strangeness, of inertia, of irregularity and idleness *[désœuvrement]* to which we open when we seek to receive the speech of the Outside" (*The Infinite Conversation,* 71–72). The "depth of strangeness" would therefore be a region more transcendent than that of the ethical relation of myself and another: for Blanchot it would be the region of poetry or writing (the region of exile or absolute nonidentity). See Gerald L. Bruns, *Maurice Blanchot: The Refusal of Philosophy* (Baltimore, Md.: Johns Hopkins University Press, 1997).

31. See Edith Wyschogrod, *Spirit in Ashes: Hegel, Heidegger, and the Era of Man-Made Mass Death* (New Haven, Conn.: Yale University Press, 1989).

32. See also Levinas, "The Ego and Totality" (EN30–38/CPP29–35).

33. See Habermas, "Philosophy as Stand-in and Interpreter," *Moral Consciousness and Communicative Action,* esp. 14–20.

Chapter 4

Gadamer and Romanticism

ANDREW BOWIE

The contemporary Western philosophical scene can be characterized in terms of divisions and interactions between approaches to philosophy which assume that their task is inextricably linked to the development of the natural sciences and approaches which often regard this assumption with considerable suspicion. Philosophers who adopt the former approach have the obvious advantage that the project of which they see themselves as a part produces more and more results which are in principle—if not in practice—publicly testable and which appear to confirm their underlying assumption that science is converging towards an already constituted reality as it is "in itself". One disadvantage of this project for its philosophical adherents, however, is that it becomes, as the work of the later Heidegger already suggested, increasingly unclear what its "philosophical" aspect is actually for. As Richard Rorty's remark against representational theories of truth—"Instead of seeing progress as a matter of getting closer to something specifiable in advance, we see it as a matter of solving more problems" — makes clear, it is possible to adopt realist or antirealist assumptions (or neither) as a working scientist (or as a philosopher) without that affecting one's belief in the value of a particular scientific theory; and even if philosophical arguments help in the genesis of theories, this cannot, on pain of circularity, legitimate either the arguments or the theories themselves.[1] Those who suspect the close link between philosophy and natural science, on the other hand, face the evident disadvantage that the explanatory and technical success of the modern sciences seems to render philosophical questions of their kind about the truth generated by those sciences redundant. The advantage they have over their opponents, though, is that even if it is the case that natural science has now developed so far that it does not need philosophy, they can still make appeals to the stubbornly persistent intuition

55

that the legislative capacity of the sciences does not extend as far as their more scientistically oriented advocates would like to claim. This view is summed up in Rorty's contention that "natural science has skewed philosophy" because "we philosophers still tend to take 'cognition' as the highest compliment we can pay to discourse."[2] The most bitter controversies here arise between positions at the extremes of the debate, when hard-line physicalists, for example, wish to reduce even their own theoretical activity to their physicalist presuppositions, or when some sociologists of science try to demonstrate that a generally accepted scientific theory is in fact merely the result of a locally dominant discursive formation. Such almost totally divergent positions exemplify a persistent divide in contemporary culture which it is important to try to understand in an adequate manner. Indeed, it could be that this cultural divide itself will be what keeps philosophical reflection about the sciences alive, despite the reduction in the scope of philosophy occasioned in modernity by the development of the sciences.

What is at issue here, of course, is a version of the debate between what are often thought of as "Enlightenment" and "Romantic" forms of thinking, which has also, in this century, been termed the debate between "positivism" and "Romanticism."[3] Given the nature of academic philosophy, the gap between the sides has in recent times led to an ever more specialized concentration on trying to account for how the sciences represent or converge on the truth about the world on the part of much "Enlightenment" philosophy, and to a sometimes equally rarefied concern with interrogations of the technological domination of nature made possible by the success of the sciences on the part of some "Romantic" philosophy. However, the rigidity characteristic of the worst versions of both sides has contrasted unfavorably with the attitude of those who have sought ways of mediating between the sides, and it will be one of my contentions that such mediation is in fact part of the thought which has the best claims to the title of "Romantic." A number of notable American philosophers trained in the analytical tradition have, for example, come to think that scientism may be as much a danger as antiscientific irrationalism.[4] John McDowell sees the problem with scientism as follows: "When we ask the metaphysical question whether reality is what science can find out about, we cannot, without begging the question, restrict the materials for an answer to those that science can countenance."[5] On the other hand, "continental" thinkers like Jürgen Habermas, while articulating worries about the effects of the dominant technological role of the sciences, have given often very necessary reminders that the alternatives to a modernity founded to a large extent upon the results of the natural sciences are not necessarily as appealing as the more extreme critics of "Western rationality" might suggest. Despite their very different backgrounds, such thinkers evidently meet on territory established by Kant that is further explored in Romantic philosophy, and in the hermeneutic tradition which emerges with Romanticism. At a time when such convergences are becoming more and more common, the stories told about the relationship between the "Enlightenment" and the "Romantic" sides of the debate will inevitably play a significant role in the future direction of philosophy.

As is well known, Gadamer offers, in *Truth and Method* and other work, one of the most influential postwar "Romantic" stories about the development of modernity, which questions perceived distortions introduced by the Enlightenment into Western philosophy. A major motivation of Gadamer's story is summed up in his assertion that "I wanted to show that it is not right to separate the question of art from the question of truth and to deprive art of all the knowledge it can communicate to us" (GW8:203). He outlines the origin of the problem this entails as follows: "Only when philosophy and metaphysics got into crisis in relation to the cognitive claims of the sciences did they discover again their proximity to poetry which they had denied since Plato. . . . Since then it makes sense to acknowledge the autonomous claim to truth of literature, but this takes place at the price of an unexplained relationship to the truth of scientific knowledge" (GW8: 287). In the wake of Kant's attempt to overcome the crisis of cognitive foundations occasioned by Hume and others, the first thinkers seriously to work out philosophical ways of thinking about the truth communicated by art were the early German Romantics, among whom I count, besides Friedrich Schlegel and Novalis, Schleiermacher and, at times, Schelling.[6] As we shall see later, in the light of the work of Manfred Frank, the aspect of Romantic philosophy which leads these thinkers to the question of art is their conviction that the attempt to ground modern philosophy in the activity of the subject cannot succeed, because the subject is not fully transparent to itself. It is now widely accepted that the main contribution of Gadamer's own work to contemporary philosophy is a rearticulation of the relationship between the claims to truth of art and of the humanities, and the truths of the sciences. However, part of that contribution involves a story about Romantic philosophy which includes a number of questionable contentions. I shall make some interpretative, philological, and historical points against that story in what follows, but I am also concerned to offer a few fragments of an account that is different from Gadamer's of how the interrogation of the truth of art and the truth of the sciences that begins with Romanticism plays a role in reflections about the nature of philosophy today.[7]

Just what is meant by "Romanticism" is still essentially contested, and it is pointless to try to conjure away the tensions now present in the term. Let us, then, take a specific historical example of a phenomenon often linked with Romantic thinking in order to see how this tension becomes apparent. In his essay "Poetry and Mimesis" of 1972 Gadamer discusses the move away from an aesthetics of "representation" in the eighteenth century, claiming that, as a consequence of this move, "The concept of expression rose to dominant significance. It has its original significance in music aesthetics. The immediate language of the heart spoken by notes now becomes the model according to which the language of art which rejects all rationalism of the concept is thought about at all" (GW8:81). In place of the "connection of poetics and rhetoric . . . a new proximity between music, which at that time was elevating itself to its classical development, and poetry" emerged (ibid.). At the time when the methods of the modern sciences appear to be giving grounds for thinking that they will eventually be able to represent reality "in itself," many of the arts and theories of the arts actually move away from the concept of representation, a move which is exemplified, as Gadamer suggests, by the emergence both of the idea of "absolute music" and of the instrumental music of Haydn, Mozart, Beethoven, and others that was seen as instantiating this idea.[8] Importantly, these moves against representation need not just be seen as taking place within the preserve of art and aesthetics: they rely on the more general idea that, in the light of the decline of theological conceptions of the ground of truth and meaning manifest in Kant's philosophy and in the overthrow of the idea of the divine origin of language, one can no longer be certain that what was previously thought of as being, in the literal sense, "re-presented" in concepts, or in language, or in art, is really accessible as such. This is because the condition of possibility of objective representation of what is "out there" is now regarded as necessarily linked in some way to the constitutive or spontaneous activity of the subject and to the language and other means of articulation employed by that subject. In this sense, a medium like music may be just as capable of revealing vital aspects of our being in the world as forms of articulation which were previously regarded as superior to music because of their representational qualities.[9]

The major philosophical questions which emerge at the end of the eighteenth century and which remain significant today concern how one should respond to this situation, especially given the success of the sciences in producing results despite the epistemological doubts that accompany that success. Gadamer's remarks refer to one extreme—and putatively "Romantic"—response, which is to valorize a language supposedly wholly constituted by the subjective, the "immediate language of the heart," that can be construed as refusing to partake of the objective realm. Toward the end of the eighteenth century music comes to be regarded by a particular group of thinkers as a language which articulates the emergent inner individuality of the subject. The need for such a language relates to the fact that this individuality is threatened simultaneously by some of the very advances in knowledge and the social changes in modernity which enabled it to emerge in the first place. The perception of music in question is apparent, for example, in Wilhelm Heinse's claim in 1776–77 that "The main source of music lies . . . in the heart, and not in . . . the usual way of speaking [*Aussprache*]. A composer cannot imitate this like a painter his model; he is . . . more of a creator than any other artist." [10] The problem is, however, that the "language" in question as characterized in this view seems simply to surrender any claims to truth by its exclusive relation to interiority, and thereby to preclude Gadamer's aim of showing that art is able to communicate truth. Because music is regarded as representing only feelings—if it represents anything at all—it can also be understood as Hegel understood it, namely as failing to reach the higher forms of modern scientific and philosophical truth which emerge via the subject's engagement with the resistance of the object world.

Gadamer's own view of music is more differentiated than this—he claims, for example, that "Every composition of 'absolute music' has [the] structure of being a relation to meaning [*Sinnbezug*] without a key [*Schlüssel*]" (GW8:324)—but he does share Hegel's suspicion of the notion of mere subjective expression associated with music, and this suspicion is carried over into aspects of his conception of Romanticism. The question is, then, whether this suspicion will allow an adequate characterization of the philosophical consequences inherent in the move away from representationalism associated with the change in status of music in the early Romantic period. Before this issue can be addressed we need to look at other aspects of Gadamer's conception in order to clarify his relationship to Romantic philosophy.

Gadamer's account of the wider significance of the constellation sketched here relies on his particular story about modern philosophy. In this story, both the suspicion of "prejudice" in the Enlightenment that follows from the demand to bring everything established before the "tribunal of reason" and the concomitant disempowering of tradition lead to the idea that the only reliable truth is arrived at by the methods of the natural sciences, which objectify the natural world. Other forms of articulation therefore come to be seen, in the manner we have just observed with regard to music, as being reliant on individual taste and individual feeling, so that the ground of the new philosophical discipline of aesthetics is thereby "subjectified." Gadamer's alternative to aesthetic theory's supposed adoption of a narrow conception of truth from the natural sciences relies on the demonstration that "understanding is never a subjective relationship towards a given 'object', but belongs rather to the effective history, and that means: to the being of that which is understood" (WMxix). This is because the model of the subject confronted with the art object in a manner analogous to the scientist with her object of investigation is untenable as an account of the experience of art:

We never find ourselves in the situation of being the pure contemplator of or listener to a work of art, for in a certain sense we are always participants in the transmission. The aim of grasping the inner structure and the connectedness of a work is, as such, not sufficient to remove all the prejudices which stem from the fact that we are ourselves within a tradition. (AP30)

Being in a tradition means being subjected to a happening of meaning which always transcends the individual's ability to articulate that meaning. In Gadamer's terms "effective historical consciousness" is "more being *[Sein]* than consciousness *[Bewusstsein],* i.e. more historically effected and determined than conscious in its being effected and determined" (GW3:221). Consequently, the very idea of a division between a subject and its object cannot be sustained, because the individual subject's meanings are—even before the subject develops a reflexive ability to think about them—inextricably bound up with already disclosed meanings which constitute the world it encounters, and which form, via the notion of "effective historical consciousness," what Gadamer means by "tradition."

The method of the natural sciences, Gadamer maintains, requires the elimination of merely contingent subjective apprehensions of their object, in order to arrive at what the object has in common with other objects of the same kind.[11] In the wake of one aspect of the work of Dilthey, Gadamer understands the development of nineteenth-century historiography and the other *Geisteswissenschaften* as leading to the attempt to objectify what has been historically transmitted, in order to establish a method for the human sciences that is analogous to that of the natural sciences.[12] His own project, on the other hand, is to "seek out the experience of truth which exceeds *[übersteigt]* the realm of control of scientific method . . . and to interrogate it as to its own legitimation" (WMxxvii). As such, "along with the experience of philosophy, the experience of art is the most emphatic warning to scientific consciousness to acknowledge its limits" (WMxxviii). Gadamer's response to the "subjectivism" of Kantian and post-Kantian aesthetics is, therefore, a conception in which "The 'subject' of the experience of art, that which remains and persists, is not the subjectivity of the person who experiences it, but the work of art itself" (WM98). A decisive methodological and historical link is thus established between the idea of natural science as the subject's means of control over the object and the rise of aesthetics, in which both are interpreted as part of the subject's attempt to arrogate to itself the right to determine truth. Gadamer's alternative conception relies on the subversion of that subject by the fact that it can never finally step outside the ways in which it is formed by tradition, so that "we are always very much more and other than what we know of ourselves, and . . . what exceeds us and our knowledge is precisely our real being" (GW8:327). How, then, does this relate to what I mean by "Romanticism"?

Given my remarks at the outset, one might have expected that a project which regards the limits of self-knowledge as a crucial aspect of our self-interpretation and aims to salvage a truth not countenanced by the analytical method of the natural sciences would see itself as at least partly in line with a Romanticism which produced such claims as Friedrich Schlegel's that—because of our inherently temporal nature—"Every person is only a piece of themselves,"[13] and his wonderful dictum that "If the chemist thinks a thing is not a whole because he can dissect it, that is just the same as what bad critics do to literature.—Didn't the world emerge from *slime*?"[14] Such parallels occur in other areas as well. Remembering the close connections between the idea of "philosophy" and the idea of "science" of the time, Schelling's claim in 1800 that art is "the only true and eternal organ and document of philosophy, which always and continuously documents what philosophy cannot represent externally"[15] initiates the explicit link of art and philosophy which Gadamer regards as so important. When Gadamer says of poetic language that "Where language exists in such a manner it is absolved of the function of pointing something out that is also presentable in another manner and thereby shows itself in its own function" (GW8:59), it is easy to think of Novalis's provocative antirepresentationalist speculation on "Poems, just pleasant sounding and full of beautiful words, but also without any meaning or context . . . like fragments of the most diverse things. True poetry can at the most have an allegorical meaning as a whole and an indirect effect, like music etc."[16] Gadamer's remark that "It is a mysterious form of the non-differentiation of what is said from the way it is said which gives art its specific unity and lightness and precisely thereby its own way of being true" (GW8:294) suggests a complex relationship between language and music, of the kind present in Novalis's assertion that the poet's "words are not universal signs—they are notes—magic words which move beautiful groups around themselves . . . for the poet language is never too poor but always too universal."[17] Furthermore, when Gadamer claims "It is paradoxical enough that one . . . speaks of art-criticism. It does not actually consist in differentiating good and bad in the work of art, but in differentiating something as a 'successful' work of art from an unsuccessful one or from something that has just been thrown together" (GW8:252), he echoes Novalis's contention that "Criticism of literature *[Poesie]* is an absurdity. It is already difficult to decide, yet the only possible decision, whether something is literature or not."[18] However, despite all these parallels—and there are plenty more—if one looks at *Truth and Method,* the only appearances of the Romantics are a few remarks by Schlegel, with little or no reference to the wider context of Romantic thought, and the more extensive critical appraisal of Schleiermacher's hermeneutics as part of the process of reduction of truth to what is produced by the method of the natural sciences that is inaugurated by Kant's "subjectivization of aesthetics."

The immediate objection to the parallels just cited between the Romantics and Gadamer might be, given the intellectual context of the Romantics at the end of the eighteenth century, that what they meant by these assertions is very different from what Gadamer means. However, things are not that simple. Gadamer's own account of interpretation is meant to reveal why interpretation can never be a simple historicist representation of aspects of thought of the past—that would be precisely the kind of objectification the theory is intended to counter—but is rather a "fusion of horizons" with what is to be interpreted, as part of the happening of "tradition." Furthermore, an awareness of the context of the Romantics, of the kind which Gadamer himself invokes for his presentation of the thinkers upon whom he does concentrate, soon makes it clear that his story offers only one—often very selective—perspective on these issues. It is therefore no longer obvious how the criteria of selection for the figures he concentrates on are to be legitimated, if not by the story he constructs about modern philosophy's being almost wholly dominated by the idea of objectification. I shall look at some consequences of this question later, but it is worth pointing out already that if the content of Gadamer's story is put into question by the proposal of an equally compelling or superior narrative, the conclusions he draws from his story concerning the nature of modernity themselves also cease to be wholly compelling, because they rely on the "effective history" of the texts he invokes to establish his story in the first place.

The central problem can be illustrated by the following example. In *Truth and Method* Gadamer gives an account of the difference between what he presents as two opposed strands of thought, epitomized by Schleiermacher's and Hegel's views of the hermeneutic task, in which Schleiermacher stands for the objectifying *"reconstruction"* of the "original determination of the work" (WM158), and Hegel for the *"integration"* of the work into a *"thinking mediation with contemporary life"* (WM161). According to Gadamer, Schleiermacher objectifies interpretation in a manner which Hegel does not, Hegel's procedure being closer in this respect to what Gadamer himself intends. The problem is that Gadamer's interpretation of Schleiermacher is tendentious at best, and in certain respects demonstrably misguided. He claims, for example, that the conception of Schleiermacher's which had the most influence was, rather than the early conception influenced by his friendship with Friedrich Schlegel in the 1790s, probably his later conception in *Hermeneutics and Criticism,* published by Friedrich Lücke in 1838.[19] According to Gadamer, in the later conception subjectivist "technical interpretation," in which, as Schleiermacher puts it in 1805, "language with its determining power disappears and only appears as the organ of the person, in the service of their individuality," plays a more dominant role than "grammatical interpretation," in which "the person . . . disappears and appears only as the organ of the language."[20] However, Wolfgang Virmond has now convincingly demonstrated that Schleiermacher used and worked on the text on "technical interpretation" that he had composed in 1805 as part of his first lectures on hermeneutics, for his *last* lectures on hermeneutics in 1832–33.[21] This text was wrongly assumed by Gadamer's pupil Heinz Kimmerle, who first edited and published it, and by others, to be a late text. As such it is now no longer clear that there *was* any substantial change in Schleiermacher's idea that, as he already put it in the 1805 notes, the two sides of interpretation are not separable: "Grammatical. Not possible without technical. Technical. Not possible without grammatical."[22] If we take, as Schleiermacher does, the grammatical to include the wider historical linguistic horizon of the text, and then accept, also with Schleiermacher, that this horizon is both a never fully graspable condition of possibility of communication for the author and the interpreter of the text, *and* that which the subject can yet re-form in individual ways, the idea that Schleiermacher relies on subjective *"feeling,* thus an immediate sympathetic and congenial understanding" (WM179), already becomes untenable. How can one understand the lexical, syntactic, and semantic resources of a particular historical "language-area" (Schleiermacher), which are then re-formed by a particular writer, simply by empathy (which is a word Schleiermacher does not use)? As Schleiermacher puts it in the 1809–10 lectures, "There is nothing purely objective in discourse; there is always the view of the utterer, thus something subjective, in it. There is nothing purely subjective, for it must after all be the influence of the object [i.e. the topic of discourse] which highlights precisely this aspect."[23] When Gadamer claims that Schleiermacher's assertion that interpretation is an art means that hermeneutics "completes its work, i.e. understanding itself, like a work of art" (WM179), he does not examine closely enough what Schleiermacher meant, assuming, in historicist manner, that the word "art" is linked with a subjectivist aesthetics based on the idea of the genius, who, in Kant's phrase, "gives the rule to art." The fact is, though, that for Schleiermacher the sense of "art" in question here includes *any* activity that relies on rules, for which there can be no rules for the applying of those rules, on pain of a regress of rules for rules that would render the activity impossible.[24] As Schleiermacher puts it, "Every single language could perhaps be learned via rules, and what can be learned in this way is mechanism. Art is that for which there admittedly are rules, but the combinatory application of these rules cannot in turn be rule-bound."[25] This conception is most obviously relevant in primary language acquisition, where the first words cannot be learned in terms of rules, because that would lead into the regress of rules for rules, and Schleiermacher often refers to the experience of children in acquiring language to suggest what he means.

Schleiermacher in fact uses "art" *(Kunst)* both in the sense of the Greek *"techne,"* meaning ability, capacity, and in the sense related to the new aesthetic notion usually associated with Kant's *Critique of Judgement*. Even in the latter case, though, what is meant has to do with the question of rules. Art in this sense cannot itself be taken to be art in terms of rules: i.e., there cannot be a concept of—a rule for identifying—art that would allow us to judge in every case whether something is art or not (the—Kantian—idea here is one source of Novalis's idea of the centrality of the decision as to whether something is literature or not). All Schleiermacher means with regard to hermeneutics, however, is that, even though it relies on indispensable methodological presuppositions, interpretation cannot be circumscribed by a definitive objectifying method. Anybody who wishes to understand a text has to make never fully groundable inductive judgments about its meaning, in the manner of Kant's "reflective judgement," or—to suggest the continuing importance of the idea—of Donald Davidson's "passing theories" that are required for "radical interpretation" because "there are no rules for arriving at passing theories, no rules in any strict sense, as opposed to rough maxims and methodological generalities."[26] I do not wish here to go into the detail of Gadamer's misapprehension of Schleiermacher, as this has already been done most effectively elsewhere, by Manfred Frank in particular, and Gadamer himself admits these days that he was mistaken in certain respects.[27] The more important issue is to establish a different account of Romanticism, which further questions Gadamer's idea that Romanticism involves a subjectivism that can only be overcome by a new kind of hermeneutics.

"Romanticism" is still widely regarded as the movement in modern European society which gave primacy to the creative and autonomous aspects of the subject over what could be understood about that subject in objectifying "Enlightenment" terms. This image has, though, increasingly come to be seen as inadequate to the complexity of what we mean by Romanticism, as the following example from the present discussion can suggest. Gadamer himself now regards his distorted picture of Schleiermacher in *Truth and Method* as being a result of his failure to take adequate account of Schleiermacher's *Dialektik,* which relates to Schleiermacher's hermeneutics in the following manner: "Language only exists via thought, and vice versa; each can only complete itself via the other. The art of explication and translation [hermeneutics] dissolves language into thought; dialectic dissolves thought into language."[28] As such, given the role of hermeneutics and dialectic as the necessary complements of each other in Schleiermacher, it cannot be the case that the ground of understanding is some kind of direct intuitive contact with another subject, or a direct apprehension of objects in the world. At the same time, though, Schleiermacher is also convinced that language alone does not determine the access we have to the world: if the determinacy of thought requires the fixity provided by the limited number of elements in a language, language in turn requires the spontaneity of the individual subject for it to be able to function in an indefinite number of un-accustomed contexts. It is therefore not possible to reduce understanding either to an account of the rules of language or to an account of the think-ing subject, because we can *neither* wholly isolate the world, including lan-guage, from what our minds spontaneously contribute to it, *nor* wholly iso-late our minds from their receptive involvement with the world. It is, of course, not a great distance from this conception to many of Gadamer's own contentions (nor, as we shall see, to those of Rorty). Gadamer considers his path in relation to Hegel, for example, to be a "path from dialectic back to dialogue" (GW2:368), and this is in many ways how, because of his rejec-tion of the idea of "absolute knowledge," Schleiermacher saw the difference of his dialectic from that of Hegel.[29]

The reason for Gadamer's failure in relation to Schleiermacher is, though, less contingent than his failure to consult one particular text, be-cause his misconception actually follows quite straightforwardly from part of the larger story that he presupposes as the basis of his desire to formulate an alternative conception of hermeneutics. Despite all Gadamer's invalu-able revisions of, and improvements to, Heidegger's conception—notably his rejection of the untenable idea of the "language of metaphysics"—his story still relies upon aspects of Heidegger's account of modern philosophy, an account which has continued to have enormous effects on the most var-ied kinds of contemporary theory, particularly via the influence of post-structuralism's adoption of its diagnosis of the role of the subject in moder-nity (see Frank for the best critical account of this issue). From Descartes, to Hegel's claim that "the substance is subject," to Husserl's search for the "principle of all principles," Heidegger maintains, the "concern *[Sache]* of philosophy . . . is subjectivity."[30] This startling assertion is explained by what Heidegger regards as being behind Descartes's adoption of the *cogito* as the *fundamentum inconcussum:* "To the essence of the subjectivity of the *subjectum* and of man as subject belongs the unconditioned de-limitation of the do-main of possible objectification and of the right to decision about this ob-jectification,"[31] so that man himself "guarantees the certainty of the know-able."[32] Heidegger's development of this position into a verdict on the whole of "Western metaphysics," which he later comes to equate with nat-ural science itself, is well known and need not detain us for long here, not least because Gadamer, while still claiming that "in the background of the whole of modern thought stands the Cartesian characterization of con-sciousness as self-consciousness" (GW2:148), is rather more circumspect about the implications of such a view of the subject in modern philosophy.

If philosophy is, as Hegel put it, its "age grasped in thought," philoso-phers who correspond to what is assumed about the age in other respects are likely to become part of a self-confirming picture. The philosophical story about the foundational status of the subject which begins with Descartes, for example, maps effortlessly onto an account of the history of modern science as the growing success of the subject in manipulating nature for its own purposes, so that the happening of science and the happening of philosophy mirror each other as the essential truth of modernity, with the consequence that the later Heidegger ends up attempting to divorce his thought from philosophy altogether in order to find ways of understanding which cannot be said to be part of the dominant story. However, this linking of the philosophical and the historical involves several short-circuits, one of the most significant of which has been identified by Dieter Henrich and further explored by Manfred Frank, to which I shall return in a moment. The simple point, in the terms with which we began, is that the Cartesian story is essentially an Enlightenment story, which fails to take account of a Romantic counternarrative.

Gadamer is in certain respects aware of this when he suggests that "It is the philosophy of German Idealism, Romantic literature, and the discovery of the historical world in Romanticism which have shown themselves up till now to be an effective countermovement within the process of Enlightenment in modernity" (GW8:163). The problem in Gadamer's approach, though, is that radical reassessments of our self-understanding are homogenized into a narrative of tradition which, as has often been pointed out, has similarities with the movement of Hegel's all-consuming *Geist,* the ultimate dominating "super subject."[33] Hegel's view of the subordination of the individual subject to *Geist*—which was precisely what Schleiermacher opposed in Hegel—is also consistent with Gadamer's view of the relationship of the subject to the work of art, in which the work of art "subjects" its recipient to its truth, rather than the recipient, as Schleiermacher saw her, also generating this truth by enabling new aspects of the work to reveal new aspects of the world. Gadamer wants to account for the indisputable fact that certain great works of art, which have transcended their context of genesis and which have remained significant in ever new contexts, are not susceptible to the kind of temporality encountered in the sciences, where validity is often very ephemeral. His underlying idea is apt to experiences like being subjected to the power of a musical work which always transcends our ability to exhaust its potential, a potential which is never fully realized in the work's performances, and in the thoughts and feelings the work evokes at any particular time. However, the approach is also too one-sided in that it transfers too many of the attributes of an admittedly inept conception of the aesthetic subject into the work itself, as though the (metaphorical) active authority of the work from the past always took precedence over the new possibilities of understanding which depend on the activity of its present and future interpreters.[34]

Behind all these matters lies the question of the subject and its relation to truth in modernity, and it is here that the Romantic contribution has rarely been adequately grasped. What is at issue was already implicit in the rise of the idea of absolute music as a nonrepresentational form of articulation, which emerged at the same time and in the same places as the most profound philosophical reflections in modernity on the nature of self-consciousness. How, though, can the question of truth be understood in relation to something whose significance lies in what cannot be propositionally stated? Here, unsurprisingly, matters become both complex and controversial, and I can only sketch the beginnings of a response to the question. The first thing is to establish a clearer picture of a specifically Romantic conception of self-consciousness, of the kind shared, albeit with certain differences, by Novalis, Schlegel, Schleiermacher, and the later Schelling. Gadamer claims that the "primacy of self-consciousness," in the sense of the ability of the modern subject to objectify the world, including itself, in the name of technical manipulation, is undermined by Nietzsche's and Freud's insights into the subversion of self-consciousness (GW8:158). The work of Henrich and Frank has shown, however, that the relevant reassessment began much earlier, and that the most convincing accounts of subjectivity are not susceptible to Heidegger's and Gadamer's interpretation of modern philosophy, in which Heidegger regards Nietzsche's "Will to Power" as the culmination of the theory in which the subject dominates the object.

It was J. G. Hamann who probably first explicitly proposed the inversion of the *cogito,* in which being is understood as preceding consciousness, rather than vice versa, in a letter to F. H. Jacobi in 1785,[35] and Jacobi developed the idea in some detail immediately after this. The fact is that Jacobi revealed the problems of grounding modern philosophy in a way that directly or indirectly affected nearly every significant subsequent German philosopher.[36] His decisive argument is simple: if all our knowledge is of determinate facts, and such knowledge is only intelligible via its relation to other determinate facts, and if, furthermore, each thing depends for its identity on its relations to other things, we are left in both cases with the threat of an infinite regress that renders incomprehensible our undoubted sense of a world of intelligible things.

This problem has reappeared in a variety of guises, suggesting the continuing centrality of Romantic thought within modern philosophy. Hans Albert's Popper-influenced "Critical Rationalism," which played a crucial role in the Positivism Dispute of the 1960s between Adorno and Habermas, and Popper and Albert, talks, for example, of the "Münchhausen Trilemma" that results from the attempt to use Leibniz's "principle of sufficient reason" to ground knowledge.[37] The attempt definitively to ground knowledge is either, as Jacobi already showed in relation to precisely this principle, an infinite regress of reasons for reasons, or a circular argument that relies on reasons which themselves require grounding, or a breaking off of the attempt at grounding in the name of something which is taken as dogmatically self-evident. Jacobi adopts the last of these possibilities in opting for a theological grounding of the fact that being is disclosed at all, a fact which he thinks is not philosophically explicable. The most influential "Cartesian" version of the third possibility, which Jacobi's arguments did much to undermine with the help of the Romantics,[38] is the philosophy of the early Fichte.[39] Fichte aims to counter the regress entailed in the fact that everything particular is "conditioned" by something else with the idea that the subject must therefore itself be "unconditioned" as the absolute founding principle of the world's intelligibility. This status is evident for Fichte in the subject's immediate spontaneous access to itself in "intellectual intuition," which is unique in that all other existents are only accessible in terms of their determined relations to other things, whereas the subject's access to itself cannot rely on determination from elsewhere. The task of philosophy for Fichte is, therefore, to establish that subjectivity, whose essential attribute, in the light of Kant, is its freedom from the determinism of the world of phenomena, is the necessary prior ground of truth, providing the explanation of what Kant failed to explain via the notion of the "transcendental unity of apperception."[40]

A vital problem which Fichte himself came to be aware of, and which the Romantics explored in detail, is that there seems to be no way of explicating the structure of subjectivity which does not entail just presupposing what is to be explicated. In what Henrich terms, in the light of Fichte's "essential insight" into the problem in 1797, the "reflection model"—the model common to Descartes and others in the Enlightenment tradition—the circle in the explanation results from the attempt to explain the phenomenon that is myself in the same way as any part of the objective world. As Novalis put it in 1795–96, "Can I look for a schema for myself, if I am that which schematizes?"[41] If I am to know the object that is myself *as* myself I must already be familiar with myself in a way which does not depend upon an objectifying reflection. One can look in a mirror and be infallibly aware that one is seeing someone without being aware that the someone is oneself, so that the object side of the reflection makes no contribution to this kind of self-awareness. Consequently, reflexive, propositional self-knowledge, knowledge of oneself as object, is fallible in a way that immediate self-knowledge is not. The experience of "qualia" and the ability to ascribe experiences to myself as my experiences are the increasingly widely accepted nonobjectifiable aspects of self-consciousness which the contemporary philosophy of mind sees as confirming both that the reflection model cannot provide an adequate account of self-consciousness and that the language via which self-consciousness is articulated is only a necessary, not a sufficient, condition of self-consciousness.[42] Henrich sums up the core idea in his dictum that "cognition of the real can never completely integrate itself into its conception of the whole of reality."[43] This means, of course, that the model which sees the subject as transparent to itself as its own object and as that which asserts its power against the other—including itself, in reductionist physicalist accounts of the mental, for example—which is the idea behind Heidegger's conception, and which Gadamer sees as subverted by the subject's relation to language, is not adequate as an account of the history of thinking about the subject in modernity.

The question therefore becomes how to think about that which resists objectification and representation and yet is essential, as Kant had shown in his demonstration of the necessity for that which will bind together different intuitions, to the possibility of truth. Schleiermacher gives a good condensed version of a Romantic conception of the subject in the following passage from his *Dialektik:*

> as thinkers we are only in the single act [of thought]; but as beings we are the unity of all single acts and moments. Progression is only the transition from one [reflexive] moment to the next. This therefore takes place through our being, the living unity of the succession of the acts of thought. The transcendent basis of thought, in which the principles of linkage are contained, is nothing but our own transcendent basis as thinking being. . . . *The transcendent basis must now indeed be the same basis of the being which affects us as of the being which is our own activity.*[44]

Frank explains the basic conception as follows: "Being—the Absolute— is no longer a content of consciousness, but rather a presupposition which we must necessarily make if we want to explain the unity of our self-consciousness, which is split into a subject- and an object-pole."[45] The nature of this being is bound up with the Romantic understanding of art in a manner close to Gadamer, because both positions regard the transcendence of being over reflexive consciousness as best understood via the experience of art.

As we have seen, Gadamer regards the truth manifest in art as a happening of tradition which transcends the contingent responses of the individual subject. Frank has suggested, though, that Gadamer's own idea of tradition may itself involve the aporias of the reflection model, because the truth about myself can only be approached via the recognition of myself in the mirror of linguistic "effective historical consciousness," which results in another version of the problem of objectifying the subjective outlined above. Frank finds an alternative conception precisely in the early Romantics, who reject Fichte's idea of the subject as prior constitutive ground of philosophy and connect this version of antifoundationalism to the experience of art— in which the failure to be ground of oneself is experienced in the failure to articulate the meaning of the work in concepts—while insisting on the irre-ducibility of the individual subject either to the symbolic orders via which it articulates itself or to naturalistic explanation.

The question which links the different approaches here is how to re-spond to the ever more widespread doubts about the possibility—or even desirability—of foundationalism. In this respect the conception of science as founded on the self-certainty of the subject proposed by Heidegger, al-though historically mistaken, does have the virtue of suggesting how "En-lightenment" positions of many kinds rely on something which has to claim to be self-confirming, if the regress discussed above is to be avoided. The point of *both* idealist *and* materialist views for Heidegger is that they require a final, articulable ground, for example in the self-certainty of the subject, or in the assumption of the ultimate possibility of a physicalist reduction of that subject to its material ground. How, then, is the relationship between the "Enlightenment" and the "Romantic" sides of modern philosophy now to be understood, given the problems in the story upon which Gadamer relies?

Two differing "Romantic" alternatives seem to me most revealing in the light of the questions with which we began. One is the early German Ro-mantic conception, now reestablished by the work of Frank, in which the recognition of the inability of philosophy to establish an absolute ground in the manner sought by the Cartesian tradition leads to the idea of truth as a regulative idea to be approached in "endless approximation," an idea which is understood, though not explained, via the subject's experience of the inexhaustibility of the work of art. The other, highly influential—and re-lated—contemporary alternative, which highlights issues also raised by Gadamer, is Rorty's Nietzsche-influenced conception of a pragmatist "Ro-mantic polytheism," which regards even a regulative idea of truth as re-maining within the Christian-Platonist representationalist tradition. Given that, for Rorty, there is nothing which can unite the differing senses in which the word "truth" is used, the very notion of a goal of inquiry or a moral ideal which is supposed to be endlessly approached but never at-tained is at best a *focus imaginarius,* albeit one which "is none the worse for being an invention rather than (as Kant thought it) a built-in feature of the human mind."[46] As we shall see, Gadamer's conception involves aspects of both alternatives.

Gadamer comes close to Rorty—though in a manner which Rorty re-gards as being too reliant on a big philosophical story—because he also does not regard truth as a goal, thinking of it instead as a temporal hap-pening which becomes manifest in the transmission of the work of art. How-ever, this conception is open to questions that were already being asked in early Romantic philosophy. The basic problem is that the conception can be seen as too readily surrendering the—admittedly only counterfactual—

aim of universal truth in the name of local agreement, and thus as being open to a relativism which puts the possible validity of the conception itself into question. What, for example, allows it to be decided when the truth revealed by art actually happens? Is it based on a consensus of the recipients of the work, or is it, as Gadamer suggests, something which transcends this? If it is the latter, what criteria do we have for what is at issue at all? Gadamer actually insists that "hermeneutic reflection is limited to revealing cognitive possibilities which would not be perceived without it. It does not itself provide a criterion of truth" (GW2:263). This does not really make the matter any more transparent, however, because Gadamer seems to be making a distinction between what hermeneutic reflection reveals and the method via which this is assessed as to its truth, which makes it unclear whether what is revealed is itself a happening of truth at all. Gadamer notoriously refuses to accept that we can use a notion of "better understanding" and thinks "it is enough to say that one understands *differently, if one understands at all*" (WM280). In this sense "better understanding" supposedly involves another kind of objectification in the manner of Enlightenment thinking, which fails to acknowledge the inherent temporality of all understanding, in which "time is the basis which carries the happening in which what is present is rooted" (WM281). It is, he claims, only because of the temporal distance of ourselves from what is to be interpreted that there is space for a new happening of its truth, which derives from the "fusion of horizons" that constitutes tradition.

Clearly the difficult problem here is how to cash out the notion of truth if we do not accept a correspondence theory. Perhaps surprisingly, Rorty is happy to admit that " 'true' is an absolute term,"[47] and he claims that "Davidson has helped us realize that *the very absoluteness of truth is a good reason for thinking 'true' indefinable and for thinking that no theory of the nature of truth is possible. It is only the relative about which there is anything to say.*"[48] These assertions take us right to the heart of the Romantic conception, as these characteristic remarks from Novalis's so-called "Fichte-Studies" of 1796 make clear. Novalis ponders the idea of philosophy as the search for the ultimate ground of truth and asks what would be the case if "the absolute ground" were unattainable, claiming that "the drive to philosophy would [then] be an endless activity," and that, in consequence—and this is compatible with Rorty's assertion—"The absolute which is given to us can only be known negatively by our acting and finding that what we are seeking is not attained by any action."[49] As such, "All seeking after the First is nonsense—it is a regulative idea,"[50] so that grounding, either from the outset, as in Fichte, or in anticipation of the absolute Idea at the end, as later in Hegel, is never definitive. Rorty's Nietzschean question here is whether there is therefore any point in pursuing something whose existence is merely hypothetical, on the assumption that, despite all, this is what most of the Western philosophical tradition has already been unsuccessfully doing since Plato (though as we saw, he does think a *focus imaginarius* a useful notion). If one adopts Rorty's Davidsonian assumption, which is also partly shared by Gadamer, that truth and meaning cannot be separated, and that most of what is said is—even though we cannot definitively provide a theory of truth—in some sense "true," because it is good enough to achieve what we need to in communication in real contexts, or because it discloses the world to the members of a community, any more emphatic sense of truth may indeed be more trouble than it is worth. Is the impulse to retain a sense of the absolute as somehow inherent in our awareness of the relativity of particular thoughts therefore to be rejected?

Schlegel suggests a partial difference from Rorty when, while asserting, like Novalis, that "There is no absolute truth," he also claims that "this spurs on the spirit and drives it to activity."[51] To counter the obvious objection to such assertions, Schlegel also admits that "If all truth is relative, then the proposition is also relative that all truth is relative."[52] Any proposition has, as Rorty also suggested, to introduce relativity into the absolute, because, as Novalis puts it, in relation to "A is A" as the statement of the absolute, "The essence of identity [of the "ideal" and the "real"] can only be established in a pseudo-proposition *[Scheinsatz].* We leave the identical in order to represent it."[53] Schlegel therefore claims that "For a positive *criterion of truth* the *truth itself* would have already to be present and *be given*—which is therefore a contradiction,"[54] because we would have presupposed what the criterion is supposed to enable us to discover. What lies behind Schlegel's assertions is apparent in his declaration elsewhere, which brings him close to Gadamer, that "In truth you would be distressed if the whole world, as you demand, were for once seriously to become completely comprehensible."[55] Complete understanding would render the pursuit of better—or other— ways of understanding redundant and the world would therefore become meaningless, because postfoundational meaning in this sense resides precisely in the idea that there is always more to be revealed, not in the convergence on a "ready-made world."

The question is, though, whether one therefore renounces any notion of the totality on the grounds that, in Rorty's terms, the notion requires either the idea of an ultimate correspondence between thought and the world as it is independently of how we describe it, or the idea of an ultimate rendering commensurable of all vocabularies. The two kinds of idea in question are, of course, not necessarily the same, as the history of subsequent philosophy will make clear. With regard to the first idea, Rorty thinks that if there is no identifiable aspect of the world that definitively could be said to be what makes our sentences true, "there is nothing that can plausibly be described as a *goal* of inquiry, although the desire for further justification, of course, serves as a *motive* of inquiry."[56] Any more emphatic concern with truth in this sense takes us into the realm of the ineffable, which offends against his views that language is a "tool rather than a medium", and that a concept is therefore "just the regular use of a mark or noise,"[57] there being nothing useful to be said about what is "subpropositional." The "philosophical" question here is how one interprets the relativity of particular knowledge, which can, remember, also be understood in terms of the second idea. *Does* one, then, give up on any sense of the absolute in favor of a relativization of truth to language games or to tradition, or does one follow Putnam, who is more in line with Schlegel, Novalis, and Schleiermacher when he insists that "The very fact that we speak of our different conceptions as different conceptions of *rationality* posits a *Grenzbegriff*, a limit-concept of the ideal truth"?[58]

There is, of course, a further dimension to this issue. Rorty's rejection of the "subpropositional" also excludes precisely the dimension of "language" that becomes manifest when Romanticism takes seriously the meaning of the non-propositional form of music, a form which relies for its significance on agreements within a community about the need for articulations which transcend what can be said. If one takes a narrowly semantic view of "truth," as Rorty sometimes does, there is no problem here, because music does not have meaning in this sense, but if "meaning" is what we understand when we understand something, there is evidently a sense in which music has to be meaningful to be music at all. Gadamer reminds one of the importance of this dimension even in everyday language use when he remarks that "The word which one says or which is said to one is not the grammatical element of a linguistic analysis, which can be shown in concrete phenomena of language acquisition to be secondary in relation, say, to the linguistic melody of a sentence" (GW2:196).

Before trying to establish which differences make a real difference here, it is important to remember that the differences we have been exploring are accompanied by a substantial degree of agreement on some basic issues. For the Romantics, Rorty, and Gadamer we are always, albeit in different senses, in contact with reality, and all agree that this contact should not be thought of as based on representing the object world in an adequate manner. Schlegel says, thereby refusing the scheme/content division in the manner of Rorty, but at the same time retaining the regulative idea of the whole also seen in Putnam, that "One has always regarded it as the greatest difficulty to get from consciousness to reality *[Daseyn]*. But in our view this difficulty does not exist. *Consciousness* and *reality* appear here as the connected parts *[Glieder]* of a whole."[59] He takes the very fact that we come to refute previously held beliefs as the source of our inarticulable sense of truth: truth "arises where opposed errors neutralize each other . . . if we destroy error truth arises of its own accord."[60] Although new beliefs are themselves in turn open to revision because they are only partial, and they depend for their confirmation on other as yet undisclosed beliefs, the regulative idea of their being coherent with all other beliefs takes one beyond relativism, in the name of the idea that the system of statements that cohere with each other is closer to being complete, even though ideas about the nature of that completion are only hypotheses. Schlegel's view of art as the key to the proper understanding of the failure of philosophy to be able to articulate the absolute depends, therefore, on the way in which art can show that there is always another way in which we can evoke or articulate aspects of the world, because the being of things is more than can be articulated in thought. Music therefore takes on a philosophical significance which cannot be explained by philosophy itself because of the new ways in which this Romantic thought comes to be understood.

To this extent Schlegel's (and Novalis's) position can be seen as congruent with many of Gadamer's contentions about art as a corrective to the objectifications of the natural sciences, which aim to reduce the being of the thing to the aspect which renders it subsumable into an explanatory theory. Frank, in *"Unendliche Annaherung,"* though, actually sees Schlegel's position as pointing to the need for a "metaphysical realist" interpretation of Romantic philosophy, because the conviction that being transcends consciousness leads to the idea of thought as correspondence to a reality which is independent of what we think about it. The problem here lies in the ever more tangled nature of the debate over realism: can the realist "view from nowhere" meaningfully be termed a "view" in the same way as a view from somewhere, and how would we articulate a view from nowhere in a language which is itself always a view from somewhere? The fact is that Schlegel's position is equally compatible with a pragmatism or a hermeneutics which regards the realism/antirealism and realism/idealism divisions as futile because of their reliance on a representational conception, which the world-disclosive nature of art undermines by its reminder of the constant possibility of rearticulation of what there is. Indeed, Schlegel himself explicitly rejects the correspondence theory of truth, which is generally regarded as essential to a realist position, because in it "the object would, as such, have to be compared with the representation; but that is not at all possible, because one only ever has a representation of the object, and thus can only ever compare one representation with another."[61] Truth cannot be seen as the "agreement of subjective and objective" because "reality . . . cannot be called either subject or object."[62] In a similar vein, Schleiermacher also says that "One could say that correspondence of thought with being is an empty thought, because of the absolute different nature and incommensurability of each."[63] Apel makes the basic point as follows, thus emphasizing one of the continuities I am concerned to establish here: "If one asked about the criterion of the presence of . . . *adaequatio,* then the answer would have to be given by an observer who located themselves outside the subject-object relation of cognition and could judge this relation like a relation between objects."[64] Such a position is not available, on pain of a regress of observers of the observers.[65] For Schlegel, then, it is the regulative idea of coherence between beliefs which can correct mistaken apprehensions of the real, not the idea of correspondence.

However, the problem remains that if something is postponed to infinity, there are grounds for assuming that it has no role to play in what we actually do that could not be better dealt with either in a more pragmatic manner, or in terms of Gadamer's notion that the temporality of understanding does not involve a privation but rather a multiplication of horizons. In common with the Romantics, Rorty rejects the notion of truth as correspondence, and he also uses attenuated notions of coherence of beliefs and communicative consensus, but the difference is that he thinks there is no substantial point in approaching these issues in terms of truth as regulative idea. As we saw above, Schleiermacher gave reasons of the kind Rorty also gives for questioning whether we can finally make distinctions between what the world contributes and what we contribute to knowledge, but he retained a more emphatic sense of truth, of the kind suggested by Putnam and Apel, insisting that "in language as well there is error and truth; even incorrect thought can become common to all."[66] Rorty refers to this idea as involving the "cautionary" use of "true," which he sees as "a gesture toward future generations"[67] who may find the contrary of what is now universally accepted a better way of talking about the world, rather than as involving truth as a regulative idea. So how are we to adjudicate between these differing conceptions of "Romantic" thought?

It should now be evident that the discussion has led into some of the most contentious debates in contemporary philosophy, and, of course, to the (intended) sense that we are in some senses little further on in resolving these debates than people were at the end of the eighteenth century.[68] One point does, though, seem to be decisive, and it is encapsulated in the title of Apel's critical essay on Gadamer, cited above: "Regulative Idea or Happening of Truth?" which also sums up the difference which has underlain much of the preceding discussion. Let us conclude, then, by looking very briefly at the investment entailed by allegiance to one or the other side of the divide suggested by Apel's title in relation to the question with which we began. Rorty and Gadamer share with Schlegel and Schleiermacher the conviction that, although the natural sciences are indispensable to human survival, as Gadamer puts it, "this does not mean that people would be able to solve the problems that face us, peaceful coexistence of peoples, and the preservation of the balance of nature, with science as such. It is obvious that not mathematics but the linguistic nature of people is the basis of human civilization" (GW8:342). The strength of this position lies in its widening of the focus of philosophical reflection beyond the narrow analytical concern with whether our thought can really converge on or represent the way the world is independently of our thought. The problem it involves lies precisely in interpreting the relationship between the happening of truth in world disclosure and the regulative idea of truth.

The vital hermeneutic idea which Gadamer has done so much to render convincing, and which was made possible by Romantic thought, is that the method of the sciences depends upon world-disclosing preunderstandings which themselves cannot be scientifically explained—hence the link of his hermeneutics to art. In the early Romantic view, the limits of what can be explained are understood in terms of the way in which the subject's being is always more than it can explain to itself, which leaves it with an endless task of self-exploration via its relations to the world: natural science is therefore only one part of that exploration. The significance of music lies, in this sense, precisely in its meaning being independent of what science can say about it as sound. Rorty has, as we saw, no time either for "subpropositional" modes of articulation or for reflections on self-consciousness, but this surely tries to obviate too much too quickly, giving us no way, for example, of understanding the difference of intentional language use or the playing of music from the mere mechanical production of signifiers and patterned noises. Do reflections on self-consciousness necessarily lead back in the last analysis to the paradigm of representation if the essential issue is not the empiricist problem of how sensations ever get to the point of becoming reliable knowledge, but rather the Romantic problem, which Rorty accepts in its psychoanalytical version, of how to come to terms with the fact that the being of the self is more than it knows?

One of Rorty's most productive ideas in this context is his separation of "projects of social cooperation and projects of individual self-development": the "paradigm" of the former is natural science, of the latter, "romantic art," and another "may be" religion.[69] The former demands the kind of communicative consensus which is vital to the functioning of any society—which Apel, Habermas, and others try, in Rorty's opinion unsuccessfully, to elevate into a substitute for earlier forms of transcendental philosophy—the latter is left to the individual, provided they do no harm to others. Gadamer, of course, wishes to use engagement with what Rorty sees in terms of a private search for transcendence in art as a means of revealing the culturally damaging implications of the exclusive concentration on rule-based "method" in the sciences. The dangers in this area are familiar: in its extreme versions the rendering public of the private need for transcendence is precisely what makes Habermas and others so suspicious of what they mean by "Romanticism," especially in the light of the course of German history. Rorty therefore says that he reads "people like Heidegger and Nietzsche as good *private* philosophers," contrasting himself with Habermas who "reads them as bad *public* philosophers."[70] This is because they offer resources for the kind of

"Romantic" transcendence which allows one to imagine utopian possibilities, even though they are useless, or worse, for the "philosophical" task of advancing democracy. Their value lies, then, precisely in the world-disclosive element of their thought, not—and Rorty suggests something similar about Gadamer, whom he regards in this respect as sharing a suspect Heideggerian nostalgia in relation to the "public" aspect of modernity[71] in their contribution to solving political, economic, and technical problems in the modern world.

Rorty himself seems here to rely on questionable radical dichotomies between two fundamentally different kinds of project, and two different uses of language, of the kind he elsewhere seeks to avoid, though the distinctions are in many ways merely strategic. He claims against Habermas, for example, that what happens in "private" world disclosure can, if it happens to become part of the problem-solving resources of a society, move from one to the other side of the divide, from mere disclosure to the realm of argument about truth based on the consensus of a community. If one accepts this view in the form in which Rorty presents it, Gadamer's desire for an emphatic sense in which great art involves a happening of truth entails the equivalent with regard to art of what Rorty wishes to escape via the rejection of the correspondence theory of truth, namely a kind of deeper legitimation that needs to be backed up by a big philosophical story, in this case of the need for something opposed to the idea of "science and technology as something like our historical fate."[72] On the other hand, if one accepts Rorty's more emphatic formulations, one is left with a questionable schematic distinction between "arguments," in which "the same vocabulary" must "be used in premises and conclusions" as part of the same "language game," and "suggestions about how to speak differently."[73] All the latter can do is "fluidize old vocabularies."[74] In real language use, of course, this distinction is being transgressed all the time, and it is the spontaneous interpretative capacity of subjects most obviously exemplified in their ability to make sense of art which prevents the confusion that would ensue if Rorty's model were really determining.

Gadamer is actually prone to make an analogous kind of distinction, from the other direction, in order to sustain his story about the difference between rule-bound, objectifying language use in scientific and technical work, and revelatory language which escapes objectification: "Both kinds of discourse, poetic as well as philosophical . . . share a common trait. They cannot be 'false.' For there is no criterion outside them by which they can measure themselves, to which they could correspond" (GW8:239). This seems to mean that scientific discourse does correspond to the world in itself, as opposed to being seen as a way of making predictions to solve problems. As such, in wishing to avoid the—in any case questionable—idea that all evaluation involves objectification, Gadamer ends up leaving the door open for an implausibly positive view of the truth of art in modernity, of the kind Adorno did so much to discredit.[75] The more plausible version of what Rorty intends in this area, which is inherent in the early Romantic project and which seeks to circumvent this sort of problem in Gadamer, involves the demand constantly to renegotiate the borders between world disclosure and the regulative idea of intersubjective validity, rather than adopt Gadamer's overhasty Heideggerian story, which sees the two as inherently distinct (on this see Apel). However, Rorty's relegation of art, along with religious belief, to the "private" on the grounds that it is not engaged in the process of "achieving democratic consensus" of the kind required in the sciences seems in certain respects to repeat Gadamer's problem from a different angle, because it underestimates what Novalis referred to as the "aesthetic imperative," the importance of the counterfactual aim—or regulative idea—of democratic consensus in relation to culture as part of any successfully functioning public sphere. Given the increasingly debased nature of commodified contemporary culture, where apparent increased diversity in fact involves a dangerous leveling of discrimination, it seems vital to sustain, as Gadamer's work—despite all—does, the impetus behind the Romantic idea that art should be true rather than merely pleasing.

NOTES

1. Richard Rorty, *Achieving Our Country: Leftist Thought in Twentieth-Century America* (Cambridge, Mass.: Harvard University Press, 1998), 28.

2. Richard Rorty, *Objectivity, Relativism, and Truth* (New York: Cambridge University Press, 1991), 162.

3. See, e.g., Tugendhat's review of Gadamer in Ernst Tugendhat, *Philosophische Aufsätze* (Frankfurt: Suhrkamp, 1992).

4. Rorty terms scientism "the doctrine that natural science is privileged over other areas of culture, that something about natural science puts it in closer—or at least more reliable—touch with reality than any other human activity." Richard Rorty, *Truth and Progress: Philosophical Papers,* vol. 3 (Cambridge: Cambridge University Press, 1998), 294.

5. John McDowell, *Mind, Value, and Reality* (Cambridge, Mass.: Harvard University Press, 1998), 72. As will become apparent below, this is essentially a formulation of the problem of the "absolute" as it is seen in early German Romantic philosophy. On this see Andrew Bowie, "John McDowell's *Mind and World* and Early Romantic Epistemology," in *Revue internationale de philosophie,* 50.197 (1996): 515–54.

6. On this see Manfred Frank, *"Unendliche Annaherung": Die Anfänge der philosophischen Frühromantik* (Frankfurt: Suhrkamp), 1997.

7. For a much more detailed account, see Andrew Bowie, *From Romanticism to Critical Theory: The Philosophy of German Literary Theory* (London: Routledge, 1997).

8. See Dahlhaus, *Die Idee der absoluten Musik* (Munich: DTV, 1978); and Andrew Bowie, *Aesthetics and Subjectivity: From Kant to Nietzsche* (Manchester: Manchester University Press, new ed. 2003).

9. One of Gadamer's aims is to establish a nonrepresentational concept of "mimesis" as the "essence of all constitutive activity in art and literature," in which "Mimesis is . . . not so much that something points to something else that is its original image *[Urbild]*, but that something in itself *[in sich selbst]* is there as something meaningful" (GW8:85). There is nothing incompatible in this with the idea that music can be world-disclosive: neither position assumes that music is essentially the representation of interiority.

10. Quoted in Paul Moos, *Die Philosophie der Musik von Kant bis Eduard von Hartmann* (New York: Georg Olms, 1975), 27.

11. It is questionable, in the light of the hermeneutically influenced postempiricist history of science, whether this is an adequate view of the practice of science, but it does correspond to a widely held view in the traditions Gadamer refers to.

12. See my *From Romanticism to Critical Theory* for a more differentiated account of Dilthey.

13. Friedrich Schlegel, *Kritische Schriften und Fragmente 1–6* (Paderborn: Ferdinand Schoningh, 1988), 38.

14. Ibid., 48.

15. Friedrich Wilhelm Joseph Schelling, *Sammtliche Werke,* ed. K. F. A. Schelling, I Abtheilung vols. 1–10, II Abtheilung vols. 1–4 (Stuttgart, 1856–61), I/3.627. On this, see Andrew Bowie, *Schelling and Modern European Philosophy* (London: Routledge, 1993); and Bowie, *Aesthetics.*

16. Novalis, *Band 2: Das philosophische-theoretische Werk,* ed. Hans-Joachim Mahl (Munich: Hanser, 1978), 769.

17. Ibid., 322.

18. Ibid., 840.

19. In F. D. E. Schleiermacher, *"Hermeneutics and Criticism" and Other Texts,* ed. and trans. Andrew Bowie (Cambridge: Cambridge University Press, 1998).

20. Ibid., 94.

21. See Wolfgang Virmond, *Schleiermacher-Archiv, Band I* (Berlin: W. de Gruyter, 1985), 575–90; Schleiermacher, *"Hermeneutics."*

22. Schleiermacher, *"Hermeneutics,"* 94. In the *General Hermeneutics* of 1809–10 Schleiermacher sees the two sides as follows: "The grammatical side puts the utterer in the background and regards him just as an organ of the language, but regards language as what really generates the utterance. The technical side, on the other hand, regards the utterer as the real-ground of the utterance and the language merely as the negative limiting principle" (ibid., 230).

23. Ibid., 257.

24. See Bowie, *Romanticism,* and my Introduction to Schleiermacher, *"Hermeneutics."* As Frank shows in *"Unendliche Annäherung,"* the insight into the regress of rules, which Kant already describes (see Bowie, *Romanticism,* chapter 2), was a commonplace of the post-Kantian thinkers who prepared the way for Romantic thought.

25. Schleiermacher, *"Hermeneutics,"* 229.

26. Ernest Lepore, ed., *Truth and Interpretation* (Oxford: Blackwell, 1986), 446.

27. On this see, e.g., Manfred Frank, *Das Individuelle-Allgemeine: Textstrukturierung und interpretation nach Schleiermacher* (Frankfurt: Suhrkamp, 1977); Christian Berner, *La philosophie de Schleiermacher* (Paris: Cerf, 1995); and Bowie, *Romanticism.*

28. F. D. E. Schleiermacher, *Dialektik,* ed. L. Jonas (Berlin: Reimer, 1839), 261.

29. See my Introduction to Schleiermacher, *"Hermeneutics."*
30. Martin Heidegger, *Zur Sachen des Denkens* (Tubingen: Niemeyer, 1988), 70.
31. Martin Heidegger, *Holzwege* (Frankfurt: Klostermann, 1980), 107.
32. Ibid., 105.
33. See Frank, *Individuelle-Allgemeine;* Bowie, *Schelling.*
34. Karl-Otto Apel, *Auseinandersetzungen* (Frankfurt: Suhrkamp, 1998), 572–74.
35. See Frank, *"Unendliche Annäherung,"* 676.
36. See Dieter Henrich, *Der Grund im Bewusstsein: Untersuchungen zu Holderlins Denken (1794–5)* (Stuttgart: Klett-Cotta, 1992); Andrew Bowie, "Re-thinking the History of the Subject: Jacobi, Schelling, and Heidegger," in *Deconstructive Subjectivities,* ed. Simon Critchely and Peter Dews (New York: SUNY Press, 1996); Frank, *"Unendliche Annäherung."*
37. Gadamer sees correspondences between his position and that of Popper (GW2:4).
38. See Bowie, "Re-thinking"; Bowie, *Romanticism;* Frank, *"Unendliche Annäherung."*
39. The contemporary counterpart of Fichte in relation to the question of grounding is Karl-Otto Apel, who insists against Albert that a "final foundation" is to be discovered in the fact that if one does not accept an absolute presupposition concerning the possible intersubjective validity of what is being argued about, one would be involved in the "performative self-contradiction" of claiming validity for a position which excludes the possibility of validity. I shall return to some of the less controversial and more productive aspects of Apel's arguments below.
40. Fichte's subjectivism has often led him to be regarded as the essential Romantic philosopher. It was Walter Benjamin who first showed why this is an invalid view of Fichte, for reasons similar to those suggested below; on this see Bowie, *Romanticism,* chapter 8.
41. Novalis 162.
42. See Manfred Frank, *Selbstbewusstsein und Selbsterkenntnis* (Stuttgart: Reclam, 1991).
43. Dieter Henrich, *Fluchtlinien: Philosophische Essays* (Frankfurt: Suhrkamp, 1982), 166.
44. F. D. E. Schleiermacher, *Friedrich Schleiermachers Dialektik,* ed. Rudolf Odebrecht (Darmstadt: Wissenschaftliche Buchgesellschaft, 1976), 274–75.
45. Frank, *"Unendliche Annäherung,"* 717.
46. Richard Rorty, *Contingency, Irony and Solidarity* (Cambridge: Cambridge University Press, 1989), 196.
47. Rorty, *Truth and Progress,* vol. 1, 2.
48. Ibid., 3.
49. Novalis 181.
50. Ibid.
51. Friedrich Schlegel, *Philosophische Vorlesungen* (1800–1807), Kritische Friedrich Schlegel Ausgabe, vol. 12 (Munich: Ferdinand Schöningh), 95.
52. Friedrich Schlegel, *Transcendentalphilosophie,* ed. Michael Elsasser (Hamburg: Meiner, 1991), 95.
53. Novalis 8.

54. Friedrich Schlegel, *Philosophische Lehrjahre II (1798–1828)* (Kritische Friedrich Schlegel Ausgabe, vol. 19) (Munich: Ferdinand Schoningh, 1971), 58.

55. Schlegel, *Kritische Schriften,* 240.

56. Rorty, *Truth,* 38.

57. Richard Rorty, *Essays on Heidegger and Others: Philosophical Papers,* vol. 2 (Cambridge: Cambridge University Press, 1989), 126.

58. Hilary Putnam, *Reason, Truth, and History* (Cambridge: Cambridge University Press, 1981), 216.

59. Schlegel, *Transcendentalphilosophie,* 74.

60. Ibid., 92–93.

61. Schlegel, *Vorlesungen,* 316–17.

62. Schlegel, *Transcendentalphilosophie,* 92.

63. Schleiermacher, *Dialektik,* 18.

64. Apel 92.

65. The further complicating factor lies in the fact that representations require linguistic articulation if they are to be agreed on, which gives a further reason why the correspondence model is untenable, at least in its traditional form.

66. Schleiermacher, *"Hermeneutics,"* 274.

67. Rorty, *Truth,* 60–61.

68. Indeed, it is arguable that for much of this century most English-speaking philosophy at least was, with respect to these specific issues, not even at the level of the Romantic debate.

69. Richard Rorty, "Pragmatism as Romantic Polytheism," in *The Revival of Pragmatism: New Essays on Social Thought, Law, and Culture,* ed. Morris Dickstein (Durham, N.C.: Duke University Press, 1998), 37–46. See also Rorty, *Contingency.*

70. Rorty, *Truth,* 310.

71. Ibid., *Truth,* 288.

72. Cited in ibid.

73. Rorty, *Essays,* 125.

74. Ibid., 126.

75. See Bowie, *Romanticism,* chapter 9.

Chapter 5

Literature, Law, and Morality

GEORGIA WARNKE

Richard Posner lists several reasons to think that morality and law are enterprises distinct from literature: the fact that the heinous actions of German lawyers and citizens in the 1930s and 1940s coexisted with Germany's status as one of the most cultured nations of the world; the circumstance that one of the well-known abilities of many well-read people is to remain insensitive to the suffering of others; the fact that moral atrocities fill the literary canon without affecting either the aesthetic virtues of the work or its reader's own moral attitudes; and, finally, the distance between the concerns of law and those of literature.[1]

For these reasons Posner is skeptical about what he calls the edifying school in legal scholarship, an approach to the relation of law and literature that claims that the study of literature is crucial to the ability of judges to judge responsibly and sensitively. Alexander Nehamas is equally skeptical about the ability of literature to teach people in general to act morally or to live moral lives. In this chapter I want to show the force of both positions. But I also want to turn to Gadamer's hermeneutics to develop suggestions he makes about the relation between literary criticism on the one hand and moral and legal reflection on the other. I shall argue that these suggestions help redirect our attention away from the solitary reader or critic toward the participant in dialogue. Moreover, I shall argue that the form this participation takes serves to strengthen rather than weaken the relation between literature, law, and morality. I shall begin with Martha Nussbaum's claims for the edifying potential of a particular novel, Henry James's *The Golden Bowl*, which is the focus of problems both Posner and Nehamas pose for attempts to connect literature, law, and morality.[2]

The Golden Bowl involves the relations between four people: two rich Americans, Maggie and her widowed father Adam; Maggie's husband, a poor Italian prince; and Charlotte, a poor American who is also Maggie's best friend, her husband's lover and, eventually, her father's wife. Nussbaum's interest in the novel centers on the sensitivity and attentiveness toward others as well as on the relentless self-consciousness with which Maggie confronts the crisis of her husband's adultery. For Nussbaum, the novel is "about the development of a woman. To be a woman, to give herself to her husband, Maggie will need to come to see herself as something cracked, imperfect, unsafe" (Nussbaum 133). But Posner argues that this analysis of the text articulates only one of its possible meanings. Moreover, to equate the novel with its moral teaching is reductive and, in any case, its moral implications remain ambiguous. One can view Maggie either as moral exemplar or as an "insufferable rich girl." One can cherish or wonder about the intimacy between Maggie and Adam. Indeed, Posner continues,

> The novel may be warning readers that it is a mistake for women to make marriage their whole career, that men and women alike should work rather than live off inherited wealth like Maggie and her prince. It may even be presenting a "grim parody" of the marital ideals of nineteenth-century England and America and of the capitalist system in which those ideals are embedded and which they reflect. (Posner 317–18).

If the moral implications of *The Golden Bowl* are ambiguous, then Posner thinks it is odd to suppose, as Nussbaum does, that reading literature is the only or best way to improve judicial decision making. For his part, Nehamas questions not only the limitations of Nussbaum's moralistic reading of James's novel, but also the assumption she appears to make that readers, whether judges or not, can transform that moralistic reading into lessons for their own lives. The problem in doing so, Nehamas thinks, is illuminated by the implications that Nussbaum tries to draw from the scene that describes the ultimate parting of Maggie and her father, a parting both see as the only way to resolve the situation in which all four characters find themselves. What James describes, as Nehamas puts Nussbaum's point, is how Maggie and Adam "loving each other as they do, become capable of letting go without harming one another, without selfishness and without cause for regret."[3]

For Nussbaum, the importance of this description is the contrast it marks between the abstract moral theories that form the content of moral philosophy and the particular situations to which they must ultimately be applied. Her point, as Nehamas understands it, is that they can only be appropriately applied "when the particular situations to which they are relevant are characterized in the detailed, fine-grained, minuscule manner of which only literary language is capable and to which only sensitive readers are attentive" (Nehamas 35). The conclusion for Nussbaum is that the sensitivity of good readers is necessary for the capacity to act morally because it is part of know-

ing how to apply the moral principles by which we live. There is no paraphrase or summary of such scenes through which we can learn their essential insights. Nor can moral philosophy give them to us because of its
necessary abstractions. Rather, we learn to act morally in the situations we
confront by expanding our "active sense of life" (Nussbaum 74) through the
resources offered us by literature.

Nehamas suggests two ways in which Nussbaum's argument might be understood. According to the first, the moral relevance of *The Golden Bowl* lies
in our capacity to expand our active sense of life to include the exquisite
sensibility Maggie and Adam exemplify. The problem here, however, according to Nehamas, is that this capacity seems to require precisely the ability to paraphrase that Nussbaum rejects. We must be able to abstract the
main features of plot, character, and reaction from a piece of literature and
show their relevance for our own lives. But works of literature are unified
wholes, Nehamas insists, unities of meaning in which no details are extra-
neous. They are not reports of real life but real life ordered around a particular sense of coherence and meaning. As he quotes William Gass, "nothing is simple happenstance, everything has meaning, is part of a net of
essential relations. Sheer coincidence is impossible" (Nehamas 37). But if
all the details of a novel have meaning only within this net of essential relations, it remains unclear how we are to extract particular moral lessons from
out of the net.

The second way in which Nehamas claims we might understand Nussbaum's argument looks to the education in attentiveness and discrimination that reading itself is meant to offer us. According to this argument, the
gravest moral problem in both reading and life is an inattentiveness to detail, an insensitivity to others, and an inability either to recognize or avoid
the cruelty that such inattentiveness and insensitivity produce. We may not
be able directly to transpose the sensibilities and actions of others to our
own lives. Still, by becoming good readers, we are supposed to become sensitive to the needs, problems, and points of view of the diverse individuals
we meet in literature and, according to Nussbaum, we are thus supposed to
be able to become better moral actors in our own lives.

In questioning these suppositions, Nehamas takes up Vladimir Nabokov's
Pale Fire, the central character of which, Charles Kinbote, is obtuse and
largely insensitive as well as terribly inattentive as a reader. The book *Pale
Fire* consists of a poem "Pale Fire," which was written by a professor at a small
college, John Shade, together with a foreword, commentary on the poem,
and index supplied by Kinbote after Shade's death. What is striking about
the commentary, however, is that it appears to be a complete misappropriation of the poem for Kinbote's own purposes. The poem concerns, in part,
the poet's daughter's suicide; Kinbote's commentary sees in it the story of
what he suggests is his life, the story of the deposed king of Zembla. Kinbote

thus fails to recognize the pain his daughter's suicide has caused Shade and fails to take seriously the poet's own intentions with regard to his poem. He appears to be a bad reader of both texts and people. For Nussbaum, then, the contribution of the book would presumably be to show the link between insensitive reading and insensitive relations to others. Moreover, it would suggest that were Kinbote to become a better reader he might also become a more sensitive and understanding person.

Nehamas understands Nabokov's book somewhat differently, however. In the first place, he wonders how deep Shade's pain is. Shade's poem is fair to middling at best, Nehamas thinks, and the suffering it expresses is banal. Shade's life is not particularly altered by his daughter's death. "He continues to work, teach and give dinner and cocktail parties, to lecture and take vacations, to be a regular, lively and witty participant at collegial lunches, to provoke . . . crushes on the part of beautiful undergraduate students." Moreover, he never talks to Kinbote very much about his pain, his daughter, or any other matters. Hence, according to Nehamas, Kinbote's supposed "insensitivity to Shade's pain appears to be due at least as much to the fact that Shade's pain is minimal as to his own insane egotism" (Nehamas 43).

In the second place, Kinbote's moral and interpretive deficiencies have literary value, Nehamas thinks. They allow Kinbote largely to ignore Shade's poem and, in appending a mad commentary to it, create a much better book. According to Nehamas, Kinbote is a better writer than Shade; the book he creates of the poem and his commentary is a better piece of literature than the poem alone. But Kinbote can engineer this literary feat only because he is so insensitive to Shade's own meaning. Moreover, Nehamas insists, Kinbote's cruelty here is the cruelty of interpreters in general "who take another person's words, redescribe them in a way that may have nothing to do with what the author consciously meant in the first place and by that means produce a greater work" (Nehamas 44). In this analysis interpretive cruelty, or what Nussbaum might consider inattentive reading, possesses creative merit. Indeed, Nehamas suggests that just this merit explains the reference to "pale fire" that in the play *Timon of Athens* refers to the moon's "arrant" thievery insofar as its light is a reflection of the sun's. It is only because of Kinbote's obtuse commentary that Shade's poem becomes noteworthy and burns with a reflected fire. Obtuse reading, as opposed to the attentive reading Nussbaum emphasizes, turns out to be necessary both for Kinbote's artistry and for the possibility of Shade's posthumous literary life.

But if an interpretive insensitivity can engender good literature, can it also lead to moral action? Nehamas suggests that Kinbote is a better man than Shade precisely because he is so interpretively insensitive. In failing to recognize the numerous ways in which Shade tries to avoid him, in attributing Shade's gruffness to a "dignity of the heart" as opposed to an impatience with Kinbote himself, and in refusing to see Shade as blameworthy or to be insulted by his failure to invite him to his party, Kinbote is more generous toward Shade than Shade is to him. Kinbote's insensitivity and obtuseness as a reader of both texts and people turn out to form the conditions of both his art and his moral attitudes toward Shade.

Of course, Nussbaum can object to this line of argument that her concerns are directed not at the relation of morality to bad readings or misinterpretations of either texts or people, but rather at the relation of morality to good and valid interpretations. Inattentiveness to the feelings of others and the literature they meant to produce may sometimes lead to better literature as well as to actions and attitudes that are generous and forgiving. Her point is that attentive reading always has the capacity to improve our ability to act morally in particular circumstances because it gives us insight into the diversity and details of circumstances beyond our experience. Yet Posner adds to his list of bad actions on the part of good readers with which we began. Sensitivity to and understanding of the needs, problems, and points of view of diverse individuals that literature is meant to give us are also the source of the success of great demagogues "who understand people," he claims, "all too well" (Posner 316). Moreover, Nehamas notes, an ability to understand others is a moral problem if it means that we can no longer condemn them. "That, at least, was the disturbing argument Bruno Bettleheim made against Robert Jay Lifton's study of the German physicians who worked in concentration camps: understanding them might lead us to forgive them" (Nehamas 50).

There thus appear to be four conclusions to be drawn from Posner's and Nehamas's reflections on Nussbaum's claims for literature, reading, and morality. First, to focus on the moral lessons a piece of literature has to teach us is to subtract from other meanings the work possesses and to ignore the different ways even its moral meaning might be understood. Second, an interpretive sensitivity that allows us to understand the moral grace in the actions of characters in literature such as Maggie and Adam in James's *The Golden Bowl* does not directly lead to a capacity to act gracefully in the different circumstances in which we find ourselves. Hence, both the moral meaning and the moral consequences of literature remain ambiguous. Third, an interpretive sensitivity can as easily provide the basis for immoral actions as it can for moral ones, for it may provide demagogues with dangerous insights into others and others with the means to forgive and excuse them. Finally, an interpretive insensitivity and the inability to read either texts or others well can lead to a generosity to others that makes better literature out of their efforts and fails to register their personal faults. The idea that literature or interpretive sensitivity is connected in any one or necessary way to morality or judicial insight seems definitively laid to rest.

Nehamas and Posner do not deny that literature can teach us how to live. What both deny, instead, is that insights into the form of a well-lived life translate into either moral or legal insights. What we learn from literature, Nehamas concludes, are models of coherent narrative in terms of which we might shape our own lives in our attempts to give them unity and meaning. Unity and meaning, however, are aesthetic values, not moral ones. In Posner's view, literature helps us understand who we are and even to become who we are. Becoming who we are, however, or enhancing our recognition of ourselves is a question of authenticity, not morality. The self we discover ourselves to be "need not be a *moral* improvement over the reader's present, less authentic self" (Posner 331). The values involved in the consideration of literature, then, are aesthetic values or the values of an improved authenticity. They are not, however, moral values, nor do they necessarily translate into the values of sound judicial judgment.

In what follows I want to examine the connections between literature, law, and morality once more to see if there is yet another way they might have significance for one another. In order to do so I shall examine Gadamer's account of the character of interpretive understanding, an account that tries to elucidate the conditions of literary interpretation by considering first, the interpretive or hermeneutic significance of Aristotle's ethics, second, the "exemplary significance of legal hermeneutics," and third, the moral experience of the "Thou." All three accounts seem to point to some relation between literary interpretation and the sphere of law and morality. What exactly this relation is meant to be remains the question. I shall begin with what Gadamer sees as the hermeneutic significance of Aristotle's ethics.

Aristotle's concern, as is Nussbaum's, is the application of moral universals to particular circumstances and to the necessity of action: we encounter the question of the good in concrete situations in which some action or response is required of us. Importantly, when we know how to act or respond, the knowledge we have is not, for Aristotle, an objective knowledge or the knowledge that an observer has of necessary or constant relations between objects. It is rather a practical knowledge of what we are to do in a specific situation with its specific characteristics.

What sort of knowledge is this? Gadamer emphasizes the difference between a practical knowledge and technical or instrumental one. Whereas the latter allows for a straightforward derivation of the proper action from the result one wants to obtain, a practical knowledge of which action is morally appropriate in a particular circumstance circumscribes both means and ends. In the first place, the end, the good, is not separate from the action or means that leads to it. Rather, the good of the end depends, in large measure, on the actions through which it is realized. The success that Maggie attains by the end of *The Golden Bowl* is not just that she has warded off a threat to her marriage but that she has done so in a particularly graceful way such that the end is not a mere victory but a good. The good of the end is defined in terms of the means or actions that lead to it, and this definition means that we cannot look to an independent result we want to obtain and simply find the best means to it. Rather, we must engage in a form of deliberation in which the means to the good and the good itself are interrelated.

In the second place, if means and end are interrelated in moral deliberation, so that we cannot simply specify some end and look for the most efficient means to it, neither can we simply learn a series of moral virtues and principles and then apply them to particular situations. Knowing how to act, according to Gadamer's interpretation of Aristotle, is not a question of learning a skill and performing it when asked to do so. Rather, moral knowledge encompasses both a training or education in proper principles and virtues as well as an adequate understanding of the particular situation in which we are required to behave morally. In order to act morally, we must already understand the situation in a way that sees the relevance of the moral virtues and principles we are to apply to it. Part of Maggie's understanding of the particular situation in which she finds herself is that it imposes a moral requirement on her to act in such a way as to injure no one while resolving the situation. To this extent, her understanding of the situation is inextricable from her understanding of the relevant moral principles and virtues. On the one hand, then, her understanding of the virtues and principles she seeks to realize is an understanding constituted by the circumstances in which she finds herself. These provide the horizon from which the meaning of those virtues and principles is illuminated for her and, to this extent, her understanding of the principles and virtues at stake is already an applied understanding. On the other hand, it is significant for Gadamer that she also understands the situation in terms of moral principles and virtues, as a situation requiring of her a heightened sensitivity. This understanding presupposes that she is oriented toward the situation by a conception of tact and generosity she already holds. Hence, just as her understanding of the situation in which she finds herself offers her a particular perspective on the virtues and principles she takes seriously, her understanding of the situation is itself oriented by her initial projection of it as one requiring particular virtues and falling under the province of certain principles.

The relevance of this analysis of practical knowledge of the good transfers, Gadamer thinks, to legal hermeneutics. Here again, just as we can understand the good only through the means we take toward achieving it, we need to apply to a particular case a law the meaning of which we do not understand independently of the case itself. And just as we do not understand what action to take independently of our previous understanding of the good, we do not understand the case independently of the law as it has been previously understood in the legal tradition to which we belong. A man has been convicted of a crime based on a confession acquired by the police before the man had obtained a lawyer or realized he should obtain a lawyer. The issue here is not simply whether the due process requirement of the United States Constitution requires the police to inform him of his right to legal counsel. Rather, we must first understand the situation as one to which the application of the due process requirement is appropriate. The issues raised by the situation are not ones to which we apply the due process clause but instead ones we first understand as issues precisely because of our understanding of that clause. By the same token, the way we understand the due process requirement and the issues of interpretation raised for us are ones framed by this particular case. Does due process refer to certain procedural rights so that those charged with a crime are entitled to obtain a lawyer, or does it entail more substantive rights such as the right to be informed of their right to a lawyer and even the requirement that the court provide them with a lawyer if they cannot afford one on their own? The way these questions are answered together with the way different questions have been raised and answered about due process in the past constitutes what due process means. Its meaning, then, or the meaning of any law, is not one that can be determined apart from the cases to which it has been taken to apply or apart from the way it is applied in the present and future.

Gadamer insists that this relation between meaning and application entails that judicial review and legal history do not radically diverge. The meaning of the due process clause is a historical one. It has been understood in specific ways in the past because of specific cases and the issues they raised. This historically and interpretively constituted clause is the one that we possess as part of our constitutional tradition and it is therefore the one through which we understand new cases and the one on which those new cases shed new light. What a law means is thus constituted by the history of its application, the way that history orients us toward the present situations to which we now apply it, and the way our present situation orients us toward the meaning we inherit.

Significantly, Gadamer thinks that the same relation holds of the understanding of literature. We understand the texts with which we are concerned from the vantage point of our lives. No more than the due process clause does a work of literature hold a meaning apart from the way it holds meaning for an interpreter who comes to the work or the law from within a particular social, cultural, and historical context with particular concerns and issues. Further, as in legal hermeneutics, the work that an interpreter seeks to understand is a work that has already been understood from within particular social, cultural, and historical contexts and has been conceived of in terms of particular concerns and issues. The work the interpreter confronts is, to this extent, a work as it has been handed down to the interpreter within a cultural and literary tradition, just as a law has been interpreted and reinterpreted within a legal tradition. At the same time, interpreters must understand the meaning of the text handed down to them and they do so from within their own historical situation and the issues or situations it involves. To this extent, they are oriented from within a present, historically constituted set of circumstances toward a text that has already been interpreted within the tradition to which they belong and which they are now to interpret in light of their own situation.

This relation between a historically situated interpreter, the perspective or "horizon" which that historical situation lends to a work of literature, and the work itself as it appears in a historically developed literary tradition is only one side of the overall interpretive situation, according to Gadamer's analysis. For if an interpreter must understand a work of literature from the horizon constituted by a particular, historical, cultural, and social situation, he or she also understands that very situation in terms informed by the work. If I am to understand it at all, in other words, I must understand the way in which it addresses me and requires a response from me. The issues and concerns it raises are issues and concerns I must take seriously if I am to understand it. If I am to understand that and why Maggie commits herself so completely to marriage, fidelity, and friendship, I must take these values and institutions seriously and consider their limits and extent. Moreover, I must examine my own assumptions about their place in my life; indeed, in asking why Maggie acts as she does, I consider why I act as I do and what I might do in her place. The point here is that in reading a work of literature I apply it to my life and circumstances to no less an extent than in trying to understand a law or moral principle: I ask what it requires of me in the situation in which I find myself. For Gadamer, this dimension of textual understanding means that all understanding is situated, not only in the sense that we always understand from a particular perspective, but also in the sense that we always understand for a particular situation. As he puts the point, the reader does not exist "who, when he has his text before him, simply reads what is there. Rather, all reading involves application, so that a person reading a text is himself part of the meaning he apprehends. He belongs to the text that he is reading" (TM340). When we read *The Golden Bowl* our understanding of it is one that includes our lives as part of its meaning. We have a certain orientation toward the text because of those lives and because of the cultures and traditions to which they belong. Similarly, what we understand of *The Golden Bowl* provides us with a perspective on those lives, one that can reconcile us to aspects of them or reveal to us assumptions and expectations we did not know we had and require us to change.

The conclusion of Gadamer's analysis, then, is that the understanding of literature is a form of practical knowledge just as moral and legal knowledge are. Reading and literary criticism are not related to morality or law in the

sense that Nehamas and Posner criticize, namely in the sense that we can reduce literature to its moral and subsequently apply that moral to our own
lives or the situations judges must adjudicate. We do not store Maggie's actions in our memory for use if our husbands should become adulterous.
Nor does reading *The Golden Bowl* lead necessarily to an increase in our own
virtues of tact and sensitivity. Nussbaum transposes Aristotle's account of the
relation of universal and particular to the relation between morality and literature in such a way that moral principle is to provide the universal and literature is to offer the insight into the particular. For Gadamer, in contrast,
Aristotle's account of the relation between universal and particular is a relation to be found in morality, law, and literary interpretation insofar as they
are all forms of practical knowledge. The conditions of understanding are
the same whether we are concerned to understand what we should do, how
we should judge, or what the meaning of a text is. All involve a situated kind
of knowledge in which universal and particular inform one another.

It is not clear that either Posner or Nehamas would necessarily reject this
analysis since neither denies that literature can have a practical effect on
our lives. Nehamas claims that we can look to literature for exemplars of
how to shape and create well-formed human lives, while Posner argues that
literature can aid in our attempts to discover who we authentically are and
would like to be. What we create or discover, however, need not be specifically moral and need not have any relevance to the abilities of judges to render sound judgments. The literature we read is rather practical in the sense
that it can change the way we view ourselves and even motivate us to re-
structure our lives. Gadamer adds to this conception of the way literature
can affect us a recognition of the impact of our lives on the literature we understand. We come to works of literature from the horizon of our lives; we
bring to those works certain questions and issues, whether we have articulated them explicitly or not, and the answers we find in literature are answers to our questions, just as the questions literature asks of us are questions we apply to our lives. Gadamer thus sees the interpretation of works of
literature as a dialogue in which both work and interpreter must raise and
answer questions they address to one another. This structural homology
to our relations to law and moral principle, however, does not mean that
works of literature can be understood as themselves laws or moral principles
for us.

Yet Gadamer's suggestions for the relation between morality, law, and literature go further. If literary interpretation is a form of practical as opposed
to specifically moral or judicial knowledge, it nonetheless has what seems to
be a moral condition. The understanding of a text is a kind of knowing how
to reveal its meaning for a particular situation and arises from a particular
situated perspective. But this relation between the universal, which is the
text for Gadamer, and the particular situations to which it is applied and in

terms of which it is understood raises a question: how can we determine that a particular situated perspective provides a horizon that can illuminate the text for us rather than deceiving us about it? How can we be sure that when we understand a work of literature we have engaged in a genuine dialogue with it in which we illuminate and are illuminated by it? How can we be sure that we have not simply imposed our own concerns on the text and thought it was illuminating them only because we mangled its "true" meaning? Will our interpretations of texts not always be prejudiced ones that distort meaning for our own purposes or, at least, blind us to real meaning because our own parochial concerns and questions impose an artificial interpretation on them? How can we be sure we are not all Kinbote and all misappropriating Shade's poem for our own purposes?

Nehamas, of course, thinks that most good interpretation does involve this sort of opportunistic and even cruel relation to works of literature. Gadamer, as well, thinks that all understanding is prejudiced insofar as it is circumscribed by the light a particular history and historical situation sheds on that which an interpreter is trying to understand. Indeed, he argues that prejudices are the condition for the possibility of any understanding since they provide the framework only within which we can first appropriate or try to grasp the meaning of that which we are trying to understand. We are situated in particular histories, cultures, and circumstances, and these necessarily provide any orientation we have toward that which we are trying to understand. We can understand a certain text as a novel, for example, because we belong to a history and culture that knows what a novel is. We can understand the meaning of a particular novel because we project tentative determinations of meaning on the whole as we begin to read its initial parts. Without such projections we have no context for beginning to appropriate or understand the text, and by calling these preliminary projections prejudices Gadamer points to their relation to the historical situation from which they emerge. Prejudices or projections are not simply subjective or personal understandings of meaning. Rather, they indicate the degree to which our interpretations of meaning are grounded in the expectations we acquire from our history and situation and from the interpretations of the texts we are trying to understand that have been handed down to us as part of the culture and tradition to which we belong.

Still, for Gadamer, this structure of understanding describes only its initial condition, not its task. For if all understanding is prejudiced, we must, he thinks, nonetheless distinguish between those prejudiced and situated understandings that are simply opportunistic in that they impose a meaning and relevance on a work of literature for the present purposes of the interpreter and those understandings that genuinely do serve to illuminate the work. And accomplishing this task, Gadamer suggests, requires a specifically moral attitude: it requires a respect for the otherness or difference of the work. If, on the one hand, we are to understand a piece of literature, if we are to allow it to illuminate our situation, and if, on the other hand, we cannot but understand from a situated and prejudiced point of view, then we must presuppose that the text is autonomous, that rather than necessarily conforming to our prejudices it has a substance and meaning of its own. A "hermeneutically trained consciousness must be," Gadamer insists, "from the start, sensitive to the text's alterity" (TM269). If we are to understand a text, we must acknowledge that we are prejudiced and that what we are trying to understand has its own meaning, not ours. Such an acknowledgment cannot involve suspending our prejudices since they remain the condition for the possibility of understanding. Rather, Gadamer writes, "The important thing is to be aware of one's own bias, so that the text can present itself in all its otherness" (TM269). And, he continues, "what another person tells me, whether in conversation, letter, book, or whatever, is generally supposed to be his own and not my opinion; and this is what I am to take note of without necessarily having to share it" (TM268).

That this acknowledgment of the autonomy of the text constitutes a specifically moral form of experience for Gadamer is implied by his account of what he calls the moral experience of the Thou, an experience he thinks has its counterpart in the hermeneutical experience of literature. There are, he argues, three forms in which we might experience the Thou. The first is a kind of objectifying experience in which we understand the other person as a means to our ends. Our concern is to be able to explain and predict his or her behavior so that we might more efficiently achieve our own goals. Such objectification, which is necessary to game theory and rational choice models of ethics and politics, Gadamer calls a contradiction of the "moral definition of man" and purely "self-regarding." Referring to Kant, he continues, "the other should never be used as a means but always as an end in himself" (TM358).

Gadamer thinks that the equivalent in the attempt to understand texts is a naive faith in our ability to extract ourselves from the horizon or prejudices through which we understand texts and to reduce them to objects. In this way, we attempt to understand them as if the meaning they had possessed no relation to who and what we understand ourselves and our experience to be. We understand them, instead, objectively, from no particular point of view. If interpretation involves a form of practical reason, however, this idea that we could achieve an objective understanding of a text or that the meaning of the text betrayed no relation to our own situation remains mythological. More importantly, in supposing the objectivity of our understanding we allow our prejudices to prevail without constraints. We make the text into an object for our own use because we assume that we have no interest in it and that its meaning has nothing to do with us. In so doing, we mistake our prejudices about the text for the object we take the text to be.

The second way of experiencing the Thou is equally self-regarding, Gadamer thinks, but it is self-regarding not because it uses the other for one's own purposes but because it assimilates the other to oneself. This experience of the Thou presumes to understand the other better than he or she understands him or herself, a presumption Gadamer associates with welfare work but that also seems to be at the root of Kinbote's relation to Shade in *Pale Fire*. In this case, "by understanding the other, by claiming to know him, one robs his claims of their legitimacy" (TM360). The fallacy here, Gadamer suggests, is the idea that one can dispense with the tension between distance and closeness in a human relationship and simply experience the other as one experiences oneself.

The equivalent to this experience of the Thou in textual understanding Gadamer calls historical consciousness. Once again, the presumption is that one can extract oneself from one's own situation and hence from the temporal relation between that situation and the situation of the text. One assumes that one can understand the text, not objectively, not now from no particular point of view as in the first relation to texts, but rather in the exact way that the author or his or her original audience understood it. But in making this presumption one simply substitutes one's present understanding for the original understanding of the author or his or her first audience. Again, one allows one's prejudices to prevail unchecked because one simply takes them for the original meaning of the text itself. If understanding is practical in the sense that it is always for and from a particular perspective, however, a historical consciousness or empathetic account of understanding misses what Gadamer considers the essential point about understanding: that it is both historically situated and capable of disclosing autonomous meaning.

The third way of experiencing the Thou, according to Gadamer, is the moral experience of the Thou in which one allows "him really to say something to us." In this moral relationship we neither objectify the other nor claim to speak for him or her. We are rather engaged in a dialogic relation in which we are open to the other as someone who has his or her own autonomy and own claims. This relationship differs from the objectifying social scientific situation in which the scientist is to understand his or her object by learning how to predict his or her behavior. It also differs from the empathetic situation in which the empathizers deny any confinement to their own situated horizons and claim to understand the object as well or better than he or she understands him or herself. Rather, the relationship is one between two subjects who understand each other by orienting themselves to the independent claims each makes.

To see the experience of literature in the same terms is to emphasize the symmetry in the relationship between text and interpreter. For Gadamer, a genuine understanding of a work of literature is not as much a question of a subject understanding an object as it is a question of a conversation in which the reader addresses the text's claims and is, in turn, addressed by them. The presupposition of this understanding of texts, for Gadamer, is a respect for the otherness or the difference of the text. One must assume its autonomy as the source of its own claims. Otherwise one understands in it only what one already knows or assumes because one has extracted oneself out of the genuinely dialogic relation and treated the text as an object to be either explained or absorbed by one's superior understanding.

Gadamer's point is a methodological one to the extent that it answers the question of how we are to construct valid interpretations of literary texts given that we are prejudiced and can understand them only from a situated point of view. The answer he gives is that we must assume that they are potentially other than what we suppose them to be and, in making this assumption, create a space in which their claims can be voiced. But Gadamer's point is also a moral one to the extent that it suggests that respect for difference is fundamental to the ability to treat people as ends rather than simply as means. In other words, treating other people as ends involves allowing their voice and their claims to their own autonomy, neither speaking for them nor reducing their claims to elements of a verbal behavior to be causally explained. To this extent, morality and literature make the same demand: that of allowing others to be and to express themselves. Rather than reducing them to either objects or ourselves, we must take them as independent beings against whose claim we can check our own prejudices and understanding. Our attempts to act morally and to understand texts require the same assumption: that others are autonomous of our ends and our ideas and must be given the space to speak their own claims.

Gadamer suggests that the same holds of the law. We cannot understand particular laws opportunistically, imposing our own purposes on them, if we are to come to a genuine understanding of them. Nor can we presume to understand them empathetically, as we think the framers of the particular laws themselves understood or intended them. Theories of legal interpretation that look to original intent mirror theories of literary criticism that equate understanding with empathy. The presumption in both cases is that one can extract oneself from one's own historical situation, with its contemporary concerns and the frameworks of interpretation it has developed, to understand the law or the literary text the way its authors or its original audience understood it. But in making this presumption, interpreters must presume a set of other conditions as well: that the authors of the law knew and understood all of their intentions with regard to it so that what they claim to have been their intentions can be taken to really accord with them; that the various contributors to the final formulation of a law, act, or constitutional amendment as well as all those who voted for it or ratified it in a state convention all had the same intentions with regard to it; that all these intentions were simple rather than complex; and that the authors, ratifiers, and voters all understood and articulated their thoughts on all the issues that the law would raise for future generations and future situations. If interpreters cannot assure themselves that all these conditions have been met, then in claiming to know the original intent of a law, they simply substitute their present understanding for it and allow their prejudices to prevail unchecked because they simply take them for the law's original meaning.

For Americans, the Supreme Court's 1896 decision in *Plessy v. Ferguson* remains a prime example of just such an opportunistic and falsely intentionalistic reading of both the Fourteenth Amendment and alternative interpretations of it. Moreover, the decision seems to confirm the suggestions Gadamer makes about the links between moral, legal, and literary knowledge. *Plessy,* as is well known, upheld a Louisiana law providing for separate accommodations for blacks and whites in railway cars. Although the black community protested, the Supreme Court (with Justice Harlan dissenting) claimed that "in the nature of things" the equal protection clause "could not have been intended to abolish distinctions based upon color, or to enforce social, as distinguished from political equality, or a commingling of the two races upon terms unsatisfactory to either." It added that if African Americans thought that separation stamped them with a "badge of inferiority," this badge was issued not "by reason of anything found in the act, but solely because the colored race chooses to put that construction upon it."[4]

Of course, the Fourteenth Amendment makes no mention of a distinction between social and political equality; nor is it clear what the nature of things is meant to be or how it shows what the intentions of the authors of the Fourteenth Amendment were. By claiming to know what these intentions were, the Supreme Court simply allows its own prejudices to hold sway. By dismissing "the colored race's" interpretation of the act as a construction they "choose" to put on it, the Court also dismisses the autonomy of African Americans and the difference their interpretations reflect. But the Court's failure here is not one only in legal interpretation or in the interpretation of texts. It is also manifestly a moral one. If the 1954 decision in *Brown v. Board of Education* began to correct this moral, legal, and interpretive failure, it did so in part, at least, because it restored dignity and independence to both the meaning of the amendment and the understanding African Americans had of it.

If we are to follow Gadamer's suggestions, *Brown* is a better decision than *Plessy* in moral, legal, and interpretive terms not because it is an unprejudiced one. *Brown* understands both the Fourteenth Amendment and black interpretations of the doctrine of "separate but equal" from a perspective that is as historically, culturally, and socially situated as *Plessy* is, one in which education has a different role than it did in 1896, in which the conscience of the nation had been awakened by the Holocaust and the sacrifices of black Americans in World War II and in which the NAACP had been struggling to be heard for decades. But if the *Brown* decision cannot therefore take credit for its historical horizon, it remains a better decision than *Plessy* because it understands both the Fourteenth Amendment and black interpretations of segregation within a dialogic relation. As *Plessy* does, it continues to address the amendment and African American interpretations of segregation from the framework of questions and concerns its horizon makes available to it, but it is also finally open to the way the answers given to those questions may differ from its traditional biases about them. In Gadamerian terms, the lesson of *Plessy* and *Brown* is not that we can learn to become better people or judges through reading but that as readers, judges, and moral agents we must treat others, including texts, laws, and the interpretations of others of them, with a respect for their autonomy from our own prejudices about them and with an appreciation of the independence of their claims.

Still, we might ask how we are meant to realize this demand. We cannot suspend our prejudices or interpretive frameworks in order to create the space in which others can speak their independent claims. We can create it only by assuming that we are prejudiced and that what we are trying to understand or what is trying to speak to us is potentially different from those prejudices. To respect the otherness of a text, law, or the claims of others is thus to respect its possible difference from what we think we already know. But, Gadamer suggests, to assume that the meaning of a text differs from what we already know is to suppose that in understanding this meaning we can learn something. To this extent, genuine understanding requires that we approach texts, laws, and the interpretations of others with a respect not only for their otherness but also for their possible superiority in knowledge. We read, examine a law, or listen to others because we are interested in what they perhaps know that we do not.

The foundation here is what Gadamer calls the *docta ignorantia* or the Socratic wisdom of knowing that one does not know (TM362). If we are situated in our historical horizons and if we are therefore prejudiced, but if we also want to create the space in which others can speak and in which we can listen, then we must assume that those others can say something new, something beyond what we already know. We cannot dismiss what they say in advance unless we are willing to be content with the prejudices we already have. And if we do want to learn, we must assume that what they say is at least potentially true. As Gadamer writes, "And just as we believe the news reported by a correspondent because he was present or is better informed, so too are we fundamentally open to the possibility that the writer of a transmitted text is better informed than we are, with our prior opinion" (TM294).

This move from otherness to superiority appears to raise a problem, however. Understanding in the context of either morality, law, or literature may require a respect for difference, and a respect for difference may require that we acknowledge the possible superiority of the claims we are trying to understand. But, if so, does respect not threaten to become deference? Suppose African Americans had deferred to the supposed superiority of the claims of the *Plessy v. Ferguson* decision. Suppose they had tried to learn from it in the way Gadamer intimates and had even used it as a guide to rethink what they thought they knew about the principle of equality and conceptions of dignity? The concern here is that if respect for the superiority of a text or claim is a condition of understanding it, we may accord a dignity to texts, laws, and interpretations of principle that do not deserve it and learn from texts, laws, and interpretations from which we should not. Furthermore, we may overlook the extent to which their claims are ideological or pathological. To respect even the ideological content of a text or principle is to ignore what we know in deference to it and even, it would seem, if interpretation is indeed a form of practical knowledge, to pervert our own relation to ourselves.

Moreover, is it not possible to respect others by *not* taking their claims at face value, by realizing that the claims they raise are not those they would raise if they were behaving well or thinking at their best? This suggestion is the one Nehamas makes about Kinbote: in depriving Shade of his own voice, in assuming that he knows how to speak for him and knows his actual goodness despite his actions, Kinbote is able to make Shade into a better poet and a better man. From a Gadamerian point of view, however, it would seem that we are moral people and good interpreters not when we speak for others, even when doing so makes them into people better than they are, but when we allow them their autonomous being and meaning, whatever that may be.

A Gadamerian response to the first question of whether we might not defer to ideological claims in our efforts to respect difference and possible legitimacy looks, I think, to the distinction between accepting the claims of others and respecting them as possible paths to understanding the issues involved. We must inspect the *Plessy v. Ferguson* decision, for example, in terms of the possible knowledge or legitimacy contained in its account of both the equal protection clause and black Americans' account of the meaning of segregation. But to do so is not to defer ultimately to its prejudices. Rather, it is to set that "knowledge" against our own reading of the case. From a Gadamerian point of view, it is precisely by trying to see the legitimacy of *Plessy,* by trying to understand the truth of what it means by the nature of things, by trying to discover how it finds in the Fourteenth Amendment a distinction between social and political equality and trying to see how its understanding of African Americans' understanding of segregation might possibly be right, that we see all too clearly its ideological components.

Gadamer's insistence that we approach a text, law, or interpretation of a practice or principle with a prejudice in its favor, a presumption that what it says could be true or valid, is meant to provide a check against the unexamined reign of our own prejudices. He does not insist that the presumption must work out. Rather, a presumption in favor of the truth of what we are trying to understand illuminates our own prejudices and therefore grants us the possibility of confirming or rejecting those prejudices against those of that which we are trying to understand. To approach a text or claim with the idea that one might learn from it is not to set aside one's own prejudices but to illuminate them, and it allows one to test the two conceptions, our own understanding and the one that we are trying to understand, against one another.

Still, this analysis may not be sufficient to overcome the problem, for it presupposes that the 1896 Supreme Court is simply prejudiced as opposed to ideologically motivated. Moreover, it supposes that although we ourselves are prejudiced, we are not ideologically motivated. But suppose the two interpretations that are supposedly illuminating one another are equally ideological? Suppose our understanding is such that we can accept *Plessy v. Ferguson* and require state governments simply to comply with it and to establish equal facilities for blacks. Such facilities might go beyond the law school Texas set up for blacks in a basement a few blocks from the regular University of Texas law school, and they might even require that black elementary school children be admitted into white schools until substantively equal facilities could be built for them. But if this understanding of *Plessy* were to replace an older one allowing for unequal facilities or tying the existence of any facilities at all to the number of blacks actively seeking them, it would be no less ideological an understanding. What can prevent or correct an endless spinning out of claims that are not simply situated accounts with their own vocabulary of understanding but are instead ideological accounts with a distorted vocabulary?

For Jürgen Habermas this possibility is similar to the case of pathologically distorted vocabularies with which mental health patients try sincerely to understand themselves and their lives.[5] The problem here is that the language through which they try to understand is itself confused by the very set of problems they are trying to solve. The problems trace back to an original trauma, the language for which the patient has repressed and for which he or she has also found substitutes in the form of symptoms. Clarity and understanding thus require a wholly reconstructed language. The same might be said for racism. If one approaches *Plessy* or the Fourteenth Amendment with a series of racist assumptions, then the achievement of substantive equality becomes impossible, no matter how sincere one's efforts, because one is trying to fit the principle of equality into a vocabulary that is distorted by the racism one has to fix.

Gadamer does not deny the gravity of this sort of problem, but he does deny that the recourse to social theory that Habermas suggests can resolve it since any social theory will itself be subject to the hermeneutic conditions of prejudice and a horizontally circumscribed understanding. Rather, Gadamer looks to what he calls the productivity of temporal distance. Time allows the prejudices that blind understanding to fall away and the prejudices that support it to emerge. "It not only lets local and limited prejudices die away, but allows those that bring about genuine understanding to emerge clearly as such" (TM298). This analysis can be only cold comfort when we remember the generations of schoolchildren who had to wait while our prejudices adjusted themselves. Nor did our prejudices do so on their own. That the United States was able finally to rethink *Plessy v. Ferguson* owes its good fortune, in part at least, to the struggles of African Americans and their allies from the moment the decision was reached. But Gadamer does not think either understanding or morality progresses in any other way. Certainly he does not think there are any guarantees in the social theory to which Habermas appeals. Rather, he thinks that morality, law, and literature are texts that we must constantly rethink in new situations and in the light of new understandings. We have to struggle over our texts; we must disagree, argue, and look for answers to our questions, answers that we all, or most of us, find compelling.

What about the second problem we noted earlier? Surely, it is a moral virtue to be good-hearted, to look past a person's failures in judgment or action and to understand him or her as he or she could be. And surely we appreciate those who see us as we could be if we were better people, rather than as we are. Gadamer does not address this problem explicitly as he does the issue of ideology. Still, it would seem that from a Gadamerian point of view, this rose-colored relation to others is as dogmatic as one that sees only their failures. If others understand us only as they want to understand us or are used to understanding us, then, whether their orientation in doing so renders us better or worse than we are, they fail to respect our autonomy. They fail to allow us to differ from who they take us to be and hence fail to respect who we are. Respect for our difference, however, may be the basic moral virtue we are owed, and respect for their difference may be the basic moral virtue we owe others. Certainly it is a fundamental feature of struggles for recognition by women and minorities. Women struggled, in part, against an ideologically motivated enhancement of their goodness, as creatures too pure and gentle to engage in competitive careers or dirty politics. African Americans struggled against an equally ideological denigration of their abilities and character, as creatures too little developed to engage in competitive careers or important politics. Moreover, individuals continue to struggle against the requirement that they be representative of their groups, that they be like all other blacks or women with a pre-established set of opinions and characteristics. But struggles for recognition suggest that what is morally required here is simply a respect for autonomy and difference. To be sure, we cannot simply suspend our prejudices or either judge or understand others without presuppositions. What is both morally and interpretively required of us, however, is that we not be dogmatic, that we recognize that we are prejudiced and, by doing so, allow others their own voice. We shall often argue with the content of what others say and we shall sometimes convince them. We cannot accomplish the latter, however, if we refuse to acknowledge that what they say and think may differ from what we think they must do or say and think.

What do these Gadamerian considerations mean for the conclusions that Nehamas and Posner reach about claims for the relation of literature, law, and morality? First, to focus on the moral lessons a piece of literature has to teach us may be to subtract from other meanings the work possesses and to ignore the different ways even its moral meaning might be understood. Yet if we always understand from a situated horizon, to understand a piece of literature as a moral lesson may be as legitimate as other ways of understanding it. Second, an interpretive sensitivity that allows us to understand the moral grace in the actions of characters in literature such as Maggie and Adam in James's *The Golden Bowl* may not directly lead to a capacity to act or judge gracefully in the different circumstances in which we find ourselves. Still, if understandings of moral principle and virtue as well as of law and literature are all forms of practical knowledge, they all reflect an ability to apply universals to particular situations in ways that illuminate and develop the meaning of both. Third, an interpretive sensitivity may as easily provide the basis for immoral actions as it does for moral ones, but a moral acknowledgment of the autonomy of others, including texts, laws, and the interpretations of others of them, remains a condition for adequate interpretation. Finally, an interpretive insensitivity and the inability to read either texts or others well may lead to a generosity to them that makes better literature out of their efforts and better people out of their characters. It may also lead to a lack of generosity that makes worse literature out of their efforts and worse people out of their characters. Neither a blind generosity toward others nor a lack of sufficient generosity seems to have the moral weight of another virtue, however: that of a respect for difference. This respect includes an appreciation of the autonomy of others, a recognition of the possible independence of their claims from one's own prejudices, a willingness to learn from them even if this willingness bears no fruit, and an acknowledgment of their possible difference from oneself and from what one wants them or needs them to be. Struggles for recognition demand no less.

NOTES

1. See "The Edifying School of Legal Scholarship," in Richard A. Posner, *Law and Literature* (Cambridge, Mass.: Harvard University Press, 1988, 1998), 304–44.

2. Martha C. Nussbaum, "Form and Content: Philosophy and Literature," in *Love's Knowledge: Essays on Philosophy and Literature* (New York: Oxford University Press, 1990).

3. Alexander Nehamas, "What Should We Expect from Reading? (There Are Only Aesthetic Values)," *Salmagundi* 111 (Summer 1996): 35.

4. See *Plessy v Ferguson,* 163 U.S. 537 (1896). See also Richard Kluger, *Simple Justice* (New York: Vintage Books, 1977), 73–83.

5. See "The Hermeneutic Claim to Universality," in *Contemporary Hermeneutics: Method, Philosophy and Critique,* ed. Josef Bleicher (London: Routledge and Kegan Paul, 1980).

Chapter 6

A Critique of Gadamer's Aesthetics

MICHAEL KELLY

There are three main critiques through which Hans-Georg Gadamer develops his conception of aesthetics, which has a central role in his philosophical hermeneutics, which in turn is his principal contribution to philosophy in the twentieth century, all of which he amazingly witnessed. He offers a critique of the philosophy of art which regards art as a lie and that denies it is capable of making truth claims; a critique of aesthetic consciousness as an alienated abstraction from the experience of truth in art; and a critique of the subjectivization of modern aesthetics, which he traces back to Immanuel Kant's *Critique of Judgment*. These three critiques are integrally linked in Gadamer's work; for he thinks that the subjectivization of aesthetics is the conceptual twin of aesthetic consciousness, and that it is only from the perspective of subjective consciousness that art is unable to have any truth. These are powerful critiques and Gadamer makes strong arguments for each of them, as well as for their connectedness. Nevertheless, I would like to try to decouple and challenge these critiques separately. Specifically, I would like to defend Gadamer's critique of any philosophy of art that considers art to be a lie, though without conceding that art makes truth claims of its own; to challenge his critique of aesthetic consciousness because it reinforces rather than overcomes a fissure between consciousness and experience; and, finally, to resist his critique of the subjectivization of aesthetics because aesthetics, as well as art, is undeniably and unproblematically subjective, as is Gadamer's own aesthetics, or so I shall argue. I begin with the critique of truth since it concerns the ontology of art, which serves as the normative basis of the other two critiques.

ART AND TRUTH

Gadamer makes a very strong and unequivocal claim about the role of truth in art: "The fact that through a work of art a truth is experienced that we cannot attain in any other way constitutes the philosophical importance of art, which asserts itself against all attempts to rationalize it away."[1] He makes this claim while arguing against any philosophy of art or aesthetic theory that maintains that art is a lie, but his claim goes beyond the ontology of art. He argues that we can experience truth in art and even that art can make truth claims.[2] In making these last points, Gadamer goes too far, I believe. For although I agree with his truth claim *about* art, namely, that it is not a lie and that it has its own truth, I do not agree that truth claims can be made *by* art. I think that Gadamer unintentionally converts the *truth about art* into the *truth content of art,* and that this conversion is a mistake because, besides being unconvincing in its own right, it weakens his philosophical insight into the truth about art.[3]

The truth issue in Gadamer's aesthetics arises with his discussion of Plato's well-known critique of the poets, in Book X of the *Republic,* that a work of art is an imitation of an imitation of the truth. A picture of a bed, for example, is a mere appearance of a bed made by a carpenter, which in turn is an appearance of the Form of the bed, which is the one and only true bed. So the truth about art, for Plato, is that it is ontologically incapable of truth. Because art is unaware of this limitation, it continues to lay false claims to truth. In short, art is a lie. Gadamer rightfully challenges this ontology of art by arguing that a work of art is not to be understood in terms of its relationship to any other thing: "in the realm of art above all, it is self-evident that the work of art is not experienced in its own right if it is only acknowledged as a link in a chain that leads elsewhere"; we are compelled, he adds, "to dwell upon the individual appearance itself" (RB16). A work is still an appearance, but it is not the appearance *of* anything other than itself; it presents itself. Art qua appearance, and in the mode of self-presentation that distinguishes it, is its own truth.

Gadamer makes these points more concretely in *Truth and Method* while discussing how a picture is ontologically distinct from a mirror image and a copy, two things with which Plato and many philosophers after him mistakenly associate it.[4] A mirror image is dependent for its being and truth on the thing, such as my own face, that it mirrors; take my face (or the mirror) away and the image disappears as well. So long as the image remains, its truth is understood in terms of the thing it mirrors, so much so that the image is self-effacing; it reflects my face more or less adequately, and such adequation determines the truth of the image. A copy of something, such as a photocopy of this page, is initially dependent for its being on the original page but, once it exists, it attains a relatively independent being: for somebody could just as easily read a photocopy of this page as the original. Yet despite the copy's ontological independence, its truth is still a function of how adequate it is relative to the original page; for a good photocopy is also self-effacing, while a poor one can obscure the content and truth of the original. By contrast, a picture is neither a mirror image nor a copy, though it shares some features of both and, for that reason, is often confused with them. Rather, a picture has a distinct being because it is not self-effacing, and its truth is to be understood accordingly. In Gadamer's words, a picture, qua appearance, is its own original because it results in an "increase in being,"[5] that is, the being of a representation as distinct from that of what is represented: "Every such [re]presentation is an ontological event and occupies the same ontological level as what is represented."[6] The truth *about* a picture is thus that it has an independent being, or, in the terms of modern aesthetic theory, that it is autonomous. To say that a picture is autonomous means, for Gadamer, that it does not depend on any external source of validation and is thus "self-fulfilling."[7] Thus, contrary to Plato, to begin to understand a work of art we need not—and should not— compare it to anything external to it.

I think the starting point of Gadamer's ontology of a picture—and, by extension, the ontology of art as a whole—is correct, but I think he draws an unwarranted conclusion from it. He concludes from the truth about the ontology of art that art itself has truth content. He would assert, for example, not only that the being of a work of art is autonomous, but also that a work has truth content beyond what it may reveal to us about art. But what is this content, and how do we recognize it? This second question is particularly problematic for Gadamer, I believe, because he can appeal only to the experience of a work of art in which a truth is allegedly disclosed to confirm that a truth has in fact been disclosed.[8] Gadamer acknowledges and, in fact, underscores this point when, in the quote at the start of this section, he says that the claim that truth is experienced in art asserts itself against any and all who would deny that there is truth in art; the truth experienced in art is thus self-evident. What is self-evident, however, is only *that* truth is experienced; the actual truth experienced is anything but self-evident: "The experience of art acknowledges that it cannot present the full truth of what it experiences in terms of definitive [that is, conceptual] knowledge" (TM100). For more detail on this truth, even the truth about art itself, we have to turn from experience to aesthetics, whose task it is "to legitimate the experience of truth that occurs in the experience of art itself."[9] This suggests that aesthetics provides us with definitive knowledge of the truth experienced in art, which means the certainty that some truth has been experienced depends ultimately on aesthetics. For how can we be sure that truth has been experienced if we do not have a definitive sense of the truth that has been experienced? If aesthetics provides the certainty here, however, then the truth in art is hardly self-evident.

This is a result Gadamer would presumably not accept, as the cornerstone of his aesthetics seems to be the self-evidence of our experience of truth in art.[10] If we look more closely at what he means by truth, however, it is not clear to me that the concept is needed to serve his own purposes, even concerning the ontology of art. He discusses truth in at least three different ways, though without ever quite defining it. First, based on a literal translation of the German word *wahrnehmen,* Gadamer links the notion of truth to that of perception: to perceive is to take *(nehmen)* something as true *(wahr)* (RB29). That is, what is presented to the senses, such as a work of art, is seen and taken *as* something. But does this mean anything other than that the work is autonomous, that is, that it is there to be perceived rather than to be regarded as something that is either merely imagined or a copy of some other thing?[11] If this is what it means, we could just say that a work is autonomous rather than that it is true, since saying the work is true does not add anything to the claim of the work's autonomy. Second, and in a vein similar to the first, to say that a work of art is "true" seems to mean no more than that it is real in the sense that we say real gold is true gold, which means that it really exists and that it is what it appears to be (RB108, 133). Gadamer could establish this point without relying on the concept of truth; in fact, he already did so in his account of a picture as an autonomous self-presentation. Third, and more metaphysically, truth means "openness," a notion that Gadamer derives from Martin Heidegger's concept of *aletheia* (unconcealment). The appeal to truth in this sense is that we remain open to what addresses us in the work of art. Such an appeal is used by Gadamer in his critique of modern aesthetics because it abstracts from the content of art in order to achieve the purely aesthetic (see "The Subjectivity of Art and Aesthetics," below). In this context, he seems to be taking away some of the autonomy of art for which he advocated earlier. Now he is emphasizing that art also has nonaesthetic content, which he interprets in terms of the concept of truth. But what is addressing us in art and what does truth have to do with it? Is Gadamer claiming here anything more than the truth *that* art has content or meaning beyond its purely aesthetic qualities?[12] He could make such a claim without arguing that the content of art is truth itself; that is, he could again make a claim about the truth of art (in this case, about its meaning or content) without arguing that the actual content of art is truth.

The common thread running through all these senses of "truth" is that something shows itself as what it is (self-presentation); for, according to Gadamer, we say of whatever shows itself as it is that it is "true" (RB108). The meaning of 'true' here is "unconcealed." Applied to art, it means that the truth about art is that it discloses itself qua appearance. If that is the case, however, then I repeat my point that this is a truth *about* art, not a truth that art discloses about something other than itself. Moreover, Gadamer does not need the second point to make the first; in fact, as we shall see, the second only weakens the first by putting more cognitive pressure on art than it can bear.

Perhaps it would be best, for art, to take it out of the truth game entirely (except for the truth(s) about art), a game into which Plato forced art by claiming it is a lie, as even something that is a lie is part of the truth/falsehood game. I believe Gadamer himself unwittingly opens up this possibility in four different ways. First, his demonstration that art is not a lie is enough to take it out of the truth game, if he were to stop with that demonstration alone instead of going on to try to argue that art makes truth claims. Second, Gadamer's argument that poetic language (and the language of art in general) cannot ever be false could have the same effect if, again, he were to leave it at that; for in the truth game, if something cannot be false, it cannot be true either (RB139). Third, the reason Gadamer says poetic language cannot be false is that there is no external standard against which it should be measured or to which it ought to correspond. If this is the only or even the principal reason, as it seems to be, then we can speak here (again) of *autonomous* rather than *true* poetic language. Fourth, Gadamer's argument that there is truth unique to art is unconvincing and indirectly reveals that truth may not be the concept he has in mind. In saying, for example, that it is incontrovertible that poetic language enjoys a unique relationship to truth, Gadamer offers two reasons: (a) poetic language is not equally appropriate at all times; and (b) content given poetic form acquires legitimation (RB105). But "appropriateness" and "legitimation" are neither the same as truth, nor does either necessarily require truth. What Gadamer's reasons reveal here, I think, is that his real concern in talking about the truth of art is it legitimacy—as an autonomous being—or its appropriateness—in the sense of the particularity of each sensuous appearance (linguistic, visual, or otherwise). He has already made a convincing case for the first and more basic issue and, I think, did not need truth to do so.

There is yet another option here, however, besides dropping truth altogether: instead of saying that the experience of truth in art is self-evident, say only that the truth that art is autonomous is self-evident, though only in a historical context, as Gadamer himself argues. Beyond that, we could say not that art makes truth claims but that it introduces candidates for truth claims. The notion of "candidates" can readily, if indirectly, be linked to several of Gadamer's own ideas. First, the notion of truth as openness or unconcealment allows for the disclosure of possible truths in art without requiring that art itself make any truth claims.[13] Second, Gadamer's idea of pre-understanding also opens art up to the realm of truth without implying that any truth claims are actually made by art. He says, "prior to all conceptual-scientific knowledge of the world, the way in which we look upon the world, and upon our whole being-in-the-world, takes shape in art" (RB164). Although the meaning or content of art provides us with a pre-understanding of the world, it is up to aesthetics—or perhaps science—to validate the specific truths (not the fact) of this pre-understanding. As Gadamer says, truth is ultimately guaranteed by "a discipline of questioning and inquiring" (TM491). Art's role in this discipline is important, but only because of the possible truths it introduces into the inquiry. This option relieves art of the pressure to validate the candidates that it introduces. And it is important to release this pressure because, according to Gadamer's own argument, art cannot provide such validation; for when he says art is self-validating, he means that it validates its own (but not necessarily any other) truth.[14] All that art would ever need to validate would be its own autonomy, which it does just by being there.

This alternative position about truth in relation to art is clearly different from Gadamer's, but I believe that it is consistent with many of his principal aims, for it allows him to argue that art is cognitive, even if it does not make any truth claims of its own. Evidence of art's cognitive status, for Gadamer, is its central role in human self-understanding, of which he gives a very good account in *Truth and Method* and subsequent writings. All cognition is recognition, and recognition is ultimately *self*-recognition, albeit through the mediation of something other than the self (RB98–100). So to say that art is cognitive is to say that it is part of the process of human self-recognition (knowledge, understanding). In Gadamer's words, art imposes "an ineluctable task on existence, namely, to achieve that continuity of self-understanding which alone can support human existence" (TM96). We come to self-understanding by understanding something other than ourselves, such as a work of art: "Since we meet the artwork in the world and encounter a world in the individual artwork, the work of art is not some alien universe into which we are magically transported for a time. Rather, we learn to understand ourselves in and through it" (TM97). Art is thus cognitively important because of its contribution to human self-understanding. Here, too, art's cognitive contribution is confined to introducing us to candidates for truth—about the world as well as ourselves, since self-understanding is mediated by our experience of the world. Now, if the restoration of this cognitive role is the aim in claiming that art has truth content, as I believe it is, it could be achieved without the further argument about truth claims made by art.

Of course, since truth serves as the normative basis of Gadamer's aesthetics, to challenge truth is to challenge this basis. Yet his discussion of truth in art could be reframed, I think, as a discussion of the normativity of art, and in two senses: first, the normativity of art itself, principally with respect to its autonomy and subjectivity; and second, the normativity of what is revealed through art, namely, the self-understanding and pre-understanding just discussed. Gadamer himself suggests in *Truth and Method* that normativity is his concern when he criticizes Kant and others for eliminating the normative validity of four humanistic and aesthetic concepts: *Bildung,* taste, *sensus communis,* and judgment (TM9–41). I believe their normativity could be restored without appeal to the notion of truth; for the significance of these four concepts for Gadamer is that each represents what he calls an extra-scientific experience, that is, an experience of truth that transcends science. But his argument here concerns the truth about such experiences, that is, their legitimacy qua normative experiences; but this argument need not involve the contention that the actual content of these experiences is truth. More specifically, *Bildung* is characterized as the process of keeping oneself open to what is "other," to other more universal points of view; the (aesthetic, moral, political, etc.) norms of common sense are what bind a community together; the logical basis of judgment cannot be taught, for it is dependent on particular cases and contexts, which means that it operates on some other (that is, hermeneutic) basis; and taste has an eye to the whole (of a work of art, of a text, or of experience in general). All these "truths" are particular to the human sciences, but paradigmatically to art, which is why art is so central in Gadamer's philosophical hermeneutics.

But, again, Gadamer could speak here of the truth about art—namely, that it has a cognitive role because we can gain certain insights from it via *Bildung, sensus communis,* judgment, and taste which we cannot get from science—without claiming that art makes truths claims. For being open to the past and to other points of view is an attitude, not a truth claim (even when what we are open to is a truth); *sensus communis* is later integrated by Gadamer into the notion of tradition where normativity could replace truth; Kant's notion of reflective judgment already captures Gadamer's point about judgment and it does so without invoking truth; and since taste is a sensibility, the truth of what it senses is not something taste can be expected to verify. To propose that Gadamer dispense with the concept of truth in his critique of these humanistic concepts is thus not to deny that art is a rich source of insights about many things; on the contrary, it is to allow art to continue to be such a source without having too many cognitive demands placed on it, demands that arise when truth claims are raised and require verification, something that art cannot possibly provide, as Gadamer himself acknowledges.

The suggestion that Gadamer dispense with the concept of truth in art (though only after he establishes the truth(s) *about* art) will seemingly cause a major shift in what it means to understand a work of art, since the task of aesthetics on his account, as we have already noted, is to legitimate the truths experienced in art. But aesthetics still has plenty to do without truth, namely, the articulation and critical analysis of the truth candidates introduced by art, along with the self-knowledge and pre-understanding of the world achieved through art. Moreover, aesthetics is also still accountable for the ontology of art, which alone is a major task: for to establish that art is not a lie, to clarify the status of art as appearance, and to show what implications these points have for our understanding of works of art are enough to keep aesthetic theory occupied. And Gadamer still has much to offer on these matters.

AESTHETIC CONSCIOUSNESS

The purpose of Gadamer's critique of aesthetic consciousness is "to do justice to the experience *(Erfahrung)* of art" as an experience of truth (TM100). So this critique is clearly linked to the truth question just discussed. At the same time, however, the two critiques can and, I think, must be separated, especially if I am right that a significant step in Gadamer's truth critique is unconvincing and unnecessary. The claim about truth as the content of art is not needed to make Gadamer's case against aesthetic consciousness, which is, in short, that it abstracts from what makes art possible. Although I agree in part with this analysis, I think the alienation of aesthetic consciousness, as Gadamer describes it, is not due to the fact that aesthetics is subjective; rather, it is due to the wrong conception of subjectivity, which I shall discuss in the final section. Moreover, such alienation can be overcome without giving up aesthetic consciousness, for all that is needed here is for art to be understood as being capable of having nonaesthetic content.

Gadamer's critique of aesthetic consciousness is part of his critique of Kant, and involves the philosophical consequences of the autonomy of aesthetics as well as of art. According to Gadamer, Kant's "main concern . . . was to give aesthetics an autonomous basis freed from the criterion of the concept, and . . . to base aesthetic judgment on the subjective a priori of our feeling of life, the harmony of our capacity for 'knowledge in general'" (TM59–60). Kant thus grounded aesthetics in a priori subjectivity in order to secure the autonomy of aesthetics (not of art, which had already been secured, at least in principle). Although Gadamer agrees with Kant that aesthetics should be "freed from the criteria of the concept," he regards the subjective turn in aesthetics which Kant formalized as an unfortunate event for the ontology of art. Although art "becomes a standpoint of its own and establishes its own autonomous claim to supremacy," it is now "contrasted with practical reality and understood in terms of this contrast"; that is, "the concept of art is defined as appearance in contrast to reality."[15] Moreover, there is a profound irony in art's autonomy, according to Gadamer, for once art qua appearance becomes autonomous from reality and is seemingly related only to itself, it continues to be defined by the very reality from which it won its autonomy, at least so long as appearance is defined as such only in opposition to reality—as it was for Plato and Kant. If it is defined in this way, autonomous art has no truth. At the same time, it has no efficacy in the world and is thus alienated from reality (even as it is defined by it); its only remaining relation to reality is to mask or veil it. So Plato's ontology of art seems to resurface in Kant: art qua appearance is—again—a lie.

According to Gadamer, this alienated conception of art is the product of aesthetic consciousness, which itself is the effect of the autonomy of art; that is, aesthetics becomes autonomous after art does, but then aesthetics (too) is alienated, and its conception of art reflects this alienation. To overcome such alienation, Gadamer critiques aesthetic consciousness, particularly its process of aesthetic differentiation, which is as follows. Once aesthetics becomes autonomous, judgment replaces taste and consciousness becomes "the experiencing . . . center from which everything considered art is measured" (TM85). Whereas taste differentiates (that is, selects and rejects) on the basis of some content, "aesthetic differentiation is an abstraction that selects only on the basis of aesthetic quality as such" (TM85). Aesthetic consciousness thereby disregards everything in which a work of art is rooted (its original context of life, and the religious or secular function that gave it significance) so that it becomes visible as a "pure work of art" (TM85). Continuing with this same point, Gadamer concludes: "It practically defines aesthetic consciousness to say that it differentiates what is aesthetically intended from everything that is outside the aesthetic sphere" (TM85).

The consequences of "aesthetic differentiation" are mixed, according to Gadamer. What is good about it is that it separates the aesthetic from everything nonaesthetic and thus, in principle, allows the work of art to be seen in its true being as autonomous appearance.[16] What is negative, and ultimately outweighs the positive contribution, is that the work is abstracted from the world in which it has meaning and now belongs only to the world of aesthetic consciousness: the work is autonomous but meaningless. What is at stake here, however, is not just the meaning of the work but, more fundamentally, its being a work in the first place. "What we call a work of art and experience *(erleben)* aesthetically depends on a process of abstraction" (TM85). In its extreme form, according to Gadamer, aesthetic consciousness "even abstracts from art" (TM89). The work of art is thus reduced to an aesthetic object, that is, to an object of aesthetic consciousness (rather than of experience). As such it is an object but not a work.

This is a very strange history indeed. Art struggles for centuries to become autonomous—from reality or, more concretely, from religion, politics tied to monarchic rule, and metaphysics—and once it succeeds, aesthetics becomes autonomous as well. Understood only from the perspective of aesthetic consciousness, however, the work of art is alienated from reality. This means, however, that art is alienated from what makes it art—not just in terms of what makes something the particular historical work of art that it is, but in terms of what makes something a work of art in the first place. In effect, art stops being art once it becomes autonomous, at least so long as art is defined as appearance only in contrast to reality. To recover the work of art, which is the aim of Gadamer's critique, he proposes that we renounce aesthetic consciousness, thereby giving up the "purity" of the aesthetic, which in turn seems to imply, more significantly, that we give up the autonomy of art, at least to some degree.[17]

These are very strong claims Gadamer is making. To understand them better, it is helpful to note their general philosophical context. Following Heidegger, Gadamer aims to break from the philosophical dichotomy between subject and object which is characteristic of modern philosophy. He claims, for example, that a general purpose of *Truth and Method* is "to show that understanding is never a subjective relation to a given 'object' but to the history of its effect; in other words, understanding belongs to the being of that which is understood" (TMxxxi). In the case of art, this means that "understanding belongs to the encounter with the work of art itself" (TM100). This belonging can, in turn, "be illuminated only on the basis of the *mode of being of the work of art itself*" (TM100). In other words, it is the mode of being of a work of art that determines our understanding of that work; so our understanding of the work is an *effect* of its mode of being. To capture this sense in which our understanding is an effect, Gadamer introduces the notion of "historically effected consciousness" *(wirkungsgeschichtliches Bewusstsein)*, by which he means "at once the consciousness effected in the course of history and determined by history, and the very consciousness of being thus effected and determined."[18] In the case of art, aesthetic consciousness is therefore an effect of the mode of being of art qua autonomous appearance. It is thus an effect of art's autonomy; that is, aesthetic consciousness is what is achieved when aesthetics, following art, becomes autonomous.

Although discussion of Gadamer's notion of historically effected consciousness helps to clarify how aesthetic consciousness is formed and what is at stake in his critique of it, it also raises a new question. If aesthetic consciousness is indeed an effect of history and specifically of the autonomy of art and aesthetics, how can Gadamer (or we) resist it? The basis of such resistance must be historical, if he is going to be consistent with his own notion of historically effected consciousness. Presumably, his answer would be that the basis is the experience of art, which he insists has priority over aesthetic consciousness; for example, on the question of whether there is any truth experienced in art, experience says "yes," while consciousness says "no," and Gadamer defends experience. Since such truth is not as perspicacious as he believes, however, his answer does not explain how experience can trump consciousness; for, again, we cannot be sure, based on experience alone, of the truth that allegedly gives experience an advantage. Truth aside, the more basic problem here, I think, is the fact that Gadamer opposes experience to consciousness and sides with the former.[19] For example, he says, "The significance of that whose being consists in expressing an experience cannot be grasped except through an experience" (TM70). This suggests that no form of consciousness, even of the hermeneutic variety, could possibly understand experience. But if consciousness is simply the effect of our experiences of the mode of being of art, then the aesthetic consciousness Gadamer resists is but an effect of the experience of art that he favors.[20] If this is the case, then clearly experience (art) and consciousness (aesthetics) have to be reconciled rather than opposed to one another.

Perhaps Gadamer has overstated his case. His criticism of aesthetic consciousness is, as we have seen, that it loses sight of the work of art and ends up with *only* an object. But he also says, more provocatively, that the being of art cannot be defined as an object at all, not just of aesthetic consciousness, "because the aesthetic attitude is more than it knows of itself."[21] Gadamer's claim is that experience is more than it knows of itself, and also that it is more than consciousness could ever know of it. Although this claim points to the limits of consciousness relative to the work or experience that it has taken as its object, such limits alone do not imply that art cannot be taken as an object at all. In addition, from the perspective of aesthetic consciousness, there is a relevant sense in which art (or the experience thereof) is an object, that is, an object of reflection. This object is not the same as the work of art that has been experienced, for reflection is not the same as experience. Yet the work that Gadamer is trying to recover is always already implicit in the object of aesthetic consciousness, so long as "object" here is understood as "the experience of the work of art." Of course, the specific thing about the work of which aesthetic consciousness has allegedly lost sight is truth, but the principal truth about art that consciousness needs to acknowledge in order to understand the work properly is the truth that the work is autonomous. Surely, consciousness is capable of grasping this truth. Since it is precisely the extreme or absolute version of this same truth that has led to the problem of aesthetic consciousness in the first place, however, what is needed is a moderation of the autonomy of art (and of aesthetics) so that it does not undermine the very possibility of art. This is precisely what Gadamer proposes, and he can achieve this end, I believe, without abdicating aesthetic consciousness.

What Gadamer ultimately wants here, I think, is for art to have some content other than "aesthetic quality," which means his aim is to recontextualize art while respecting its autonomy. But there are other ways of accomplishing this aim without abandoning aesthetic consciousness entirely. For example, in Gadamer's own earlier discussion of the cognitive dimension of art, namely, its role in human self-understanding, it was already established that what we experience in a work of art is a world other than that of consciousness; for self-understanding is possible only through mediation of something other than the conscious self, such as a work of art. Gadamer offers other examples of what he means by the content of art beyond "aesthetic quality": art is intuition, a worldview, an intuition of the world; and the significance of art is that it opens us up to the "message of the whole."[22] Even without going into detail here about each of these claims, their common ground is that art is not (and never has been) just an alienated object of consciousness. Moreover, this point can be made without appeal to the concept of truth (except for the truth about art, namely, that it has rich content), and, as we shall see in the next section, the best way to achieve the recontextualization Gadamer is seeking is, I think, to reconnect art with subjectivity rather than, as he recommends, to divorce them.

THE SUBJECTIVITY OF ART AND AESTHETICS

Gadamer critiques the subjectivization of aesthetics, a process that developed throughout the eighteenth century and culminated in Kant's *Critique of Judgment*. One of the principal motivations for Gadamer's critique is his interest in restoring the cognitive dimension of art, which he believes requires a new, nonsubjective foundation for aesthetics. What he is aiming for here, in short, is a conception of aesthetics "that transcends thinking from the perspective of subjectivity" (TM100). I do not think such transcendence is either possible or desirable, even given Gadamer's own aims, as I interpret them.

According to Gadamer, "it was a methodological abstraction corresponding to a quite particular transcendental task of laying foundations which led Kant to relate aesthetic judgment entirely to the condition of the subject" (TM97). The basis of Gadamer's challenge to Kant is, as we have seen, that an account of aesthetic judgment that excludes knowledge and truth from art runs into indissoluble contradiction with the "true experience of art." He then counters the Kantian conception of aesthetic judgment with a hermeneutic ontology of art—characterized by play, symbol, and festival—as a mode of being that possesses knowledge and truth. Yet however attractive Gadamer's conception of art is, Kant—and no other theorist—is responsible for the subjectivization of aesthetics. There simply would be no aesthetics at all, at least not as we know it, had there not been—for complicated philosophical and social reasons—a subjective turn in our thinking about the production, experience, taste, and judgment of art.

Although the term 'aesthetics' (or at least 'aesthetic') has origins in Greek philosophy and a rich genealogy up to and beyond the Renaissance, it is well known that aesthetics did not emerge as an autonomous discipline within philosophy until the eighteenth century. One of the principal philosophical insights that contributed to this emergence is the realization that beauty (and, following it, any other aesthetic predicate) is neither a transcendens (as it was from Plato through at least medieval philosophy) nor a property of objects (as it was until, say, John Locke). Gadamer's own negative formulation of this insight, with reference to Kant, is that in taste "nothing is known of the objects judged to be beautiful" (TM43). That is, a judgment that an object is beautiful is neither a judgment that the object participates in a transcendent idea of beauty nor a judgment about an objective property of that object. The judgment and the taste that it embodies are a reflection of how the object affects the subjective consciousness of the person making the judgment: if the subject experiences pleasure, the object that occasions the pleasure is judged to be beautiful.[23] This is the sense in which an aesthetic judgment is subjectively grounded and also the sense in which Gadamer considers aesthetics as a whole to be subjective. What he objects to in particular here is that, from the perspective of the subjectivization of aesthetics, aesthetic judgments do not involve knowledge; since knowledge is what conveys truth, such judgments also lack truth value. So we are once again back to the truth question.[24]

Clearly, Gadamer does not mean to argue that we can uncritically revive the premodern philosophical belief in a nonsubjective conception of beauty (and of art in general). He is too historically minded in his thinking for such an argument. Yet he does believe that a contemporary version of the classical (principally Platonic/Aristotelian) conception of beauty linked to the good and truth could be hermeneutically appropriated if we could only overcome subjectivism in aesthetics.[25] But this is the whole problem, I think: aesthetics is irreversibly subjective and so such an overcoming is impossible. The best way to argue this point against Gadamer, I think, is not to defend Kant or any other aesthetician or to criticize Plato and Aristotle, but rather to show that Gadamer's own aesthetic theory is more subjective than he would have us believe, given his earlier account of the cognitive role of art in human self-understanding.

To begin with, Gadamer acknowledges in a positive spirit that "modern aesthetics has fully recognized the 'contribution of the subject' to the construction of aesthetic experience" (RB127). But what such theory overlooks, he adds, is that "the experience of art also presents that other dimension in which the play-like character of the creation, the very fact of its being 'played', comes to the fore" (RB127). Although the concept of play is intended to capture the sense in which our experience of art is an event that happens to us beyond (and prior to) aesthetic consciousness, it is not opposed to subjectivity. Gadamer's underlying concern is rather to balance subjectivity with its other "dimension" rather than to overcome it. He is not always careful or consistent about this concern for balance, however. For example, the concept of art as play is explicitly introduced in *Truth and Method* as a way to overcome the subjectivity of aesthetics. In Gadamer's later writings, however, he uses the same concept to balance subjectivity, saying that it is through art as play that we catch sight of "what we are, what we might be, and what we are about" (RB130). In fact, he emphasizes the cognitive contribution of "art as play" to human self-recognition in order to offset any tendency to interpret such play as spurious freedom. And there are other indications that Gadamer's later view of the subjectivity of art and aesthetics is more tempered than it first appears to be in *Truth and Method*. For example, he calls the subjective turn in aesthetics an "anthropological turn," and writes in *Truth and Method* as if he were against such a turn in principle (TM82). But it is clear in his writings after *Truth and Method* that play itself is anthropologically grounded (RB5, 22, 46–47). Since play is one of Gadamer's main aesthetic concepts, his aesthetics is anthropologically grounded as well. As he himself asks: "And is not art really defined by the fact that, whatever may be represented in it, humanity encounters itself?" (RB167). Even when Gadamer discusses tragedy, which is the exemplar of play transformed into the structure of a work of art which is beyond subjectivity ("primacy of play over the players"), he says that it dissolves our disjunction from what is, thereby allowing a return to ourselves (TM129–34).

Gadamer is therefore not against subjectivity *tout court;* rather, he is offering an alternative conception of it. It is this alternative, however sketchy it remains here, which provides evidence that Gadamer's aesthetics is more subjective than he claims. What he is interested in is a historically situated subjectivity rather than an abstract, alienated subjectivity in the form of aesthetic consciousness, as we saw in the previous section.[26] In effect, he aims to recontextualize autonomous art. If so, then he must already acknowledge that the subjectivity of aesthetics—which, like the autonomy of art, is a historical achievement which both predates Kant and has still not been fully realized—cannot be transcended. We cannot transcend subjectivity because, as Gadamer himself emphasizes through his notion of historically effected consciousness, we cannot transcend our historicity. The task of aesthetics, in this light, is to understand the philosophical meaning and implications of the historical and ontological fact of art's subjectivity (along with its autonomy and historicity).

CONCLUSION

Gadamer is right that contemporary aesthetic theory is still marked by profound philosophical transformations in art that took place in the eighteenth century. Art was indeed severed from truth in that period, aesthetic consciousness did arise then along with the autonomy of art, and aesthetics, following art, did become deeply subjective. Although Gadamer's critiques of these transformations are rich with philosophical insights, I think it is a mistake to try to rehabilitate classical aesthetics. It is one thing to attain a better understanding of our contemporaneity by situating it in the context of its classical and modern genealogy; it is another thing entirely to think that we can understand contemporary art in a classical manner. After all, according to Gadamer's principal philosophical notion, "historically effected consciousness," our understanding of art is an effect of the mode of being of art. As that mode changes, so too does our understanding. Thus what is appropriate for Plato and Aristotle's time is not for ours, because art today is very different, even ontologically, than it was in ancient Greece.[27]

I agree with Gadamer that understanding the contemporary mode of art is the task of aesthetics today, and that recognizing that aesthetic understanding is historically effected is a philosophical precondition of this task.[28] Although this recognition is by no means a guarantee that we shall get art right, getting it right is what aesthetics must constantly try to do as art continues to change its mode of being. Such is the hermeneutic nature of the historical dialogue about art to which Gadamer has contributed in ways that have only begun to be explored. My aim here has been to open up such exploration through a critical analysis of his aesthetics, which I believe may still help us to understand contemporary art, if only truth would not get in our way.

NOTES

1. TMxxii–xxiii. For Gadamer's claim that such truth is unique to art, see RB37, 105. I will return to this issue below.

2. On the issue of truth claims in art see, for example, TM97. Although the expression 'truth claim' suggests a notion of propositional truth, that is not what Gadamer has in mind; he works with a notion of truth as disclosure, which is discussed below. So, among other problems with this expression in Gadamer's aesthetics, his use of it is simply misleading.

3. Joel Weinsheimer makes a three-way distinction regarding truth and art: the truth *about art*, the truth *of art*, and the truth *about truth* as revealed through the truth of art. *Gadamer's Hermeneutics: A Reading of* Truth and Method (New Haven, Conn.: Yale University Press, 1985), 99. In effect, I am confirming the first truth while criticizing the last two, and especially the second.

4. Gadamer discusses other art forms, of course, but a modern picture is paradigmatic for him because it exists only along with "aesthetic consciousness" and, for that reason, it best exemplifies the results of "aesthetic differentiation"—two notions discussed below.

5. TM140; RB35. The notion of "increase in being" is tied to (and, I think, could be replaced by) the notion of autonomy because it implies that a work of art is not a means to something else the way, for example, a mirror image is.

6. TM140. Gadamer makes much of the distinction between *Darstellung* (presentation) and *Vorstellung* (representation).

7. RB110. For Gadamer, such self-fulfillment is what defines beauty, as the beautiful "fulfills itself in a kind of self-determination and enjoys its own self-

representation" (RB14); "Beautiful things are those whose value is of itself evident" (TM477). Self-fulfillment is also self-presentation, which is a feature of play and of the beautiful (TM116). On Gadamer's use of the notion of autonomy, see, for example, TM139–40.

8. "The significance of that whose being consists in expressing an experience cannot be grasped except through an experience" (TM70). This quote is discussed in more detail below.

9. TM98; cf. RB16–17; and TM100: "We do not ask the experience of art to tell us how it conceives of itself, then, but what it truly is and what its truth is, even if it does not know what it is and cannot say what it knows."

10. Gadamer does acknowledge, however, that the experience of art constitutes a kind of evidence that is both too strong and too weak: too strong because nobody would venture to develop a model of progress in art as an analog to progress in science, too weak "in the sense that the artwork withholds the very truth that it embodies and prevents it from being conceptually concise" ("Reflections on My Philosophical Journey," PHGG6).

11. RB33: "the meaning of the work of art lies in the fact that it is there."

12. Another issue here is whether the aesthetic qualities of a work of art can ever be isolated in the pure terms to which Gadamer claims aesthetic consciousness aspires. He may be mistaking their aspirations for achievements, aspirations which his own critique shows to be impossible to achieve.

13. This point could also be tied to Heidegger's acknowledgment that it is misleading to call *aletheia* (unconcealment) truth because it is "not yet truth"; rather, *aletheia* "first grants the possibility of truth." "The End of Philosophy and the Task of Thinking," in *On Time and Being,* ed. and trans. Joan Stambaugh (New York: Harper and Row, 1972), 69–70.

14. Gadamer says that a text—and, by analogy, a work of art—"captivates us" before we are in a position "to test the claim to meaning that it makes" (TM490).

15. TM82. Cf. also PHGG44: "This was really the starting point of my whole hermeneutical theory. The artwork is a challenge for our understanding because over and over again it evades all our interpretations and puts up an invincible resistance to being transformed into the identity of the concept."

16. "In performing this abstraction, aesthetic consciousness . . . shows what a work of art is, and allows it to exist in its own right. I call this 'aesthetic differentiation'" (TM85).

17. In Gadamer's words, "In order to do justice to art, aesthetics must go beyond itself and surrender the 'purity' of the aesthetic" (TM92). Cf. also TM81: "Is the aesthetic approach to a work of art the appropriate one? Or is what we call 'aesthetic consciousness' an abstraction?" And "Heidegger's Later Philosophy" (PH218): "In the last analysis, we need to overcome the concept of aesthetics itself." Based on interpretations of these quotes, some people consider Gadamer's aesthetics to be *anti*-aesthetics. I think, rather, that he critiques one type of aesthetic theory (the one based on what he calls "aesthetic consciousness") and defends another, hermeneutic type (based on the experience of truth in art). I, in turn, am challenging Gadamer's aesthetics and proposing another, neither of which involves a critique of aesthetics *tout court.*

18. TMxxxiv. Elsewhere, Gadamer says that historical consciousness in relation

to aesthetics is "simply the fact that our senses are spiritually organized in such a way as to determine in advance our perception and experience of art" (RB11).

19. Gadamer discusses two distinct notions of experience, *Erlebnis* and *Erfahrung*. He is not satisfied with the former because it stresses the fragmentariness of experience and thus cannot capture the truth of the hermeneutic continuity that constitutes human existence (TM95–97). The concept of *Erfahrung* is introduced to capture this continuity (TM97–99).

20. Is Gadamer setting up an opposition here between (the experience of) art and aesthetics, and siding with the former? Is this part of what some have referred to as his anti-aesthetics? If so, I again think that reconciliation rather than conflict is what is needed here.

21. TM116. See also PHGG43–44: the work of art distinguishes itself in "that one never completely understands it"; and RB34: the fact that a work exists at all "represents an insurmountable resistance against any superior presumption that we can make sense of it all."

22. RB164, 32. There are some passages, however, that reaffirm the role of truth. Gadamer says, for example, that it is by virtue of the beautiful that we are able "to acquire a lasting remembrance of the true world" (RB15).

23. A major philosophical issue that the subjective ground of aesthetic judgment raises, of course, is how such judgment can be objective or universal. This is one of the issues which first gave rise to philosophical aesthetics in the eighteenth century and which has continued to trouble philosophers ever since.

24. This confirms, I think, that truth is the normative basis of Gadamer's aesthetic critiques.

25. Cf. RB, passim. Such appropriation is as much the means as the result of the overcoming of subjectivism Gadamer proposes. It consists of the redefinition of a number of central aesthetic concepts; in addition to beauty, see, for example, mimesis: TM113–15 and RB92–104, 116–22.

26. Also at issue in Gadamer's critique of the subjectivization of aesthetics is its universality. Since the inception of modern aesthetics in the eighteenth century, subjectivity has been a virtual given because of the subjective status of beauty and, by extension, all other aesthetic concepts, and universality has been a problem because, prima facie, such subjectivity seems to preclude universality. For Gadamer, however, universality is a given (RB13) because of the truths we experience in art, and subjectivity poses a problem because it threatens to undermine the universality of such truths. Despite Gadamer's emphasis on universality, however, he acknowledges in his later writings that it is rather weak. For example, he says, "The only thing that is universally familiar to us today is unfamiliarity itself, momentarily illuminated by an ephemeral glimmer of meaning. But how can we express that in human form" (RB79)? He also says "there is no longer a unified symbolic language capable of commanding our acceptance" (RB75); in fact, contemporary art is characterized by "the dearth of the symbol, the very renunciation of the symbolic" (RB74). Such doubts put the universality of art seriously into question.

27. Gadamer would not agree that the ontology of art changes over time. On this point he is an essentialist, which enables him to claim that what Plato and Aristotle say about art still has truth for us today. Although I agree, as I have said, that we can

learn from the classics, it is not because art is ontologically constant. This essential-ism question is clearly a crucial issue, but I cannot pursue it here.

28. In his later writings on art, those after *Truth and Method,* Gadamer stresses the problem raised by contemporary art, namely, that it breaks from all the traditional ways in which art has been legitimated by philosophy (RB7, 10, 22, 46, 77–78, 83). Although I agree that contemporary art makes such a break, I also think that part of the break is a challenge to the assumption of traditional aesthetics that art is some-thing that needs to be legitimated. It is only from the perspective of the theories that regard art as a lie that art needs to be legitimated. Once the ontology of art is altered in the way that Gadamer himself proposes, the need for legitimation ends.

PART TWO

Gadamer and Dialogue

Chapter 7

On Dialogue

To Its Cultured Despisers

DONALD G. MARSHALL

The terms "conversation" and "dialogue" lie at the heart of Hans-Georg Gadamer's description of understanding. In a phrase that draws together many lines of his thought, he speaks of "the conversation that we ourselves are" (TM378).[1] Although "understanding a text and reaching an understanding in a conversation" appear to be very different (TM378), Gadamer's analysis enables the insight that describing "the task of hermeneutics as entering into dialogue with the text" is "more than a metaphor" (TM368). To understand something is to reach an understanding with another about it, and that can only be achieved through a conversation that sustains the interplay of question and answer.

Much can be said—and has been said, by Gadamer and others—to explain, support, and elaborate these claims. It is true, I think, that some who read the preceding paragraph may form the impression that they already understand it. Within a contemporary American context, the terms "conversation" and "dialogue" seem immediately familiar. We have seen any number of public meetings, large and small, advertised as "conversations" or "dialogues." The former director of the National Endowment for the Humanities presented as his main goal setting up a program of conversations across the country about what America means. Religious leaders tirelessly call for dialogue both within and between religious bodies. The president proposed a national "dialogue on race" and participated in small-group discussions that were nationally televised. Nor are the terms uncommon in the narrower area of understanding texts. Robert Maynard Hutchins's introductory volume to the set of *Great Books of the Western World* bore the title *The Great Conversation: The Substance of a Liberal Education,* and the philosopher Michael Oakeshott wrote a famous pamphlet called "Poetry in the Conversation of Mankind."

This ceaseless drumming predisposes many to think of dialogue and conversation as self-evidently good without much reflection on why they are or even on what they are. Such people will feel little temptation to read a difficult 600-page book that demonstrates what they already know—or think they know. Even if they read it, they may well substitute their own preconceptions for Gadamer's specific ideas. They may be more dangerous to a just appreciation of Gadamer than are his critics. It is difficult to correct the misunderstanding of someone who feels certain that he agrees with you.

In the spirit of hermeneutic philosophy, however, my concern here will be with the critics of dialogue, for Gadamer argues that only by confronting objections to one's ideas, and indeed only by strengthening as far as possible the arguments against oneself, can one attain genuine insight. I divide criticisms of dialogue into two groups. The first responds to the ubiquity of calls for dialogue in contemporary life that I have sketched. Dialogue's status as a dominant but unexamined value irresistibly provokes critical examination from those who are suspicious of all received ideas, particularly those whose invocation lays automatic claim to good faith. Criticisms of dialogue as a currently conventional value may be legitimate, but there is still room to ask whether suspicion of an ideological use—or abuse—of dialogue may lead to objections to Gadamer's thought that miss the mark. The second line of criticism challenges in more fundamental and rigorously philosophical terms the very idea and possibility of dialogue. Together, I believe, they will throw into sharper relief Gadamer's understanding of dialogue.

A first line of objection to Gadamer is that he is silent about the concrete identity of persons as they have entered into dialogue, or been excluded from it. In the Socratic dialogues, for example, women have no place, even though the *Republic* acknowledges that men and women are equally qualified for philosophical training. St. Paul counts it a disgrace for a woman to speak in church, even as he asserts that in Christ there is neither Jew nor Greek, slave nor free, male nor female. The law in some Southern states made it a capital offense to teach a slave to read or write, yet Jefferson thought it self-evident that all men were created equal. Not even the silencing of the Jews, who had contributed so much to German philosophy and culture, seems to disturb Gadamer's equanimity. This objection turns into bitter accusation when John Caputo writes,

> For deconstruction, tradition is largely the story of the winners while the dissenters have been excommunicated, torched, castrated, exiled, or imprisoned. . . . If Gadamer is interested in how the metaphysical tradition passes along its stored-up treasures, Derrida is on the look-out for the police state that inevitably accompanies theories of infinite wealth. Philosophical hermeneutics takes a stab at recognizing the finitude and flux that inhabits all human institutions, but deconstruction doubts that hermeneutics has its heart

in it. Deconstruction suspects that hermeneutics has something else up its sleeve—or hidden in the closet.[2]

Caputo's remarks are notably impertinent, in every sense of the word. Like every other human being, Gadamer doubtless has his shortcomings, but he is innocent of the blind self-righteousness that speaks this sort of violent language. Gadamer is not Dietrich Bonhoeffer, but neither is Professor Caputo. Genuine moral authority is quite distinct from cheap indignation.

The spirit of dialogue, however, is not to triumph over intemperate eristic but to strengthen the other's argument. Gadamer has himself stressed that understanding is neither a method nor something abstractly mental but a mode of being. His rehabilitation of prejudice aims to account for understanding's dependence on the resources of existence a person brings to dialogue with a text or another person. Gibbon's *Decline and Fall of the Roman Empire* is palpably a work of the Enlightenment. This is not a limitation, which would suggest that later histories will supersede it with the advance of research; on the contrary, this is exactly what is unsurpassable about Gibbon's interpretation. *Truth and Method,* published in 1960 when Gadamer was sixty, could not, of course, anticipate the categories of group identity that are so central to contemporary American culture. At that time, the murderous history of this century had made any such categories seem beyond the pale. Given that context, it took some boldness to insist that an adequate account of understanding could not do without such particularities. At the same time, nothing in Gadamer countenances a reductive and essentialist identity politics. To the dialogue in which understanding takes place, each individual brings a horizon, "the range of vision that includes everything that can be seen from a particular vantage point" (TM302). The word indicates how "thought is tied to its finite determinacy" (TM302). But on the other side, it also "means not being limited to what is nearby but being able to see beyond it" (TM302). Horizons can be too narrow, but they also can be expanded and new horizons can open up. Horizons are not fixed or static, but they move and change with individual and cultural life. Hence, "the closed horizon that is supposed to enclose a culture is an abstraction" (TM304). In dialogue, the participants' individual horizons "fuse" (TM306). The term may not be happily chosen, but the context makes clear that what is implied is not any surrender of individuality nor subordination under an alien outlook. If prejudices "constitute the horizon of a particular present" (TM306), that horizon is constantly being formed by a process of testing prejudices. When Gadamer says that through dialogue we rise "to a higher universality that overcomes not only our own particularity but also that of the other" (TM305), the terminology is legitimate because "universality" is not abstract. The whole force of the term "horizon" is to reject any biological or cultural determinism without turning under-standing into an empty abstraction.

Gadamer's thought, then, can allow for and even insist on the indispens-ability of the particularities each person brings into dialogue. But a person accomplishes this by bringing those particularities into the language of di-alogue. Here, too, "Being that can be understood is language" (TM474). This, however, occasions a second line of objection. For in what language—or whose language—will a dialogue be conducted? Gadamer intends his stress on the diversity of languages as a critique of any dream of a universal language or of the idea that thinking can transcend the actual languages that are the accomplishments of specific historical communities. The prob-lem becomes clear even in a thinker as judicious as Martha Nussbaum. In a carefully considered argument for cosmopolitanism in outlook and con-duct, she acknowledges the appropriateness of paying special attention to our local reality:

> A useful analogy is one's own native language. I love the English language. And although I have some knowledge of some other languages, whatever I express of myself in the world I express in English. If I were to try to equalize my command of even five or six languages, and to do a little writing in each, I would write poorly. But this doesn't mean that I think English is in-trinsically superior to other languages. I recognize that all human beings have an innate linguistic capacity, and that any person might have learned any lan-guage; which language one learns is in that sense morally irrelevant, an acci-dent of birth that does not determine one's worth. That recognition of equal worth has practical consequences for the ways in which I react to and speak about others.[3]

This shows an admirable effort to check ego- and ethnocentrism. But can the goal be achieved by an exercise of moral will? English is in fact a world language. Someone whose native language is Xhosa or Inuit-Inupiaq has access to a much more restricted group. Some languages do not have a de-veloped philosophical tradition or, even if they do, the works of that tra-dition are known to few outside the language. A speaker of Hungarian or Dutch who wants to reflect on certain philosophical issues will have to take up terms and ideas articulated in languages with an established tradition. What is opened here is the problematic ethical situation of all dialogues in which the aim is genuine mutuality and yet the relation is inherently asym-metrical. In the political and historical world, it is not in the power of in-dividuals to establish equality, for the asymmetry results from historical institutions and realities. Thus, a call for "dialogue" with persons from the third world proffered by someone who enjoys the security of the European-American world is quite different from the opposite invitation by someone who has access only to the limited power and resources of the third world, a world made precarious by a history of colonial subjection.

The apparent plausibility of this argument testifies to language's constitutive disappearance in favor of the world it brings into view. The asymmetry of actual power relations is attributed to language itself and thus mys-
tified. The fact that nothing we can do to the language of dialogue will
eliminate these distorting asymmetries bears witness that language is not
an instrument subject to our will. It is not a place where power is stored up
or exercised. When Gadamer says that the being of language lies in dialogue, that is, in "coming to an understanding," he immediately draws the
conclusion:

> This is not to be understood as if that were the purpose of language. Coming
> to an understanding is not a mere action, a purposeful activity, a setting up of
> signs through which I transmit my will to others. Coming to an understanding
> as such, rather, does not need any tools, in the proper sense of the word. It is
> a life process in which a community of life is lived out. (TM446)

Communities do not simply have a language, they form it. In dialogue, language "places a subject matter before those communicating like a disputed
object set between them" (TM446). It discloses the world as "the common
ground, trodden by none and recognized by all, uniting all who talk to one
another" (TM446). "Every conversation," Gadamer claims, "presupposes a
common language, or better, creates a common language" (TM378).

As Gadamer describes dialogue, there can thus be no decision, whether
unilateral or mutual, about the language of dialogue that precedes the
dialogue itself. If we imagine a dialogue between an English speaker and a
speaker of Inuit-Inupiaq, it is a mistake to think that it is the speaker of
Inuit-Inupiaq who is at a disadvantage. Such a dialogue offers the speaker
of English occasion to ask what his or her words really mean. The more apparently "impoverished" the language of the person addressed, the deeper
and more fruitful this self-questioning can be. The loss of the presumed
sufficiency or self-evidence of one's own words is the dawn of thinking. To
enter into a dialogue means to give hearing—oneself as well as the other—
priority over speaking. Heidegger's excavations of the philosophical tradition tirelessly teach the dangerous advantage an established terminology
confers. This does not mean that the tradition is a record of error but only
that it must be reanimated and appropriated for thinking to take place.
Gadamer refers to Kleist's essay "On the Progressive Elaboration of Thoughts
in Discourse" to bring out this point: "A word becomes real when it proffers
itself in our speaking on its own out of however thoroughly pre-schematized
a thesaurus and customary usage. We speak that word and it leads to consequences and ends we had not perhaps conceived of" (TM548). Language
is not an "infinite text" that we learn to "recite" (TM548). Language is
not "a stock of words and phrases, of concepts, viewpoints and opinions"
(TM549). On the contrary,

> Speaking is only speaking if we accept the risk of positing something and fol-
> lowing out its implications . . . . In fact, language is the single word, whose
> virtuality opens for us the infinity of discourse, of speaking with one another,
> of the freedom of "expressing oneself" and "letting oneself be expressed."
> Language is not its elaborated conventionalism, nor the burden of pre-
> schematization with which it loads us, but the generative and creative power
> to unceasingly make this whole once again fluent. (TM548–49)

This is why Plato's dialogues retain their power to stimulate thinking. Their
language arises out of the consideration of the subject under inquiry. It
does not harden into a terminology. This certainly presents a challenge to
commentators, who for two millennia have striven to contain and codify this
power of thinking. But the dialogues remain unsubdued.

Of course if two persons speak different languages, a translator will be
needed. But translation does not consist in letting one language dominate
the other—a notion that makes no sense. Donald Davidson has elaborated
the argument of W. V. O. Quine against any claim that a meaning in one language could be radically untranslatable into another language. It is in fact
a secret bias in favor of a language like English or German to suppose that
anything that can be said in it would be untranslatable into or unintelligible
in Xhosa or Inuit-Inupiaq or any other language. The particularity of a given
language is not a barrier between its speakers and the world that is disclosed
in any other language. Precisely because that world is disclosed in language
it is "of itself always open to every possible insight and hence to every ex-
pansion of its own world picture, and is accordingly available to others"
(TM447).

These contrasting views of language need testing against a particular instance. Derek Walcott's *Omeros* suggests itself precisely because it embraces
a polyglot and palimpsestic world.[4] The central characters—Achille, Hélène, Hector—bear the names of those in Homer's epic, but the names are
mocked and treated with contempt by French slave masters who thereby implied that the superiority of their civilization legitimated their dominion.
Although the slaves were eventually liberated by the British, their descen-
dants' poverty and situation at the edge of empire prolong an economic
submission. Yet Walcott's transposition of Homer's story discloses the dignity of these lives. The power of this revelation does not merely restore the
inhabitants of a fishing village on St. Lucia to their full humanity, but even
more it restores Homer to himself from the misappropriation of the colo-
nizers. It is Homer who gains the most, since the claim of his poem to truth
depends on the confirmation of its applicability in the Caribbean. Without
that, his poem shrivels to a mere "masterpiece" and his name shrinks to the
pretentious moniker of a New England farmer. In this interaction between
the founding poem of the Western tradition and the creole of a colonized
people, it is the colonized whose lives and experience disclose the poem's

truth. This state of affairs speaks in myriad ways through the densely woven language—or more accurately, languages—of Walcott's poem.

But even if these responses to Gadamer's critics are persuasive, do they not pave the way to a third and more fundamental line of objection, of which the others are perhaps only variants or, rather, exfoliations? This objection turns against dialogue Gadamer's own argument that "the goal of all attempts to reach an understanding is agreement concerning the subject matter" (TM292). If dialogue presupposes "sharing in a common meaning" (TM492), does it not follow that it precludes an acknowledgement of differences, which are not always resolvable? If all horizons fuse into "a single historical horizon," "the one great horizon" (TM304), what happens to the variety and even conflict of traditions? Understanding "consists in subordinating ourselves to the text's claim to dominate our minds" (TM311). In language, "a totality of meaning" is disclosed. But if that is so, is not dialogue inherently coercive, concealing or erasing difference and yielding an agreement that can only be an extension of received opinion, of the status quo? Does not the language of "agreement" and "sharing" and "the common" turn here into the language of domination and totality? Must the person who enters into dialogue surrender his one real power, the power of resistance? If we listen to the Socratic dialogues with the ears of Callicles and his kind, these victims of Socratic openness refuse to speak or else withdraw into resentful and angry silence perhaps because they feel, viscerally as much as mentally, that the first word anyone proffers Socrates becomes the end of a string with which he will, in the end, tie his interlocutor's tongue with Gordian knots.

This is likewise the point of John Milbank's startling rejection of calls for "dialogue" between religions:

> The very idea that dialogue is a passage for the delivery of truth, that it has a privileged relationship to Being, assumes that many voices are coalescing around a single known object which is independent of our biographical or transbiographical processes of coming-to-know. It then follows that the many different biographies (experiences) and traditions can be appropriated by all as angles upon the truth, which are themselves radiations from the truth.[5]

But in fact, dialogue "is not relevant to the poor and dispossessed, because justice toward them is not primarily a matter of listening to them, but constructing for them and with them the circumstances in which they can join in many conversations, no longer as the poor" (183). Far better than this pretense, Milbank suggests, would be acknowledgment that any serious religious faith is seeking not the sacrifice of its own difference but rather the conversion of those it addresses (190). In a similar vein, Stephen Tyler finds in the image of "faces suffused with the glowing light of reasonable reason, cooperation, consensus, harmony, and agreement, . . . a cloying Franklinesque sense of smug self-righteousness, . . . a kind of braying colonial authoritarianism wrapped in the flag of undistorted communication."[6] The images of "symmetry, egalitarianism, mutuality, harmony, agreement" put a happy face on "a form of expression that constrains the hearer's belief and understanding by making her a willing accomplice in the domination that suppresses her voice by invoking a unity of desire in which opposing voices sing in complicitous harmony as a single voice" (297).

It is not surprising that some of Gadamer's words would be a stumbling block to some, like many Americans, who pride themselves on resisting authority, and a scandal to others, like many Germans, who blame themselves for not resisting it enough. Feelings run so strong here that it may not help—one thinks of the title of one of Wayne Booth's books, "now don't try to reason with me"—to say that a careful reading of *Truth and Method* shows that these very words point in precisely the opposite direction. When Gadamer speaks of the submission required by dialogue, he always speaks of the first person, not the second or third: "Openness to the other, then, involves recognizing that I myself must accept some things that are against me, even though no one else forces me to do so" (TM361). To say that "only what really constitutes a unity of meaning is intelligible" (TM294) is to assert that discovering the true meaning of a text or work of art is "an infinite process" (TM298). Just as is the case with natural law according to Aristotle, 'no dogmatic use can be made' of this meaning" (TM320). It lies at the heart of Gadamer's thought that understanding has the character of experience, and that experience "in the genuine sense" is always negative (TM353): we only possess our knowledge clearly when we discover that it is in some way wrong, limited, inadequate. The genuinely experienced person is radically undogmatic and therefore open to new experience.

What is being lost sight of is that Gadamer's is not in fact a theory of dialogue. It is a theory of understanding. His core claim is that if we understand a text that comes down to us from the past, then that understanding has the character of dialogue. Since it would seem very strange to argue that no one ever has or ever could understand a past text, it is usual to say that we do not "really" or "fully" understand, or at least not in any "rigorous" sense of "understand." What such terms could mean is left unexplored. It is part of Gadamer's argument, not his critics', that understanding cannot be measured against abstract, impossible, and unexamined idealizations. The strict question, therefore, is whether, conceding that understanding does take place, a description of dialogue as the conduct of question and answer best characterizes understanding. Gadamer is not recommending dialogue either for its presumed ethical or humanizing qualities or as a method for achieving understanding. His idea is quite far from anything like Jürgen Habermas's procedural conception of uncoerced, undistorted communicative rationality. The latter may be defensible as a prescription for legitimating political action, though it too has drawn the usual complaints that such a process secretly excludes persons or groups of persons or turns an abstract consensus into a coercive instrument. In fact, Gadamer's thinking might be more sympathetic to Hegel's critique of Kant's ethical formalism, which asserts that without substantive agreement on a conception of the good, a pure formal proceduralism has already abstracted itself out of the substantive concerns that give ethical or political questions their meaning in the first place. Gadamer is indeed Hegelian to the extent that he believes that substantive solidarity rooted in our concrete historical life—call it "prejudice"—must exist for understanding to occur at all. This does not imply a cheery harmony, since historical life encompasses fundamental conflicts. Gadamer parts company with Hegel in believing that it is inherent to historical life that it can never constitute a totality for us (this is the point of his lengthy critique of historicism from Ranke to Dilthey [TM197–242]). "Reason exists for us," he writes, "only in concrete, historical terms" (TM276). The consequence is that we cannot stand outside this historical process and see it as a whole (Gadamer insists on "the point of view of finitude") and therefore never possess an understanding we could use dogmatically against another person. Understanding is an infinite dialogue, so that all who participate in it must accept that their views will eventually be superseded. No one ever has the last word. It is possible that exactly this is what lies behind the impassioned rejection of dialogue. The suspicion that one may be coerced betrays a fear that one may not be able to hold fast to one's prior view against whatever the other says. If all one is seeking is to confirm an opinion, then it will indeed be the right move not to risk that opinion by engaging in dialogue.

It would be a mistake, however, to let replying to Gadamer's critics lead one to acquiesce in the unstated premise that he universalizes the role of dialogue in human affairs. In an essay that takes a broad view of Gadamer's thought, Dieter Misgeld shows that those who assert that Gadamer "has underestimated the place of power or coercion in social life and therefore has failed to address the phenomenon of domination as a social problem in modern societies are mistaken."[7] Precisely because he recognizes the limited sphere of dialogue oriented toward understanding, he refuses to pretend that hermeneutics is a critique of domination or an answer to the problems of political life. Politics is a realm of power from which differences and inequalities can never be eradicated. As Misgeld puts it, Gadamer even asserts that "*Disorder* . . . is the natural condition of a political world-order" (172). Ordinary politicians do not seek understanding in dialogue, but "test the limits of the other's convictions in order to see where he or she can be overwhelmed and where his or her real *power* lies" (174). But it does not follow that politics is simply relations between allies and foes. For Gadamer, "politics is the art of transforming enmity into a *negotiable* opposition of interests" (172). The prudent politician accepts differences and inequalities and the limits set by the power of others. For Gadamer, civility and tolerance are the central civic virtues (173–74) precisely because public life is a sphere where necessities surface and decisions that are not in everyone's interest must be made. In the sphere of politics and public negotiation, Gadamer "makes prudent suggestions for the maintenance of minimal conditions of tolerance and understanding, rather than proposing that what he means by dialogue can become a measure of fully public communication" (169).

Far from taking a triumphalist tone, Gadamer is acutely aware both of the limited sphere within which dialogue can be carried on and of the forces in the contemporary world that threaten its survival. In a highly politicized, overadministered society in which the individual "feels dependent and helpless in the face of its technically organized forms of life" (Gadamer, cited on 166), instead of identifying with a history and a world with which he or she feels some solidarity, the individual can only adapt to "a managerial and administrative apparatus that demands responsiveness to externally established behavioral clues, be it in the form of media images, advertising, or bureaucratic regulation" (167). Gadamer is deeply skeptical about any politics of emancipatory resistance to this social formation:

> Any form of utopian politics aiming at the achievement of an *ideal* order or any form of planning (be it piecemeal or total planning) is suspect to him, as long as both forms of politics or administration and management do not respect the fact that political decisions are finite and that they are based on limited knowledge gained in the interpretation of situational constraints and subject to a great variety of standards of measurement and evaluation. (170)

The history of utopian politics in the last century lends some support to Gadamer's reservations. He invokes instead the old image of piloting, the art of seeking and maintaining "an equilibrium among different and often conflicting forces," making "decisions under conditions of uncertainty," working for "an always-to-be-reestablished fragile, common ground" (170). Admittedly, there is here no magic to stir men's blood or rally them to the great cause of liberation, but perhaps what Gadamer suggests is all we may prudently hope to achieve and in the long run quite enough.

Because Gadamer rarely has a specifically political question in view, articulating the interplay between his conception of understanding and any potential political position requires at least the care Misgeld brings to it. His essay makes clear that Gadamer has a more comprehensive and well-proportioned understanding of contemporary social and political realities than some—one might even say most—of his critics, who parrot the shibboleths of oppositional and identity politics. But using political labels to accuse and dismiss Gadamer's ideas not only requires reductive and distorting misreadings, it also exhibits in a blatant way precisely the dogmatic and co-ercive imposition of categories of which it accuses Gadamer. To adapt Karl Kraus's remark about psychoanalysis, such accusations themselves commit the political offense of which they claim to be the critique. By contrast, the range of terms Misgeld deploys—conservative, aristocratic liberalism, elit-ism, antiutopianism, quietist, prudent—aim, quite rightly, not to pigeon-hole Gadamer, but to bring him sympathetically but by no means uncriti-cally into the tangled web of contemporary political and social thought. For his ideas can be seen to be in agreement at least sometimes with those of thinkers who would never be labeled conservative or liberal and who cer-tainly are not thinking of Gadamer at all.

Consider, for example, an essay by Judith Butler, "Universality in Cul-ture."[8] The paradox she asserts is that while "standards of universality are historically articulated" (47) and hence "culturally variable" (45), exposing this fact is itself "part of the project of extending and rendering substantive the notion of universality itself" (47). To assert a political norm as univer-sal need not require "an idealizing presupposition of consensus, one that is in some ways already there" (49). On the contrary, that the universal is as-serted only in particular situations shows that it is "a postulated and open-ended *ideal* that has not been adequately encoded by any given set of legal conventions" (48). The universal is therefore "articulated precisely through challenges to its existing formulation, and this challenge emerges from those who are not covered by it" (48). So conceived, the universal antici-pates a future "that has not yet arrived, one for which we have no ready con-cept, one whose articulations will only follow, if they do, from a contestation of universality at its already imagined borders" (49). When political claims conflict, it would be a mistake merely to enumerate them as "radical partic-ularisms between which no communication is possible" (51). Nor is it in-evitable to treat one claim as merely either ruled out by or one more ex-ample of the universal asserted by the other. What is required instead is a "difficult practice of translation among the various languages in which uni-versality makes its varied and contending appearances" (49). If each is ac-cepted as a claim to universality, each becomes able to provoke in the other "a radical rearticulation of universality itself" (46). There is always the risk that that rearticulation will be short-circuited, but it is "the movement of that unanticipated transformation [that] establishes the universal as that which is yet to be achieved and which, in order to resist domestication, may never be fully or finally achievable" (52).

Butler's thought exactly matches Gadamer's description of understand-ing. Aristotelian ethics and legal interpretation are exemplary for Gadamer because they make manifest a kind of universal that exists only in its con-crete expressions. To say that every interpretation anticipates a completion, whole, or "totality" (TM474) of meaning is to say that meaning cannot be grasped apart from particular interpretations and yet is never exhaustively present in them. Its own nature therefore demands that a particular interpretation confront a conflicting interpretation in a dialogue that "strengthens the argument of the other" so as to provoke reconsideration of itself. That the claim to understand is dialogical means that it demands its own critical self-examination and that this demand can be met only by openness to the other. Although it would be unjustified to claim that this line of thought implicitly constitutes a political theory or even to claim that it can be immediately projected into the terms of a political theory, it is nevertheless true that with appropriate care and precision it can be brought into fruitful relation, that is, opened to translation into a thinking about political and social matters.

In calling the first class of objections to dialogue political and the second class, to which I will now turn, philosophical, I do not intend any invidious distinction. There is no sharp divide, though I believe there is a difference in what questions or issues are uppermost. However philosophical they may be, the critics I have been discussing are directly concerned with political and social matters. Such questions are rarely to the fore in Gadamer's writing (though they are in some of his essays, especially), and they are certainly not in *Truth and Method.* As I have suggested, there is considerable danger of distortion or misunderstanding when one tries to make a thinker answer questions he or she has not posed. At the very least, it is unlikely that one will get a direct response and care must be taken not to pounce on a few terms or remarks and force them into an alien frame. At a minimum, a complicated process of translation that keeps in view the whole of a line of thought and therefore the situation of particular terms or ideas within that whole is indispensable.

The case seems to be different when another thinker offers a view radically opposed to the same or a closely related question. But similar care will be needed when the thinkers never encountered each other's thought directly but are brought together by a third party, who must then find a language that establishes common ground without distorting either thinker or favoring one over the other. It was the hope that a direct encounter might take place—a thing rare enough in the history of thought—that led to a public meeting between Gadamer and Jacques Derrida in Paris in 1981. Hermeneutics and deconstruction seemed so obviously to be opposed on fundamental matters of language, reading, interpretation, and understanding that an exchange of views between the thinkers most closely associated with each line of thought seemed highly promising. The results, as is well known, were disappointing. For whatever reason, Derrida virtually ignored Gadamer's writings and even his remarks on the specific occasion. Diane P.

Michelfelder and Richard E. Palmer tried to save the opportunity by publishing a volume that included Derrida's and Gadamer's remarks at their meeting and essays by a number of scholars who were invited to consider the exchange and to offer their own views on hermeneutics and deconstruction.[9] It is no criticism of this valuable book to say that the results are somewhat mixed and again show the difficulty of bringing two opposed lines of thought into conversation. But it is doubly difficult to do so when one side puts dialogue itself at the heart of its thinking and the other believes it has good grounds for arguing that language is by no means to be understood as conversation and that the very linguistic resources that seem to establish dialogue also make it impossible, an event that never takes place, a message that never arrives.

Aware of these difficulties, I want to take a step back and try a more indirect approach. I want to begin by considering Maurice Blanchot, a writer and thinker of the highest importance for Derrida, who has nevertheless pursued an autonomous path. Blanchot has never, so far as I know, shown any awareness of Gadamer, and though they share some philosophical sources, notably Heidegger, they seem to have carried Heidegger's legacy along quite original lines toward apparently opposed conclusions. I will not attempt to bring these opposed conclusions into a direct confrontation but rather to consider whether Blanchot's thought may be more complicated, perhaps even internally divided, than is sometimes supposed. If so, then even if a dialogue between Blanchot and Gadamer cannot be opened here, at least a precondition for such a dialogue may be met.

The record of Blanchot's thinking is found not only in philosophical essays but in a number of haunting and disquieting narratives. It may seem at first impossible to locate these strangely abstracted narratives within the time and space of ordinary experience, and yet they do not seem allegorical or symbolic in any obvious way. There is, I think, a sense in which Blanchot's narratives do belong to experience, but to experiences that are at once extreme and yet cannot be treated as exceptional or marginal, so that everyday life could be screened from the limitless disturbance they introduce. In the narrative *Thomas the Obscure*,[10] Blanchot situates in this way an experience of the impossibility of dialogue that his philosophical writings present in the language of argument:

> Although she did not expect to hear him answer and even if she were sure that he would not answer she would not in fact have questioned him, there was such a presumption in her manner of assuming that he could give an answer (of course, he would not answer, she did not ask him to answer, but, by the question she had posed him personally and relating to his person [she asked, "But, what are you?"], she acted as if she might interpret his silence as an accidental refusal to answer, as an attitude which might change one day or another), it was such a crude way to treat the impossible that Anne had suddenly

revealed to her the terrible scene she was throwing herself into blindfolded, and in an instant, waking from her sleep, she perceived all the consequences of her act and the madness of her conduct. Her first thought was to prevent him from answering. For the great danger, now that by an inconsiderate and arbitrary act she had just treated him as a being one might question, was that he might in turn act like a being that might answer and make his answer understood. She felt this threat deposited in the depths of her self, in the place of the words she had spoken. He was already grasping the hand held out to him. He seized it cruelly, giving Anne to believe that he understood her reasons, and that after all there was in fact a possibility of contact between them. Now that she was sure that, pitilessly unrelenting as he was, if he spoke he would say everything there was to say without hiding anything from her, telling her everything so that when he stopped speaking his silence, the silence of a being that has nothing more to give and yet has given nothing, would be even more terrifying, now she was sure that he would speak. And this certainty was so great that he appeared to her as if he had already spoken. He surrounded her, like an abyss. He revolved about her. He entranced her. He was going to devour her by changing the most unexpected words into words she would no longer be able to expect. (48–49)

What emerges here is a radical questioning not just of communication in a particular instance but of the anthropological and ontological presuppositions that assure that dialogue is possible at all. Questioning and answering seem to go on in our lives all the time. But the most fundamental question—"what are you?"—may occasion a recognition that my being is not at my disposal to be turned into an answer. Posing a question requires that I hold myself back, that I permit a determinate void to open in my world into which an answer can emerge. What is there is a question—"what are you?"— that would require my holding back, voiding my whole world, because nothing less would provide adequate room for the answer. By asking the question, I would erase myself as a participant in the very exchange I had initiated. The one who answers would likewise have exhausted himself, said everything he had to say, but now with the very person addressed no longer there (or here) to hear it. The only adequate answer would then have become no answer at all, in the absence of the question it answered. The effacement of the questioner and the exhaustion of the answerer leave nowhere for the exchange to go. Having lost both its origin and its anticipation of a future, the exchange would have cancelled the structure of time and therefore lost its present as well. With the self-elimination of the questioner and answerer as "beings who can be questioned," the space and time within which dialogue could take place have also been eliminated.

What *Thomas the Obscure* offers as represented experience is explored discursively in *The Infinite Conversation*.[11] Implicitly recognizing the received idea of dialogue that underwrites its importance for many contemporary philosophical and cultural projects, Blanchot attends to overlooked aspects of dialogue that overturn its received idea. For instance, nothing seems more obvious than that dialogue consists of all the speeches exchanged between interlocutors. But Blanchot points out that in conversation, two people do not speak together but in turn. What one says is interrupted when the conversation passes to the other. Whatever term may be used to articulate successive speeches with each other—as confirmation, contradiction, elaboration, change of topic—it is the interruption or pause "that alone permits speech to be constituted as conversation" (75). Oscar Wilde, a great writer of dialogue, already said so: "the essence of good dialogue is interruption."[12] On the one hand, discontinuity "promises exchange" (76) and thus aims ultimately at "a unitary truth" within the horizon of common sense. On the other is a more enigmatic interruption that registers an irreducible distance between the interlocutors. In this case, I regard the other not as an object, nor as a first person the same as myself, nor as joined through shared knowledge or personal comprehension. All these presuppose a continuity of being. But what if instead I base my relation to the other on everything that separates us and separates us infinitely, that is, on an "interruption of being" (77)? Blanchot calls this alterity the neutral. In it, language is no longer thought "solely with a view to unity" (77) but as "an essentially dissymmetrical field governed by discontinuity" (77). Here speaking is not just intermittent (as in conversation), but intermittence itself speaks—a "non-pontificating" speech that does not bridge the abyss between two sides (78). But this would mean that what is outside any language, indeed, "the outside of any language," is expressed "in language itself" (78–79).

What makes dialogue serious is that in it language is essentially dual, exposed to "the indecision of Yes and No" (80; Gadamer makes the point in TM364–65). The advantage we gain from distributing this duality between the equal and reciprocal partners in dialogue is that we escape the false unity of monologic self-enclosure and orient our thinking toward a unity of being that presents itself. In contrast, Blanchot points to difference, which cannot be reduced to unity or even equalized, but which "gives voice to two instances of speech by keeping them separate even as they are held together only by this separation" (81). In such a dialogue—but "rather than dialogue, we should name it plural speech" (215)—the other is left in a strangeness that is empty, since to give it any content whatsoever would violate precisely its strangeness. Where understanding has "always already posited ends and values" in a language that speaks "our will to clarity" (182), this other speech gives voice to the absurd, the impossible. If the possible is what has the power to be, only in the space "where the essence of man is the impossible" can language escape power, force, violence, and thus lay bare "this limit of man that is no longer a power, not yet a power. A space from which what is called man has as if in advance always already disappeared"

(183). Such a speech is not one kind among others, but the "infinite task" (82) of proposing, expressing, affirming "a truly plural speech" (82) whose exigency arises out of interruption and rupture, in which thought is "called to itself through the discontinuity of writing" (82). Although it brings terms into relation, neither term relinquishes itself "in favor of a measure supposed to be common" (128). The strange or foreign is received into speech as such, not thereby to be at home but as "always Outside" (128). Here meaning finds its source in "exile, exodus, existence, exteriority, and estrangement" (128), in the "ex-" that designates distance and separation.

Within the space of a short essay, it is not possible to surround these excerpts with enough prose to bring out their plausibility and relation to features, however extreme, of ordinary experience. Fortunately, Gerald Bruns has already performed that necessary task brilliantly.[13] The general theme, however, is clear enough. Blanchot rejects dialogue because he sees it as confining its participants, their language, and what they say to the realm of the possible. It deploys a limiting, coercive force—he does not hesitate to call it "violence"—a force that is both political and ontological, to impose uniformity and obliterate difference. Instead, Blanchot seeks the language of a thinking not oriented to unity. This is the language of the infinite conversation, of plural speech, that is not an alternative to dialogue but the other of dialogue that attentive reading and hearing uncovers already within it. I have chosen excerpts that set forth this conception in terms that appear directly opposed to Gadamer. But it is worth repeating that caution is in order. Only a hasty and simplistic reading would allow one to leap to conclusions by contrasting Gadamer's talk of a whole, a unity, a totality of meaning with Blanchot's rejection of unity. A careful reading shows that Gadamer too opposes the Hegelian kind of dialectic that issues in unity, just as he rejects a knowledge that conceptually or empirically dominates either the world or other persons. And on the other side, a reader might suspect that Blanchot's call for plural speech commits a performative self-contradiction, since his own writing over more than fifty years is traversed by rigorously consistent restatements of a few closely linked insights. Notoriously, everyone Blanchot writes about ends up sounding like Blanchot.

Yet it is more important and more in the spirit of dialogue to ignore obvious objections. As Blanchot says, "Criticism has little hold on me. What is weak does not need us to grow weaker, but we ought to preserve and reinforce what is strong" (267). We must consider whether it unduly constricts Blanchot if we ask only how he differs radically from Gadamer. Have we really understood him if we extract only the statements that seem to put dialogue into question? For a number of the pieces in *The Infinite Conversation* would conventionally be called "dialogues"—a fact of which Blanchot could hardly be unaware. Perhaps we should ask whether he wants to show another form of conversation, of "this back and forth of words between us"

(326), rather than dialogue as conventionally understood. Blanchot offers a striking example, perhaps not merely imagined:

> I recall being present at a conversation between two men who were very different from one another. One would say in simple and profound sentences some truth he had taken to heart; the other would listen in silence, then when reflection had done its work he would in turn express some proposition, sometimes in almost the same words, albeit slightly differently (more rigorously, more loosely, or more strangely). This redoubling of the same affirmation constituted the strongest of dialogues. [!] Nothing was developed, opposed, or modified; and it was manifest that the first interlocutor learned a great deal, and even infinitely, from his own words repeated—not because they were adhered to and agreed with, but, on the contrary, through the infinite difference. For it is as though what he said in the first person as an 'I' had been expressed anew by him as 'other' *[autrui]* and as though he had thus been carried into the very unknown of his thought: where his thought, without being altered, became absolutely other. . . . Just as there was no relation between these two repeated instances of speech, these two men had in a certain sense nothing in common, except the movement (which brought them very close) of turning together toward the infinite of speech, which is the meaning of the word conversation. (341)

We cannot speak here of "unity," for there are not in this case two perspectives entering into a dialectical synthesis. And yet each speech is doubled, sutured by the pause that separates it from itself. Instead of different speeches dialectically united, speech itself differs from itself; difference speaks.

Such a speech is impossible, which means that it does not belong to the realm of the possible, to what lies within our power to say. We are perhaps not far from Hoffmansthal's "Letter of Lord Chandos," whose fictional writer says that he is convinced that to save his soul he must speak a language of which he knows not a single word.[14] The impossibility of such a speech points to a speech beyond possibility. If Lord Chandos does not know this language, perhaps that indicates that when we know a language we do not stand toward it in a relation like the perceptual or conceptual knowing epistemologists describe—and describe accurately enough, for all that. Only such a language might save our soul instead of merely expressing it, merely emptying it out in words. "We live upon the bread of faithful speech," writes Wallace Stevens. If there is such a language, that might put *Thomas the Obscure* in a different light, as in this passage:

> And in each of his reasonings, more mysterious still than his existence, he experienced the mortal presence of the adversary, of this time without which, eternally immobilized, unable to come from the depths of the future, he would have been condemned to see the light of life die out on his desolate peak, like the prophetic eagle of dreams. So he reasoned with the absolute

contradictor at the heart of his argument, he thought with the enemy and the subject of all thought in the depths of his thought, his perfect antagonist, this *time,* Anne, and mysteriously receiving her within himself he found himself for the first time at grips with a serious conversation. (61)

Perhaps to understand Blanchot we must find this moment where his thought turns on itself—not a dialectical reversal, but a repetition or redoubling that is an infinite difference, the difference between, say, "dialogue" or "conversation" and, after reflection has done its work, "dialogue" or "conversation." This is just as true of Gadamer. Blanchot, Gadamer: same difference.

Both Blanchot and Gadamer have learned much from the later Heidegger. Blanchot continues in Heidegger's line of thought through his own chiastic language to unexpected and logically extreme positions. The originality and audacity of many of Gadamer's ideas are concealed beneath a language that he has deliberately chosen (and for philosophical reasons) to keep calm and conversational. But it seems certain that Gadamer's feel for dialogue comes from his lifelong study of Plato. It may be useful to remind ourselves of what Platonic dialogue is like, since it could scarcely be more divergent from the straw man most critics of dialogue knock down. We should recall, for instance, that Socratic dialogue begins not in eagerness to state a view, but in ignorance, with a question, and it often, after a perplexing array of views and many dialectic twists, ends without a conclusion. Socrates' rejection of long speeches and insistence on the give and take of short interchanges shows that dialogue provokes thinking by interrupting the flow of opinion and its prefabricated language. Along the way, Socrates repeatedly asks his interlocutor to say whatever he thinks, completely without shame or fear, and not to abandon his view until he feels compelled by the argument. Nor is Socrates satisfied with agreement. Instead, he often rebukes the interlocutor by pointing out that a view has been accepted too easily, that objections have not been considered, that aspects of the position have not been examined. Many of the interlocutors are far from pliant. They become mocking, contemptuous, stubborn, angry, occasionally withdrawing into a silence that is more ominous than any alleged "violence" Socrates' questions and answers could perpetrate. Noncitizens are welcomed to these discussions, and in some dialogues Socrates himself says little or nothing, stepping back (or is it stepping forward?) into the role of the listener. Nor does Plato draw a sharp line between argument and character. Dialogue calls for the lifelong development of the whole person. He makes clear that whether someone accepts an argument as convincing depends very much on his willingness to surrender his own position and on the depth, quality, and passion of his commitment to truth before all else. When some position is reached at the end of a dialogue, Socrates is rarely contented but usually says all this will have to be examined again to make sure the view is right and also, implicitly, to bind the character of the inquirers more closely to truth. Even Socrates' closest friends fail to experience this binding relation. As he prepares to take the hemlock, his disciples seem to follow with close attention Socrates' elaborate and decisive proofs that the soul is immortal and that death is nothing to fear or mourn. But once their master drinks the hemlock, they burst into wailing and tears like men of the commonest clay. Socrates' thinking is coherent without being systematic. His real skill is raising objections and exposing deficiencies. When he states his deepest convictions, he often resorts to myths or tales, admitting that he can only hope to say something "like" the truth. He knows the weakness of reasons and words, and he is occasionally rebuked for his plain and conversational language, which lacks technicalities and eschews the treacherous power that rhetorical elaboration lets loose—as often to the harm of a speaker as to his benefit. This world of dialogue has all the complexity, irony, and passion, the uncertainty and inconclusiveness of ordinary life. Both those for whom dialogue is an unexamined slogan and those for whom it is an unanswerable anathema have substituted a bloodless shade for this richly imagined and densely presented world.

While the study of Plato has nourished Gadamer's lifelong reflection on understanding, his work also bears a deep imprint from a specific group of contemporaries, namely, German-language lyric poets. When asked whether hermeneutics applies primarily to what is old or also to contemporary literature, Gadamer replied, "It is entrusted with all that is unfamiliar and strikes us as significant. That is why I have written about Celan, one of the most inaccessible poets of world literature."[15] In a wonderful essay, "Are the Poets Falling Silent?"[16] Gadamer indicates the special importance of poetry today and for hermeneutics above all. It lies especially in poetry's endangerment, its vulnerability in a world "increasingly ruled by anonymous mechanisms and where the word no longer creates direct communication" (73). Poetry is important precisely because its necessity, even its possibility, come into question "in an age where social unrest and the discomfort with our social life in an anonymous mass society is felt from all sides and where the demand for rediscovering or reestablishing true solidarities is advanced over and over again" (73). The poets are not falling silent, but they are becoming, in a phrase Gadamer takes from Rilke, "indescribably discreet" (74): "As discreet messages are spoken quietly so that an unintended person cannot overhear them, so has the poet's voice become. He shares something with the one who has an ear for it and who is sympathetic. He whispers something to him in his ear and the reader, who is all ears, nods finally. He has understood" (81).

Gadamer calls one of Celan's poems "a hermetic dialogue" (*On Education* 120), and the phrase could apply to most of them. This is Celan's special importance, for his poetry is at the limit of the possibility of dialogue in our time. This lies behind the question Gadamer poses as the title of his short book on Celan, *Who Am I and Who Are You?* The same question emerges in Gadamer's comments on the following short lyric by Celan:

> In den Flüssen nördlich der Zukunft
> werf ich das Netz aus, das Du
> zögernd beschwerst
> mit von Steinen geschriebenen
> Schatten.

> In the rivers north of the future
> I cast out the net, that you
> hesitantly weigh down
> with stone-written
> shadows.

The tension between throwing out the net and weighting it resonates with the tension between the I and you. The poet cannot catch the poem without a you who burdens it with the weight of meaning. Yet the you must hesitate, must find exactly the right weight, so that the net neither floats away nor sinks, but, "as the fisherman says," stands (*Gadamer on Celan* 75). The poet's experience is, however, common to each and every one of us, for "No human can look into the future except as always hoping . . . always beyond any justified expectation concerning what comes next" (76). But if the reader is in this sense the I, once again, who is the you? Because the poem does not say, "the answer is not left to our interpretive wish" (77). As with the commandment to "love your neighbor," the question "who is my neighbor?" is already a failure of understanding. The you "is the you of the I": "one can first comprehend what is being said when one understands himself to be the one who should always already know, here and now, who the you is: everyone" (77). In this indescribably discreet way and against everything in our historical situation that makes it seem impossible the poem tries to catch the I who cannot not always already share language with each and every you. "The question," Gadamer says, "is not whether the poets are silent, but whether our ear is acute enough to hear" (78).

Nothing, of course, forces us to enter into this relationship. In fact, almost everything in our world militates against it. The horrors that have been and continue to be perpetrated in our century seem to divide humankind into the oppressors and the oppressed and demand action to end injustice, not idle chatter with the oppressors or false consolations for the oppressed. The din and racket of mass media, the "floods of informational chatter that wash over us" (178), deafen us to the only word—a whispered word—that might open dialogue. The manipulation and debasement of language deprive us of the very ground on which there could be any possibility of meeting. No one knew this better than Celan. He decided "to live out to the end the destiny of the Jewish spirit in Europe."[17] "There remained amid the losses," he said, "this one thing: language." That was no consolation, for language had to pass through "the thousand darknesses of deathbringing speech" (114):

> Whichever word you speak—
> you owe
> to destruction (289)

And yet, if poetry can exist at all, it remains what it is, *Gespräch*, conversation, dialogue, even though "often it is despairing dialogue" (163): "A poem, as a manifestation of language and thus essentially dialogue, can be a message in a bottle, sent out in the—not always greatly hopeful—belief that somewhere and sometime it could wash up on land, on heartland perhaps" (115). Without assurance, Celan continued to write, as long as he could stand it, poems sent on their way "toward something standing open, occupiable, perhaps toward an addressable Thou, toward an addressable reality" (116).

Dialogue is not a method. It is not at the disposal of our will, even our good will. We cannot be exhorted, cajoled, or sermonized into it. No one can be forced into it—or out of it. We do not enter into dialogue, we find ourselves already in it—but only if we are already listening with the most intense attention, all ears to the discreet, the whispered word. Dialogue has no guarantees, being pure risk. In contemporary poetry like Celan's, dialogue comes to itself, to its essential, its inalienable weakness. But if—a large if—anyone is left in this world who wants to understand, dialogue has already begun.

NOTES

1. Han-Georg Gadamer, *Truth and Method,* 2d rev. ed., trans. Joel Weinsheimer and Donald G. Marshall (New York: Crossroads, 1989).

2. John Caputo, "Gadamer's Closet Essentialism: A Derridean Critique," in *Dialogue and Deconstruction: The Gadamer-Derrida Encounter,* ed. Diane P. Michelfelder and Richard E. Palmer (Albany: State University of New York Press, 1989), 258–64; here 264.

3. Martha C. Nussbaum, with respondents, *For Love of Country: Debating the Limits of Patriotism,* ed. Joshua Cohen (Boston: Beacon, 1996), 136.

4. Derek Walcott, *Omeros* (New York: Farrar, Straus and Giroux), 1990.

5. John Milbank, "The End of Dialogue," in *Christian Uniqueness Reconsidered: Myth of a Pluralistic Theology of Religions,* ed. Gavin D'Costa (Maryknoll, N.Y.: Orbis, 1990), 171–91; here, 175.

6. Stephen A. Tyler, "Ode to Dialog on the Occasion of the Un-for-seen," in *The Interpretation of Dialogue*, ed. Tullio Maranhão (Chicago: University of Chicago Press, 1990), 292–300.

7. Dieter Misgeld, "Poetry, Dialogue, and Negotiation: Liberal Culture and Conservative Politics in Hans-Georg Gadamer's Thought," in *Festivals of Interpretation: Essays on Hans-Georg Gadamer's Work*, ed. Kathleen Wright (Albany: State University of New York Press, 1990), 161–81; here, 171.

8. Judith Butler, "University in Culture," in Martha C. Nussbaum, with respondents, *For Love of Country: Debating the Limits of Patriotism*, ed. Joshua Cohen (Boston: Beacon, 1996), 45–52.

9. Diane P. Michelfelder and Richard E. Palmer, eds., *Dialogue and Deconstruction: The Gadamer-Derrida Encounter* (Albany: State University of New York Press, 1989).

10. Maurice Blanchot, *Thomas the Obscure*, trans. Robert Lamberton (New York: D. Lewis, 1973).

11. Maurice Blanchot, *The Infinite Conversation*, trans. Susan Hanson (Minneapolis: University of Minnesota Press, 1993).

12. Richard Ellmann, *Oscar Wilde* (New York: Vintage, 1988), 237.

13. Gerald Bruns, *Maurice Blanchot: The Refusal of Philosophy* (Baltimore, Md.: Johns Hopkins University Press, 1997).

14. Hugo von Hofmannsthal, "The Letter of Lord Chandos" in *Selected Prose*, trans. Mary Hottinger and Tania and James Stern (New York: Pantheon, 1952), 129–41.

15. Hans-Georg Gadamer, *Gadamer on Celan: "Who Am I and Who Are You?" and Other Essays*, trans. and ed. Richard Heinemann and Bruce Krajewski (Albany: State University of New York Press, 1997), 70.

16. Hans-Georg Gadamer, *On Education, Poetry, and History*, ed. Dieter Misgeld and Graeme Nicholson, trans. Lawrence Schmidt and Monica Reuss (Albany: State University of New York Press, 1992), 73–81.

17. John Felstiner, *Paul Celan: Poet, Survivor, Jew* (New Haven, Conn.: Yale University Press, 1995), 267.

Chapter 8

Gadamer's Philosophy of Dialogue and Its Relation to the Postmodernism of Nietzsche, Heidegger, Derrida, and Strauss

RONALD BEINER

There is such a thing as being too profound. Truth is not always in a well.
EDGAR ALLAN POE, *The Murders in the Rue Morgue*

The reflections that follow are a response to Catherine Zuckert's interesting and provocative book, *Postmodern Platos*.[1] The premise of the book is that there is a widely perceived crisis in the status and identity of Western philosophy, and leading thinkers since Nietzsche have felt obliged to return to the origins of philosophy in Plato in order to clarify what philosophy means and what it might continue to mean in the light of this crisis. In addition to Nietzsche, Zuckert examines four other thinkers—Heidegger, Hans-Georg Gadamer, Leo Strauss, and Jacques Derrida—who share the conviction that Plato must be confronted as a privileged philosophical interlocutor in order to illuminate our contemporary crisis:

> [Nietzsche, Heidegger, Gadamer, Strauss, and Derrida] look back to the origins of philosophy from an explicitly "postmodern" position. That is, they return to Plato and ask what the character of philosophy was at its origins explicitly on the basis of a conviction that modern rationalism has exhausted its promise and its possibilities. They are all seeking a way of making a new beginning, of moving beyond "modernity" to something better, by articulating a new and different understanding of the distinctive characteristic of "the West." (Zuckert 1–2)

Zuckert assumes that Strauss is the one for whom it would be "most questionable or controversial" to attach the label "postmodern" (Zuckert 279, n. 1). She says, "I am using the term 'postmodern' to mean literally 'after the modern,' as applied specifically to philosophy" (ibid.), and she argues that for Strauss the crisis of philosophy is sufficiently profound that it doesn't suffice simply to go back to the ancient understanding of philosophy. The modern Enlightenment and modern rationalism, through their own inner evolution, have thrown themselves into such philosophical crisis that modern thought now looks as discredited and in need of supersession as premodern thought did at the dawn of modern philosophy. The chief reason a straightforward return to ancient intellectual horizons is no longer viable is that modern thought offered a deeper insight than was available in antiquity into the radical breach and incompatibility between reason and revelation, between philosophical rationalism and biblical morality. This is what Zuckert calls "the untraditional character of [Strauss's] view of the tradition" (Zuckert 197). Because Plato, for example, lacked access to biblical religion, the deepest philosophical problem is not a problem for him, so Strauss's awareness of the antinomy between philosophy and biblical religion as the deepest problem must situate his thought beyond the boundaries of ancient philosophy. On the other hand, Strauss's conviction of "the end or untenability of modernity" (ibid.) also precludes any allegiance to modern philosophy. Therefore, Zuckert concludes, it seems legitimate to apply the description "postmodern" to Strauss's thought. Again, the assumption is that if Strauss is postmodern, it's easy to grant the postmodernity of the other thinkers considered in her book. In this essay I don't want to challenge Zuckert's thesis concerning the postmodern character of Strauss's thought (on the contrary, I'll present some arguments of my own that yield the same conclusion). I do, however, wish to contest the idea that Gadamer belongs happily in the company of the other thinkers who figure in Zuckert's intelligent study of the postmodern tradition.

Is Gadamer a postmodernist, and is his Plato a postmodern Plato? Obviously, what answer one will give to these questions will depend on how one defines postmodernism; and if there is one thing we *know* about postmodernism, it is that there is an almost infinite malleability in how one defines it. So in order to approach an answer to the questions that I've posed, I want to consider a few possible definitions of postmodernism.

I think it is relatively easy to show what is postmodern about the approaches to philosophical texts in Nietzsche, Heidegger, and Derrida. For each of them, Plato is not a dialogical partner whose reasons must be weighed against one's own within a shared intellectual enterprise. Rather, Plato's commitment to philosophy is to be understood as belonging to (in fact, as having initiated) a form of intellectual activity—the search for eternal essences—that is no longer credible, and one must apply to it a diagnostic interpretation from a superior position *beyond* the boundaries of philosophy. Nietzsche, of course, offers the most extreme instance of the postmodern refusal to engage Plato at his own level, on the level of rational debate, of reasons and counterreasons. Instead, we get diagnosis of the So-cratic-Platonic disease, for example, in Nietzsche's analysis of what he calls "the problem of Socrates" in *Twilight of the Idols:* Socrates and Plato are mere "symptoms of degeneration" *(Verfalls-Symptome),* and it suffices to deal with them as such.[2]

In Heidegger we get another version of Nietzsche's conception of his relationship to the philosophical tradition, which Nietzsche compares to a physician diagnosing an illness. Zuckert reports Strauss's comment that Heidegger's interpretation of Plato was "the most brazen thing he [had] run into" (Zuckert 321, n. 120). This isn't surprising. For example, near the end of "Plato's Doctrine of Truth," Heidegger writes, "Nietzsche's concept of truth is an example of the last reflection of the extreme consequence of that changing of truth [enacted by Plato] from the unhiddenness of beings to the correctness of the glance."[3] In other words, if Nietzsche represents the triumph in the West of the will to will, the blind worship of technologi-cal mastery, and "humanism" as all-consuming subjectivism, then we ulti-mately have Plato to blame for this, for Plato, with his definition of Being as *idea,* invented Western metaphysics, and the history of metaphysics is the history of the oblivion of Being, which in turn means the eventual undoing of the West. So Plato must be deconstructed.

In Derrida's "commentary" on the *Phaedrus,* we get a remarkable illus-tration of the postmodern subversion of philosophical dialogue. Consider the following passage (cited in Zuckert 221), which occurs in the midst of an entire section devoted to a word *(pharmakos,* scapegoat) that, Derrida in-forms us, is *absent* from the Platonic corpus:

> We do not believe that there exists, in all rigor, a Platonic text. . . . provided the articulations are rigorously and prudently recognized, one should simply be able to untangle the hidden forces of attraction linking a present word with an absent word in the text of Plato. . . . the so-called "presence" of a quite rel-ative verbal unit—the word—while not being a contingent accident worthy of no attention, nevertheless does not constitute the ultimate criterion and the utmost pertinence.[4]

That is, in reading a text one shouldn't privilege words that are in the text over words that are absent from it! For Derrida, the boundary between text and nontext is in large measure a metaphysical construction. Not surpris-ingly, this deconstruction of the text is accompanied by a deconstruction of the author. On the page preceding this passage Derrida twice places "Plato" in quotation marks and refers to what is "concealed from the author him-self, if any such thing [i.e., an author] exists."[5]

This leaves Gadamer and Strauss. Each, I think, yields a different way of carv-ing up the philosophical turf, one of which I will try to defend and the other

I will criticize. *One* way of drawing the battle lines, Strauss's, is to give central-ity to the antinomy of nature and history: those thinkers who take their bearings by "nature" are faithful to the Socratic-Platonic philosophical tra-dition, whereas those who take their bearings by history turn their back on that tradition. One can presume that as Strauss himself would have applied this criterion, Gadamer would fall on the Nietzsche-Heidegger-Derrida side of the barricades, with Socrates, Plato, and Strauss on the opposite side.

Up to a point, Strauss's critique of historicism seems perfectly warranted. For example, Strauss's critique of Heidegger seems to me more or less cor-rect: one cannot engage dialogically with a philosophical position that one regards as merely a historically contingent emanation of the "history of Be-ing." In that sense, the encounter between Heidegger and Plato, as seen from Heidegger's side, is not an encounter between two philosophers, each of whom has reasons to adduce why they think they have apprehended the truth, and it is therefore not rationally adjudicable by philosophical dia-logue (a parallel analysis applies to both Nietzsche and Derrida).

How does Gadamer fare in the light of this critique? "I am a Platonist," Gadamer flatly declares in an interview with Ernest Fortin.[6] An important part of what it means to be a Platonist, for Gadamer, is the belief that inter-rogating the nature of the Good dialectically, and therefore dialogically, is part and parcel of what it is to be human. So, far from agreeing with the Hei-deggerian or Derridean thesis that the reign of philosophy/metaphysics is coming to an end, Gadamer's view is that philosophy is and must be inter-minable. As Gadamer puts it, "Philosophy is a human experience that re-mains the same and that characterizes the human being as such. . . . there is no progress in it, but only participation" (cited in Zuckert 71).

From Strauss's point of view, historicism represents *the* great breach in the philosophical tradition, and therefore, as a resolute antihistoricist, he alone of Zuckert's five thinkers remains entirely faithful to the Western (Socratic-Platonic) philosophical tradition.[7] Is Gadamer a historicist in the culpable sense? Well, the notion that we all *start off* within some historical horizon is surely uncontroversial. It seems fully consistent with the Platonic notion that every human society is a cave habituating its inhabitants to a particular set of opinions. One would be a historicist in the culpable sense only if one thought that each of us is locked into our initial horizon, in-capable of ever getting outside its fixed boundaries. But this is clearly not Gadamer's view. The very notion of a "fusion of horizons" as Gadamer pre-sents it means that we can open ourselves dialogically to rival horizons: the boundaries are expandable, and we can in principle—through intercivili-zational dialogue (in a spatial *and* temporal sense)—liberate ourselves from the opinions of our own cave. But this presumably wouldn't fully satisfy Strauss, for the process of self-liberation, in Gadamer's view, always proceeds in an incremental and partial fashion (though the process is open-ended, and hence the possibility of its further extension is never foreclosed).[8] Strauss, on the other hand, seems committed to the possibility of *complete* liberation from the modern horizon, so that one could in effect set aside millennia of intellectual and moral history and see the ethical world *exactly* as Plato and Aristotle saw it. This is a stunningly ambitious thesis, and it is not clear that one can blame Gadamer for being reluctant to embrace it.[9] In any case, it is worth noting that Stanley Rosen, in his contribution to the recently published Library of Living Philosophers volume devoted to Gadamer's work, presents a version of Gadamer's "fusion of horizons" doctrine that is deliberately intended to be entirely free of historicism in the culpable sense, and Gadamer says he fully accepts Rosen's version of the doctrine.[10]

Let us now consider a second way of surveying the philosophical landscape, this time inspired by Gadamer. According to this alternative delineation, Strauss is the one who gets aligned with Nietzsche, Heidegger, and Derrida, whereas Gadamer gets aligned more closely with Socrates and Plato. I think Catherine Zuckert's book is actually quite helpful in getting us to appreciate this realignment, in two ways: 1) by her efforts to distance Gadamer from Heidegger (Zuckert 72–73); and 2) by her suggestions about surprising affinities between Strauss and Derrida.[11] As regards the latter of these two themes, Zuckert offers the crucial comparison between Strauss and Derrida in the following passage:

> When we compare Derrida and Strauss, we seem to confront an irony, if not a paradox. By showing that the roots of the Western tradition are fundamentally incompatible, Strauss thought he was preserving the secret core or nerve of its vitality. By revealing a fundamental fissure, cleft, or instability at its roots, Derrida thinks he is showing how the West is necessarily deconstructing itself. To what extent, we are led to ask, do Derrida and Strauss actually have different views of the West, in general, and its Platonic origins, in particular? (Zuckert 200)

This suggests a radical contrast between Gadamer on the one hand and Strauss and Derrida on the other, for of course Gadamer's basic sense of the Western tradition is not one of incommensurabilities and "fissure," but of continuities and unbroken dialogue.[12] If what defines the postmodern sensibility is a profound sense of discontinuity, then again, Gadamer, with his confidence in philosophy as a unitary dialogical tradition, has less reason to be called postmodern than the other thinkers surveyed in Zuckert's study.

As Zuckert observes (332, n. 8), Gadamer is set off against the other three twentieth-century philosophers she considers—Heidegger, Derrida, and Strauss—because the other three, unlike Gadamer, all take Nietzsche as their starting point.[13] If we interpret all positions in the philosophical tradition as mere assertions of will to power, dialogue is radically subverted.[14] If we interpret all positions in the philosophical tradition as pathological emanations of the history of the forgetfulness of Being, philosophical dialogue is radically subverted. If, as Derrida suggests, "there is no Platonic text" in the rigorous sense, and in interpreting Plato, words that are present in the text shouldn't be privileged over words that are absent, dialogue is impossible. And if, finally, all authentically philosophical utterances are merely the publicly salutary mask of a wisdom that cannot be spoken (except to the initiated), then philosophical dialogue is, once again, radically subverted.[15] One cannot engage dialogically with a consistently ironic interlocutor, and this leads to a stymieing of philosophical dialogue whether the irony is Straussian irony or Derridean irony.

What distinguishes Gadamer from Nietzsche, Heidegger, Derrida, and Strauss is that for each of the latter four, in their different ways, the "subtext" is more meaningful than the text.[16] One doesn't confront the text, "face-to-face" so to speak, in order to open oneself to a dialogue with it, but one tries to read under the text, through the text, behind the text. The basic meaning of Gadamer's famous "fusion of horizons" idea is that one's relation to the text one is trying to interpret is that of a dialogical encounter: one not only seeks to fathom the meaning of the text by bringing to bear one's own judgments and commitments, but at the same time one exposes those judgments and commitments to possible revision and transformation by reassessing them in the light of what one has been able to understand of the text with which one is in a dialogical relationship.[17] This idea of dialogue is put into practice in Gadamer's two Plato books, *Plato's Dialectical Ethics* and *The Idea of the Good in Platonic-Aristotelian Philosophy*. One might say that the purpose of these books is to show that it is possible for a sympathetic twentieth-century reader of Plato (even one schooled in the Heideggerian critique of Western metaphysics!) to restate and make a plausible case for the central tenets of Platonic metaphysics. There is no presumption whatsoever that a Platonic understanding of virtue, dialectic, the Good, or the relation between reason and desire is outdated; that Plato's arguments, addressed to the contemporary reader, will succeed in vindicating themselves remains a real possibility. Gadamer is in dialogue *with* the text rather than trying to read under or through or behind the text.

This Gadamerian way of formulating the basic issues is nicely illustrated by the exchange between Gadamer and Derrida (hardly a dialogue!) published in *Dialogue and Deconstruction*. In "Text and Interpretation," Gadamer argues that, contrary to the arrogance of presuming to penetrate the metaphysical determinations of the text of one's philosophical interlocutor, any genuine philosophical (or any other kind of) dialogical encounter takes the form of an open dialogue that presupposes mutuality, namely the possibility of either side receiving instruction from the other (and opening itself to the interlocutor's meaning in its quest for better insight).

> The dialogical character of language . . . leaves behind it any starting point in the subjectivity of the speaker. . . . What we find happening in speaking is not a mere reification of intended meaning, but an endeavor that continually modifies itself, or better: a continually recurring temptation to engage oneself in something or to become involved with someone. But that means to expose oneself and to risk oneself.[18]

> For a written conversation basically the same fundamental condition obtains as for an oral exchange. Both partners must have the good will to try to understand one another.[19]

Inexplicably, Derrida relates this dialogical impulse to "a metaphysics of the will,"[20] and he expresses his own skepticism about the very notion of a universal ground of dialogical experience, which Derrida cannot help but regard as a "metaphysical" residue:

> I am not convinced that we ever really do have this experience that Professor Gadamer describes, of knowing in a dialogue that one has been perfectly understood or experiencing the success of confirmation.[21]

Gadamer, in his compelling reply, points out that the very posing of questions in a philosophical encounter presupposes the hermeneutical intention that Derrida insists is impossible (or at least fatally compromised by metaphysics):

> Whoever opens his mouth wants to be understood: otherwise, one would neither speak nor write. . . . Derrida directs questions to me and therefore must assume that I am willing to understand them.[22]

> Surely this is not at all a kind of metaphysics, but the presupposition that any partner in a dialogue must assume, including Derrida, if he wants to pose questions to me. Is he really disappointed that we cannot understand each other? Indeed not, for in his view this would be a relapse into metaphysics. He will, in fact, be pleased, because he takes this private experience of disillusionment to confirm his own metaphysics. But I cannot see here how he can be right only with respect to himself, be in agreement only with himself. Of course I understand very well why he invokes Nietzsche here. It is precisely because both of them are mistaken about themselves. Actually both speak and write in order to be understood.[23]

It would be hard to improve upon this demonstration of the incoherence of Derrida's radical skepticism concerning the possibility of a hermeneutically motivated dialogue.

The activity of interpretation, in the postmodern view, is not a matter of engaging in dialogue with a text concerning a shared subject matter, but of *see-*

ing through the text, of penetrating its disguises and its subterfuges, of diagnosing its pathology (as the psychoanalyst sees through the evasions and
compulsions of his or her patient) [24]—what Paul Ricoeur has labeled the
"hermeneutics of suspicion." The notion that philosophers throughout the
Western tradition are caught in inescapable conundrums that overpower
their intention to offer rational arguments, so that the object is not to engage with the public arguments at the level of their intended rationality, but
to exhibit the conundrums that necessarily defeat this intention of public
rationality: this is the fundamental meaning of deconstruction. As we saw in
our brief discussion of Derrida's "interpretation" of Plato, deconstruction is
an activity of literary subversion—subversion of the boundaries between inside and outside, text and nontext, philosophy and sophism.[25] But Straussian hermeneutics, too, is subversive of dialogue where each side presumes
that it encounters an interlocutor whose speech expresses what the interlocutor really thinks, and where each side opens itself to discursive challenge from the other side. It seems to me that philosophy as it is understood
by Strauss and his followers is not fundamentally an activity of giving an
account of one's position by adducing public reasons. Rather, philosophical activity is conceived primarily as an art of seduction used to draw young
men into a certain way of life; and esotericism serves a central function not
only in excluding those who aren't fit for that way of life but in seducing
those who are.

In a strange and paradoxical reversal, one might say that the way Nietzsche, Heidegger, and Derrida encounter Plato is more dialogical than
Strauss's encounter with Plato, because each of *them* takes the Platonic theory of the ideas at face value, whereas Strauss takes *nothing* at face value.
(From a Straussian point of view, it could be said that Plato did such a convincing job of pretending to be committed to the doctrine of ideas that he
not only inspired Christian Platonists like Augustine but also befuddled anti-
Platonists like Nietzsche and Heidegger.)[26] According to Stanley Rosen,
Strauss's failure to uphold (some version or other of) the Platonic ideas
turns out to be fatal to his vindication of philosophy. Unless the philosophical way of life can be grounded in some kind of theoretical teaching,
Strauss's defense of the philosophical life inevitably degenerates into either
Gadamerian historicism or, worse, Derridean deconstruction.[27] According
to Rosen, Zuckert never gets beyond Strauss's exoteric teaching.[28] But as
soon as one postulates the distinction between esoteric and exoteric teachings, it is unclear how one could *ever* know whether *anyone* had succeeded
in penetrating to the (final) esoteric level, since each esoteric level of understanding may be merely exoteric in relation to some further, yet more
inaccessible esoteric level. In fact, Rosen himself is unsure whether there *is*
an esoteric teaching in Strauss (the "golden apple concealed within the sil-
ver filigree"), in the sense of a theoretical teaching that could in principle

be displayed publicly. And his point is that until we see what Strauss's own theoretical position is, the appeal to philosophy as a way of life (which constitutes Zuckert's defense of Strauss as being elevated above the forms of historicism and relativism that plague other postmodern thinkers) is useless: contrary to Zuckert, Strauss's para-philosophizing is "on a par with" Derridean "chatter."[29]

Once we enter the labyrinth of esotericism, how do we know that the philosophical position with which we are trying to engage dialogically isn't merely another veil intended to admit the few and deceive the many? To illustrate, let me just mention the tortuous question of Strauss's theism/atheism.[30] In *Hermeneutics as Politics,* Rosen quotes Strauss's view that we are "compelled from the very beginning to make a choice [between Biblical wisdom and Greek wisdom], to take a stand," and then comments: "No competent student of Leo Strauss was ever in doubt as to his teacher's choice. . . . Strauss's own respect for and attention to the detailed statements on behalf of revealed religion were primarily intended as extensions of his own elusive propaganda for philosophy. . . . It was part of his attempt as a political philosopher to convince the city that philosophers are not atheists."[31] There is a startling symmetry between this claim and the contradictory claim offered by a leading student of Strauss, Thomas Pangle, when he writes that it is "evident from any responsible reading of Strauss's published works . . . that Strauss emphatically embraced theism."[32] Something has surely gone wrong with the Straussian practice of political philosophy if two immensely careful and intellectually sophisticated readers of Strauss can disagree on such a fundamental question as whether Strauss is or isn't a theist. How can we be sure that Strauss isn't dissembling his real view about his relation to Western theism? For that matter, how can we be sure that Pangle's avowal of Strauss's "emphatic theism" isn't itself another merely exoteric device intended to help protect the city from corruption or subversion by philosophical wisdom? And how can we engage dialogically with a position where we can never be sure that our interlocutor isn't dissembling? Again, one can only engage dialogically with positions one can presume are literally (nonironically) held by one's interlocutor, and in a Straussian philosophical universe, there's *always* a lurking question mark about just how far esotericism really extends.

It's hard enough to pursue a philosophical dialogue without tossing in the wild card of esotericism! There's also the related problem of the narcissism of the Straussian conception of philosophy.[33] The fundamental topic of political philosophy as Strauss understands it is philosophy itself: the *only* properly Platonic teaching, according to Strauss, is the superiority of the philosophical life.[34] Okay, so is there a public argument showing (or even trying to show) why this way of life alone is a happy or satisfying form of human life (for the thesis is, after all, hardly self-evident)?[35] No, none that I know of. Nor should we expect to get a public argument demonstrating why one way of life is superior to every other, for to argue explicitly for this one Platonic doctrine would betray Platonic esotericism—based on insight into the need to obscure the radical gulf separating philosophers and non-philosophers.

If dialogue is impossible, then philosophy is impossible; and if philosophy is impossible, then we indeed find ourselves in a postmodern intellectual universe. My conclusion, then, is as follows: If postmodernism fundamentally means the end of philosophy as an activity of rational dialogue, as an enterprise of public reason giving and response to reason-based challenges, then Gadamer is the only one of the five thinkers in Zuckert's book who is not a postmodernist.

NOTES

1. Catherine H. Zuckert, *Postmodern Platos: Nietzsche, Heidegger, Gadamer, Strauss, Derrida* (Chicago: University of Chicago Press, 1996). All parenthetical references in the text are to this book.

2. *The Portable Nietzsche,* ed. Walter Kaufmann (New York: Viking Press, 1968), 474. Philosophers and their judgments concerning life "have value only as symptoms, they are worthy of consideration only as symptoms."

3. Martin Heidegger, "Plato's Doctrine of Truth," in *Phenomenology and Existentialism,* ed. W. Barrett and H. D. Aiken (New York: Random House, 1962), 267.

4. Jacques Derrida, *Dissemination,* trans. Barbara Johnson (Chicago: University of Chicago Press, 1981), 130.

5. Ibid., 129.

6. "Gadamer on Strauss: An Interview," *Interpretation* 12, no. 1 (Jan. 1984): 10. The context is a response to Fortin's challenge to the universality of hermeneutics in reference to notions of a "pre-hermeneutical" and "post-hermeneutical" situation in Strauss and Heidegger respectively.

7. Zuckert suggests that Strauss makes more concessions to history than he professes. See, for instance, Zuckert 197 on "the untraditional character of [Strauss's] view of the tradition"; cf. 276. As discussed earlier, what Zuckert has in mind is that Strauss cannot simply return to the ancients because the need to deal with the tension between ancient political philosophy and biblical morality complicates his philosophical task in a way that wasn't the case for the ancient political philosophers themselves (see 329, n. 67). This strikes me as a vindication of Gadamer's view of Strauss's (necessarily historically mediated) relation to the tradition.

8. Cf. "Gadamer on Strauss," 11–12: "Finitude corresponds to Hegel's 'bad infinity'. . . . The emphasis on finitude is just another way of saying that there is always one step more. Bad infinity in the Hegelian sense belongs to finitude. As I once wrote, this bad infinity is not as bad as it sounds."

9. Ibid., 3: "I tried to convince Strauss that one could recognize the superiority of Plato and Aristotle without being committed to the view that their thought was immediately recoverable and that, even though we have to take seriously the chal-

lenge which they present to our own prejudices, we are never spared the hermeneutical effort of finding a bridge to them."

10. Stanley Rosen, "Horizontverschmelzung" (PHGG207–18); and Gadamer's reply (PHGG219–21). Gadamer writes, "Rosen's contribution seems to me to confirm precisely that which I had in view in my analysis of understanding" (221). In general, Gadamer seems to agree with Strauss that "human thought is capable of transcending its historical limitation or of grasping something trans-historical" (Zuckert 128, quoting *Natural Right and History*).

11. "The similarities between Strauss and Derrida are both surprising and striking" (Zuckert 201). "Derrida and Strauss arrive at a remarkably similar understanding of the problematic character and foundation of our common life" (Zuckert 267). See also 225 and 244–45 on Derrida's acknowledgment of Platonic esotericism. The affinities are not hard to locate—for instance, in Derrida's reading of the *Phaedrus*. Like Strauss, Derrida embraces the *Phaedrus*'s doctrine of "logographic necessity" (*Dissemination* 69, 78, 79–80, 85–86, 95–96) and applies his own version of that doctrine to his reading of the dialogue. Derrida, too, is on the lookout for "a more secret organization of themes, of names, of words" (67). Derrida, too, is not above counting lines in order to calculate the center of a text (68). And Derrida, too, attends not just to what is present in the text but equally to what is absent—the silences of the text: what the text should but *doesn't* say (129–30).

12. Cf. Zuckert 270: in contrast to Strauss and Derrida, Gadamer's view is that "there are [in principle] no unbridgeable rifts or differences."

13. Cf. Zuckert 102–3 on how *both* Derrida and Strauss reject universal dialogue. Also, p. 270: Nietzsche, Heidegger, Strauss, and Derrida share the view that "there is an irreducible conflict at the heart of things." Gadamer's view, by contrast, is less conflictual; as he puts it in his interview with Fortin, "I think that without some agreement, some basic agreement, no disagreement is possible. In my opinion, the primacy of disagreement is a prejudice" ("Gadamer on Strauss" 9).

14. I take it for granted that this applies not only to Nietzsche himself but also to his most influential twentieth-century disciple, Michel Foucault. Cf. Charles Taylor: "[Foucault] is . . . the most profoundly antidialogical thinker" ("Living with Difference," in *Debating Democracy's Discontent: Essays on American Politics, Law and Public Philosophy*, ed. Anita L. Allen and Milton C. Regan, Jr. [Oxford: Oxford University Press, 1998], 224).

15. In chapter 1 of Zuckert's book, one is struck by the extraordinary resemblance between Nietzsche's Plato and Strauss's Plato: Plato is a liar (18, 22, 25), a legislator (21–22, 28), someone who believes above all that philosophy is "the only form of human life truly worth living" (30), and someone who propagates salutary untruths in order to mask and minister to this esoteric wisdom.

16. Cf. Zuckert 202: "According to both Strauss and Derrida, what an author does not say can be more important than what is said." Needless to say, I have no interest in denying that each of them, Derrida and Strauss as well as Nietzsche and Heidegger, makes available genuine insights in their interpretations of, for instance, Plato, and that someone who rejects their conceptions of philosophy can nonetheless profit enormously from their interpretive insights.

17. Cf. "Gadamer on Strauss," 6–7: "As I see it, the hermeneutical experience is the experience of the difficulty that we encounter when we try to follow a book, a

play, or a work of art step by step, in such a way as to allow it to obsess us and lead us beyond our own horizon. It is by no means certain that we can ever recapture and integrate the original experiences encapsulated in those works. Still, taking them seriously involves a challenge to our thinking and preserves us from the danger of agnosticism or relativism." What more could a critic of historicism ask for?

18. Gadamer, "Text and Interpretation" (DDe26).

19. Ibid., 33. Cf. Gadamer, "Reply to Jacques Derrida" (DDe55): "one does not go about identifying the weaknesses of what another person says in order to prove that one is always right, but one seeks instead as far as possible to strengthen the other's viewpoint so that what the other person has to say becomes illuminating. Such an attitude seems essential to me for any understanding at all to come about."

20. Derrida, "Three Questions to Hans-Georg Gadamer" (DDe53).

21. Ibid., 54. Gadamer, of course, never appeals to knowledge of being perfectly understood. Mutual understanding is an *aspiration,* in the absence of which it would be pointless to engage in any act of communication at all.

22. Gadamer, "Reply to Jacques Derrida" (DDe55).

23. Ibid., 56–57.

24. Cf. ibid., 56: contrary to the hermeneutical intention of mutual understanding, "psychoanalytic interpretation does not seek to understand what someone wants to say, but instead what that person doesn't want to say or even admit to him or herself." Gadamer argues very persuasively that "it is a mistake to privilege these forms of distorted intelligibility, of neurotic derangement, as the normal case in textual interpretation" when in fact they are aberrations in relation to the norm of attempted mutual understanding ("Text and Interpretation," DDe40).

25. See, for instance, *Dissemination,* 103, 107–8, 110, 112, 127–33, 149, 158, 169.

26. See Zuckert 164: both Nietzsche and Heidegger read Plato in terms of the doctrines concerning the ideas and the soul. See also 154 (citing Thomas Pangle on "Strauss's discounting of the doctrine of the ideas"), 155, 164 ("Farabi led Strauss to question the status of the doctrines concerning the ideas and the soul"), and 178.

27. See Rosen's review of Zuckert's book in *The Review of Politics* 59, no. 1 (Winter 1997): 162–64. "The praise of the Socratic way of life makes sense as a contranihilistic celebration of philosophy if and only if Socrates' way of life is guided by or culminates in knowledge of what we may call here 'the Ideas'" (164).

28. Ibid., 164.

29. Ibid.

30. Cf. Zuckert 162 and 167 on the need of philosophical atheists to hide their unbelief (or to disclose it "only to sensible friends"); and 175 on Socrates' "dissimulation." According to Zuckert, the fundamental meaning of the Platonic virtues of justice and moderation (as Strauss interpreted them) is the need to hide one's skepticism about the existence of god and the immortality of the soul out of deference to the needs of the city.

31. Stanley Rosen, *Hermeneutics as Politics* (New York: Oxford University Press, 1987), 112; cf. 17 and 107.

32. Thomas Pangle, contribution to APSA Roundtable on Leo Strauss and Religion (1994), manuscript, p. 1. Pangle explains that in calling Strauss an emphatic theist, he has in mind a radical dichotomy between natural theology and revealed

theology, which he says was strongly emphasized by Strauss as well: what Strauss embraced was natural theology, which required esotericism with respect to revealed theology. But in a letter to me dated March 22, 1997, Pangle concedes that even in regard to natural theology, one may ask, "Or is this still [for Strauss] an exoteric level, meant to inspire and console those of us who are not (yet) strong enough to accept the more austere but serene pleasure of appreciating through understanding the ultimately mortal universe, which is constituted in part by our mortal awareness and contemplation of it?" This is left as an unanswered question.

33. Cf. Laurence Lampert, *Leo Strauss and Nietzsche* (Chicago: University of Chicago Press, 1996), 109: "the philosophic spirit points to itself, points to its own nobility as a primary ground for gratitude for the goodness of the world."

34. Cf. Zuckert 148: "*The* secret Strauss thought he discovered by studying Farabi's *Plato* was that Socrates represented the only fully satisfying form of human existence . . . but the open presentation of that fact was apt to provoke popular envy"; see also 276.

35. Zuckert 132: "To ask why a human being should pursue philosophy is to ask why human beings should devote their efforts to acquiring knowledge rather than power or wealth; it is to ask what is the best way of life." Why is it power and wealth that are presented as the alternatives? Why not beauty, or pursuit of justice, or saintliness? It may be relatively easy to demonstrate the superiority of the philosophic life if the alternative is living the life of a sophist or tyrant (cf. *Theatetus* 172c ff.); a much more ambitious argument is required if one also considers the life of a sculptor, dancer, poet, journalist, community activist, pastor, or jurist.

Chapter 9

Meaningless Hermeneutics?

JOEL WEINSHEIMER

Ronald Beiner's contribution to this collection strikes me as particularly far reaching, especially with respect to his argument that Gadamer avoids "the labyrinth of esotericism." Beiner contends that unlike Nietzsche, Derrida, Heidegger, and even Strauss, Gadamer does not try to "read under or though or behind the text." That is, he does not assume that "the 'subtext' is more meaningful than the text." For this reason, according to Beiner, Gadamer must be (for better or worse) excluded from the ranks of postmodern thinkers. This argument, I believe, opens up something important about Gadamer, but its implications extend far beyond the question of his postmodernism. Virtually all interpreters during the last two millennia, and not just the postmodern ones, have been "esotericists" of various stripes, insofar as all posit some "deep meaning" or other. Thus, if Gadamer does not do so, if he has no need for the surface/depth distinction, then his theory of interpretation marks a momentous change in the history of interpretation theory, because a hermeneutics without deep meaning amounts to a hermeneutics without any meaning at all.

This is not the place to attempt even a thumbnail sketch of the hermeneutic theories over the centuries that have depended on the surface/depth distinction.[1] It is enough to recall that in the West this distinction dates, at the very latest, from allegorical readings of the Greek epics, a practice that Christians have modified and continued to our own day. During the medieval period, the metaphor of the integument or cover was most predominant, branching out into figures of the shell or chaff on the one hand and the veil on the other. Correlative to expression as covering, understanding comes to be figured as dis-covery of what lies beneath, once the veil has been rent, the nut cracked, or the grain winnowed. The dichotomies of spirit and letter, figural and literal, content and form, involve a similar topography of surface and depth, with the concomitant implication that understanding requires penetration through the container to the contained. Traditionally, then, interpretation consists in finding hidden meanings.

Gadamer, by contrast, says no such thing. He offers many descriptions for various aspects of understanding, but none of them involves "finding" or "meanings." Among these descriptions, Beiner emphasizes Gadamer's dialogical model. This avoids esotericism by placing both interlocutors on the same plane. Historically, the author occupied the superior position, since he knew the real meaning hidden from the reader; now, if postmodern interpreting implies no more than reversing the relative superiority of the two, with the interpreter instead of the author privy to the real meaning, then such interpreting is not nearly radical enough. Gadamer—more radically—accords neither interlocutor privileged possession of the subtext, and so his might be called a two- rather than three-dimensional hermeneutics, a hermeneutics without depth, indeed without (real) meanings.

On the dialogical model understanding means "coming to an understanding" (TM385), not discovering meanings. No moment that could be called "finding the other's meaning" need occur in a conversation. Admittedly Gadamer does use the language of "finding" when he says, "Hermeneutical conversation, like real conversation, finds a common language" (TM388). What is found, however, is a language, not a meaning. And finding a language does not imply that the common language pre-exists the conversation, such that it could be hidden or lost or "found" in an epiphany of understanding. Whatever Gadamer does mean by "finding," it overlaps with what he means by "creating"—as when he remarks that "Every conversation presupposes a common language, or better, creates a common language" (TM378).

Paralleling the dialogical notion of understanding as the creation of a common language, Gadamer's famous thesis that understanding is the fusion of horizons (TM306) just as clearly avoids the need for any hierarchized surface/depth distinction. The concept of fusion rejects the superiority of the author (and the author's meaning) implied in the alleged need for empathy or historical transposition (that is, the need to "disregard ourselves" and subordinate ourselves to the other's standards). It is in opposition to the notion of finding as reconstruction that Gadamer asserts, "Understanding is not merely a reproductive but always a productive activity as well" (TM296). If understanding is a production, not a reconstruction of a pregiven meaning, "we understand in a different way [from the author] if we understand at all" (TM297). Yet it does not follow that "different from the author" means "same as ourselves." The fusion model just as surely rejects the superiority of the interpreter (and the interpreter's meaning) implied by the alleged necessity of assimilation, that is, of "subordinating another person to our own standards" (TM305). Fusion subverts the hermeneutics of depth by eliminating the dualism upon which the whole notion of meaning depends, the dualism that bifurcates the work into meaning and something that is not the meaning, whether the latter is conceived as the author's expression of the meaning (the form) or the reader's expression of the meaning (the interpretation). Where there is no dualism, there is no meaning.

Like the dialogue and fusion models, Gadamer's performance model of understanding also moves toward a monistic—or "meaningless"—hermeneutics. Here the paradigmatic example for conceptualizing what it means to interpret a work is Lawrence Olivier's interpretation of *Othello,* say, or Van Cliburn's interpretation of Beethoven. On this model, to interpret a work is to perform it; and performance does not distill out something that could be called a meaning, separable from the work. That is because, in Gadamer's view, the performance cannot be differentiated from the work itself. "It is in the performance," Gadamer writes, "and only in it—as we see most clearly in the case of music—that we encounter the work itself" (TM116). Unless we are willing to say that the real music is actually the score and the real play is the script, then we must concede that the work is nowhere to be found more authentically than in the performance of it. This performance— whether on stage or in a scholarly article—is not an adventitious concealment that needs to be stripped away in order reach the work itself. Quite the contrary, Olivier's interpretation is "the coming-into-existence of *[Othello]* itself" (TM116). Just as the work of art cannot be bifurcated into genuine meaning and arbitrary form, so the understanding of it cannot be split into the real work itself and an arbitrary interpretation of it.

This indivisibility or "non-differentiation" (TM117), as Gadamer terms it in the context of aesthetics, marks the fundamental character of beauty, and explains why the beautiful is so important that *Truth and Method* begins and ends with it. Gadamer is no Platonist if that means being a dualist who radically distinguishes the Ideas above from the dim shadows that merely represent them here below. Yet that is not how Gadamer understands Plato at all, and it is precisely Plato's description of beauty in the *Phaedrus* that indicates why Plato should not be thus understood:

> Now in the earthly likeness of justice and temperance and all other prized possessions of the soul there dwells no luster; nay, so dull are the organs wherewith men approach their images that hardly can a few behold that which is imaged, but with beauty it is otherwise. . . . Beauty, as we said, shone bright amidst these visions, and in this world below we apprehend it through the clearest of our senses, clear and resplendent. For sight is the keenest mode of perception vouchsafed us through the body; wisdom, indeed, we cannot see thereby . . . nor yet any other of those beloved objects, save only beauty; for beauty alone

this has been ordained, to be most manifest to sense and most lovely of them all. (*Phaedrus*, 250b, d) [2]

For Gadamer "the metaphysical crux of Platonism" consists in explaining *methexis,* "the relation of the appearance to the idea" (TM481). (As we will see, this is the crux of Gadamer's hermeneutics as well.) All the "beloved objects" except beauty can be apprehended only indirectly, through "the earthly likeness." Justice, temperance, wisdom, and the good generally must be represented in order to be understood. But beauty, as Plato describes it, has its own luster, and so requires no extrinsic mediation. "Obviously what distinguishes the beautiful from the good," Gadamer infers, "is that the beautiful of itself presents itself, that its being is such that it makes itself immediately evident. This means that beauty has the most important ontological function: that of mediating between idea and appearance" (TM481). Unlike the good, there is no mistaking beauty. It seems exactly what it is. For this reason it makes no sense to ask, "This seems beautiful, but it is really?" All beauty is true beauty.

This insight has implications not just for the nature of interpretation but also for the kind of truth that interpretation can have. Negatively expressed, the truth of interpretation conceived on the model of beauty cannot be a correspondence kind of truth because beauty lacks the duality on which correspondence depends. If beauty "presents itself," as Gadamer says, then the presentation of beauty is not something other than itself. That is, the presentation is not an extrinsic representation distinguishable from the thing but an action of the thing itself. As we see from the performance model and from the example of beauty, interpretation is not an adventitious process but the work's own self-presentation. Positively expressed, to say that beauty presents itself is to say that it evidences itself. The particular kind of truth conceived on this model is therefore self-evident truth—traditionally called common sense—which Gadamer considers foundational for all other types of truth.

Gadamer opens himself to misunderstanding in this respect, because all his talk of "truth claims" gives the impression that he thinks of truth as something requiring verification, proof, or evidence.[3] The main thrust of his argument, however, points in exactly the opposite direction. Art works do not have meanings in the form of propositional contents that may or may not turn out to be true, depending on further investigation: they are themselves the evidence of their truth. In the case of self-evident truth, no other evidence than itself is either necessary or possible. Such truth presents itself. On the model of self-evident truth, then, just as on the model of beauty, interpretation does not involve finding the meaning of a work, and true interpretation does not involve finding the real meaning. The history of interpretation, the *Wirkungsgeschichte,* is the history of the work's presenting, evidencing, "proving" itself.

More specifically for Gadamer's hermeneutics, interpreting is the history of the work's presenting itself in language. Not unexpectedly, given what we have seen thus far, Gadamer's phenomenology of language takes a nondualistic form, one that runs quite counter to the familiar semiotic theories of this century. The dualism of signifier and signified, Gadamer contends, has no phenomenological basis, for in speaking we have no awareness of the world distinct from the word, and no awareness of the word distinct from the world. Quite the contrary, "We may speak of an absolute perfection of the word, inasmuch as there is no perceptible relationship—i.e., no gap— between its appearance to the senses and its meaning. . . . In this sense all words are 'true'—i.e., their being is wholly absorbed in their meaning" (TM410–11). To describe words as "true" clearly wrenches our notion of truth because of the firmly entrenched notion that only propositions bear truth-values. And yet it is easy to see that the notion of true words coincides with Gadamer's focus on self-evident truth, where the nondifferentiation of presentation and presented, interpretation and interpreted, constitutes the truth-value. In any case, Gadamer is not really talking about individual words (or even sentences) as being true, but of languages. Every language fits its world perfectly—is self-evidently true—precisely insofar as signifier and signified do not correspond but rather coincide, dissolve in their distinctness, so that language does not represent the world. It is the world's self-presentation, the world interpreting itself.

These considerations make it clearer why Gadamer begins with aesthetics on the way to ontology. His is a hermeneutic ontology in that what is true of the work of art interpreting itself in language—namely that this process does not dichotomize the work from its interpretations—is also true of being generally. "Being that can be understood is language" (TM474). This, Gadamer explains,

> means that [being] is of such a nature that of itself it offers itself to be understood. . . . To come into language does not mean that a second being is acquired. Rather, what something presents itself as belongs to its own being. Thus everything that is language has a speculative unity: it contains a distinction, that between its being and its presentations of itself, but this is a distinction that is really not a distinction at all. (TM475)

The ontological nondifferentiation between being and its presencing in language stands as the broadest implication that Gadamer draws from the nondifferentiation between a work and its meaning.

It would seem to follow from Gadamer's hermeneutics, then, that we should move beyond nondifferentiation to speak of the identity of the work and its interpretations—that is, we should simply dispense with the whole notion of meaning as anything other than the work itself. Notably, however, Gadamer never makes this move, never takes his argument to what seems its obvious conclusion. He does indeed say that there is a unity between being and its presentations of itself—but this, he insists in the language of Hegel, is a "speculative unity," not an identity. A speculative unity "contains a distinction" that is "really not a distinction." But then why say it involves a distinction at all? Why not affirm a monistic hermeneutics in which there is always and only the work itself? Put differently, what indispensable conceptual functions are performed by the concept of meaning and the hermeneutic dualism on which it depends, such that we cannot simply dispense with them?

With regard to legal hermeneutics, a paradigmatic example for Gadamer, the work/meaning or work/interpretation dualism serves to explain the distinctiveness of judicial interpretation as such. The process of interpretation needs to be kept distinct from that of legislation, lest the judge assume the powers of the legislator; and one distinctive characteristic of interpretation is that it can be wrong. A judge can be mistaken. But legislators are never wrong—not because they are particularly far-sighted, but because "wrong interpretation"—and, more broadly, interpretation as such—does not pertain to the process of legislation. One function of legal dualism, then, consists in making it possible to distinguish between the law and some of its interpretations, that is, the wrong ones.[4] One might say, further, that where there is no possibility of misinterpretation—getting the meaning wrong—we are not dealing with interpretation at all but something more like legislation. A monistic or "meaningless" hermeneutics cannot explain wrong interpretation because that is simply the extreme instance in which an interpretation differs from the text. Dualist hermeneutics best explains that difference.

Gadamer does not use the legal argument against monism, however, because it is a two-edged sword: whatever the theoretical desirability of distinguishing between the legislative and judicial branches of government, in practice the two overlap. We know that legislators cannot make law without acting like judges—namely by interpreting, insuring that the proposed law coheres with the body of existing law—and likewise judges cannot interpret the law without making it, something like legislators. The notion of "judge-made law" derives from the fact that applying old law to new cases results in interpretations sufficiently novel that they amount to "judicial legislation." Judicial creativity makes it unusually difficult to define the very notion of misinterpretation, because not all new and different interpretations, not all "legislative" interpretations that create law, are wrong. The example of legal interpretation, then, does not constitute decisive evidence for hermeneutic dualism and against monism.

Quite the contrary, if anything, this example shows that sometimes we

need a dualistic hermeneutics (because judges are fallible and some putative interpretations are not presentations of the law itself), and sometimes
we need a monistic hermeneutics (because the most perfect subservience to
existing law still refashions it in an ongoing process of evolution without a
decisive break). My thesis is that Gadamer's hermeneutics acknowledges
just this double need. Although, as Beiner rightly points out, by way of re-
dressing a long-standing imbalance, Gadamer emphasizes the nonrepresentational, monistic aspect of hermeneutics over the meaning-based, dualistic
aspect of hermeneutics, he does not in fact dispense with either one. The
question is how the two relate. For Gadamer, we have seen, "the metaphysical crux of Platonism" consists in defining "the relation of the appearance
to the idea" (TM481). The crux of Gadamer's hermeneutics, likewise, consists in reconciling the unity of meaning with the multiplicity of understandings. For him, interpretation constitutes the site of this reconciliation,
where the distinction between the one and the many is superseded.

In the famous passage of *Truth and Method* explicating the fusion of horizons, Gadamer seems oddly indecisive about whether there is one horizon
or two. Perhaps now we are in a position to understand why.

> We are familiar with the power of [the fusion of horizons] chiefly from earlier
> times and their naiveté about themselves and their heritage. In a tradition this
> process of fusion is continually going on, for there old and new are always
> combining into something of living value, without either being explicitly fore-
> grounded from the other.
>
> If, however, there is no such thing as these distinct horizons, why do we
> speak of the fusion of horizons and not simply of the formation of the one
> horizon? . . . To ask the question means that we are recognizing that under-
> standing becomes a scholarly task only under special conditions. . . . Every en-
> counter with tradition that takes place within historical consciousness involves
> the experience of a tension between the text and the present. . . . Historical
> consciousness is aware of its own otherness and hence foregrounds the hori-
> zon of the past from its own. On the other hand, it is itself, as we are trying to
> show, only something superimposed upon a continuing tradition, and hence
> it immediately recombines with what it has foregrounded itself from in order
> to become one with itself again in the unity of the historical horizon that it
> thus acquires . . . which means that as the historical horizon is projected, it is
> simultaneously superseded. (TM306–7)

The metaphor of fusion is often taken as proof that Gadamer never comes
to grips with fission, multiplicity, otherness of all kinds, personal, cultural,
historical. This seems an implausible charge when directed at a hermeneutics that takes as its motto: "we understand differently, if we understand at
all." Yet in the above passage, admittedly, Gadamer does begin with the non-

differentiation of old and new that characterizes their ongoing unification in a naive tradition. But second, just as Heidegger distinguishes between everyday *Auslegung* and scholarly *Interpretieren,* Gadamer moves on to acknowledge that, unlike naive tradition, a more sophisticated historical consciousness knows that times change, new and old are different, and historians must recognize the otherness of history to do their job well. And yet, third, the historian's job is not just to recognize difference but to understand it. And understanding means discovering that the otherness of the past (however arcane and unfamiliar) is never absolute; it means discovering history's continuity with the present, and correlatively discovering the historian's own hitherto unrecognized continuity with history. Understanding consists in sophisticated historical consciousness forever coming to grips with its own naiveté.

Postmodernism has not moved much beyond historicism, insofar as both insist upon difference and inveigh against assimilation. Both historicism and postmodernism leave understanding quite unexplained because they conceive of all understanding as assimilationist and hence equivalent to misunderstanding; but this makes the different simply unintelligible. The other thus becomes the very embodiment of inscrutability, and all injunctions to respect this unintelligible other come to have a hollow sound. For Gadamer, too, fusion means discovering sameness, kinship, continuity. And yet, however assimilationist this seems and is, understanding in his view not only finds sameness in difference: "we understand differently, if we understand at all." Sameness and difference are indivisible in Gadamer's hermeneutics, and neither can be suppressed if interpretation is to be made intelligible. An interpretation that is not the same as what it interprets is not an interpretation but a new creation; an interpretation that is not different from what it interprets is not an interpretation but a copy. What distinguishes Gadamer's hermeneutics in this regard is that for him interpretation involves this interminable interplay between sameness and difference, the irreducible *methexis* of the one and the many.

NOTES

1. For a good overview, see Jean Grondin, *Introduction to Philosophical Hermeneutics,* trans. Joel Weinsheimer (New Haven, Conn.: Yale University Press, 1994).

2. Trans. R. Hackenforth, in *The Collected Dialogues of Plato,* ed. Edith Hamilton and Huntington Cairns (Princeton, N.J.: Princeton University Press, 1961), 496–97.

3. Gadamer's notion of a claim comes from Kierkegaard and Lutheran theology, where it signifies the basis upon which an unspecified demand could be concretized in the future (TM127).

4. False interpretations and their causes, the centerpiece of every critical her-

meneutics, lie mostly outside Gadamer's purview insofar as (for better or worse) his is an uncritical hermeneutics, focusing on self-evident truth, for which no proofs or arguments can be offered other than itself. Concerning self-evident truth, like beauty, *non est disputandum*. An interpreter who fails to see what is self-evident is more blind than mistaken (TM322), and so the notion of (wrong) meaning never comes into play.

PART THREE

Gadamer in Question

Chapter 10

Radio Nietzsche, or,
How to Fall Short of Philosophy

GEOFF WAITE

Radio-activity
It's in the world for you and me.
KRAFTWERK, *"Radioactivity"*

I grant you also a very general but not universal agreement could come
from a transmission diffused throughout the whole of mankind.
LEIBNIZ, *New Essays on Human Understanding*

A good place to start is from where and whom we distance ourselves, even if ultimately we all think, make our decisions, and act "in the emptiness of a distance taken."[1] Well-known statements by Gadamer observe a certain distance from Nietzsche, and Gadamer is not the explicit subject of my intervention in this anthology devoted to him and his repercussions. An essay on Nietzsche may be out of place, *hors de saison et de combat,* so I should justify my inclusion here with a prologue.

Distance from Nietzsche demarcated Gadamer from other philosophers in what *mirabile dictu* has just been dubbed "Gadamer's century."[2] Heidegger and Derrida are the ones he publicly highlighted in his "Nietzsche connection," but it is crucial not to forget Strauss. As for "Gadamer's century," I'd prefer the term "current period of the globalizing tendency of liberal-parliamentarian free-market capitalism," though perhaps they amount to much the same thing—both promoting "moderation," "dialogue," and the like. Two of Gadamer's remarks about Nietzsche are especially well known and yet insufficiently analyzed individually or together.

Gadamer welcomed part of Strauss's epistolary response to *Wahrheit und Methode.* In Gadamer's published paraphrase, whereas "the point of critical orientation for Heidegger was Nietzsche, for me [it was] Dilthey."[3] This distanced him also from Strauss, who is by common consensus Nietzschean, though not qua Heideggerian (and certainly not Diltheyan).[4] Gadamer never mentioned that Dilthey and Nietzsche had had a brief but intense contretemps in the 1880s over the then new concept of "inner experience" or "inner world, and that Dilthey had ended up rejecting Nietzsche *tout court* on the grounds that he lacked historical consciousness to the point of a subjectivism and solipsism leading necessarily to insanity.[5] As for Heidegger's view of Nietzsche, as of everything, there are at least two faces. In public he viewed Nietzsche as the consummate post-Platonic metaphysician of will to power, and critiqued him as such, though he accepted a will to power as his own hermeneutic procedure when interpreting other thinkers (as contrasted to interpreting Being). "Force" *(Gewalt)* is required to read all great thinkers; and every authentic "engagement *[Auseinandersetzung]* with them operates on the ground of an interpretation that is already decided and removed from any debate."[6] All this is due to the fact, Heidegger says in regard to Plato and Nietzsche especially, that all great thinking is not merely "unwritten" but "unsaid."[7] More privately Heidegger (especially in the late 1930s and early 1940s) embraced precisely the figure Dilthey had shunned, namely, the solitary Nietzsche who was *"ver-rückt"* (insane simply but also "dis-placed" and" de-ranged"), and as such the main harbinger (alongside Hölderlin) leading beyond the otherwise inescapable ambit of post-Platonic metaphysics into a future "other beginning."[8] When he affirmed that part of Strauss's response to *Wahrheit und Methode,* Gadamer did not say that he was adapting Dilthey's prior position against Nietzsche. And the Diltheyan Gadamer likely found Heidegger's closeted promotion of Nietzschean "insanity" (in his philosophical sense, if no other) hard to swallow—along with Heidegger's not-unrelated "Chinese" language games and equally infamous public visit to "Syracuse." Also left unsaid by Gadamer was something that Strauss would be the last person who needed to be told. The exceptionally important thing Dilthey shares with Nietzsche and Heidegger is that all three are highly tuned to the rhetorical techniques of philosophical esotericism and quite prepared to use them.[9]

The second of Gadamer's two relevant statements about Nietzsche still involves Heidegger but expanded to Derrida. It was published in "Destruktion und Dekonstruktion" (1985), Gadamer's postmortem on his contretemps with Derrida that had begun four years earlier but symptomatically terminated before it began. Gadamer summed up the difference between philosophical hermeneutics and deconstruction by remarking that "evidently Nietzsche marks the critical point," and then stated bluntly that, unlike and against Derrida, "I am in fact convinced by Heidegger's interpretation."[10] This concession would require viewing Nietzsche as the famous "completion" or "perfection" of the history of metaphysics leading back at least to Plato and the purported "fall away from Being." Yet Gadamer's own Plato was sooner the originator of the "unwritten" or esoteric philosophy expressed in open-ended dialogic form, a seminal hermeneutic model with perduring significance. And this is how Gadamer had interpreted Nietzsche a year earlier in his only detailed analysis of what he called "Antipode Nietzsche." That is, he read *Thus Spoke Zarathustra* as a "drama" by focusing more attention than had even Heidegger (in the 1950s) on Zarathustra's consideration of his intended listeners or interlocutors, including the animals.[11]

We have observed four things so far, the first three mostly obvious, the last tacit. 1) Gadamer agrees with a relatively friendly Nietzschean interlocutor (Strauss) that Nietzsche for him (unlike for Heidegger, or Strauss) was not his "point of critical orientation," and takes for his own such point one (Dilthey) opposed to Nietzsche. 2) Gadamer reacts to a quite hostile Nietzschean non-interlocutor (Derrida) by averring that he himself (contra Derrida) is "convinced" by the interpretation of Nietzsche by the philosopher (Heidegger) with the rival point of orientation, Nietzsche. 3) When Gadamer produces his extended reading of Nietzsche it is in terms less of Platonic metaphysical closure than of open-ended Platonic dialogue. 4) Two thematic threads emerge from what Gadamer precisely does *not* say. These are the history of philosophy's two most embarrassing problems, each in its own way "unwritten" and "unsaid": insanity and esotericism.

Observation number 4 may be controversial, but there's no doubt that Gadamer's "Nietzsche connection" has ushered us into a hermeneutic circle that is "political." I mean this (thus far) in the wholly uncontroversial sense that Gadamer's dialogue with different partners in the *polis* is differently *policed* by certain prejudices or prejudgments (more or less explicitly stated) about who that partner is, and what that partner stands for. In the properly Platonic tradition, *politeia* (the political, politics, or constitution) "designates . . . the way of life of a society . . . decisively determined by hierarchy," and "implies . . . something like a right of un-wisdom, a right of folly" because "the polis as polis is characterized by an essential, irremediable recalcitrance to reason."[12] In any case, the Gadamerian hermeneutic circle, or circle of dialogue, is at once closed-and-open, open-and-closed, and so forth. This is one of the most rudimentary features of the subtending system—not just its politics, but what I'd call its political economy. There's nothing novel or interesting here, either, at least in formal, procedural, or theoretical terms, and certainly not for the true believers. Jean Grondin, for one, has argued that the circle of philosophical hermeneutics is not the circle of fundamental ontology due in part to their differing views of the circle's limit qua metaphor. Whereas Heidegger sees its explanatory power as overly restricted existentially and ontologically, Gadamer's objection is comparatively epistemological and hermeneutic. For Gadamer, still according to Grondin, "there is not really a circle, because it only expresses a requirement of coherence that calls for a constant revision of the hypotheses of interpretation (following the anticipation [of] perfection)."[13] My own focus is not only on the allegedly ongoing and open-ended processes of Gadamerian understanding, interpretation, and dialogue, but also and even more on Grondin's parenthetically stated phrase, "anticipation [of] perfection," which translates what (a quite Heideggerian) Gadamer in *Wahrheit und Methode* calls "der Vorgriff der Vollkommenheit." Grondin's allusion must be to Gadamer's assertion (using another common translation of the key phrase):

> Here . . . we see that understanding means, primarily, to understand the content of what is said, and only secondarily to isolate and understand another's meaning as such. Hence the most basic of hermeneutic preconditions remains one's own fore-understanding of completeness *[Vorgriff der Vollkommenheit]*, which comes from being concerned with the same subject. This is what determines what can be realized as unified meaning and thus determines how the fore-conception of completeness is applied.[14]

But it is here that Gadamer adds to the authoritative edition of *Wahrheit und Methode* what is its most remarkable footnote—indeed "passage" in all senses. As stated:

> There is one exception to the anticipation of perfection: the case of disguised or encrypted writing *[den Fall des verstellten oder verschlüsselten Schreibens]*. This case poses the most difficult hermeneutic problems *[die schwierigsten hermeneutischen Probleme]*.[15]

Way back in 1809 Schleiermacher (Nietzsche's "veil-maker") had memorably written that "the difference between easy and difficult writers only exists via the fact that there *is* no complete understanding."[16] So why is Gadamer's only admitted exception—to all of Gadamer, in effect—big news? We will return to *der Vorgriff der Vollkommenheit* shortly, but first a word about its exception.

Without mentioning the term, Gadamer's footnote refers to the great tradition philosophical esotericism, as the reference to Strauss in the note's continuation makes clearer. (Gadamer's objection to Strauss is so cursory and imprecise that it may be intentionally misleading, but that is a demonstration for another time.) Gadamer refers to Strauss on several other occasions in his collected works, but in terms far less of the basic problem of esotericism than of the merely subsidiary one of taking different sides in *les querelles des anciens et des modernes* and debates about natural right.[17] On other occasions, Gadamer alludes to the general problem of esotericism, as is well-nigh unavoidable in so many reflections on what Aristotle famously dubbed Plato's "unwritten" philosophy and its first principle, though he has comparatively little to say anywhere about the ensuing "logographic necessity" of the "noble lie."[18] In any event, Gadamer's stated single exception (qua *énonciation*) to what philosophical hermeneutics can understand is itself exceptional (qua *énoncé*). Given all his fine attunements to *subtilitas legendi, prudentia,* and *der richtige Takt,* it is note- and question-worthy that Gadamer never treated esotericism with anything remotely like the attention demanded if "disguised or encrypted writing" indeed is "the *one* exception" to "*the* most basic precondition" to which it "poses *the* most difficult hermeneutic problems." Our own problem in reading Gadamer becomes no less difficult. What if the greatest contemporary hermeneutic philosopher and promoter of dialogue did not adequately treat esotericism because he was somehow a practitioner? For precisely such reticence or prudence is what the "unwritten" tradition mandates, having stipulated that any reference to esotericism be just barely enough to alert "those in the know" that they are in its presence. *Sensu stricto* there can be no "completeness" or "perfection" to solving this problem, obviously enough, but at least we should set it.

Once again summarily and crudely stated, the hermeneutic structure of Gadamer's relation to the "Nietzsche connection" is indeed not fully circular. But nor is it (*pace* Grondin) fully open through "constant revision of the hypotheses of interpretation (following the anticipation [of] perfection)," though that is precisely its public or exoteric face. The unsaid and esoteric structure is that of a political economy adjustable to specific interlocutors and situations, and ultimately closed to full disclosure or debate.[19] As such, Gadamer's "Nietzsche connection" is homologous with his foreclosure of open dialogue about esotericism, which is the one exception to the basic precondition of hermeneutic understanding called *der Vorgriff der Vollkommenheit*. The *tertium quid* articulating the two terms of this homology is the signifier "Leo Strauss" insofar as it represents, at once: 1) the point of critical departure *not* shared by Gadamer; and 2) the exceptional problematic of philosophical esotericism *not* analyzed by Gadamer. Since what I call Radio Nietzsche is an esoteric Nietzsche, and since Strauss is more help in identifying its existence than anyone else, the justification I give for the inclusion here of my essay on Radio Nietzsche is a type of argument *per negationem*. Perhaps the best I can hope for is that the Gadamer Industry will now be informed (to paraphrase John Cage) by "a space, an emptiness, that it formally lacked."[20] But because I want to dispel any impression that my argument is merely *ad hominem,* I want to devote the remainder of this prologue to *der Vorgriff der Vollkommenheit.* This is the axial point around which philosophical hermeneutics and the major exception to it are said by Gadamer to turn, and with which any interpretation of Nietzsche must settle accounts.

German *Vollkommmen* is "complete" or "absolute" in addition to "perfect"—whatever has "come-to-full." Thus, for example, a philosopher is said to "perfect" the history of metaphysics. This word is easy enough to translate, but the phrase *der Vorgriff der Vollkommenheit* is not, and not only because of *Vorgriff,* to be considered presently. The phrase is a genitive metaphor and as such semantically duplicitous. There is no way to tell grammatically whether *der Vollkommenheit* is *genitivus obiectivus* or *genitivus subiectivus*.

In the one case, one reads "perfection's *Vorgriff*" and, in the other case (of particular interest to us), "*Vorgriff*'s perfection." Either we live with the ambiguity or we make one of two incompatible decisions. Thus, as we'll see, we confront *in nuce* at the level of grammar a deep philosophical, ethical, and political question, which the genitive metaphor thus not merely constates for us but asks us to perform. Since, however, this demand is true in principle of all genitive metaphors, we won't see the exceptional importance of *der Vorgriff der Vollkommenheit* until we recognize the complexity of the second of the two subjects and/or objects: *Vorgriff* (verb, *vorgreifen*).

Vor-griff is "pre-grip" (as *Be-griff* is "con-cept"—"a taking in" from Latin *capere,* "to take"). Gadamer depends for his term on section 32 of *Sein und Zeit* in which Heidegger famously articulates *Vorgriff* to *Vorhabe* ("intention," also "what lies before us") and *Vorsicht* ("foresight," "circumspection," also "caution" or "prudence"). All these significations can and do overlap and merge. Heideggerian *Vorgriff* had decisively resituated the age-old question of whether any interpretive act "draws from the entity itself" or instead "forces the entity into a concept to which it is opposed in its manner of being" because, as Heidegger concludes, "in either case the interpretation has already decided in favor of a definite way of conceiving the entity, be it with finality or with reservations." [21] It is in this sense that "prejudice or prejudgment" *(Vorurteil)* is "philosophically vindicated" by Heideggerians and Gadamerians alike. But why stop at the philosophical? Does not its political vindication follow sooner or later? It is here that hermeneutics became "a subdivision of ethics," to say the least. [22] A related problem is that even if we could determine degrees of prejudice (though it seems we cannot), then on what basis could that ever be, inasmuch as that, too, would be always already a function of prejudice—and so forth. Moreover, Heidegger's distinction between conceiving "with finality" and "with reservations" indeed becomes moot, but so do all others. There is no center to hold, and mere anarchy is loosed upon a groundless world. If Gadamer's *Vorgriff der Vollkommenheit* has no answer to this problem (read also: is part and parcel of it), then Hans Albert would be correct in saying that, many appearances to the exact contrary, Gadamer's "urbanization of the Heideggerian province"—their shared "rehabilitation of prejudice"—"has the extreme consequence for textual interpretation of a sort of immunization of interpretation from all relevant criticism whatsoever." [23]

Now, had Heidegger and Gadamer written in Greek (and effectively they did), *Vorgriff* would be *prólēpsis (pro + lambanein,* "prior grasp" and "preconception" or "anticipation"—the latter two also derived from *capere*). In grammar, the proper name "X" in the phrase, "When he joined the National Socialist Teachers Union in August 1933, X was widely respected as . . . ," is anticipated by the proleptic shifter "he," its referent determined only retroactively. In rhetoric, prolepsis is the more or less sly anticipation or forestalling of an opponent's expectations or objections. (Recall my choice of grammatical example, indicative also of my *Vorurteil.*) In Epicurean and Stoic epistemology, prolepsis (related to *katálēpis,* "grasping," "apprehension"—a major truth criterion) results from the repeated perception of the same object (for example, individual esotericists), and in that sense is a universal concept ("esotericist"), that is, a residual composite derived from those prior perceptions or "preceptions." In ancient theology, prolepsis is the anticipation of the perfection of the gods. In periodizations of philosophy, if the "classical" philosopher is differentiated from the "modern" on the grounds that, whereas the former spoke to a present audience, the latter writes for the future, then an entire era is defined in terms of its proleptic intent, an ever-updated version of *actio in distans.* Prolepsis can signify any "premature" conceptual, physical, or discursive "leap ahead." This includes—*nota bene*—a "taking or gripping or possessing beforehand" that is not merely grammatical, rhetorical, epistemological, theological, and historiographical. For it is also legal, economic, and military. (Greek rhetorical terms were commonly derived from or related to martial strategy and trickery.) [24] For example, it is prolepsis when one gains possession of a parcel of land in anticipation of future use, or makes a preemptive strike against an enemy, which in German is *ein Präventivschlag* or *Präventivangriff.* ("Preempt" is from Latin *praeemere,* "to buy beforehand"; compare Latin *praevenire,* "to come before," which in German could also be *zuvorkommen.*) It has been too rarely noticed that in crucial section 74 of *Sein und Zeit,* Heidegger articulated the entire nexus around *Vorgriff* to "*vorlaufende* Entschossenheit."[25] This not only signifies "anticipatory resoluteness" in a hermeneutic sense or in terms of abstract historicality. It also implies "vanguard resolve" in a quite specific martial sense. This extended (bellicose) semantic field is crucial because, qua prolepsis, *Vorgriff* includes the "handicapping intention" *(Vor-gabe)* to "fore-stall" in advance (and in *that* sense prejudge, prejudice, and police or "fore-guard") any counter to one's vanguard attack *(Angriff).* ("Vanguard" evolved from Old French *avant-garde,* "fore-guard.") In short, fully or perfect open-ended dialogue is rendered a priori impossible, and the only real question becomes whether the standpoint from which the preemptive strike is sent forth is open to discussion or not—and it would be lethal to believe it could be in all situations. The fact that *der Vorgriff der Vollkommenheit* is a genitive metaphor means that even though we cannot decide this question, nevertheless we must make a decision. Both fundamental ontology (Heidegger) and philosophical hermeneutics (Gadamer) are—more or less tacit or encrypted—modes of decisionism. (Carl Schmitt might have said shamefaced modes, but that qualification need not distract us here.)

Pace Gadamer's footnote, no *external* "exception" ("disguised or encrypted writing" being the only one admitted) is required to problematize *der Vorgriff der Vollkommenheit* and the understanding ostensibly grounded on it. To the exact contrary, *Vorgriff* qua prolepsis already always forecloses the possibility of open-ended or uncoerced dialogue. The translation without commentary of *Vorgriff* as "fore-understanding" or "anticipation" nicely disguises that it entails radical *fore-closure*. (*Forclusion* and *extimité,* to speak Lacanian; *exergue* and *supplément* to speak Derridian; *ideologie,* to speak Althusserian.) What is *incepted* is *excepted* and vice versa. The *Ausnahme* is a *Vorwegnahme* and vice versa. What "begins by being taken in hand" (*incipire,* again from *capere*) is simultaneously "excepted by being taken out" (*excipere*), and so on. And exactly the same applies, I suggest, to Gadamer's way of distancing himself from Nietzsche and Heidegger. They are expelled or repelled as exoteric points of critical orientation for philosophical hermeneutics only because they inform its esoteric core. Esotericism is a constitutive, informing principle of philosophical hermeneutics—hence the need to divert attention away from it by positing it as singular external exception, and immediately forgotten as such.

If at day's end Gadamer's work remains (in Hans Albert's phrase) "a continuation of Heidegger's thinking" or even *im Banne Heideggers,* then their only major difference (*pace* Albert) would not be that they began "with different premises."[26] It would be that Heidegger and Gadamer differed on how to employ esotericism (the "unwritten" and the "unsaid") to remarkably similar ideological and political-economic conclusions, which they shared *à tout prendre* with Nietzsche. And if Nietzsche's work can be read as the "completion" or "perfection" of metaphysics (or, more precisely, its "closure effect"), as Heidegger and as many Heideggerians assert (though perhaps not Gadamer), then this claim is valid only in the following reformulation. If Nietzsche does return to the purported "origin" or "primal fissure and leap" (*Ursprung*) of metaphysics, he does so only to its constitutive form, namely, the paradoxical fact that any most esoteric "first principle" can be exoterically expressed only as "unwritten doctrine." Radio Nietzsche remains the most powerfully retrofitted response under modern (and postmodern) conditions to *that* origin. Its ultimate significance lies in the success of its *Vorgriff der Vollkommenheit,* that is, its proleptic strike against effective philosophical opposition to the globalizing tendency of liberal-parliamentarian free-market capitalism. Take it or attack it.

RADIO-ACTIVITY AS EXO/ESOTERICISM

> *The concept of dissimulation has to do with a* practical *problem. And the blurred outlines of the concept don't change anything about that.*
> WITTGENSTEIN, *Last Writings on the Philosophy of Psychology*

Radio Nietzsche is a covert project of secular modern "oral" transmission by means of which Nietzsche intended to produce proleptic subliminal "radio-

active" effects on what might today be called aural virtuality or aural ideology.[27] These effects were programmed to be potentially lethal to some "listeners." To expose even the existence of Radio Nietzsche requires not only
"reading between the lines" of Nietzsche's written texts but also "hearing between the lines."[28] The expressions "radio-active" and "Radio" (hence also
"listeners" and "hearing between the lines") are clearly "metaphoric" in the
sense of being figurative. Any attempt to express their meaning in "un-
metaphoric," or rather nonfigurative, language would lead to the discovery
of a terra incognita, a field whose very dimensions are as yet unexplored.
These terms are also anachronistic insofar as Nietzsche preceded the
discovery of radium and the invention of radio. And, although Nietzsche
slightly antecedes these actual developments of science and technology, he
was well aware of the basic principles of covert, subliminal, and potentially
dangerous communication involved therein. These principles Nietzsche
knew from his detailed study of classical philology, rhetoric, music, and the
history of philosophy. His written texts were designed to exceed the limits
of the written medium insofar as they entailed techniques of transmission
and structures of reception more commonly associated with sound than
with the written, including sound's omnidirectionality, mood, and closer
proximity and sensitivity to the (Schopenhauerian and Wagnerian) "will" or
unconscious.

By Nietzsche's design, the precise content or meaning of the resulting
transmissions of Radio Nietzsche was to remain concealed or, more precisely, to appear to exist only in its subliminal effects within what he anticipated would be changing but largely hostile historical conjunctures. A
single surplus content or center of his transmission nonetheless does exist
in the form of what he called—appropriately only in private—"my *centrum.*"

On January 3, 1888, Nietzsche remarked in a letter to Paul Deussen (one
of his oldest friends, with whom he had almost lost contact) that some German critics who had just begun to be interested in his work were given
to characterize it in pejorative medical terms as "'eccentric,' 'pathological,'
'psychiatric,' *et hoc genus omne.*" But, Nietzsche continued, "These gentle-
men, who have no clue as my *centrum,* as to the great passion in the service
of which I live, will have difficulty casting a glance even where I previously
have been outside of my center, where I was *really* 'eccentric.'"[29] The last
term has little to do with any pathological eccentricity, or with the well-
known Romantic trope of "eccentric circle" as a figure of irony or poetic
and conceptual rigor. It has far more to do with Nietzsche's principled refusal, in public or even private, fully to reveal his center of radio-active
transmission.

But he concealed this center so well that it arguably cannot be identified.
It is certainly premature to assign it any ideological value before its logical
structure has been articulated. This is not to say that Nietzsche's center is

not ideological. Nor is it to say that it was not unconscious—either to him or to us—insofar as ideology is unconscious and as such not fully accessible to any subject. Rather, I mean to say that for Nietzsche the existence of the unconscious is not primarily something to be exposed to view by analysis (in any enlightenment or psychoanalytic sense) but rather put to his own *use*. Specifically, he put to use the gap or surplus that exists between the traditional (Marxist) definitions of "ideology" as "false consciousness" and the "systematic articulation of ideas." And this is also why, in listening to Radio Nietzsche, we should perhaps share Althusser's stubborn private insistence (his own version of Lacanian theory to the contrary) in regarding the "'relations' between ideology (or concrete ideological formations) and the unconscious" as "a problem provisionally without solution."[30]

Critiquing the dependence of psychoanalytic theory and practice on the concept of negation *(Verneinung)* as the basic way to "transgress" ideology—when negation in fact is one of ideology's main ways of functioning—an Althusserian argument has recently been developed to suggest that "somebody who knows about the mechanisms of negation can instrumentalize them as a code of communication."[31] Furthermore, "everything that negation says—even what it says at the level of its enunciation—belongs to its enunciated content. Only the fact that it is a negation remains on the level of enunciation. Everything that can be falsified or verified is a part of the constative level of the enunciated—not the performative level of enunciation, where the question of truth does not play any role."[32] Translated into terms of Radio Nietzsche, this means that although any of us is free to falsify or verify the manifest content of Nietzsche's code of communication, to accept or reject it—in short, to read it as unconscious negation—it was Nietzsche's intent to instrumentalize the mechanisms of such negation so as to render the performative level of his enunciations concealed from view in inverse relation to their perlocutionary effectivity. So, to anticipate, when Nietzsche's enunciation explicitly defends, say, human slavery, we appear free to read him as saying the opposite, whereas the real slavery here is being transmitted not at the level of the enunciated but at the level of the enunciation itself—where it remains impervious to detection, let alone verification or falsification. Unless a new way of reading be developed—one which will necessarily be dictated proleptically by Nietzsche, to some extent, but which will explore the possibility of escape.

The effect of Radio Nietzsche's transmission was also designed to be mainly *formal* (as opposed to semantic) and *prophylactic* (as opposed to positive or constructive). In spite and because of his fervent and publicly expressed desire to produce, say, the "superman" in an age he diagnosed as increasingly democratic and permeated by "slave morality," he was pessimistic, prudent, and practical enough not to limit himself to the superman's production, and certainly not to his immediate production. Nietzsche did not merely design safeguards against the disclosure of his *centrum* or content (which is not reducible to the "superman"—and after *Thus Spoke Zarathustra* the term effectively disappeared from his diction). He attempted—with remarkable success—to impose severe, untranscendable limits on the possibility of finding viable alternatives to what his transmission was to insure: a permanently imprisoning, more or less voluntarily accepted structure of conceptual and social "order of rank" *(Rangordnung)*. And, in the event, the dominant aftereffect of Radio Nietzsche in our particular historical conjuncture takes the form of a very general, though not quite universal, unacknowledged consensus that imagines itself to allow all manner of "debate" or "dialogue"—including about Nietzsche—regardless of the content, which in any case is assumed not to exist. One such debate (seminal, though not well known) will be under scrutiny here in due course. But first a few preliminaries.

Now, the world has hardly needed Radio Nietzsche to produce or reproduce "order or rank." But, for more than a century now, Nietzsche's effects have been particularly enervating. They constitute postmodernity's necessary, if not sufficient, logical condition. Radio Nietzsche was produced to be "radio-active" in both senses of the word: a transmission across distant space, and especially time, more or less subliminally received, and, as such, debilitating or even lethal for those unaware that this transmission indeed has a content and who persist in the mistaken belief that Nietzsche's thought must—somehow—be liberating. Responding to Radio Nietzsche, then, real philosophical struggle cannot occur at the level of "free debates" grounded in an unacknowledged consensus appealing always already to Nietzsche, but in as yet uncharted radio-active waves. And precisely these are what is exo/esoteric or "aesoteric."[33]

FALLING SHORT OF PHILOSOPHY

Premises of the machine age. — *The press, the machine, the railway, the telegraph are premises whose thousand-year conclusion no one has yet dared to draw.*
NIETZSCHE, *The Wanderer and His Shadow*

By falling short *of philosophy, I mean stating propositions as "conclusions without premises," as Spinoza and Althusser would have put it.*
BALIBAR, *The Philosophy of Marx*

The juxtaposition of these enthymematic epigraphs indicates that Nietzsche was not merely a philosopher *sensu stricto,* but also a philosopher of the indefinite technological future.

It is insufficiently recognized that Nietzsche was "Hegelian" not only in his concern with techniques of ideational incorporation (described in Hegel's analysis of the death of Socrates) and the ruse of reason (the way that world-historical individuals ruthlessly dominate history), but also in the matter of the concept or *Begriff*: expressed epistemologically, the *concept*, expressed politically, the *grasp*. And what Nietzsche's concept is always most prepared to grasp is the Nietzschean corps/e.[34] At the same time in history, Marx was translating Hegel's *der Begriff* into *die Ware* or commodity— today the commodity of the global capitalism subtending each and every mode of socioeconomic, intellectual, and cultural transmission. In his 1885 notebooks Nietzsche wrote that philosophers "must no longer merely permit themselves to accept concepts as gifts *[die Begriffe nicht mehr sich nur schenken lassen]*, merely purifying and polishing them, but rather first of all *make* them, *create* them *[sie schaffen]*, present them and render them convincing *[zu ihnen überreden]*. Hitherto one has generally trusted one's concepts *[Begriffe]*, as if they were a wondrous *dowry [Mitgift]* from some sort of wonderland."[35] Understandably, this passage is cited approvingly near the beginning of Deleuze and Guattari's *What Is Philosophy?* Indeed, it leads directly into their core thesis that the object of philosophy is "to create concepts that are always new." To which they add, "We can at least see what philosophy is not: it is not contemplation, reflection, or communication."[36] And certainly not "dialogue"—except to the extent that the Platonic dialogues, too, were in fact a monologue *in disguise*. And as we will see presently, *this* is much closer to Nietzsche's own position than to that averred by many others (notably Gadamer). But in the process of beginning to cite Nietzsche's text verbatim, these two Nietzscheans (who rival Derrida in influence) suddenly stop short, and hence fall short of producing non-Nietzschean philosophy, at the very least. Instead, they themselves paraphrase or translate—that is, they *incorporate*—the continuation of Nietzsche's argument. They continue, "but trust must be replaced by distrust, and philosophers must distrust most those concepts they did not create themselves (Plato was fully aware of this, even though he taught the opposite)."[37] That makes it sound as if these last words are their own. In fact, they have incorporated only a transmission of Radio Nietzsche.

The *philosophical* problem whenever "reading" Nietzsche is always *philological*: we must grasp the conceptual peculiarity of his "love of words" as well as of his "love of wisdom." Generally speaking, to paraphrase or translate him is not merely to say something slightly different from what he openly said—*all* paraphrase or translation unavoidably does this *(traduttore, traditore)*—but is also to incorporate unwittingly something *else* he said between or behind the lines, namely, his unstated, enthymemic premise. Actually, the last part of this notebook text breaks down, as Nietzsche's notebooks frequently do, under a certain pressure. In addition to contingent physiological pressures (Nietzsche's health) it is also the pressure of coming dangerously close to putting in print what ought never to be uttered explicitly to the great unwashed multitude in the long tradition of esoteric elitism. Nietzsche's clear text in 1885 ends: "At first what is necessary is absolute skepticism with regard to all inherited concepts (as *may* have been possessed once by One philosopher—Plato: naturally [he] *taught the opposite*— —)."[38] It is at this precise point that Nietzsche's text stutters, becomes unintelligible (as his editors' double dashes indicate). Whenever one's handwriting disintegrates completely—becomes illegible to others or even oneself—this is not necessarily by chance, however, nor necessarily *un*consciously motivated. And it is precisely this breakdown, this static, that is smoothed over and filtered out by Deleuze and Guattari's paraphrase or translation.

Basically, such postmodern post-Marxists *trust* Nietzsche, who gives them their root definition of philosophy as "the creation of concepts that are always new." But why, returning to Nietzsche's elided words, is it *"natural"* that perhaps the "One" philosopher before Nietzsche would have "taught the opposite" of what that philosopher believed? Why should he have given off the *appearance* of skepticism with regard to all inherited concepts? Arguably, because Plato had some hidden agenda in mind that neither he nor Nietzsche states publicly because it would be illogical and counterproductive to do so. This agenda is shared elitism with regard to politics. In this context, Nietzsche's attack on Plato's metaphysics is *too* well known.[39] It has to do with the concomitant requirement to speak exo/esoterically at once to those both "in" and "out of the know." This requirement—at once Platonic and Nietzschean—logically entails the subliminal incorporation of concepts. This thesis emerges between the lines (with Hegel's help) from Plato's depiction of the death of Socrates and its mortally transformative, bi-suicidal relation to society via the (Hegelian *and* Nietzschean) ruse of reason.

But then it would follow *against* Deleuze and Guattari that if we are philosophers in *their* Nietzschean sense (i.e., conceptually creative), then among the "newly" minted concepts we must *most* distrust are those created *by Nietzsche*. The dowry (German *Mitgift*) of this *pharmakos* is always already poison *(Gift)*. So I argue that the trust Nietzsche most betrayed is ours, namely, our trust that the "object of philosophy"—its joy and its terror, as Deleuze and Guattari also say—is the "creation of concepts that are always new," when in fact Nietzsche's concepts were created surreptitiously to serve ideological interests and agendas that are premodern, archaic in their commitment to social, conceptual, and rhetorical hierarchy of the kind that, paradoxically, Nietzsche affirms and that Deleuze and Guattari reject. Therefore, our task is to grasp the paradox of philosophy as being, at once, "the creation of concepts that are always new" (Deleuze and Guattari) and/ or "the possibility of univocal translation" (Derrida) and/or "struggle"—not least "class struggle in the specific element of theory" (Althusser) and not most the struggle not to fall short of philosophy.

ACTIO IN DISTANS

New Battles. —*After Buddha was dead, his shadow was for centuries still exhibited in a cave—a gigantic, terrifying shadow. God is dead; but, as is the way with humans, there will perhaps be caves for millennia in which his shadow will still be exhibited.*
    NIETZSCHE, *The Gay Science,* 1882

The true formula of atheism is not God is dead . . . the true formula of atheism is God is unconscious.
    LACAN, Seminar XI, 1964

Kleist wrote somewhere that what the poet would most like to be able to do would be to convey thoughts by themselves without words. (What a strange admission.)
    WITTGENSTEIN, *Culture and Value,* ca. 1931

To advance intercourse within the borders of the four corners of the earth, an electrical telegraph has recently been invented, a telegraph that by means of dynamo and electrical wire communicates information at the speed of thought, I mean to say in less time than any chronometric instrument can register.
    KLEIST, "Letter Bomb Project," 1810[40]

I stand down before One who does not yet exist [Ich trete vor Einem zurück, der noch nicht da ist], and make my bow, a millennium in advance, before his spirit.
    KLEIST, letter of 1803 (also cited by Heidegger in the documentary film *Im Denken unterwegs,* 1975)

Philosophy acts at a distance, in a void (mine!)
    ALTHUSSER, *L'avenir dure longtemps,* 1985

Obviously it is anachronistic to attribute to Friedrich Nietzsche (1844–1900, and who effectively ceased writing in 1888) any serious thoughts—neutral, negative, or positive—about current "technoculture" (the tendency increasingly to fuse culture, in the broad and narrow sense, with digital technologies that can "freely" manipulate and synthesize images and sounds) and hence about his own technocultural afterlife as techno-Nietzscheanism. Nonetheless, speculative attempts linking Nietzsche to various forms of wireless communication are already underway, at least *en passant.*[41] But the deeper problem lies elsewhere. As parsed by Charles Grivel in his work on radio, "since God is dead the voice, without reservation, dissolves."[42] And so it is that Nietzsche's parable of the ear in *Thus Spoke Zarathustra* (also the central exhibit of Derrida's *otobiographie*) has been called "a parable of the effects of radiophonic art."[43] But Grivel is simply wrong. God *is* not dead, *is* "not-dead." We recall, with Lacan, that the most radical statement of atheism is not "God is dead" (any more than God is eternal), but rather "God is unconscious."[44] This is what enables Radio Nietzsche to transmit subliminally from an apparent distance, from one mountain cave to another. Paraphrasing Lacan, we can say that it was Nietzsche's exo/esoteric position that "precisely because God is dead, and always been dead" that permitted Nietzsche-as-God to "transmit a message via all those beliefs which made Him appear always alive, resurrected from the void left by his death."[45]

Now, radio qua technology (as opposed to its concept or possibility, both of which came much earlier) was arguably created in 1913; and the first commercial radio broadcast was in 1920. Radium had been isolated chemically and radioactivity discovered in 1898 (by Marie and Pierre Curie). In the words of radio's historian and theorist Allen S. Weiss (whose *Phantasmic Radio* analyzes the way the medium disembodies *and* reembodies what I call corps/es), it was on January 31, 1913, that

> Edwin H. Armstrong notarized his diagram of the first regenerative circuit, an invention which was to be the basis of radio transmission. His discovery was that the audion (vacuum tube) could be used not only as a detector of electrical waves but also, through regeneration or feedback, as a signal amplifier. Furthermore, as a generator of continuously oscillating electronic waves, it could be used as a transmitter. The very first demonstration of audio amplification, by Lee de Forest in November 1913, created the "crashing sounds" of a handkerchief dropping. Radio was created—and along with it, an unfortunate electronic side-effect was first heard, that of static.[46]

In 1898 Nietzsche was still alive but not receiving broadcasts of any kind from the outside world. And by 1913 and 1920 his physical corpse had naturally long decayed; the globe had fast turned toward its first technowar, which accelerated and was accelerated by radio technology; and the basic structure of Nietzsche's influence (i.e., "immanent" or "structural causality," in the Spinozist and Althusserian senses) was firmly rooted in place qua corps/e. This was the Nietzsche who had written in *Thus Spoke Zarathustra* not of handkerchiefs dropping, it is true, but that it is the thoughts coming in our "most silent moments" and "with the feet of doves" that "guide the world."[47] Nietzsche intended this particular thought, as his thought generally, to be exoterically beautiful, esoterically chilling, and ultimately concealed by, and transmitted through, static.

As a rule of thumb, it is worse to underestimate than overestimate Nietzsche, whose influence would *be* much less had he *anticipated* less. Certainly he had taken the pulse of the mass—or, as he called it, "philistine" and "decadent"—culture of his own, early capitalist time. And this was the same time for Germany as for the rest of Europe, the United States, Japan, and increasingly the globe. He had already done so by his 1873 essay on David Friedrich Strauss, and he continued to do it in his extensive critiques of Wagner's "total work of art" *(Gesamtkunstwerk)* and, most tellingly, in his reflections on Baudelaire's *œuvres postumes,* as is revealed in Nietzsche's private notes taken near the end of his sane life.[48] And Nietzsche could have easily extrapolated the basic structures of his criticism of mass culture to take the measure of modern and postmodern spectacularization—not least radio. Although Nietzsche is widely imagined to be at the cutting edge of the avant-garde—which certainly would have included radio, had he lived to know it—it is Nietzsche's *rearguard* actions, his programming behind the scenes, that have remained in the dark.

The discovery of radium aside, basic technological prerequisites for radio were well in place within Nietzsche's sane lifetime (though my argument resists technological determinism). On December 6, 1877, "Thomas A. Edison made the first recording of the human voice onto a tinfoil roll, singing 'Mary Had a Little Lamb'"[49] Weiss continues:

> As never before voice is separated from body and eternalized in a technological mechanism—breeding the first of sundry techno-phantasies . . . where the fears, hopes, and phantasms of disembodiment are finally actualized. At the very moment that the invention of the typewriter and the practice of experimental psychophysics freed words from both their gestural significance and their meaning, and at the time that psychoanalysis dissociated meaning from consciousness, phonography transformed voice into object, marking an end to several millennia of pneumatological, ontotheological belief.[50]

To be sure, readers of the Bible accustomed to God speaking through burning bushes or prophets will find nothing new here, nor would anyone attuned to the other types of accousmatically disembodied voices. In any case, this was hardly the end, for Nietzsche, of the archaic need and desire to maintain all types of hierarchy and order of rank by the best technological means available. Rather, it was for him yet another new beginning within the great cycle of Eternal Recurrence of the Same informed by Will to Power.

Weiss suggests that "the paradox of radio" consists in the fact that "a universally public transmission is heard in the most private of circumstances; the thematic specificity of each individual broadcast, its imaginary scenario, is heard within an infinitely diverse set of nonspecific situations, different for each listener; the radio's putative shared solidarity of auditors in fact achieves their atomization as well as a reification of the imagination."[51] So it is, too, that Radio Nietzsche cannibalistically, incorporatively feeds off this paradox to produce ("interpellate") auditors receiving a universal esoteric message in the exoteric guise of maximum individuality. As pertinent for Radio Nietzsche is the fact that the omnidirectional "surround sound" of radio (in my extended, non–technologically reductive sense, and in any case unlike visually rooted, monodirectional technologies or concepts such as television) allows the consumer to do other things in the rest of the more or less private, more or less public sphere—within and without the broadcast, so to speak—yet while never being fully aware what influence the auditory experience is having on all those other activities. In this sense, sound always—ever so slightly—precedes sight (from "womb to tomb," as gynecologists and Shelley's "Ode to the West Wind" might tell us).

The properly Nietzschean articulation of aesthetics, politics, and prophecy also consists of the desire to "write"—that is, to be *"heard"* before being read—so as to have maximum possible and subcutaneous effect in the future, after the death of one's material body, under the sign of the slogan, as Nietzsche put it in 1882 (as always bastardizing Spinoza), *"sub specie trecentorum annorum"* (under the aspect of three hundred years).[52] And a year later: "To be ignited in 300 years—that is my desire for fame."[53] (Not fortuitously, Nietzsche's tercentennial timeframe was adapted by Heidegger for the proleptic dissemination of his own work.)[54] In 1881 Nietzsche spoke in social Darwinian terms of millennia, and had his own version of a millennial Reich: "The age of experiments *[Experimente]!* The claims of Darwin are to be tested—through experiments *[Versuche]!* As is the evolution of higher organisms out of the lowest. Experiments *[Versuche]* must be conducted for millennia! Raise apes into men!"[55] Raise them, that is, as work force, as the "trained gorillas" of Taylorism.[56] Now recall Nietzsche's 1880 aphorism *"Premises of the machine age"*: "The press, the machine, the railway, the telegraph are premises whose thousand-year conclusion no one has yet dared to draw." And note the striking double homology: on the one hand the relationship between Nietzsche's desire to have an effect beginning in 300 years (or millennia), his desire for prestige and its required prestidigitations, and his need for social Darwinian experiments extended into the distant future; and, on the other hand, "postmodernist" Nietzsche's implication, "prediction," or "self-fulfilling prophecy" that his effectivity would be conterminous and compossible with the development of whatever new information technologies might become available.

Lacking exposure or access to radio, film, video, HDTV, even telephones and phonographs, let alone the digital technologies of cyberspace and implant chips, and having barely discovered the typewriter, Nietzsche did know technoculture superbly well in its then most powerful mode. The Wagnerian "total work of art" was the sublime and subliminal mode of communication that is today widely viewed as a crucial protoform of virtual reality (VR).[57] Yes, Nietzsche criticized "the music drama of the future" *(Zukunftsmusik),* but not in principle, only in kind: Wagner himself had betrayed its politico-philosophical, world-historical mission to transmit "order of rank" by selling out to such epiphenomenal and counterproductive aberrations as anti-Semitism, Christianity ("Platonism for the people"), and the Germans. Presumably Nietzsche would have had the same reservations *mutatis mutandis* about any future technology, including the internet, cyberspace, and so forth. These limits of Wagner in mind, however, is precisely what led Nietzsche to produce his own "total work of art"—one much smaller in apparent scale but, it has turned out, possessing considerably greater impact and transformative power than Wagner's "artwork of the future," namely, Nietzsche's written corpus.[58] Or, more precisely, Radio Nietzsche and its corps/es.

Nietzsche's imagination as a teenager at Schulpforta turns out to have been as prescient as it was vivid. The eighteen-year-old boarding school boy dreamt of quite specific technologies of dissemination:

> It's deathly still in the room—the one sound is the pen scratching across the paper—for I love to think by writing, given that the machine that could imprint our thoughts into some material without their being spoken or written has yet to be invented. In front of me is an inkwell in which I can drown the sorrows of my black heart, a pair of scissors to accustom me to the idea of slitting my throat, manuscripts with which I can wipe myself, and a chamber pot.[59]

This text from 1862 outlines Nietzsche's subsequent project: to take advantage of the limited technology of writing to work proleptically on the "material" of the human race until more advanced techniques of subliminal and subcutaneous "imprint" might be found. And Nietzsche was to have remarkable success in sublimating and transforming the scatological, sadomasochistic, suicidal aspect of his juvenile project into a fully mature and more social process of euthanasia, one related specifically to music and to radio-active aural transmission generally. *"Compared with music,"* Nietzsche stressed, "all communication via *words* is shameless; the word dilutes and makes stupid; the word depersonalizes: the word makes the uncommon common."[60] And music is one of Radio Nietzsche's transmissions *inter alia inter pares.*

As for the precisely scatological aspect of Nietzsche's precocious teenaged fantasy of "influencing machines," it can be linked directly to radio by reference to Artaud's famous failed attempt at radio broadcast. In philosophical "translation," for Nietzsche, death is profoundly involved in the transactions between producing corpse, corpus, and receiving corps. On the one hand the mere biological contingencies of birthing and of the division of mammals into two basic (binary) sexes may all be replaced by a bio-engineering that Nietzsche's many affirmations of the necessity for the higher man's "breeding" *(Zuchtung)* give us no reason to believe he would reject.[61] On the other hand there seems to be, at least for Nietzsche, a direct homology between male birthing and the projective nature of "radio" transmission as a particular type of excrement: the expulsion of dead but potentially lethal matter. Weiss follows Freud, Bataille, and particularly Artaud to note that, like radio transmissions,

excrement, as a sign of death, is formless matter excluded from the organization of the symbolic order. It poses a threat to cultural formations both because it signifies a wasteful expenditure that circumvents societal modes of
production and because it is an originary sign of autonomous production,
of sovereign creativity bypassing societal structure of exchange. Excrement
marks the body, and not the socius, as the center of production, whence comes
the necessity, in the process of socializing the infant, of controlling anal functions and establishing the anus of possession and exclusion. This exclusion
entails, in the major irony of human ontogenesis, the rejection of one's own
body, a rejection which is the very origin of sublimation. Any desublimated return to anality in adult life marks a return of the repressed and serves as a contestation of the symbolic law.[62]

So it was in the case of young Nietzsche's prediction of imprinting technologies. But so it also was, at the outset of his academic teaching career, that
Nietzsche's then closest friend (the classical philologist Erwin Rohde) and
their harshest enemy (Ulrich von Wilamowitz-Moellendorff, an underclass-
man of Nietzsche's at Schulpforta and the dominant classical philologist of
this and the next generation) were thus not wrong to set out the terms of
debate about Nietzsche's philology in his first book *The Birth of Tragedy*—all
according to the antinomy: *Zukunftsphilologie* versus *Afterphilologie*.[63] For the
philology of Radio Nietzsche is precisely both a proleptic philology of and
for the *future* and an *anal* philology, that is, anally aggressive to maximum
effect, *ex extremis*.

Make no mistake, however. The adult Nietzsche—*Radio* Nietzsche—was
never out to contest all "symbolic orders," only those that threatened his
own "order of rank." Friedrich Kittler also cites the chamber pot passage
from the teenaged Nietzsche, whom he places at the axial passage from the
classical-romantic discourse network ("1800") to the properly modern or
postmodern ("1900"). Kittler describes this moment as "a primal scene, less
well known but no less fraught with consequences than the despair of Faust
in and over his study in the Republic of Scholars. This *(the)* scholar is replaced, however, by the very man of letters whom Faust made to appear
magically as the redeemer from heaps of books."[64] For Kittler, however,
the representative Nietzschean technology remained the typewriter, the increasingly blind Nietzsche being the first major philosopher to use this new
technology designed for, and indeed by, the blind.[65] With the typewriter
and its "psychology" (as it came to be called in 1909), a certain epistemological and ontological break arguably occurs within the discourse network:
"'in place of the image of the word [in handwriting as somatic creation]
there appears a geometrical figure created by the spatial arrangement of
the letter keys.' Indeed, a peculiar relationship to place defines the signifier: in contrast to everything in the Real, it can be and not be in its place."[66]

Whereas for Kittler the adolescent Nietzsche's "machine that could imprint our thoughts into some material without their being spoken or written," and which "has yet to be invented," remained the typewriter, I am arguing that the more radical post-Faustian, Nietzschean prosthesis of incorporation is radio and radio-activity. And it is this that *interdicts* access to the Real—at least to Nietzsche's most esoteric and unwritten version of it.

Heidegger criticized the invention of the typewriter as part of the "increasing destruction of the word" insofar as "the typewriter grabs script away from the essential domain of the hand—and this means that the hand is removed from the essential domain of the word," "degrading the word to a mere means for the traffic of communication."[67] Nietzsche, too, had no use for "mere traffic in communication"—the *very reason* to invent the more properly prosthetic and oral transmission-reception system of Radio Nietzsche. It is not (just) radio in the literal sense, say, as the extension from the writing hand to the typewriter to the telegraph already known to Nietzsche. Rather, Radio Nietzsche is (also) radio in the sense of an authorial intent to communicate influence across space and time, as a probe into the future, as a mode of Spinozist immanent causality and *actio in distans,* just slightly beneath the surface of full cognition. As Kittler notes, the physical condition of Nietzsche (and, by extension, the paradigm shift from "1800" to "1900"), including his continually worsening eyesight, undoubtedly contributed less to his abandonment of Faustian books than to the production of a particular type of book, namely, the "first experiments with telegraphic style" in 1880 in *The Wanderer and His Shadow*[68]—that is, even *before* he purchased his maladroit typewriter in 1882. But the material form of these experiments, by hand or by typewriter, was *immaterial* to Nietzsche. At stake, I argue, is a transmissive structure or discursive network of *corps/e/ing.* In *Ecce Homo: How One Becomes What One Is* (1888), in the section "Why I Write Such Good Books," Nietzsche claimed—in his now patented telegraph style— that "My eyes alone put an end to all book wormishness *[Bücherwürmerei]:* in plain language *[auf deutsch]:* philology: I was delivered from the 'book,' for years I read Nothing any more—the *most* charitable act I ever conferred upon myself!—That nethermost self *[Jenes unterste Selbst]* submerged, as it were, grown silent under the constant pressure of having to listen to other selves (—what reading means, after all!) awakened slowly, shyly, suspiciously,—but eventually *it spoke again.*"[69] And when it spoke it *(id, ça)* was radio-active.

Nietzsche's periodic and increasing near-blindness was more than a physical ailment, more than a reiterated theme in his correspondence during the last years of his sanity. In response to Nietzsche's painful near-blindness, his secretary, the musician and composer Heinrich Köselitz (known as Peter Gast), encouraged Nietzsche in September 1888: "You have dragged your artillery to the highest mountains, you have guns such as have never existed, and even if you shoot blindly you will inspire terror all around."[70] Two months later, ever closer to breakdown in Turin (1888–89), Nietzsche wrote Danish literary critic Georg Brandes, who was serving to open up synapses and receptors to Nietzsche's work in Europe: "I am an old artillery man and I can fire heavier cannons than anyone has ever dreamed existed."[71] And in one of his last published texts, the section of his "autobiography" *Ecce Homo* entitled "Why I Am a Destiny," Nietzsche famously defined himself as "dynamite."[72] Which is to say, not only an artillery man but a munitions expert, a sapper, the great Old Mole of the "right" (which is to say always slightly more than of the "left"). What Nietzsche obviously (logically) chose *not* to say was where the dynamite was planted and when it was timed to explode. But this kind of openly bellicose remark—whether about artillery in private or dynamite in public—is one of Nietzsche's many more or less public ruses or masks, his ruse of reason. In fact, the deepest mode of warfare of this near-blind philosopher and superbly trained classical philologist was not artillery or land mines but the radioactivity that remains undetected by anything but the most refined philological Geiger counter.

Much of Nietzsche's original genius and subsequent afterlife lies in his extraordinary ability to transform ("sublimate," one might suppose) his painful near-blindness and other illnesses (which appear to have been more somatic than psychological, which is also to say psychosomatic) into *concepts*—concepts that were "new" *and* hence to have these (in fact exceedingly "old") concepts incorporated by readers beneath the surface of cognition by his ruse of reason. For their part, Deleuze and Guattari follow Spinoza, Nietzsche, and Marx to say that "The concept is an incorporeal, even though it is incarnated or effectuated in bodies."[73] Spinoza's principle of immanent causality, that the cause "indwells its effects," eminently prefigures Marx's critique of leftist idealism: "The weapon of criticism cannot, of course, replace criticism by weapons, material force must be overthrown by material force; but theory also becomes a material force as soon as it has gripped the masses. Theory is capable of gripping the masses as soon as it demonstrates *ad hominem*, and it demonstrates *ad hominem* as soon as it becomes radical. To be radical is to grasp the root of the matter."[74] As most succinctly defined already by Kant, "an *argumentum ad hominem* is an argument that obviously is not true for everyone, but still serves to reduce someone to silence."[75] Nietzsche was a radical philosopher defined in just this sense; but his ideological and political commitment was the reverse of Marx's insofar as his *centrum* of radiographic transmission and incorporation was in principle esoteric and surreptitious, whereas the enlightenment commitment of Marx was to maximum possible exposure, rendering Marxism to date incapable of locating or even knowing about the Nietzschean *centrum*. In this regard Althusser was right to suggest that Nietzsche had proceeded Freud in developing "a theory of ideological hallucination."[76] Which is also certainly not the worst description of Radio Nietzsche.

If I am on the right track, tracking Nietzsche correctly, whenever it speaks, Nietzsche's voice speaks "radio-actively." Lacoue-Labarthe has suggested in his analysis of what he calls "the echo of the subject" that the modern subject has been formed—in a trajectory from Schopenhauer, Wagner, and Nietzsche to Theodor Reik—not only visually, representationally, under the sign of Apollo, but also under the sign of Dionysus. Which is to say musically, aurally, willfully, and as an echo not of "signification" but of a "significance" that is *sensu stricto* not "of the order of language."[77] Rather, in Lacoue-Labarthe's words, "it affects a language, and affects in the use of a language . . . its *musical* part, prosodic or melodic," in order to produce a mode of communication and response "that is capable of offering infinitely greater material, according to Reik, than what is given to us by conscious perception."[78] But this is also why what is crucially at stake *for* Nietzsche is the production of a constitutive problem *in* Nietzsche, that of *Stimmung*— of voice, fine tuning, and mood.[79] It remains here to illustrate how such a Nietzschean mood has been proleptically transmitted across space and time in and by Radio Nietzsche, in ways that "translators" and "creators" alike are unaware and that forge ostensibly rival "creations" and "translations" into the harmony of unacknowledged consensus. And when "class struggle in the specific element of theory" still today might be the more appropriate response, necessary though insufficient.

"THESE GOOD EUROPEANS": THE ADORNO-HORKHEIMER-GADAMER CONSENSUS

> *However far language might slip into a technical function, as language it holds the invariable things in our nature fast, those things which come to be spoken of in language again and again. And the language of philosophy, as long as it remains language, will remain a dialogue with that language of the world.*
> GADAMER, *Hegel's Dialectic*

> *Everything that is thought, written, painted, composed, even built and formed, belongs either to monologic art or to art before witnesses. Among the latter is to be taken into account even that apparently monologue-art which involves faith in God, the entire lyric of prayer: because for the pious there is as yet no solitude—this invention was made only by us, the godless. I know no more profound difference in the entire optic of an artist than this: whether he looks out from his work in progress (at "himself") with the eye of a witness, or whether he has "forgotten the world," which is the essence of all monologic art. It is based on forgetting, it is the music of forgetting.*
> NIETZSCHE, *The Gay Science*

Let us now turn back to the year 1950 as the symbolic and actual halfway point between the death of Nietzsche's corpse, the concomitant birth of his corps, and the centennial of that birth and death at the turn of the next century. This is not quite the 300 years or millennia staked out by Nietzsche before his death in 1900 for his philosophical conclusions to be reached by means of the premises of the technologies that were his own written and spoken transmissions. But it is proximate enough.

Nineteen fifty marked the half century after Nietzsche's death with several public events. Above all, in retrospect, there was Bataille's remark that "Nietzsche's position is the only one outside of communism"[80]—a thought whose repercussions have only now begun to be played out in social as well as intellectual history, for we find ourselves in a situation in which, assuming "the death of communism," Nietzsche and Nietzscheanism have become totalitarian, globally hegemonic. Nineteen fifty also saw the affirmation and reaffirmation of Nietzsche as an "existentialist" philosopher, albeit one working in basic solidarity within the antifoundational tradition of enlightenment critique. This interpretation was codified philosophically in the recent republication and discussion of the 1936 Nietzsche book by Karl Jaspers, and publicized in the English-speaking world by Walter Kaufmann's obsessive and influential rehabilitation of existentialism and especially of Nietzsche. Particularly in Germany, 1950 celebrated Nietzsche with several more public occurrences, including two major radio shows. The second of these remains relatively well known (at least in Germany), namely, Gottfried Benn's broadcast entitled "Nietzsche—nach fünfzig Jahren" (Nietzsche—after fifty years). It was transmitted from Berlin on August 25, fifty years to the day after Nietzsche's death. Benn not only depicted Nietzsche hyperbolically as "the most far reaching giant of the post-Goethean epoch" but also radiophonically as "die größte Ausstrahlungsphänomen der Geistesgeschichte."[81] Which we can now translate as "the greatest phenomenon of radiation, of radio and radioactivity, in the history of consciousness." A year earlier Benn had celebrated what he called *Radardenken* (radar thinking).[82] He now turned, on radio, to Nietzsche. Benn not merely affirmatively *constated* Nietzsche's commitment to "monologic art," he also *reperformed* it in his patented monotone, producing a hagiographic levitation rite around Nietzsche's corpse. The first radio show on Nietzsche had already taken place at the end of July, and is today almost wholly unknown or forgotten. Whereas Benn's broadcast was a self-conscious monologue about a monologue, the first broadcast was to have been a dialogue. In other terms, Benn's format was far closer to the spirit of Nietzsche than had been the first transmission; if the latter had been designed as a proleptic strike against Benn's position, it failed miserably. In this respect it has justly sunk into virtual oblivion.

That an unacknowledged consensus with regard to Nietzsche cuts across virtually all ideological differences is succinctly illustrated by this second broadcast, "Über Nietzsche und uns: Zum 50. Todestag des Philosophen"

(On Nietzsche and us: for the 50th anniversary of the philosopher's death).[83] The participants in the Frankfurt studio represented supposedly rival wings of German philosophy: Adorno and moderator Horkheimer for Marxian critical theory; and Gadamer for Heideggerian fundamental ontology translated into philosophical hermeneutics and the philosophy of "dialogue." Whereas Benn explicitly embraced Nietzsche's own dictum that great art has absolutely nothing to do with communication or dialogue—being in its essence monologue—Horkheimer and Adorno (in spite of their Nietzschean lip service to true art as hermetically sealed off from mass culture) ignored this thematic entirely, choosing instead to follow the Gadamerian dictum that true philosophy is in essence dialogical. Thus, this intended "dialogue" was bipartite, incorporating 1) all three philosophers in dialogue with Nietzsche, and 2) dialogue between Gadamer on the "right" and his two interlocutors on the "left."

Now, specifically German philosophy—as well as *mutatis mutandis* continental European philosophy in the last three-quarters of the twentieth century, its high-modernist moment—was defined by three texts published in a half-decade of the Weimar period: Wittgenstein's *Tractatus logico-philosophicus* in 1921; Lukács's *History and Class-Consciousness* in 1923–24; and the never-completed torso of Heidegger's *Being and Time* in 1927. "These three works, the most influential philosophical writings of this century, originated from, and defined themselves in relation to, certain traditions which they themselves brought to an end."[84] The effect of National Socialism, on at least German academic philosophy, was to eliminate or radically diminish—and not just temporarily between 1933 and 1946—the impact of two of these three seminal works, their traditions and legacies. Both the analytic, postpositivist, and latter common-language tendency and the Hegelian-Marxist tendency were both effectively terminated or deformed during the Third Reich and its immediate aftermath. All that remained more or less intact was the Nietzschean-Heideggerian tendency, most notably represented after World War II by Gadamer. When analytic philosophy and Marxism belatedly began to return, as the latter did in the work of Horkheimer and Adorno's Frankfurt School of Social Research, they were critically but indelibly effected by the Heideggerian—hence Nietzschean—tendency.[85] This, then, is the sociological explanation for the symptomatic and exemplary modern "virtual consensus" that I identify as Radio Nietzsche. But mere sociology is never adequate even to describe, let alone explain, such complex issues.

In the 1950 Frankfurt "conversation," despite minor differences of opinion about Nietzsche (having to do, I would argue, with different views of Heidegger), there turned out to be remarkably few real bones of contention. In short, yet another consensus under capitalist hegemony. What was really at stake, in other words, was already the German complement to the later French station of Radio Nietzsche as "The New Nietzsche"—from which the ultraconservative Benn's position had been tacitly excluded. At explicit general stake for Horkheimer, Adorno, and Gadamer was the question of *whether*—but not how or why—we can take any utterance "literally or figuratively." At the beginning of the broadcast Gadamer and Adorno both quickly accepted Horkheimer's basic premise that the problem not merely with reading Nietzsche (i.e., solving the enigma of whether he was a "good enlightenment liberal" or instead a "bad fascist elitist") but also with modernity *tout court* occurs when any reader "takes what Nietzsche wrote literally." For Horkheimer, Adorno and Gadamer quickly concurring, it is specifically "American and Russian" society that takes things "too literally," with properly German thought moving with dialectical precision in between.

Now, remarkably, this is the philosophical version of the social "convergence theory" that has deep, and problematic, roots in nineteenth-century German conservative thought. As recently as the 1930s, for Heidegger and (other) Nazis alike, this theory had held that the United States and the USSR had developed into an "in-essence-the-same" syndico-technical form of society.[86] This entailed the proposition that Germany, "the heart of Europe" *(Hölderlin),* must seek its proper "third way" between and beyond the "pincers" of "Americanism and Bolshevism." (Similar national and social self-legitimations were global, most visibly in Japan.) In this matter, there was also a difference. Our three German panelists concurred that "Americanism" (read: pragmatism, Fordism, Taylorism, pluralism, multiculturalism, liberal democracy, culture industry and mass culture, and so on) necessarily entails the instrumentalization of *language* and the latter's "reduction to statements and propositions" (as Horkheimer put it). By contrast, under Soviet communism, "every word is a thesis for which one can die, if taken at one's word." But these "two cultures" have one *tertium quid* that Nietzsche is said by the consensus to expose, critique, and properly reject—definitively.

On the consensus view, the relentless, unreflecting tendency of both "rival" cultures is "to take language literally" (in Horkheimer's words), rendering it "simply impossible"—*de facto et de jure*—even to read a Nietzsche who, as Horkheimer, Adorno, and Gadamer all simply presuppose, used language in a "radically different" manner from the "American-Russian" paradigm. Gadamer prefers to say that Nietzsche was a "parodist," while Adorno (and, years later, Rorty) favors "ironist," but in the matter of celebrating Nietzsche it all amounted to the same thing.[87] And it may not have mattered much, ideologically, if others had been invited to the Frankfurt studio that evening in 1950. "When everyone is invited, it is not the hoped-for new science that is being invited (for it is never the result of a gathering of specialists who are ignorant of it), but a character no one has invited—and whom it is not necessary to invite, since it invites itself!—the *common theoretical ideology* that silently inhabits the 'consciousness' of all these specialists: when they gather together, it speaks out loud—through their voice."[88] In our case here, Nietzsche's voice transmitted from his *centrum*.

On this consensus assumption, Nietzsche never quite meant what he said, never *could* mean what he said. In short, a prohibition performatively becomes a constated impossibility. So it is, for the Frankfurt consensus, that both the Nazi "misappropriation" of Nietzsche and the "whitewashing" of his elitism by well-meaning liberal-existentialist philosophers (meaning Jaspers and especially Kaufmann) were equally misguided, equally literal, potentially "totalitarian" even. Such were the explicit terms employed in the Frankfurt studio. Paradoxically, however, this same ideological consensus holds that in *one* matter we *can* read Nietzsche literally, after all. That is, *his own* remarks ought never to be taken . . . literally. To be precise: Sometimes we can read Nietzsche literally, sometimes figuratively, or we can conflate the two, but in any case we don't need to get exercised about his intentions, because the one thing we can take at face value is his own claim to be a "free spirit," "smasher of all idols," "perspectivist," "parodist," "ironist," "thinker on stage," "enlightener," "great emancipator of humankind," and so forth, *ad infinitum et nauseam*.

This *a priori* "logic" with regard to reading Nietzsche is thus at root benevolent about what he intended to say, in spite of the subsequent "misrecognition" by all others who take him too literally in one literal direction or another. Yet this "logic" itself remains binary and dualist, rendering it impossible for Nietzsche ever to have said something different or more radical than the consensus can ever see and hear. And what it cannot see and hear is his One Aim, his ruse of reason. This "German consensus" "left," "right," and "center"—there are equivalent national variants everywhere, from the French Derrida and Deleuze to the North Atlantic Rorty and across the Pacific—*tacitly* embodies Nietzsche/anism, never worrying why "we" ought to take him literally *only* when *he* might ordain it. If by stating propositions as conclusions without premises we fall short of philosophy, then the Nietzschean consensus falls short *of* Radio Nietzsche because it is already always informed and incorporated *by* Radio Nietzsche. This is not avant-garde radio but slapstick radio—philosophically speaking, speaking with the esoteric Nietzsche himself. He would have had as little use for Gadamer as he would have had for Adorno and Horkheimer (or Benn)—*except* insofar as he was effectively using all of them to prevent access to any alternative way of approaching him.

What matters most in Radio Nietzsche *cannot* be perceptible at the level of *theme* or *dialogue*. This includes even the fact that what he meant by "fateful" is the task to split future humanity in two by subliminal rhetorical means up to and including suicide and euthanasia. Rather, what matters are his *illocutionary means to this end and their actual perlocutionary effect*. In other terms, all auditors and speakers within Nietzscheanism—alongside capital-

ism itself, the subtending instance of immanent causality in our epoch—
have been programmed by Nietzsche to be embodied as corpse and as corps
by the medium of his corpus. This incorporation or "translation" of Nietzsche's philosophical corpse and corpus by his corps was consciously *incepted*
and *produced* as *Stimmung*. As such, it is not receivable as any mere theme
or content that might ever be detected except unconsciously. Like his God,
Nietzsche himself is neither dead nor eternal, but unconscious. This in
mind, we return to Radio Nietzsche in 1950.

Here is Horkheimer introducing the radio broadcast "On Nietzsche
and Us":

> Nietzsche predicted that in Germany one would erect monuments to him
> when he could no longer defend himself. Radio he could not have fore-
> seen. What would he have indeed said if he had foreseen that we—you
> Mr. Gadamer, and you Mr. Adorno—would sit together and solemnly con-
> verse about him on the fiftieth anniversary of his death? Why are we really
> here?

These remarks at the half-century mark of Nietzsche's death were imprecise
if not simply mistaken. The question remains, as we have passed the centenary of that death: Are we any less imprecise and mistaken about Mr. Nietzsche? In any case, the reason Horkheimer, Adorno, and Gadamer were "really here" was that they had gathered unconsciously to embody Nietzsche's
corpse and voice. They all "overheard"—*and hence reiterated*—all the "punctuation marks" of Nietzsche's *centrum*.

If you listen to the finale of the 1950 broadcast you will hear—more
or less unconsciously—not Hans-Georg Gadamer but *Pastorsohn* Friedrich
Nietzsche ventriloquizing the voice of Gadamer, intoning platitudes about
Nietzsche's place of birth and burial in the context, or "horizon," of "world
history." Whereas Benn was simultaneously to perform and constate his embrace of Nietzschean monologue, Gadamer's voice performed precisely the
monologue that his own philosophy explicitly rejected at the level of constatation. This Nietzschean voice—not its message or content but its *Stimmung*—makes serious critical confrontation with Nietzsche as impossible as
does the excited, sharper, and apparently more critical theoretical voices
of Adorno and Horkheimer. *All* are modulations of Nietzsche's own voice.
All Nietzscheans speak in his medium, Radio Nietzsche, as mediums for
this near-blind living or dead man, and never fully in their own voice. This
Adorno-Horkheimer-Gadamer broadcast in 1950 was not a "conversation"
or "dialogue" about Nietzsche at all—*except* on an exoteric level handi-
capped in advance by Nietzsche exo/esoterically. And not by chance, this
broadcast was yet another preliminary, performative celebration of "the
death of communism." The "only" difference between the way Gadamer on
the one side and Adorno and Horkheimer on the other received Radio

Nietzsche is that the former was arguably a conscious collaborator with Nietzsche's project, whereas the latter were merely unconscious dupes.[89]

So I agree with Kōjin Karatani's attempt to shift the drift of what he calls "secular criticism" (at the end of a twentieth century globally marked by the purported death of communism and the factual resurgence of religious fanaticism and theocratic states) *away* from literary criticism, much psychoanalysis, and cultural studies *toward* philosophy and proper psychoanalysis (a shift I find more properly informed by Althusser, Lacan, and Karatani than by Derrida or Deleuze). Alluding to Marx's critique of Hegel's *Philosophy of Law*, Karatani interprets Marx to be arguing "that it is impossible to dissolve any religion unless the 'real suffering' upon which every religion is based is dissolved. There is no reason to criticize religion theoretically, because it can only be dissolved practically."[90] *Pace* Karatani, however, I do not regard Nietzsche as an immediate ally in any argument.[91] Nietzsche and his repercussions are a form of religion across the ideological spectrum. But this difference aside, I tend to concur with Karatani's thesis that, in our times, "religion, albeit as *Schein,* has a certain necessity inasmuch as man is an existence of passivity (pathos); it functions 'regulatively' as a protest against reality, if not a 'constitution' of reality." Karatani continues:

> Although communism as well is a mere *Schein,* to criticize its "illusion" means no more and no less than "to call on [people] to give up a condition that requires illusions." And religion will be upheld so long as this state of affairs endures. We can never dissolve fundamentalism by the criticisms or dialogues motivated by enlightenment, precisely because to criticize the "illusion" of the latter is "to call on them to give up a condition that requires illusions." The advocating of the collapse of *Idee* and the insistence on its realization are, in fact, intertwined and inseparable, and both are *Schein* that represent, each in its own way, the real (the thing-in-itself) of world capitalism, of which they themselves are members.[92]

It is *this* real that Nietzsche—and the consensus of all Nietzscheans—ultimately monologically has closed off from any "conversation" or "dialogue." If, as I argue, Nietzsche and Nietzscheanism—Nietzsche's corps/e—constitute the radically unquestioned ideological support—the *Idee*—of the fundamentalism known as late capitalist hegemony, then this would also confirm *per negationem* Bataille's 1950 thesis that communism remains the only position outside of Nietzscheanism. For worse or for better.

Closer inspection of Nietzsche's writing than is normally granted it across the ideological spectrum would reveal that it is too simple to say that he was "against" socialism or communism, at least not in any easily identifiable sense. After all, Radio Nietzsche is programmed not to be part of any enlightenment problematic, except exoterically. Here what we consciously hear is incepted to appear different from what we unconsciously get. There is never any easy answer to the question of esotericism, of radio-activity, if only because *totally* esoteric writers would leave *no* trace of this intent— "a demonstrably exoteric text is a contradiction in terms."[93] And Nietzsche *did* leave some trace—if only sigetically, in the rhetoric of allusion by silence. Nor, as obviously, should one ever assume that what Nietzsche intended to communicate covertly was always expressed with equal finesse or effectiveness. Nonetheless, the fact remains that, to date, the "right" has grasped this entire problematic of Nietzsche better than has the "left," which has never really grasped it at all.

No matter how the public face of a text like *Beyond Good and Evil* might appear to anyone, the esoteric intent was crystal clear in Nietzsche's mind, the mind of this prototypical "good European." In 1885 he wrote to himself in his now patented telegraphic mode:

> *These Good Europeans* that we are: What distinguishes us from the Men of the Fatherland? First, we are atheists and immoralists, but for the time being *[zunächst]* we support the religions and morals of the herd instinct: for these prepare a type of human that must one day fall into our hands, that must *desire* our hands. Beyond Good and Evil, but we demand the unconditional maintenance of the herd morality. We hold in reserve many types of philosophy that need to be taught: Under some conditions the pessimistic type, as hammer; a European Buddhism might perhaps be indispensable. We probably support the development and maturing of democratic institutions: They enhance weakness of the will: We see in "Socialism" a goad that in the face of comfort— — — Position toward nations [or peoples: *Völkern*]. Our preferences; we pay attention to the results of interbreeding . . . . By possessing a *disciplina voluntatis,* we are in advance of our fellow men. All strength applied to *the development of will power,* an art that allows us to wear masks, an art of understanding *beyond* affects (also to think a "supra-European" manner on occasion).[94]

That Nietzsche wears illocutionary masks is hardly news.[95] What is at issue is the *kind* of mask he adapts as the occasion demands, the fact that he intended these masks to look like one thing and yet have another effect entirely, and the more or less unconscious effect—"beyond affect"—that his masks have on "readers" and "viewers"—but above all "listeners" who for him should better die than live. And not just listeners in Derrida's sense of *otobiographie* or "biography of the ear," who still appeal to the considerable, but still merely rational, powers of deconstruction, and thus delude themselves into thinking that they can thereby deconstruct "Nietzsche's teaching" and "politics of the proper name."[96] As our *nom-du-père,* to speak Lacanian, Nietzsche has *no* proper *name.*

Any broadcaster is not only Machiavellian but also "Jesuit" or "Jesuitical," in the extended Gramscian sense, who declines, in principle or in practice, "to elaborate a modern 'humanism' able to reach right to the simplest and most uneducated classes,"[97] and who engages in conspiratorial, esoteric writing in the prophylactic project *against* the masses. Nietzsche ultimately admired only one form of "art": "The work of art where it appears without artist: e.g., as body, as organization (Prussian officer corps, Jesuit order). To what extent is the artist only a preliminary stage? What does the 'subject' mean—?"[98] Answer: anyone within "order of rank." But, like his relationship toward socialism, Nietzsche's Jesuitism is exo/esoterically complex. Even the most hostile (and sometimes accurate) things he said in public against "democracy" and the like were intended as exoteric posturing. While working out the illocutionary strategy of *Thus Spoke Zarathustra,* he noted: "Zarathustra [is] happy about the fact that class war is *over,* and now there is finally time for a rank ordering of Individuals. Hatred against the democratic system of leveling is only *foreground:* in fact he [Zarathustra] is very happy that *this has come thus far.* Now he can finish his task. —"[99] But then it was never to be *Zarathustra's* task that would be at ultimate stake in any new world order. At stake is Radio Nietzsche, and our "voluntary" way of hearing and overhearing it.

FAIRE UN ENFANT DANS LE DOS

> *What seems to happen before their eyes happens, in reality, behind their backs.*
> ALTHUSSER, *Philosophy and the Spontaneous Philosophy of the Scientists*

I'm almost tempted to conclude my counter-transmission with that old line from Leonard Cohen: "You can say that I've grown bitter, but of one thing you can be sure, the rich have got their channels in the bedrooms of the poor."[100] For so it is that we—all of us—always risk falling short of philosophy, falling on our collective face. And Nietzsche could be held responsible. But one final caveat about the problem of holding trickster Nietzsche responsible. Slapstick indeed!

The recently suicided Gilles Deleuze once turned a remarkable, untranslatable phrase to express how difficult it is to translate philosophy in general, and that of Nietzsche in specific. Deleuze remarked that, for him,

> the history of philosophy is a sort of buggery or (it comes to the same thing) immaculate conception. I saw myself as taking an author from behind and giving him a child that would be his own offspring, yet monstrous. It was really important for it to be his own child, because the author had actually to say all I had him saying. But the child was bound to be monstrous too, because it resulted from all sorts of shifting, slipping, dislocations, and hidden emissions that I really enjoyed.[101]

Now Deleuze turned to face the problem of Nietzsche. "It was Nietzsche, who . . . extricated me from all this. Because you can't deal with him in the same sort of way. He gets up to all sorts of things behind your back *[Des en-*

fants dans le dos, c'est lui qui vous en fait]."[102] In French to do something behind your back is *faire un enfant dans le dos.* In Deleuze's language, his own
epitaph might then read: *Des enfants nietzschéens dans le dos, c'est lui qui vous
en fait.* In impossible translation: Nietzsche sneaks up on you from behind
and gives you monstrous children. He does this—he makes us fall short
of philosophy and his most fundamental premises, his *centrum*—by means
of the omnidirectional "oral" emissions of Radio Nietzsche, as Radio Nietzsche. As such, like God, Nietzsche remains both dead and eternal—unconscious. If to date his effect has indeed been mainly prophylactic—not to
create the higher man but only to incorporate possible opponents into his
own corps—then this was quite sufficient and necessary for the time being.
From beginning to end, Nietzsche never intended to broadcast to any present time exclusively, but always into the future. Just like God and capitalism themselves.

NOTES

This essay is the second of a two-part essay on Radio Nietzsche originally written for
this commemoration of Hans-Georg Gadamer and his repercussions. In the meantime, Yutaka Nagahara has translated part one in the Japanese journal *Gendai shizō*
[Contemporary thought] 26, no. 14 (1998): 188–219. The two parts will be united
in my forthcoming book, *Traces of Communism in Capitalist Culture: Essays in the Premodern Postmodern.* With the exception of what I now call its prologue (including
notes) and unless otherwise remarked, the current essay is essentially the same as
the one commented upon in this volume by Catherine H. Zuckert.

1. Louis Althusser, *Machiavelli and Us* [ca. 1962], trans. Gregory Elliott (London:
Verso, 1999), 8. *Le vide d'une distance prise* is one of Althusser's several basic definitions of philosophy (which include the Platonic *synoptikos*).
2. See *Gadamer's Century: Essays in Honor of Hans-Georg Gadamer,* ed. Jeff Malpas,
Ulrich Arnswald, and Jens Kertscher (Cambridge, Mass.: MIT Press, 2002).
3. Although he refers several times to this differentiation, see especially Hans-
Georg Gadamer, "Text und Interpretation" [1984] (GW2:330–60; here 334). For
the original remark and context, see Gadamer and Leo Strauss, "Correspondence
Concerning *Wahrheit und Methode,*" *Independent Journal of Philosophy* 2 (1978): 5–12.
In his magnum opus Gadamer had analyzed Dilthey in detail and Nietzsche hardly
at all, though he did make the following passing remark. "In raising the question
of being and thus reversing the whole direction of Western metaphysics, the true
predecessor of Heidegger was neither Dilthey nor Husserl . . . but rather *Nietzsche.*
Heidegger may have realized this later; but in retrospect we can see that the aims already implicit in *Being and Time* were to raise Nietzsche's radical critique of 'Platonism' to the level of the tradition he criticizes, to confront Western metaphysics on its
own level, and to recognize that transcendental inquiry is a consequence of modern
subjectivity, and so overcome it." Gadamer, *TM* 257–58.

4. On Nietzsche as having been in effect Strauss's "point of critical orientation," see the anti-Straussian account by Shadia B. Drury, *The Political Ideas of Leo Strauss* (New York: St. Martin's, 1988), and the pro-Straussian account by Lawrence Lampert, *Leo Strauss and Nietzsche* (Chicago: University of Chicago Press, 1996).

5. Scholarly discussion of the Dilthey-Nietzsche contretemps (originally mediated by their mutual acquaintance, Heinrich von Stein) began around 1939 but reached its first important stage a decade later in two essays. Jan Kamerbeek's essay, "Dilthey versus Nietzsche," *Studia philosophica* 10 (1950): 52–84 (favoring Nietzsche), was followed by Georg Misch's attempted rebuttal (favoring Dilthey), "Dilthey versus Nietzsche: Eine Stimme aus den Niederlanden, Randbemerkungen," *Die Sammlung* 7 (1952): 378–95. (Misch, Dilthey's son in law, intended his title to be dismissive.) Several important analyses have appeared in the meantime. See Antonio Negri, *Saggi sullo storicismo tedesco: Dilthey e Meinecke* (Milan: Feltrinelli, 1959), 124–29; Helmut Pfotenhauer, "Mythos, Natur und historische Hermeneutik: Nietzsches Stellung zu Dilthey und einigen 'lebensphilosophischen' Konzeptionen um die Jahrhundertwende," *Literaturmagazin* 12 (1980): 329–72; Johann Figl, "Nietzsche und die philosophischen Hermeneutik des 20. Jahrhunderts: Mit besonderer Berücksichtigung Diltheys, Heideggers und Gadamers," *Nietzsche-Studien* 10 (1980–81): 408–41; Ernst Wolfgang Orth, "Phänomenologie und spekulative Ontologie bei Dilthey und Nietzsche," in *Dilthey und der Wandel des Philosophiebegriffs seit dem 19. Jahrhundert,* ed. Ernst Wolfgang Orth (Freiburg im Breisgau: Karl Alber, 1984), 80–120; and Alfredo Marini, *Alle origini della filosofia contemporanea: Wilhelm Dilthey* (Florence: La Nuova Italia, 1984), esp. 163–94.

6. Heidegger, *Beiträge zur Philosophie (Vom Ereignis)* [1936–38], ed. Friedrich-Wilhelm von Hermann, in *Gesamtausgabe* (Frankfurt am Main: Vittorio Klostermann, 1989), 65: 253, and *Nietzsche* (Pfullingen: Neske, 1961), 2: 110.

7. See Heidegger, "Platons Lehre von der Wahrheit" [1930–31; first published 1942], in *Wegmarken* (Frankfurt am Main: Vittorio Klostermann, 1967), 109–44; here 109, and *Nietzsche,* 1: 158.

8. See Heidegger, *Beiträge zur Philosophie,* in *Gesamtausgabe,* 65: 235. Heidegger was most explicit about Nietzsche and Hölderlin in this regard in this self-described "esoteric" and "sigetic" text written during the Third Reich, but unpublished until 1989 (though some insiders had had prior access, including Otto Pöggeler and perhaps Gadamer). But Heidegger had said much the same thing more publicly in his 1937–38 lecture course, *Grundfragen der Philosophie: Ausgewählte "Probleme" der "Logik"* (Foundational questions of philosophy: selected "problems" of "logic"), first published in 1984 as volume 45 of the *Gesamtausgabe.* This publication must have put peculiar pressure on Heideggerians to practice their "damage control"—considerably before the scandal unleashed by Victor Farías and then Hugo Ott several years later.

9. To take on Dilthey as your "point of critical orientation" hardly entails rejecting esotericism, even when done to distance yourself from more explicit esotericists like Nietzsche, Heidegger, and Strauss. As is well known and discussed at length in *Wahrheit und Methode,* a crucial text for Heidegger in developing the analytic of historicity in *Sein und Zeit* was the correspondence between Dilthey and Count Yorck von Wartenburg, then just recently published. Gadamer does not mention that the very first letter contains Yorck's stern caveat that he and Dilthey never divulge them-

selves fully even in this ostensibly private medium because the deepest thoughts must remain unwritten, at most orally transmitted. After all, "what is of superior rank wears superior garb, pearls are worthless to fatten swine." Paul Yorck von Wartenburg to Dilthey, November 23, 1877, in *Briefwechsel zwischen Wilhelm Dilthey und dem Grafen Paul Yorck v. Wartenburg 1877–1897*, ed. Sigrid von der Schulenburg (Halle [Saale]: Max Niemeyer, 1923), 1–2; here 1. Their entire exchange remained under that caution flag.

10. Gadamer, "Destruktion und Dekonstruktion" [1985] (GW2:361–72; here 368, 372). For the original contretemps between Derrida and Gadamer, see *Text und Interpretation: Deutsch-französische Debatte*, ed. Philippe Forget (Munich: Fink, 1984). If I may be allowed a personal reminiscence, I was privy to some of the thoughts that went into "Destruktion und Dekonstruktion" (which I was later to translate). Gadamer told me that he considered it to be one of his most compressed and important interventions into current philosophical debates.

11. See Gadamer, "Nietzsche—der Antipode" [1984] (GW4:448–62). On the importance of Zarathustra's animals, compare Heidegger, "Wer ist Nietzsches Zarathustra?" [1953], in *Vorträge und Aufsätze* (Pfullingen: Neske, 1954), 1: 101–26. This is a compressed version of the argument in *Was heißt Denken?* [Freiburg winter semester 1951–52 and summer semester 1952] (Tübingen: Max Niemeyer, 1954).

12. Leo Strauss, *On Plato's Symposium* [Chicago fall semester 1959], ed. Seth Benardete (Chicago: University of Chicago Press, 2001), 8, 9.

13. Jean Grondin, "Gadamer's Basic Understanding of Understanding," in *The Cambridge Companion to Gadamer*, ed. Robert J. Dostal (Cambridge: Cambridge University Press, 2002), 36–51, here 49.

14. Gadamer, *Truth and Method*, 294. Compare Gadamer, *Wahrheit und Methode* (GW1:300).

15. Gadamer, *Wahrheit und Methode* (GW1:300, n. 224). Despite its revisions of the execrable first translation, the currently official English text often remains unusable, as it does here: "There is one exception to this anticipation of completeness, namely the case of writing that is presenting something in disguise, e.g., a *roman à clef*. This presents one of the most difficult hermeneutical problems." Gadamer, *Truth and Method*, 295–96, n. 22.

16. Friedrich Schleiermacher, "General Hermeneutics" [1909], in *Hermeneutics and Criticism, And Other Writings*, ed. and trans. Andrew Bowie (Cambridge: Cambridge University Press, 1998), 225–68; here 266; emphasis added. This dictum (no. 45) follows immediately from Schleiermacher's more familiar one (no. 44), a bone of contention between Strauss and Gadamer: "Complete understanding grasped in its highest form is an understanding of the utterer better than he understands himself" (ibid.).

17. See especially Gadamer, "Hermeneutik und Historismus" [1961] (GW2: 386–424), as well as Ernest L. Fortin's interview with Gadamer in 1981, published as "Gadamer on Strauss: An Interview," *Interpretation* 12, no. 1 (1984): 1–13. This interview is particularly disappointing (innocuous and mutually congratulatory), particularly given the venue in which it was eventually published.

18. See Aristotle, *Physics* 209b14; also Plato, Second Letter 314b–c; Seventh Letter 341b, 344c–d; and *Phædrus* 264b–c, 275c–276b; also Leo Strauss, *The City and Man* [1962–64] (Chicago: University of Chicago Press, 1977), 52–62. In addition

to Gadamer's references or allusions to the unwritten philosophy in *Wahrheit und Methode* and the many other places where he privileges the spoken over the written (though not normally in the sense meant by Derrida's "logocentricity"), see especially "Dialektik und Sophistik im siebenten Platonischen Brief" [1964] (GW6: 90–115) (where he is particularly adroit in sidestepping some of the most important structures and implications of esotericism, however). Gadamer's interpretation (and indeed embrace) of the "unwritten" essence of philosophy is less radical than the additional stress placed by the most influential modern practitioners of esotericism—Nietzsche and Heidegger—on the "unsaid." They follow the ancient definition of philosophy as the capacity to be silent. See, for example, Boethius, *Philosophiæ consolationis* 2: 74–77, and Nietzsche, *Human-All-Too-Human,* preface, section 8. For Heidegger, "the capacity to be silent *[Schweigenkönnen]* is the very origin of language" and "to be silent *[Schweigen]* is the specific, excellent way and means of the capacity to speak *[des Redenkönnens].*" Heidegger, *Vom Wesen der Wahrheit* [Freiburg winter semester 1933–34], in *Sein und Wahrheit,* ed. Hartmut Tietjen, in *Gesamtausgabe* (Frankfurt am Main: Vittorio Klostermann, 2001), 36/37: 81–264, here 107, 109. In a particularly sibylline phrase, "What is merely not spoken does not preserve the unspoken." Heidegger, "'Germanien': Das Unausgesprochene" [1943], in *Zu Hölderlin [und] Griechenlandreise,* ed. Curd Ochwadt, in *Gesamtausgabe* (Frankfurt am Main: Vittorio Klostermann, 2000), 75: 279–86; here 279. Gadamer selected as epigraph for his *Philosophical Apprenticeships* the Baconian *de nobis ispsis silemus,* which is remarkable not least because this text contains one of his few extended discussions of his activities during the Third Reich. The significance of this epigraph as a traditional index of the presence esotericism has gone unnoticed or has been trivialized by Gadamer's minions, as for example by Robert J. Dostal in "Gadamer: The Man and His Work," in *The Cambridge Companion to Gadamer,* 13–35; here 28–29. Of course, at stake in all our discussions must not (only) be speaking or saying *per se* but (also) writing. Although his full reasons for saying so remained unclear, Strauss said that "writing on the highest level is higher than nonwriting on the highest level." Strauss, *On Plato's Symposium,* 250. In Stendhal's words, so dear to Nietzsche and thus likely Heidegger, "Une croyance presque instinctive chez moi c'est que tout homme puissant ment quand il parle, et à plus forte raison quand il écrit" (as cited by Nietzsche in his unpublished notebook 11 [33], used in the years 1887–88). Nietzsche's affirmation of Stendhal's remark, which Socrates could well have uttered, makes risible most attempts to read Nietzsche, but especially all those dragged behind the pious hope that by placing him in "his nineteenth-century context . . . we have a better opportunity of engaging in a meaningful dialogue with his multivalent thought." Robert C. Holub, "Understanding Perspectivism: Nietzsche's Dialogue with His Contemporaries," in *Gadamer's Century,* 111–33; here 131. Historicism has nothing to say to or about a project incepted from the proposition that "the context of a body of thought cannot be appropriately understood so long its unifying center has not been disclosed and pondered." Heinrich Meier, *Carl Schmitt & Leo Strauss: The Hidden Dialogue* [1988], trans. J. Harvey Lomax, preface to the American edition (Chicago: University of Chicago Press, 1995), xiii-vii; here xiii-iv.

19. Note the symptomatic tension—to the point of implosion—between the subject of the utterance (*énoncé*) and the subject of the enunciation (*énonciation*) in the last sentence of Gadamer's postmortem (or postpartum) response to Derrida:

"Whoever wants me to take deconstruction to heart and insists on difference, stands at the beginning of a conversation, not at its end *[nicht an seinem Ziele]*." Gadamer, "Destruktion und Dekonstruktion" (GW2:372). According to Derrida's standpoint, however, that conversation can't begin, in part because there is reason to doubt Gadamerian "good will." See Jacques Derrida, "Guter Wille zur Macht (II)," in *Text und Interpretation*, 62–77. This may help explain the flustered and even aggressive tone of Gadamer's conclusion. The subject about which the subject is speaking is dialogue and opening, but the subject who is speaking sounds as if he is prescriptively foreclosing all but his terms of approach to that other, distant subject.

20. John Cage, *Silence* [1961] (Hanover, NH: Wesleyan University Press: 1973), xi.

21. Martin Heidegger, *Sein und Zeit* [1927], 7th edition (Tübingen: Max Niemeyer), 150. Recall Heidegger's later defense of interpretive "force": because the great thought of great thinkers is "unsaid," authentic "*Auseinandersetzung* with them operates on the ground of an interpretation that is already decided and removed from any debate." (A lot of nonsense has been written about Heidegger's "turn" and thus about his student Gadamer's response to it and his own turn. For the violence required to read the unwritten there has never yet been a sufficiently radical turn. Communists take particular note.) In my next sentence, I have taken the notion of "vindicating the positive function of prejudice" from Vattimo, though he seems to assume that this is more unproblematic than I am convinced it is. See Gianni Vattimo, "Gadamer and the Problem of Ontology," trans. Stefano Franchi, in *Gadamer's Century*, 299–306; here 303.

22. Alasdair MacIntyre, "On Not Having the Last Word: Thoughts on Our Debts to Gadamer," in *Gadamer's Century*, 157–72; here 169.

23. Hans Albert, "Critical Rationalism and Universal Hermeneutics," trans. Michael Isenberg, in *Gadamer's Century*, 15–24; here 18. The first of these apt phrases, "urbanization of the Heideggerian province," was notoriously coined by Habermas.

24. See Everett L. Wheeler, *Stratagem and the Vocabulary of Military Trickery* (Leiden: Brill, 1997).

25. Heidegger, *Sein und Zeit*, 382. Indeed, one of the only readers of *Sein und Zeit* who has taken this kind of articulation seriously is Johannes Fritsche, "On Brinks and Bridges in Heidegger," *Graduate Faculty Philosophy Journal* 18, no. 1 (1995): 111–86, and *Historical Destiny and National Socialism in Heidegger's* Being and Time (Berkeley: University of California Press, 1999), esp. 1–28.

26. See Albert, *Kritik der reinen Hermeneutik: Der Antirealismus und das Problem des Verstehens* (Tübingen: J. C. B. Mohr [Paul Siebeck], 1994), 36–77. This chapter on Gadamer is entitled "Im Banne Heideggers." To be in somebody's *Banne* is to be under his or her "spell" and thus "spellbound," often with an effect that is "baneful" (Old Norse *bani*, "destruction" or "death"). If Heidegger and Gadamer and we all remain *im Banne* of any one thing, I suppose it to be Radio Nietzsche or some cognate.

27. Let me stress, here at the outset, that there is little "new" about Nietzsche's project, as I understand it. Indeed, what I call "Radio Nietzsche" (as I think Nietzsche himself must have conceived it, given his social and psychological formation) is exceptionally "old"—in its intended aftereffect in our ostensibly "postmodern" or "postcontemporary" era. His intention was to keep alive the premodern concept of "order of rank" by employing an updated version of a principle of esoteric commu-

204   GEOFF WAITE

nication that predates Plato and the pre-Socratics. In "hermeneutic" terms, Radio Nietzsche remains the most exemplary current version—on behalf of what I regard as an objectionable politico-philosophical agenda—of the archaic (Greek) concept of *kledon*. "The God Hermes is the patron of thieves, merchants, and travelers; of heralds and what heralds pronounce, their *kerygma*. He also has to do with oracles, including a dubious sort known as *kledon*, which at the moment of its announcement may seem trivial or irrelevant, the secret sense declaring itself only after long delay, and in circumstances not originally foreseeable. Hermes is cunning, and occasion- ally violent: a trickster, a robber. . . . Such operations may require the professional exercise of stealth or violence." Frank Kermode, *The Genesis of Secrecy: On the Interpre- tation of Narrative* (1977/78) (Cambridge, Mass.: Harvard University Press, 1979), 1. My analysis of Radio Nietzsche is intended, therefore, to be a form of countervio- lence to Nietzsche's "hermeneutic" violence, his "esoterrorism." Finally, I strongly suspect, but am *not* completely certain, that Hans-Georg Gadamer and philosophi- cal hermeneutics generally are part of the problem of this entire problematic, not the solution to it. In related terms, Nietzsche (like Heidegger) wrote as a *maître de verité*, that is, as a modern practitioner of the archaic art of "assertoric truth" or "efficacious speech" (Greek *krainein*), in Detienne's seminal sense, which is also attuned to the esoteric problematic. See Marcel Detienne, *The Masters of Truth in Archaic Greece* [1967], trans. Janet Lloyd [New York: Zone Books, 1996]). For a use- ful introduction to Nietzsche's appropriation of important elements of *krainein* (though the author does not take adequate account of the esoteric dimension), see Béatrice Han, "Nietzsche and the 'Masters of Truth': The pre-Socratics and Christ," in *Nietzsche and the Divine,* ed. John Lippitt and Jim Urpeth (Manchester: Manches- ter University Press, 2000), 115–36. My own analysis of Radio Nietzsche is intended as an act of counter-violence to Nietzsche's consequent "hermeneutic violence" and "esoterrorism," so to speak. (N.B.: This note was not in the original version of this essay, to which Catherine H. Zuckert responds in this festschrift for Gadamer. Yet I doubt that her response would have been substantially different had she read this note's attempted clarification earlier, if one assumes, as I do, that in both this note and in the essay I am only "making the obvious obvious," to paraphrase the Platonic Socrates.)

28. Some readers will recognize that certain phrases and concepts in this sen- tence, as well as in the immediately following ones, have been appropriated—some- times verbatim and without quotation marks—from a key passage in Leo Strauss, "Persecution and the Art of Writing" [1941], in *Persecution and the Art of Writing* (New York: Free Press, 1952), 22–37; here 24. They may also notice that I am turning these phrases and concepts against the Straussian tradition, but not necessarily against its controversial methodology and deep insight into Nietzsche.

29. Nietzsche to Paul Deussen, January 3, 1888, in Nietzsche, *Kritische Gesam- tausgabe, Briefwechsel,* ed. Giorgio Colli and Mazzino Montinari (Berlin and New York: Walter de Gruyter, 1975 ff), 3/5: 221–23; here 222; emphasis added. Henceforth I will cite this edition as *KGB,* followed by volume, section, and page numbers. (One year to the date of this letter Nietzsche was to suffer his irrevocable breakdown in Turin.) Deussen (1845–1919) had been a friend of Nietzsche's during their uni- versity days, going on to become one of the first preeminent scholars of so-called Eastern philosophy, in particular the Indic Vedânta. Deussen was a crucial source

(more so than Schopenhauer) of Nietzsche's interest in the ancient international tradition of esotericism and in the caste system based on the "Laws of Manu."

30. Louis Althusser as cited in Olivier Corpet and François Matheron, "Présentation," *Écrits sur la psychanalyse: Freud et Lacan,* ed. Olivier Corpet and François Matheron (Paris: Stock/IMEC, 1993), 7–14; here 12.

31. Robert Pfaller, "Negation and Its Reliabilities: An Empty Subject for Ideology?" in *Cogito and the Unconscious,* ed. Slavoj Žižek (Durham, N.C.: Duke University Press, 1998), 223–46; here 232. See further Pfaller's extended treatment of this problem in *Althusser: Das Schweigen im Text; Epistemologie, Psychoanalyse und Nominalismus in Louis Althussers Theorie der Lektüre* (Munich: Fink, 1997).

32. Pfaller, "Negation and Its Reliabilities," 233.

33. Were my terminology not ungainly enough already, it would be more precise to replace the term "exo/esoteric" with "aesoteric" (a-esoteric). In mind is homology with Heidegger's seminal interpretive translation of Greek *alētheia* not ("positively") as "truth" *(Wahrheit)* but ("negatively") as "unconcealment" *(Unverborgenheit).* In all cases (the epistemological and/or ontological and/or discursive), the alpha privative emphasizes that one can never access truth or the (in any case "unwritten") esoteric except by various forms of indirection—not least (or most) by deception and encryption. *And,* I add, *we must access Truth by our decisions.* (N.B.: This note was not in the original version of my essay.)

34. For a discussion of this concept and problem, see Geoff Waite, *Nietzsche's Corps/e: Aesthetics, Politics, Prophecy, or, The Spectacular Technoculture of Everyday Life* (Durham, N.C.: Duke University Press, 1996). The overhasty, but very influential, depiction of Nietzsche as anti-Hegelian was classically established by Gilles Deleuze's *Nietzsche et la Philosophie* (Paris: Presses Universitaires de France, 1962).

35. Friedrich Nietzsche, *Kritische Gesamtausgabe: Werke,* ed. Giorgio Colli and Mazzino Montinari (Berlin: de Gruyter, 1967 ff), 7/3: 206. Henceforth I will cite this edition as *KGW,* followed by volume, section, and page numbers.

36. Gilles Deleuze and Félix Guattari, *What Is Philosophy?* [1991], trans. Hugh Tomlinson and Graham Burchell (New York: Columbia University Press, 1994), 6. If one wanted to put it this way, part of my project is to dislocate what I regard as Deleuze's superior earlier work from that produced after his association with Guattari (e.g., *Anti-Oedipus* and *A Thousand Plateaus*). This is not to say, however, that I wish to denigrate all of Guattari's *other* work, most notably his collaboration with Antonio Negri in their coauthored *Communists Like Us: New Spaces of Liberty, New Lines of Alliance* [1985], with a "Postscript, 1990" by Toni Negri, trans. Michael Ryan et al. (New York: Semiotext[e], 1990).

37. Deleuze and Guattari, *What Is Philosophy?* 5–6.

38. Nietzsche, *KGW,* 7/3: 207.

39. That Nietzsche, and after him Heidegger, remains entangled to various degrees and at various times in a Platonic and post-Platonic philosophical problematic should hardly be news. I am thinking first and foremost of Stanley Rosen's ongoing reflections on the complex Platonism of Nietzsche and Heidegger (see especially *The Mask of Enlightenment: Nietzsche's* Zarathustra [Cambridge: Cambridge University Press, 1995]). For another quasi-Straussian perspective on Nietzsche's Platonism, see Laurence Lampert, *Nietzsche and Modern Times: A Study of Bacon, Descartes, and Nietzsche* (New Haven, Conn.: Yale University Press, 1993), and *Leo Strauss and Nietz-*

sche (Chicago: University of Chicago Press, 1996). And, for a "left-wing" perspective on Nietzsche's Platonism, though not esotericism, see Philippe Lacoue-Labarthe, "Apocryphal Nietzsche" [1972], trans. Timothy D. Bent, in *The Subject of Philosophy*, ed. Thomas Trezise, trans. Thomas Trezise et al. (Minneapolis: University of Minnesota Press, 1993), 37–56. Finally, for "left-wing" analyses of the problem of esotericism and modern Platonic political philosophy, see Shadia Drury, *The Political Ideas of Leo Strauss* (New York: St. Martin's, 1988), esp. ch. 9, "Post-Modernity: Plato or Nietzsche?" and Teresa Orozco, *Platonische Gewalt: Gadamers politische Hermeneutik der NS-Zeit* (Hamburg: Argument, 1995), and "The Art of Allusion: Hans-Gadamer's Philosophical Interventions under National Socialism," trans. Jason Gaiger, *Radical Philosophy* 78 (July/Aug. 1996): 17–26 (reprinted in this volume).

40. Kleist refers to the recent invention of the electrical telegraph by physician and physicist Samuel Thomas Sömmering (1755–1830). See Heinrich von Kleist, "Entwurf einer Bombenpost" [1810], in *Sämtliche Werke und Briefe*, ed. Helmut Sembdner (Munich: Deutscher Taschenbuch Verlag, 2001), 2: 385–86; here 385. I'm grateful to Rachel Magshamhráin for directing my attention to Kleist's extraordinary text—Wittgenstein's source, as the continuation of the passage I cite makes clearer. If there is an earlier reference in literature to the concept and even technology of the letter bomb, I don't know it. (N.B.: This epigraph and the following one from Kleist were not in the original version of my essay.)

41. See, for instance, Christopher Schiff, "Banging on the Windowpane: Sound in Early Surrealism," and Frances Dyson, "The Ear that Would Hear Sounds in Themselves: John Cage 1935–1965," both in *Wireless Imagination: Sound, Radio, and the Avant-Garde*, ed. Douglas Kahn and Gregory Whitehead (Cambridge, Mass.: MIT Press, 1992), 139–89 and 373–407, respectively.

42. Charles Grivel, "The Phonograph's Horned Mouth," trans. Stephen Sartarelli, in *Wireless Imagination*, 33–61; here 33.

43. Allen S. Weiss, "Radio, Death, and the Devil: Artaud's *Pour en finir avec le jugement de Dieu*," in *Wireless Imagination*, 269–307; here 293.

44. *The Seminar of Jacques Lacan, Book XI: The Four Fundamental Concepts of Psycho-Analysis 1964* [1973], ed. Jacques-Alain Miller, trans. Alan Sheridan (New York: W. W. Norton, 1981), 59.

45. *Le séminaire de Jacques Lacan, Livre VII: L'éthique de la psychanalyse 1959–1960*, ed. Jacques-Alain Miller (Paris: du Seuil, 1986), 212.

46. Weiss, *Phantasmic Radio* (Durham, N.C.: Duke University Press, 1995), 5.

47. Nietzsche, *KGW*, 6/1: 185.

48. On Nietzsche and these issues, see Waite, "The Politics of Reading Formations: The Case of Nietzsche in Imperial Germany, 1870–1919," *New German Critique* 29 (Spring/Summer 1983): 185–209, and "Nietzsche's Baudelaire, or, The Sublime Proleptic Spin of His Politico-Economic Thought," *Representations* 50 (Spring 1995): 14–52.

49. Weiss, *Phantasmic Radio*, 3.

50. Ibid.

51. Ibid., 6.

52. Nietzsche, *KGW*, 7/1: 9.

53. Ibid., 195.

54. In his *Spiegel* interview, Heidegger remarked that his thinking is "not for everyone"; that "National Socialism had gone in the direction" (correctly, in his opinion still) of using thinking to "assist technology to find its proper limits," even if individual Nazis "were much too inexpert in thinking" to succeed; that the intervening years following the Third Reich had "failed to convince" him about the value of "democracy" or of public access to thinking at its deepest levels; that true thinking can occur only in the German and Greek languages; and that "another thinking" can still "change the world," but only through "indirect influence." This, then, was the context in which he noted of his own work that "It can also be that the way of thinking today leads to silence in order to preserve it from being sold dirt cheap *[verramscht]* within a year. It can also be that it needs 300 years to have its 'effect.'" "Spiegel-Gespräch mit Martin Heidegger," in *Antwort: Martin Heidegger im Gespräch,* ed. Günther Neske and Emil Kettering (Pfullingen: Neske, 1988), 81–114; here 96, 103, 105, 109, 107–8, and 101, respectively. The interview took place September 23, 1966, but was published posthumously, as per prior agreement with Heidegger, in *Der Spiegel* on May 31, 1976, under the heading "Nur noch ein Gott kann uns retten" (only a god can save us). Compare Heraclitus's Fragment B 92 (Diels-Kranz): "The Sibyl—who with raving voice [μαινομένῳ στόματι] utters through the god what cannot be ridiculed, embellished, or beautified—reaches out over thousands of years [χιλίων ἐτῶν].

55. Nietzsche, *KGW,* 5/2: 406.

56. Contrast *Selections from the Prison Notebooks of Antonio Gramsci,* ed. and trans. Quintin Hoare and Geoffrey Nowell Smith (New York: International, 1971), 302.

57. See Michael Heim, *The Metaphysics of Virtual Reality* (New York: Oxford University Press, 1993), 124–28.

58. By contrast, Nietzsche's objection—most thoroughly in *David Friedrich Strauss as Confessor and Writer* (1873)—that the great alternative kind of writing and thinking in his time, the newspaper, was necessarily democratizing may appear rather less prescient. Critics of the newspaper on the right, center, and left—including Karl Kraus, Georg Simmel, and Walter Benjamin—have tended to conclude that its power is anything but democratic, that is, that it has rendered the newspaper reader "increasingly unable to assimilate the data of the world around him by way of experience," that "the linguistic usage of newspapers [has] paralyzed the imagination of their readers," and that "the principles of journalistic information (freshness of the news, brevity, comprehensibility, and, above all, lack of connection between the individual news items)" only serve "to isolate what happens from the realm in which it could affect the experience of the reader." Walter Benjamin, "Über einige Motive bei Baudelaire" [1939], in *Gesammelte Schriften,* ed. Rolf Tiedemann and Hermann Schweppenhäuser (Frankfurt am Main: Suhrkamp, 1980), 1/2: 605–53; here 610–11. To give the critique another leftist spin, the newspaper prevents the formations of a geopolitical consciousness of the kind necessary to produce authentic communism and with which Nietzsche has been in competition. Similarly, all "experiential" criticisms of the newspaper, e-mail, and the ostensibly "interactive" internet, which often imagine themselves to be Nietzschean, can really appeal only to Nietzsche's many *exoteric* attacks on newsprint. From his *esoteric* perspective, all such baneful effects are actively *desired* by him for a huge slice of humanity, in order to in-

crease the mechanisms of social and intellectual hierarchization. And this exo/eso-teric problematic can be expected to carry over *mutatis mutandis* into his proleptic critique of more current forms of mass-cultural spectacle and technoculture.

59. Nietzsche, *Werke und Briefe: Historisch-kritische Ausgabe*, ed. Karl Schlechta et al. (Munich: Beck, 1933–42), 2: 71.

60. Nietzsche, *KGW*, 8/2: 159.

61. Some of these remarks are conveniently assembled for the English-speaking reader as Book 4 ("Discipline and Breeding") of Nietzsche, *The Will to Power*, trans. Walter Kaufmann and R. J. Hollingdale (New York: Random House, 1968).

62. Weiss, *Phantasmic Radio*, 22

63. The German title of Nietzsche's later work *Jenseits von Gut und Böse: Vorspiel einer Philosophie der Zukunft* (Beyond good and evil: prelude to a philosophy of the future) plays aggressively both with Wagner's slogan of the "artwork of the future" *(Zukunftsmusik)* and with the classical philologist Ulrich Wilamowitz-Moellendorff's parodic ridicule of Nietzsche's first book, *The Birth of Tragedy Out of the Spirit of Music* (1872), as "philology of the future" *(Zukunftsphilologie)*. Rohde in turn ridiculed Wilamowitz-Moellendorff's detailed and hostile criticisms as *Afterphilologie:* meaning not only post- or pseudo-philology but also an ass-backwards philology of anality for assholes, "anal-philology" (German *After*, "anus," "backwards," "second-hand," "fake"—with the homophobic and/or homosexual associations being rather more closeted than open). For the facsimile reprint of this entire confrontation, see *Der Streit um Nietzsches "Geburt der Tragödie": Die Schriften von E. Rohde, R. Wagner, U. v. Wilamowitz-Moellendorff*, ed. Karlfried Gründer (Hildesheim: Olms, 1969). The abusive term *Afterphilosophie* had enjoyed a rather long history in German thought, significantly predating the contretemps between Nietzsche and Wilamowitz-Moellendorff.

64. Friedrich A Kittler, *Discourse Networks: 1800/1900* [1985], trans. Michael Metteer, with Chris Cullens (Stanford, Calif.: Stanford University Press, 1990), 181.

65. On Nietzsche's encounter with the typewriter in 1882, though not on the more sinister dimensions of Nietzschean *logographia,* see Kittler, *Discourse Networks,* 177–205.

66. Ibid., 193; citing Friedrich Herbertz, "Zur Psychologie des Machinenschreibens," *Zeitschrift für angewandte Psychologie* 2 (1909): 551–61; here 560.

67. Heidegger, *Parmenides* [Freiburg winter semester 1942–43], ed. Manfred S. Frings, in *Gesamtausgabe* (Frankfurt am Main: Vittorio Klostermann, 1982), 54: 119–20. It is small surprise that current discussions of technologies like hypertext, virtual reality, and cyberspace take their point of departure from an appreciative embrace of such passages in Heidegger (see, e.g., Heim, *The Metaphysics of Virtual Reality,* 55–72; here especially 63).

68. Kittler, *Discourse Networks,* 191.

69. Nietzsche, *KGW*, 6/3: 324; also Kittler, *Discourse Networks,* 191.

70. Nietzsche, *KGB*, 3/6: 309–10.

71. Nietzsche, *KGB*, 3/5: 482–83.

72. Nietzsche, *KGB*, 7/3: 363.

73. Deleuze and Guattari, *What Is Philosophy?* 21.

74. Karl Marx, "Contribution to the Critique of Hegel's Philosophy of Law: Introduction" [1844], in Karl Marx and Frederick Engels, *Collected Works* (New York: International, 1976), 3: 175–87; here 182.

75. Immanuel Kant, *Lectures on Logic* [1770s and 1780s], trans. and ed. J. Michael Young (Cambridge: Cambridge University Press, 1992), 241.

76. Althusser, "Sur Feuerbach" [1967], in *Écrits philosophiques et politiques, Tome II,* ed. François Matheron (Paris: Stock/IMEC, 1995), 169–251; here 227.

77. Philippe Lacoue-Labarthe, "The Echo of the Subject" [1979], trans. Barbar Harlow, in *Typography: Mimesis, Philosophy, Politics,* ed. Christopher Fynsk (Cambridge, Mass.: Harvard University Press, 1989), 138–207; here 159.

78. Ibid., 162.

79. For an astute analysis of aesthetic aspects of "mood" in Nietzsche with some mention of the combative project, see Stanley Corngold, "Nietzsche's Moods," *Studies in Romanticism* 29 (Spring 1990): 67–90; for a similar analysis of Heidegger, see Corngold, "Heidegger's *Being and Time:* Implications for Poetics" [1976], in *The Fate of the Self,* 197–218. Heidegger is most responsible for elevating mood into its properly philosophical dimension in *Sein und Zeit* but especially in his 1929–30 lecture course *Die Grundbegriffe der Metaphysik: Welt-Endlichkeit-Einsamkeit,* where philosophy itself is defined as nothing less than the capacity to create authentic mood. It was Nietzsche, however, who eventually gave Heidegger his mature notion of the concept of mood as physical embodiment. As Heidegger put it in his 1936–37 lectures on Nietzsche (punningly, in the untranslatable German), "every feeling is a bodying tuned in a certain way, a mood that bodies in a certain way." Heidegger, *Nietzsche* (Pfullingen: Neske, 1961), 1: 119. There are worse formal descriptions of the desired effect of Radio Nietzsche on us "listeners." (N.B.: This note augments one in the original version of my essay.)

80. Georges Bataille, *La part maudite* [1950–54], in *Œuvres complètes,* ed. Denis Hollier et al. (Paris: Gallimard, 1970–88), 8: 405.

81. Gottfried Benn, "Nietzsche—nach fünfzig Jahren" [1950], in *Gesammelte Werke,* ed. Dieter Wellershoff (Wiesbaden: Limes, 1968), 4: 1046–57; here 1048.

82. See Benn, "Der Radardenker" [1949], in *Gesammelte Werke,* 6: 1435–51

83. The original program was first broadcast from Frankfurt am Main on July 31, 1950, and subsequently rebroadcast (after the unification of Germany) on the same Hessischer Rundfunk, September 19, 1991, as "Gespräch über Nietzsche" (Conversation about Nietzsche). Transcripts have subsequently been printed. See, for example, Max Horkheimer (with Theodor W. Adorno and Hans-Georg Gadamer), "Über Nietzsche und uns: Zum 50. Todestag des Philosophen," *Gesammelte Schriften,* ed. Alfred Schmidt and Gunzelin Schmid Noerr (Frankfurt am Main: S. Fischer, 1989), 13: 111–20. Obviously what is crucial to radio is missing from the transcript: the modulations of voice and mood (what Adorno might call the "punctuation marks"), in short, the link to oral-aural tradition. I will cite in my translation from the original broadcast.

84. Herbert Schnädelbach, *Philosophy in Germany 1831–1933* [1982], trans. Eric Mathews (Cambridge: Cambridge University Press, 1984), 1.

85. For preliminary remarks on the constitutive influence of Nietzsche on Horkheimer and Adorno, see Jürgen Habermas, "The Entwinement of Myth and Enlightenment: Rereading *Dialectic of Enlightenment,*" *New German Critique* 26 (Spring/Summer 1982): 13–30. But on this issue Habermas places too exclusive a focus on their early *Dialectic of Enlightenment* (1944) as their "blackest, most nihilistic book" (p. 13). I have argued elsewhere that Habermas himself, in whom the Frankfurt School is ar-

guably most alive today (along with Axel Honneth), is hardly immune from Nietzsche's influence (see Waite, "The Politics of Reading Formations: The Case of Nietzsche in Imperial Germany, 1870–1919," 201–3). It is evident from Horkheimer's
drafts for *Dialectic of Enlightenment* that he was particularly under Nietzsche's influence, and had much to do with pushing Adorno in a Nietzschean direction to become yet another "leftist" corps/e.

86. For a discussion of this powerful trope of German political thought with particular focus on Heidegger's updated variant, see Hans Sluga, *Heidegger's Crisis: Philosophy and Politics in Nazi Germany* (Cambridge, Mass.: Harvard University Press,
1993), 79–81 (though this is ultimately a superficial book on Heidegger himself,
unaware as it is of even the *question* of exo/esotericism).

87. In the broadcast Adorno also alludes to Hegel's first and most basic definition of Socratic irony, namely, as a subcategory of the dialectic, insofar as irony
"grants force to what should be granted force, as if it had force, but only in order to
allow it inherent destruction to develop itself: the universal irony of the world."
Georg Wilhelm Friedrich Hegel, *Werke in zwanzig Bänden*, ed. Eva Moldenhauer and
Karl Markus Michel (Frankfurt am Main: Suhrkamp, 1971), 12: 460. But rather
more to the point for Adorno's argument would be Hegel's technical definition elsewhere of "parody" as "the use of forms in the era of their impossibility" in order
to "demonstrate this impossibility and thereby altering the forms." Theodor W.
Adorno, *Noten zur Literatur I,* ed. Rolf Tiedemann (Frankfurt am Main: Suhrkamp,
1974), 303. But note also that, for Hegel, "Hypocrisy is the truest irony," since it allows us wantonly to contradict ourselves for subjective motives (*Werke*, 12: 461).

88. Althusser, "Philosophy," in *Philosophy and the Spontaneous Philosophy of the Scientists and Other Essays,* 97.

89. In hermeneutic terms, developed by Gadamer through Heidegger, a main
technique of exo/esotericism is "giving-to-understand" *(Zu-verstehen-geben),* and
what in a different tradition Michel Pêcheux, following Althusser and semiotic theory, calls *transdiscours* (see, e.g., *Analyse automatique du discours* [Paris: Dunod, 1969]).
Gadamer's 1934 lecture on Plato's *Republic,* and on the reason why the foundation
of the State apparently requires the expulsion of poets, rigorously refused to give his
audience what they most expected, namely, the connection between this detailed
philosophical, historical question to the just recent instauration of the National Socialist state. Gadamer was thus employing a form of sigetics whereby the speaker tells
his audience everything *except* what they fervently desire to hear, *so that they are given
the illusion of having produced this meaning themselves.* Which in this case was the bridge
between Plato to Hitler. For a discussion of Gadamer in this regard, see Orozco, *Platonische Gewalt,* although Nietzsche is not a main exhibit in her argument. Orozco
has made a good circumstantial case that Gadamer's philosophical writings and professional activities during the Third Reich suggest that he was working, quite self-
consciously, within the esoteric "oral" tradition of philosophy extending, or so he
held, back to Plato, and that his success in concealing his own deepest political
agenda (in tune with what I would call Heideggerian political ontology) explains
Gadamer's speedy rehabilitation as a (if not indeed *the*) philosopher of postwar West
Germany. Yet Orozco does not really tackle the problem of the perlocutionary implementation of Gadamer's project, nor does she grasp the full dimensions of philosophical esotericism. (Orozco is not alone in this regard; a similar problem informs

the account of Catherine H. Zuckert, *Postmodern Platos: Nietzsche, Heidegger, Gadamer, Strauss, Derrida* [Chicago: University of Chicago Press, 1996]; and those of us who have been touched at all positively by Gadamer, his person or works, must read Orozco's study with particular sadness.) In any case and whatever the deficiencies of their extensive appropriation of Nietzsche may be, there is no fully comparable problematic in Adorno and Horkheimer, whose conscious grasp of philosophical esotericism was as inadequate as that of the various left-wing French tendencies had been. To begin to grasp properly Nietzschean esotericism, however, we have to turn from the "left" to the "right"—but not to Gadamer, who is prudently silent about the matter, but to Leo Strauss and Stanley Rosen.

90. Kōjin Karatani, *Architecture as Metaphor: Language, Number, Money,* ed. Michael Speaks, trans. Sabu Kohso (Cambridge, Mass: MIT Press, 1995), 187.

91. See ibid., xx, 8–9. In the Japanese version of this essay I go into this difference in detail.

92. Ibid., 188. Note that in the German idealist tradition (in which Marx is to be included here), *Idee* (idea) is defined, roughly, as "an ideal that is realized, concretized," and that *Schein* plays simultaneously with two senses, "appearance" and "illumination"; in other terms, it is phenomenal appearance of something thus rendered im/perceptible and exo/esoteric.

93. Paul A Cantor, "Leo Strauss and Contemporary Hermeneutics," in *Leo Strauss's Thought: Toward a Critical Engagement,* ed. Alan Udoff (Boulder, Colo.: Lynne Rienner Publishers, 1991), 267–314; here 277.

94. Nietzsche, *KGW,* 7/3: 234–35. Again, the long dashes indicate illegibility. The passage then concludes: "Preparation for becoming Masters of the Earth: The Legislators of the Future. At least out of our children. Basic attention to marriages."

95. For by far the best account, see Rosen, *The Mask of Enlightenment.*

96. Contrast Jacques Derrida, *Otobiographies: L'enseignement de Nietzsche et la politique du nom propre* (Paris: Galilée, 1984).

97. Antonio Gramsci, "Concept of the 'National-Popular'" [1930], in *Selections from Cultural Writings,* ed. David Forgacs and Geoffrey Nowell Smith, trans. William Boelhower (Cambridge, Mass.: Harvard University Press, 1985), 206–12; here 211. See further Gramsci's remarks entitled "Father Bresciani's Progeny," including the editors' comments (pp. 298–341). "Brescianism"—from the Jesuit priest and novelist Antonio Bresciani—was one of Gramsci's code terms for "Jesuitism," a tendency he tried to combat also within his own Communist Party.

98. Nietzsche, *KGW,* 8/1: 116–17.

99. "Zarathustra glücklich darüber, dass der Kampf der Stände *vorüber* ist, und jetzt endlich Zeit ist für sein Rangordnung der Individuen Hass auf das demokratische Nivellirungs-System ist nur im *Vordergrund:* eigentlich ist er sehr froh, dass *dies so weit ist.* Nun kann er seine Aufgabe lösen. —" Nietzsche, *Werke,* ed. Fritz Koegel (Leipzig: Naumann, 1899), 12: 325.

100. Leonard Cohen, "Tower of Song," *I'm Your Man,* © 1988 CBS Records Inc. CK44191.

101. Deleuze, "Letter to a Harsh Critic" [1973], in *Negotiations* [*Pourparles, 1972–1990,* 1990], trans. Martin Joughin (New York: Columbia University Press, 1995), 3–12; here 6.

102. Ibid. See also the translator's note on page 184.

Chapter 11

The Art of Allusion

*Hans-Georg Gadamer's Philosophical Interventions
under National Socialism*

TERESA OROZCO, *translated by Jason Gaiger*

On February 11, 1995, Gadamer reached the age of ninety-five. The tributes that were paid to him were justifiably numerous; in the *Frankfurter Allgemeine Zeitung* he was celebrated as "the most successful philosopher of the Federal Republic," placed even before Jürgen Habermas, to whom the title of philosopher was awarded only with certain reservations.[1] The worldwide influence of Gadamer's thinking is closely connected with the reception of his principal work, *Truth and Method* (1960). In 1979, Habermas characterized Gadamer's achievement as the "urbanization of the Heideggerian province." The bridges that Gadamer has built consist above all in an elaboration of Heidegger's paradigm of understanding in its application to hermeneutics; these bridges connect philosophy with all those realms in which interpretative procedures are necessary, such as literary studies, jurisprudence, theology, and even medicine (see VG).

CONCILIATORY THINKING

What is striking in the present reception of Gadamer's work is the concentration on what Henning Ritter has described as "conciliatory thinking which knows how to conceal his hardness."[2] The notion of conciliation is generally explicated through reference to the third section of *Truth and Method*. In what he terms the "ontological turn of hermeneutics oriented by the guiding thread of language," Gadamer develops a conception of language that comes close to the dictum of the later Heidegger: that, properly understood, it is not the individual subject but language itself that speaks[3]— with the difference, however, that Gadamer introduces the model of dialogue as a sort of counterbalance. In short, Gadamer's basic assumption is that truth is disclosed in dialogical speech. Decisive here is Gadamer's reinterpretation of Socratic maieutics in terms of an aleatory happening. This abstract paradigm of a dialogical situation that encompasses both the art of persuasion and an openness to the opinion of the other possesses an enormous resonance today.

In contrast, the conditions of hermeneutic understanding that first enable a successful accomplishment of understanding, as developed by Gadamer in the second section of *Truth and Method,* have retreated into the background.[4] In this section Gadamer pursues a trenchant rehabilitation of a thinking that is grounded in prejudices *[Vorurteilen],* and affirms both the power of tradition (above all through the example of the classical) and the unlimited validity of authority and authorities. He defends this as a genuinely conservative undertaking that does not need to be argumentatively justified.[5] The subjective dispositions through which this project is to be sustained are "affirmation, appropriation and care" (WM265 ff.). Because Gadamer regards "the self-reflection of the subject" as "only a flickering in the closed circuits of historical life" (WM265), "the prejudices of the individual, far more than his or her own judgments, constitute the historical reality of being" (WM261). Under these conditions, understanding "is less to be thought of as a subjective act" than, in a way that carries associations with military practices, "as conscription into an event of tradition" (WM274 ff.; italics removed). In Gadamer's view, there is no "method" for acquiring this competence in understanding.

Finally, it is characteristic of the current reception of Gadamer's work that the emphasis has shifted away from a thinking grounded in prejudices toward a more comprehensive notion of pre-understanding that is prior to every act of understanding. Through selective and sometimes critical readings, Gadamer has been drawn into dialogue with the school of Anglo-American philosophy of language, theorists of intersubjectivity such as Habermas and Karl-Otto Apel, Richard Rorty in the United States, and Jean Grondin in Canada, as well as left-oriented hermeneutic thinkers such as Gianni Vattimo in Italy and Emilio Lledó in Spain.

A LOOK INTO THE PAST

In what follows I seek to illuminate Gadamer's philosophical writings during the period of National Socialism by focusing on two important essays.[6] In light of the reception that has been awarded to Gadamer's thought there may seem something provocative about the goals of this enquiry. Gadamer himself has addressed the issue of his career under National Socialism, both in autobiographical writings and in recent interviews. The picture seems to be clear and the relevant facts already known. In contrast to his teacher and to various other colleagues, Gadamer is happy to present himself in this context as someone who was ready to accommodate himself to circumstances.

In several places he reveals that although there was no question of his joining one of the organizations of the National Socialist Party because of the importance of remaining loyal to his Jewish friends, he was nonetheless obliged to make political concessions in order to advance his career. Ultimately, he was able tactfully to organize the situation to his advantage, and in 1939 he was called to a chair in Leipzig. This took place, as he correctly observes, "as a consequence of high politics."[7]

This external accommodation in turn gave Gadamer the opportunity to pursue philosophical work in a spirit of pure "scholarship" even under National Socialism. Unlike Karl Löwith, Gadamer argues for a strict division between the scientific and political domains. And this implies that there were both accommodationists and Nazis who were otherwise thoroughly responsible scholars, such as Martin Heidegger, Kurt Hildebrandt, Erich Rothacker, Wolfgang Schadewaldt, Felix Krüger, Helmut Berve, Richard Harder, and Gerhard Fricke. The claim to "scientific excellence" provided the means by which the academic community could constitute itself internally and at the same time insulate itself from the influence of National Socialism externally. What this view fails to take into account is that this appeal to "scientific excellence" may well have been the very form in which the knowledge and skills of the human sciences could be employed in the service of National Socialism. Today, Gadamer also emphasizes his contacts with the "national conservative" resistance to Hitler. Together with other members of the Goerdeler circle, to which he belonged in the last phase of fascism during the war period, he shared an open opposition to the Weimar Republic as well as admiration for Hitler's foreign policies, which still seemed highly promising during the so-called "Blitzkrieg." Gadamer was not a Nazi and for this reason he was elected rector of the University of Leipzig by the occupying Soviet powers in 1947. Later he transferred to the University of Frankfurt and finally, as successor to Karl Jaspers, to the University of Heidelberg.

Such clarity concerning the facts would seem to render the questions I am pursuing here superfluous. Nonetheless, the crucial problem from which I started out was to arrive at a more substantial and exact definition of the concept of "national conservatism" by focusing on those philosophers who belonged to the so-called "black faction." Despite the fact that these philosophers entered into a clear and solid alliance with the Nazis that endured almost until the end of the Nazi period, it has long remained unclear exactly what contribution this faction made to the consolidation and perpetuation of National Socialism. The key to interpreting this contribution is not to be found in the attempted assassination of Hitler on July 20, 1944. According to the self-understanding of the national conservative opposition, as articulated for example by Gadamer's friend Eduard Spranger in 1947, "it was not National Socialism that led us into catastrophe but rather Hitlerism itself."[8] The studies written for the project *Philosophie im Deutschen Fascismus* (AS165) are concerned with national conservatives of an earlier generation—for example, Nicolai Hartmann,[9] Eduard Spranger,[10] and Theodor Litt[11]—and they can help us to recognize different modalities of fascism within the black faction.

It was in this context that I began to investigate Gadamer's texts from the period 1933 to 1945. Amongst other things I came across interpretations of Plato in which Nazism was never explicitly referred to. Gadamer's articles were entirely in keeping with then current research and did not appear to represent anything unusual. His goals did not extend to such ambitious projects as the question of the meaning of being or revolutionizing the discipline of philosophy. As a young university lecturer he worked unassumingly on texts of ancient philosophy, above all on a reading of Plato's *Republic*. During the course of my research, however, I discovered that this reading was multilayered, and this in turn opened up a new way of looking at Gadamer's writings of the period.

My first concern was to reconstruct the connection between what was said and the context in which it was written, to document what for us has now fallen silent. Or, to put it in Gadamer's own language, I sought to establish the historical basis on which other hermeneutic approaches could be developed and to discover the fusions of horizon between past and present that were possible at that time. In the course of my investigations I was able to give more precision to the often overgeneralized and inexact use of the notion of "context" through employing the concept of "relations of response" to Plato. We can use this concept to describe how in the process of fascization various ideas were articulated through readings of Plato: National Socialism was identified as a task that had already been laid out in antiquity. These ideas resonated not only within the domain of academic discourse but also within other fields of practice such as the National Socialist Party's policies on health, justice, education, and art.[12]

Around 1933, despite differences in interpretation, there emerged a common point of convergence: the destruction of the self-understanding of universalist humanism. This expression signified the humanism of European modernity and of Weimar classicism; above all, that humanism that was articulated through the ideals of the French Revolution. Disqualified as "apolitical" under the cipher of aesthetic humanism and identified with the "age of liberalism," it became the hegemonic critical target for the new reception of antiquity. At the basis of the denunciation of the Enlightenment as developed within the humanist camp itself, which was in opposition to the Weimar Republic, lay a new conception of law that aimed at strictly controlling society, and that attacked as "sophistic" the old human dream of a society based on self-determination and autonomy. The process of fascization supported an unparalleled project of bourgeois modernization, to

which not only radical technocratic modes of thinking but also the humanist notion of "care of the soul" made a contribution. It was on this front that
the interpretation of Plato was engaged. Alongside the lecture that Gadamer gave in occupied Paris in 1941 in the service of foreign propaganda,
and the interpretation of Max Weber (1943), in which he addressed the issue of modernizing National Socialist policy on science and education in
the face of possible military defeat, it is the two interpretations of Plato that
particularly stand out amongst Gadamer's philosophical writings between
1934 and 1942. In what follows I shall restrict myself to a consideration of
these two essays.

1933: RESPONSES TO PLATO'S *REPUBLIC*

Since we possess neither any systematic nor any definitive investigations
of the influence of fascism on the interpretation of Plato in the German-
speaking context,[13] a large part of my work consisted in studying the Plato
scholarship of the period through the original sources.[14] Decisive for understanding Gadamer's work is the transformation of the humanist image
of Plato that had already taken place during the Weimar Republic. The key
features of this transformation can be summed up as follows:

1. Classical philology stepped into line with National Socialist thinking,
    thereby bringing to an end the conflict that had raged in the Weimar Re-
    public concerning the correct interpretation of Plato. Official justifi-
    cation was provided by the work of Werner Jaeger.[15] Whereas classical
    humanism had paradigmatically interpreted Plato as a poet and a meta-
    physician and considered him the founder of the doctrine of ideas, an
    association of philologists and philosophers now sought to propagate an
    alternative "political reading" of Plato. In the course of this conflict of in-
    terpretation new interpretative principles were developed.
2. The relative importance of the various texts in the Platonic canon was
    subjected to a revaluation. Those dialogues, dialogue passages, and ele-
    ments that are concerned with metaphysics and the theory of ideas—
    that is, those texts on which the traditional humanistic interpretation of
    Plato developed by Schleiermacher and neo-Kantianism was based—no
    longer stood at the center of philological research. Instead, attention was
    focused on the *Republic*, the *Laws* and the *Seventh Letter*. The epistemo-
    logical concerns that had informed earlier readings of Plato receded
    into the background. This shift of emphasis was justified philologically
    inasmuch as the *Seventh Letter*, Plato's so-called political biography whose
    authenticity is still disputed today, was declared to be an authentic tex-
    tual source.[16]

3. Advocates of this "politicized" reading of Plato made appeal to the so-called unwritten doctrine that, according to the *Seventh Letter* (341 a–e) and other sources, represents the essence of Plato's philosophy. Out of this secret doctrine they then sought to derive new rules for philological inquiry that went beyond what could be defended on the basis of the textual material itself, and one to which they believed they enjoyed access.[17]

In this new interpretation emphasis was no longer placed on the construction of a systematic conceptual system. The hermeneutic key to Plato's writings was provided by his involvement in Attic politics. Plato's supposed biography was interpreted with categories taken from *Lebensphilosophie*, with great emphasis being laid upon Plato's "decision" to reground the state.

The most noted Plato scholars (in the tradition of Ulrich von Wilamowitz-Moellendorff) were Werner Jaeger, Julius Stenzel, Paul Friedländer, Heinrich Gompertz, and, from the George circle, Kurt Hildebrandt, Wilhelm Andrae, Kurt Singer, and Edgar Salin. It suited their purposes to depict Plato as a "philosopher of crisis." Kurt Hildebrandt maintained that "for us Germans" Plato should be "a model of a savior in an age of dissolution and decay." Plato's *Republic*, which was itself a response to the crisis of the Attic *polis*, offered material on the basis of which the crisis of the Weimar Republic could be projected back into antiquity. Plato's dream of restoring Attic aristocracy by reforming it in the form of an authoritarian educational state was elevated to the status of a "spiritual task."

As can be seen from the example of Jaeger and Hildebrandt, the ground for the subsequent fascization of the interpretation of Plato had already been fully prepared during the period of the Weimar Republic. As the philological associations fell into line with National Socialist ideas this interpretation then became orthodox teaching: "Whereas our predecessors saw Plato as a Neo-Kantian system builder and the initiator of a highly revered philosophical tradition, for our generation he has become the founder of the state and the giver of laws."[18]

THE EXPULSION OF THE POETS: A LECTURE AND ITS CONTEXT

On January 24, 1934, Gadamer gave a lecture entitled "Plato and the Poets" before the Society of Friends of the Humanistic Gymnasium in Marburg. In this lecture he set himself the task of "understanding the meaning and justification"[19] of Plato's critique of the poets in the *Republic*. For the members of the cultural elite who had gathered to hear him speak, this "represented the most difficult task confronting the German spirit in its efforts to assimilate the spirit of the ancient world" (5). The difficulty of this task resided in the fact that Plato's critique of the poets was carried out through

an attack on the "art and poetry of the ancients" and so challenged just that
ideal domain that embodied the self-understanding of German humanism.

Gadamer starts out by recalling the harmonious character of this humanist ideal, in which Plato occupies a place. Plato is recognized as one of
"the greatest representatives of the poetic genius of the Greeks," "admired
and loved like Homer and the tragedians, Pindar and Aristophanes" (5). By
identifying Plato's eminent status within the humanistic ideal as envisaged
by his audience, Gadamer finds a starting point from which he can begin to
rebuild this ideal from within. Plato himself is represented as a "hostile
critic of the art of classical antiquity" (5). The poetry he wrote in his youth,
"he burnt . . . after he became a pupil of Socrates" (6) and he "condemned
Homer and the great Attic dramatists . . . to be completely expelled from
the state" (5). The tension generated by this conflict enables Gadamer to
set the hermeneutic circle of his lecture in motion.

Following Socrates, Plato turns against the "much beloved Homer" (6).
He censors Homer in accordance with the norms of a poetry that should
work for the state and recomposes the opening of the *Iliad* so as to "purify
it of all direct speech" (10). Plato thereby chooses "a deliberately provocative example" (10), since Socrates, through whom Plato speaks, must struggle against his own deep-rooted sentiments and attitudes. But Gadamer,
too, thereby chooses a "deliberately provocative example," for the "verses
known to all" from the opening of the *Iliad*—learned by heart by entire
generations of gymnasium students—were a symbol of classical education.

Gadamer may well have disturbed his hearers by demanding that they
should bring this "monstrous attack" upon poetry and on Homer vividly
to mind rather than "pushing it away from us . . . into the distant past of a
unique historical period." Gadamer is concerned with the fact "that this decision also has something to say to us" (10). Was his audience not suddenly
confronted with the National Socialist present, with its burning of books,
and the censorship, exile, and persecution of poets and writers?

At no point does Gadamer directly mention the fascist present. His lecture remains entirely on the terrain of an interpretation of Plato. Plato's
measures against the poets are to be understood through an interpretation
of the *Republic*.[20] In the first part of the lecture Gadamer discusses the status of Plato's critique. Its full significance is derived from the project of
refounding the state. This new state is to be an educational state. At its center Gadamer places the Platonic *paideia,* the education of the youths to become its guardians. These are the youths who risked corruption by the
poets because they lacked "the binding civil *ethos* which could secure that
poetry would have its proper effect" (15). In the second part of the lecture
poetry is rehabilitated in the service of patriotic ends. Here Gadamer discusses Plato's critique of imitation. Plato develops a conception of art whose
purpose is not to give aesthetic pleasure but to strengthen the civil *ethos,* as

in the case of hymns. Finally, Gadamer presents Socrates, the critic of myths, as the restorer of myth against the Enlightenment.

Despite the textual immanence of Gadamer's reading of Plato, his audience must have been all too aware of the fascist present with its censorship, persecution, exile, and expatriation. When this lecture was delivered in January 1934, the burning of books, the symbolic high point of the "action against the non-German spirit," had taken place only six months before.

Taken as a whole, the lecture and its context are rich with interdiscursive implications and allusions. Together they provide a hermeneutic horizon that is congruent with the ideal self-understanding of National Socialism as a political decision to "renew" the state after the "decay" of the Weimar Republic. Drawing explicitly on the politicized reading of Plato that valued his thought as a "resolute expression of decision . . . directed against the entire political and spiritual culture of his age" (12), Gadamer chose to discuss the theme of the expulsion of the poets—a theme that seemed to be given in advance of the times—rather than emphasizing his status as a "metaphysician of the theory of ideas" (12).

When Gadamer demanded of his educated and cultured audience that they respect the expulsion of the poets as a decision made within the framework of the founding of the state, he indirectly attacked the reservation and skepticism about the burning of books that was widespread amongst the humanist elite. The burning of books was not only an action against the so-called enemies of the state, but it also affected authors who belonged to the cultural bourgeoisie itself. Alongside books by Marxists, pacifists, and left-wing intellectuals such as Bertolt Brecht, Kurt Tucholsky, Carl von Ossietzky, Erich Maria Remarque, and Franz Kafka, flames also consumed the works of writers like Thomas Mann, Friedrich Gundolf, Arnold and Stefan Zweig, and the Catholic pacifist Friedrich Wilhelm Foerster. Parallel with the attack against thinkers on the left there was also a second front of "action against the non-German spirit." In Goebbels's language, the so-called aesthetic humanism of the enlightened liberal bourgeoisie revealed an attitude of "non-involvement" and "standing to one side." In this respect, the burning of books could be understood as a warning against "inner emigration."

In Alfred Baeumler's inaugural lecture, which was originally planned as a speech to accompany the burning of books, the critique of the ideal of a harmonious personality and of the "aesthetic attitude"[21] entertained by the highly educated took on a key role. Baeumler's critique of the personality ideal of the cultured reappears—in almost exactly the same words [22]—in Gadamer's lecture. His interpretation of Plato's notion of *paideia* is directed against the "humanist ideal of the 'harmonious personality'" (18). Gadamer seeks to make this critique of aesthetic humanism plausible to his humanist audience by constructing it out of their most coveted cultural sources. He makes Plato's *paideia* into "the opposite of that which the Greeks themselves and we as their humanist successors conceive under the terms 'education' and 'culture'" (18).

As can be shown in greater detail, Gadamer constructed an interpretive framework for the contemporary situation in Germany that, at the same time, allowed Plato's critique of the poets to be understood in a manner that simultaneously articulated the self-understanding of the present. As a result, the passages in which Gadamer, together with Plato, argues for the unconditioned validity of authority over and against the sophistic conception of the laws of the state can be seen as a grave and unambiguous response to National Socialism in the period of its consolidation. Central here is the demand for a new *paideia* that was called upon to shape the youths into the guardians of the new state and to help them to resist the seductions of the sophistic spirit to which they may be exposed. In this way, a new form of subjectivity was to be developed that—without the recognition of basic human rights—was to bring the interior of the state into agreement with its external form. This achievement can be made visible, however, only when the meaning and scope of the *topos* of the sophists (or the sophistical), as well as the critique of the Enlightenment, is understood not only in terms of the history of ideas but also as a concrete and stigmatized way of representing the enemies of the state under National Socialism.

By drawing upon all the available material, in which Gadamer's voice is but one amongst many, we can establish the following points:

1. The genesis of this multiform interpretation of Plato was not determined by extra-academic impulses or by some sort of *Weltanschauung*, but arose at the center of academic discourse itself and was unconditionally asserted as part of the scientific canon. Popular interpretations of Plato drew upon these approaches and sought to make them productive in their own way.

2. At the same time, however, certain interpretations of Plato's *Seventh Letter* and of Plato's unwritten secret doctrine secured exclusive access to the truth for the academic elite under National Socialism. By identifying hidden "reserves of meaning" in the Platonic material, they were able to distinguish their own reading from the "simple message" contained in the popular image of Plato.[23]

3. The *topos* of interpreting the *Republic* as an ideal task that is yet to be fulfilled allowed the possibility of conceiving new ways of actualizing this task under National Socialism as it developed through its various stages. This is something that can be shown in an exemplary way in the case of Gadamer. The traditional reading of the *Seventh Letter* as an expression of Plato's disappointment at the impossibility of realizing his project of a proper ordering of the state could be functionalized in a new way with

the occurrence of "processes of disappointment" over certain unwelcome developments under National Socialism.

THE CURE FOR THE UNHEALTHY CONDITION OF THE STATE:
GADAMER IN THE SS STATE

Gadamer's essay "Plato's Educational State" was published in 1942 as part of a collection of texts whose purpose was to document the contribution made by classical philology to the "human sciences as part of the war effort." In the intervening period Gadamer had become firmly established as a professor in Leipzig. In 1977 he himself described this text as "a sort of alibi" (PL74) without providing any further explanation. In fact, Gadamer adopts an unexpected tone in this essay. He appears to resist becoming caught up in the general enthusiasm generated by the triumphal march of the German military forces. The posture of "German strength" that had informed the lecture on Herder, given in 1941 to imprisoned French officers, is no longer in evidence. Instead, Gadamer takes up a pensive attitude and appears to want to direct a word of warning to the "present" through a reading of Plato. The theme that is treated under the title of "Plato's Educational State" is the unsuspicious, familiar postulate of the "philosopher king"; that is, the idea that "the philosophers lead the rulers and the rulers are taught by the philosophers how to rule."[24] This theme, however, harbors a certain explosive force.

Gadamer presents Plato here as someone who is disillusioned with the dictatorship that has taken over from Athenian democracy. He quotes whole passages from the *Seventh Letter* in which Plato raises impassioned complaints about the general moral decay under the rule of "tyranny." In order to put an end to his decay Plato advocates "a reform of unheard of proportions" (GW5:317). For Gadamer, it is the Plato who criticizes and admonishes the tyrants of Athens and, through Socrates, seeks to show them the way to reform who provides the guiding thread by which the *Republic* is to be interpreted.[25] The shift of emphasis involved in this image of Plato is remarkable. Gadamer's Plato of 1934 was someone who had made the expulsion of the poets and the education of the guardians into a condition of the founding of the state. The hermeneutic horizon within which Plato is now presented is "the decay of the state under tyranny."

The contemporary horizon for this reading of Plato was given by the restructuring of the National Socialist ruling apparatus that took place at the start of the war. The apparatus of repression was built up and the SS state began to take shape. With the deterioration of the war situation this reorganization allowed the ideological forces of cohesion on the "inner front" to slacken and the ideological incorporation of the individual to break down.

The general change of mood was not restricted to the conservative and academic elites. Within the philosophical domain there was a proliferation of proposals for an inner reform of fascism based on readings of Plato, Hobbes, Machiavelli, and Frederick the Great. The cases of Eduard Spranger,[26] Hans Freyer,[27] and Carl Schmitt[28] belong here. Almost all the projects that became philosophically effective in 1933 sought to establish a normative foundation for developing various conceptions of an ideal fascism. Against the background of the destabilizing effects of the war, these projects consequently served to procure stability and order. This can be elucidated by looking at the model of society that Gadamer sought to distill from the *Republic*.

Under the heading of *"dikaiosyne"* (a term that is translated as *"Gerechtigkeit,"* or "justice") Gadamer opposes, as he had in 1934, the idea of the Platonic state, the state as "an order of classes" (GW5:326), to the concept of tyranny and the sophistic conception of the state. *Dikaiosyne* is used to describe government in the form of the general interest. Ideally, the rulers should use their competence in planning and leadership unselfishly—that is, for the good of all, rather than in the service of their own interests. The military uses its weapons in defense of the whole. For the rulers and those that are ruled, however, the "state as a whole" (GW5:327) presents itself in a different way. Because their special competence resides in leadership, the rulers have a position in the "division of labor" that binds them immediately to the "universal": "Every form of work is indeed there for the use of all who need it. Nonetheless, the work of a political leader or a warrior is not merely a technical skill like any other but is immediately related to the interest of the state as a whole" (GW5:327). If in this way, in a formulation that Gadamer takes up from Hegel,[29] "the universal prevails" (GW5:329), then the rulers can rely upon the *"sophrosyne"* or virtue of those who are ruled to guarantee that their decisions will meet with agreement. In opposition to real, "tyrannical" fascism, Gadamer describes an ideal fascism, a stratified community of the people brought about through the "reconciliation of the three classes to form a single unity" (GW5:328).

The system of government that Gadamer derives from Plato's ideas is only conceivable as an authoritarian state with a highly centralized concentration of power. He clearly rejects the conception of "democratically" formed decision-making procedures: "The disruption of this order of the classes is the real political misfortune, that is, the destruction of the structure of government as this became visible in the decay of the Attic democracy" (GW5:327). The concentration of power in the hands of the "governing classes" has its price: there is no guarantee, no internal power, that can prevent the "governing classes" from establishing a tyrannical government. There is a permanent danger that the governing class will succumb to the "temptations of power" and that the "order of the state will be destroyed"

(GW5:329). In regard to this problem, Plato's doctrine of the soul can be seen as a doctrine of how the state can become diseased through the actions of its rulers. The form of "legality" (GW5:324) transforms the power of leadership into the "legal force of the state," and its government into the "administration of the power of the state" (GW5:326). Such government is legitimate government that is able to survive situations of crisis without transmuting into tyranny. Since it occupies a position in the soul of those it rules over, it can count on their "inner attunement," even "in proximity to possible discord" (GW5:329).

My thesis is that this ideal of an authoritative government represents a re-action to the "tyrannical" transformations that fascism underwent during the war. Gadamer's call for "a cure for the unhealthy state" is closely related to the various proposals for providing the National Socialist system and its military policies with a "new" basis, as these were developed within the up-per ranks of the government, military, and business. Proposals for an inner reorganization of the state were not limited to the Potsdam faction of Na-tional Socialism, whose plans for transforming the *"Führer"* state into an "en-lightened" monarchy resulted in the military putsch of July 20, 1944. An impetus for reform was also generated from within the National Socialist Party itself. Paradigmatic here is the critique that was openly articulated by Hans Frank, one of the foremost lawyers of the National Socialist Party.[30] From the example of Frank's attempt to curb the development toward ty-ranny we can see the range and variety of social forces that informed Gada-mer's interpretation of Plato. In stark contrast is the option pursued by Carl Schmitt, who in 1938 sought to legitimate the establishment of a total po-lice state through recourse to the work of Hobbes. While both the national conservative opposition and certain factions within the National Socialist Party sought to discover a way of securing the relationship between "the leadership and the people" by respecting the "emotional and psychological constitution of the individual," Schmitt outdid these suggestions—among which Gadamer's is to be included—with his model of tyranny.

In summary, the results of this investigation reveal the way in which Gadamer was able to identify with the national conservative faction of Na-tional Socialism without, however, publicly declaring his opposition to its more popular forms. The contemporary relevance of his interpretations of Plato enabled him to construct bridges that allowed various connections to be drawn without the need to state them explicitly. The hermeneutic art of allusion that Gadamer invokes in his critique of Carl Schmitt's interpreta-tion of Hamlet is also relevant to Gadamer's own work: "In fact, the reality of a play is constituted by leaving an indefinite space around its theme" (GW2:380).[31]

In the end, we can agree with Jan Ross's evaluation that "Gadamer's vir-tuosity" consisted "in adapting the subject of thought to altered circumstances and, above all, to the circumstance of permanent change." After 1945 a new interpretation of Aristotle was being called for by means of which civil society could be reconstituted out of the ancient *polis,* and here, too, Gadamer discreetly took part.[32] If, as Ross claims, it is "Gadamer's secret" and at the same time "his dangerous inheritance to have smuggled the great philosophical tradition from Plato to Heidegger into the home of the prosaic *Bundesrepublik,*" then this secret demands a new reading of *Truth and Method,* one that finally begins to examine more closely the origin of such smuggled goods. For this work the hermeneutic experience garnered by Gadamer under National Socialism finally attained the prominent status of a theory of interpretation with a claim to universality.

NOTES

Translator's note: The two principal texts discussed by Orozco ("Plato and the Poets" and "Plato's Educational State") are translated by P. Christopher Smith in Hans-Georg Gadamer, *Dialogue and Dialectic: Eight Hermeneutical Studies on Plato.*

1. Ross accords philosophical predominance to Gadamer alone on the grounds that Habermas has "made too much of a mark in the social sciences and in political debates for him simply to be called a philosopher" ("Schmuggel. Gadamers Geheimnis," *Frankfurter Allgemeine Zeitung,* Feb. 11, 1995). By this criterion, however, Plato's *Republic,* Aristotle's *Nichomachean Ethics,* and Hobbes's *Leviathan* would all forfeit their status as philosophical texts.

2. Henning Ritter, "Konziliantes Denken. 'Der Philosoph Hans-Georg Gadamer wird neunzig,'" *Frankfurter Allgemeine Zeitung,* Feb. 10, 1990, 27.

3. Martin Heidegger, *Unterwegs zur Sprache* (Frankfurt am Main: Vittorio Klostermann, 1959), 243.

4. "The goal of all attempts at reaching understanding is agreement concerning the subject matter. Hence the task of hermeneutics has always been to establish agreement where there was none or where it had been disturbed in some way" (WM276).

5. It was Jürgen Habermas who critically questioned this hermeneutic postulate, thereby initiating a debate that introduced the "claim to justification" as the ineliminable foundation of a theory of interpretation.

6. These case studies form part of a larger work, *Platonische Gewalt. Gadamers politische Hermeneutik der NS-Zeit* (Berlin: Argument Verlag, 1995), in which I undertake an ideological analysis of Gadamer's philosophical interventions in important aspects of National Socialism.

7. Research into the circumstances of Gadamer's call to Leipzig reveals that he was promoted in place of the university's preferred choice, the NSDAP candidate Theodor Haering, an *ordinarius* lecturer in Tübingen, on the insistence of Professor Heinrich Harmjanz, who was the minister responsible for the social sciences section (Department W6) in the Ministry of Education. Gadamer's name occupied second place on the list, even before that of the SS "echelon candidate" Hans Lipps. See

Jerry Müller, *The Other God that Failed: Hans Freyer and the Deradicalization of German Conservatism* (Princeton, N.J.: Princeton University Press, 1987), 319. Control of Department W6, which for all intents and purposes was "already something like an SS post" (Helmut Heiber, *Walter Frank und sein Reichsinstitut für Geschichte des neuen Deutschlands* [Stuttgart: Deutsche Verlags-Anstalt, 1966], 649), was given to the SS lobbyist Harmjanz in 1937.

8. Cited in Peter Dudeck, "Kontinuität und Wandel. Wissenschaftliche Pädagogik im Nachkriegsdeutschland," in *Wissenschaft im geteilten Deutschland. Restauration oder Neubeginn nach 1945?* eds. W. H. Pehle and P. Sillem (Frankfurt am Main: Fischer Taschenbuch Verlag, 1992), 68. Spranger was still able to identify "much that was irreproachable, indeed praiseworthy, in National Socialism" (ibid., 69), such as the "Reichsberufwettkampf," the "Arbeitsdienstpflicht" and the "NS Landjahr."

9. See Wolfgang Fritz Haug, "Nicolai Hartmanns Neuordnung von Wert und Sinn," in *Deutsche Philosophen 1933,* ed. Wolfgang Fritz Haug (Hamburg: Argument-Verlag, 1989), 159–87.

10. See Thomas Laugstien, "Die protestantische Ethik und der 'Geist von Potsdam'. Sprangers Rekonstruktion des Führerstaats aus dem Prinzip persönlicher Verantwortung," in *Deutsche Philosophen 1933,* 29–68.

11. See Thomas Friederich, "Theodor Litts [?] Warnung von der 'allzu direkten Methoden,'" in *Deutsche Philosophen 1933,* 99–124.

12. Some of the results of this research are drawn together in my essay "Die Plato Rezeption in Deutschland um 1933," in *"Die besten Geister der Nation". Philosophie und Nationalsozialismus,* ed. Ilse Korotin (Vienna: Picus Verlag, 1994).

13. In the standard work on research into Plato in the German-speaking context, Ernst Moritz Manasse (*Bücher über Platon. Bd. I. Werke in deutscher Sprache* [Tübingen: Mohr, 1957] reviews all the editions of the relevant literature after 1945 and yet more or less completely excludes consideration of the obvious relations that they bear to their historical context.

14. This short outline is based upon accounts of the Plato scholarship of the period, which, studied in detail, reveal a more differentiated picture. For a fuller discussion, see Orozco, "Die Plato Rezeption in Deutschland um 1933."

15. Volker Losemann, *Nationalsozialismus und Antike: Studien zur Entwicklung des Faches Alte Geschichte 1933–1945* (Hamburg: Hoffmann und Campe, 1977), 86.

16. It is not necessary here to go into the still undecided question as to whether this biography is genuine or fake. Of central interest, however, is the role this biography played in transforming the principles on which philological investigations into Plato were conducted. The volume *Das Problem der ungeschriebene Lehre Platons* (Darmstadt: Wissenschaftliche Buchgesellschaft, 1972), edited by Jürgen Wippern, contains a number of contributions in which the attempt to reconstruct Plato's unwritten doctrine draws upon a far more complex set of sources.

17. Hans Leisegang, *Die Platondeutung der Gegenwart* (Karlsruhe: G. Braun, 1929), documents this through the example of Kurt Singer (a member of the George circle): "The conclusions to be drawn from demonstrating the authenticity of the *Seventh Letter,* the fact that Plato himself said that he did not write down his real doctrine, the attempt to discover this doctrine in the utterances of his pupils and by re-interpreting the later dialogues in light of these utterances—all this was simply

pushed to one side by Singer with a magnificent gesture of superiority. However, we have no idea on what factual knowledge or on what personal research this rejection is based" (50).

18. Werner Jaeger, "Die Erziehung des politischen Menschen und die Antike," *Volk im Werden* 3 (1933): 46.

19. *Plato und die Dichter* (Frankfurt am Main: Vittorio Klostermann, 1934), 5; reprinted in GW5; subsequent page references (to the original) appear in parentheses in the text.

20. It is this immanence that allows Gadamer to make recourse to this text again on other occasions; by interpreting Plato's work from an atemporal standpoint he is able to disregard its historical features. This is particularly clear in his polemic against Karl Popper ("Platos Denken in Utopien," *Gymansium. Zeitschrift für Kultur der Antike und humanistische Bildung* 90 [1983]: 434–55).

21. "Antrittsvorlesung in Berlin. Gehalten am 10. Mai 1933," in Alfred Baeumler, *Männerbund und Wissenschaft* (Berlin: Junker und Dunnhaupt, 1943), 131.

22. This is not to say that Gadamer is quoting Baeumler directly. Nonetheless, this coincidence is not wholly contingent. It demarcates an identical critical front. The ideal of the harmonious personality was derived polemically from a formulation of Schiller's and was widely used under National Socialism as a cipher to criticize the "apolitical intellectual." Gadamer's employment of this term represents a classic example of what Michel Pêcheux has termed a "cross-discourse."

23. In the introduction to *Platons Lehre von der Wahrheit* (Frankfurt am Main: Vittorio Klostermann, 1931–32, 1940), 201, Martin Heidegger indicated his own approach to the question of Plato's secret doctrine: "The 'doctrine' of a thinker is that which remains unsaid in what is said, that to which man is exposed in order that he might expend himself on it." Heidegger's modern interpretation of the analogy of the cave addresses the reader by mobilizing both the hermeneutic force of the esoteric and a notion of truth as something that can only be revealed. Manfred Frank (*Stil in der Philosophie* [Stuttgart: Reclam, 1992], 64) has described this phenomenon in a very clear way: "What can be 'shown' in the utterances of philosophy but cannot be 'said,' that is, what remains silent can always remain silent profoundly." Devoted disciples are attracted by the realm of the unspoken in that they imagine themselves to be among the select few who stand in the presence of a truth that can never be grasped discursively. See Andrew Bowie's translation of Frank's statement in *Radical Philosophy* 80 (Nov./Dec. 1996): 56.

24. "Platos Staat der Erziehung," in *Das neue Bild der Antike*, ed. Helmut Berve (Leipzig: Koehler & Amelang, 1942), 317 (reprinted in GW5:249–61).

25. Gadamer's various interpretations of the *Seventh Letter* reveal the variety of possible readings to which this letter is exposed. In the texts of 1934 and 1942 he discusses the first part of the letter, in which Plato provides a narrative account of his political and philosophical development. Gadamer's influential article "Dialectic and Sophism in Plato's *Seventh Letter*," dating from 1964, contains a shift in emphasis insofar as he devotes his attention to that part of the letter in which Plato addresses the question concerning "the means by which knowledge comes about" ("Dialektik und Sophistik im siebten Platonischen Brief" [GW6:92]). This essay is a meticulous philological treatise that is radically different from the pieces discussed above in its mode of presentation, style, and form of argument. It is also interesting

because Gadamer discusses the political reading of Plato at a markedly discreet distance. In the tradition of the Tübingen school of classical philology, he writes: "We are concerned to investigate the responses of Aristotle and his contemporaries [to the dialogues—T. O.]. The more we engage with Plato's philosophy in this way, the more one-sided seems the approach to Plato's dialogues which was pursued in Germany in the first half of this century. Either the 'political Plato' was pushed to the fore, as in the work of Wilamowitz, Friedländer and—in the extreme form—Hildebrandt. Or, with reference to the *Existenzphilosophie* of the 20s, prominence was given to the 'existential Plato' and the doctrine of ideas was stripped of its dogmatic form" (GW6:91).

26. See Thomas Laugstien, "Die protestantische Ethik und der 'Geist von Potsdam,'" in *Philosophieverhältnisse im deutschen Faschismus* (Hamburg: Argument-Verlag, 1990), 61 ff.

27. See Müller, *The Other God that Failed*, 267 ff.

28. See Martin Jänicke, "Die 'Abgründige Wissenschaft' vom Leviathan. Zur Hobbes-Deutung Carl Schmitts im Dritten Reich," *Zeitschrift für Politik* 3: 401–15.

29. It remains an open question whether Gadamer sought to indicate his proximity to the Kieler school with this discreet reference. According to Bernd Rüthers (*Entartetes Recht. Rechtslehren und Kronjuristen im Dritten Reich* [Munich: Beck, 1994], 43), this school did not regard the state as "a mere instrument of power for the party or for a 'movement'" (ibid.). In the tradition of Hegelian modes of thought, the state was "bound up with the incarnation of the idea of the ethical as a superpersonal form of 'law' whose central content they sought to define in a national and racist way. The very notions of general law, penal law and individual rights represented normative limits upon the holders of power because of their connection with objective and fundamental legal values (justice, ethical life). The idea of the state and of 'right' could not be instrumentalized at will. Nonetheless, the recourse to Hegel and to German Idealism could, theoretically, set limits to the misuse of the law and the state in the despotic arbitrariness of the administration of the law and the employment of the police" (ibid.). Laugstien has also drawn attention to the functionalizing of the Hegelian universal within this school: "the Hegelian discourse of the 'universal' in which everything individual knows itself to be sublated was ideally suited to consecrating as a higher necessity the removal of the basic rights of the individual" (*Philosophieverhältnisse im deutschen Faschismus*, 175).

30. Martin Broszat, *Der Staat Hitlers* (Munich: DTV, 1983), 412 ff. This source documents a statement made to the minister of justice by Frank's representative in the National Socialist *Juristenbund* on August 22, 1935. There he expressed "serious concern about the state of legal protection in Germany" (ibid.). He referred to the fact "that the refusal of legal support in cases of preventative detention" by the Gestapo stood "in contradiction to the natural sense of law of the northern peoples" and "encouraged calumny." Further, "the activities of the Gestapo—like the Russian Tscheka—w[ere] outside of the sphere of law" and "purely despotic." Frank later took a leading role in the genocide of the Jews. He was condemned to death by the Nuremberg military tribunal.

31. Gadamer criticizes Schmitt's discussion of the play's contemporary political relevance, arguing that Schmitt sought "to read *Hamlet* like a *roman-à-clef*" (GW2: 379). Gadamer maintains programmatically that, "The more that remains open, the

more freely the process of understanding succeeds, that is, the process of transposing what is known in the play into one's own world and, of course, into the world of one's political experience as well" (GW2:380).

32. Gadamer provided the introduction and commentary for a translation of Aristotle's *Metaphysics* that was published in 1948.

Chapter 12

On the Politics of Gadamerian Hermeneutics
A Response to Orozco and Waite

CATHERINE H. ZUCKERT

OROZCO

In "The Art of Allusion: Hans-Georg Gadamer's Philosophical Interventions under National Socialism," Teresa Orozco accuses Gadamer of having written "Plato and the Poets" to justify Nazi suppression of liberal humanist education and "Plato's Educational State" to support national conservative efforts to reform the regime. Geoffrey Waite repeats her accusation in "Radio Nietzsche." Whereas most twentieth-century readers of Nietzsche have unintentionally fostered his elitist politics by adopting a perspectivist reading, Waite charges, Orozco shows that Gadamer did so intentionally. In my view, there is little evidence to support either charge.

Gadamer never joined the National Socialist Party. "For this reason," Orozco admits, "he was elected rector of the University of Leipzig by the occupying Soviet powers in 1947." Although, as Gadamer has stated publicly, "there was no question of his joining one of the organizations of the National Socialist Party because of the importance of remaining loyal to his Jewish friends," she argues he nevertheless was "obliged to make political concessions in order to advance his career."[1] Orozco does not (and presumably cannot) cite any statement, vote, or action by which Gadamer explicitly supported National Socialism. Her argument depends completely upon associations she draws between the historical circumstances and things Gadamer said about Plato. "Gadamer's articles were entirely in keeping with then current research and did not appear to represent anything unusual," she concedes. The goals of Gadamer, in implicit contrast to those of his teacher, Martin Heidegger, "did not extend to such ambitious projects as the question of the meaning of being or revolutionizing the discipline of philosophy." Only by looking at the articles he wrote on Plato explicitly in the context of German politics under the Nazis did she discover the nefarious character of his apparently innocent scholarship.

One might have expected a critic examining Gadamer's scholarship during the Nazi period to have noted the explicit contrast between Gadamer's actions and statements, on the one hand, and those of his teacher, Heidegger, on the other. Orozco never makes this connection. Although Gadamer repeatedly acknowledged his *philosophical* debt to Heidegger both before and after the war, he did not follow Heidegger politically. Unlike Heidegger, he never joined the party or gave speeches defending its policies; nor did Gadamer assert the "essential truth" of National Socialism, as Heidegger did, after Germany was defeated and the party forcibly removed from power. Heidegger himself broke relatively early with the ruling authorities. If Gadamer wanted to reform the party from within, as Orozco goes on to argue, he might have tried to make some sort of "political" alliance with his mentor. He did nothing of the sort.[2]

Perhaps because Gadamer warned critics about dismissing Heidegger's thought solely on political grounds, Orozco claims that Gadamer "argues for a strict division between the scientific and political domains" (TM263; GW1:268). She does not offer any citations to support this claim, which flies in the face of Gadamer's insistence on the importance of breaking down such a strict line by asking what is the meaning of, or what is true in, historical texts for us living now. For example, in "Plato and the Poets," he states, "it cannot be our purpose to dispose of Plato's decision [to expel the poets from the city] by saying that it is merely the function of some particular distant and irrelevant moment in history" (DD41). Gadamer later reiterates this point more generally and defends it at much greater length in his theoretical masterpiece, *Truth and Method*. We cannot learn the truth of any historical writing in a merely "scientific" manner by determining its meaning solely in its own time and place; in his famous teaching about the "fusing of horizons," he argues that we must go on to ask what in the writing remains true for us here and now. Contrary to her own claims about Gadamer, that is what Orozco accuses Gadamer of doing when she criticizes him for implicitly justifying Nazi repression of intellectuals by giving an explication of Plato's expulsion of the poets in the *Republic*.

Orozco does not accuse Gadamer of believing in the truth of National Socialism. On the contrary, she charges him with a kind of political opportunism. In the two essays he wrote on Plato during the Nazi period, she suggests, Gadamer presented his teaching in a manner designed to foster his professional career by pleasing relevant groups or authorities. By demanding that "his educated and cultured audience . . . respect the expulsion of the poets [in Plato] as a decision made within the framework of the founding of the state," in 1934 Gadamer "indirectly attacked the reservation and skepticism about the burning of books [by the Nazis in 1933] which was widespread among the humanist elite." He thus demonstrated the utility or "meaning" of his particular form of Platonic scholarship to the authorities.

When he returned to Plato's *Republic* in 1941 to find a way to respond to "the decay of the state under tyranny," he was seeking a way "to identify with the national conservative faction of National Socialism without, however, publicly declaring his opposition to its more popular forms."

To see whether Orozco's charges are credible, we have to look at what Gadamer actually wrote in "Plato and the Poets" in 1934 and in "Plato's Educational State" in 1941. In his first essay he began by emphasizing the *paradoxical* character of Plato, an obviously poetic writer, turning against poetry. There was a problem here that needed explanation and explication. Although earlier philosophers and poets questioned both the truth and the morality of traditional myths, Plato attempted not merely to purify poetry of untrue mythology and bad moral examples, but also to abolish imitation entirely. Since Plato's own dialogues are imitative representations, we have to distinguish the character of Plato's own words and the effect he intended them to have from the law forbidding imitations he proposes in the *Republic*. "The meaning and intent of [Plato's] critique [of poetry]," Gadamer insisted, "can be established only by [taking account of] the place where it occurs. It is found in Plato's work on the state within a program of education for the guardians of that state, *a state which is erected before our eyes in words alone*" (DD48). As he reports in the *Seventh Letter*, Plato had become convinced that political reform would not occur until rulers were educated differently. In other words, philosophers must become kings. But Gadamer cautioned,

> One misses the full seriousness and importance of that requirement . . . if one takes the projected educational program and the ordering of the state literally. *This state is a state in thought, not any state on earth.* That is to say, its purpose is to bring something to light and not to provide an actual design for an improved order in real political life. (DD48)

What is brought to light in Plato's *Republic* is the natural conflict within the human being between the bestial and the peaceful and the consequent need to bring order to the soul through education. "Such a description seems reminiscent of the humanist ideal of the 'harmonious personality' which is to be formed by developing the whole range of one's human potential—an aesthetic ideal to be achieved by a proposed 'aesthetic education of the human race,'" Gadamer observes. "But for Plato harmony means the tuning of a *dissonance* which is inherent in man (*Republic* 375 c)" (DD54).

Orozco never mentions Gadamer's insistence, both in this essay and the next, that Plato's *Republic* does *not* constitute a blueprint for political reform or that the education described there is explicitly said to culminate in philosophy, that is, in the asking of questions. The end or goal of the "political" education Plato proposes is thus explicitly anti-authoritarian. According to Gadamer, the exposition of this ideal state in the *Republic* serves in educating the political human being, but . . . *[t]his* education . . . is anything but a total manipulation of the soul. . . . [T]his education is not authoritative instruction based on an ideal organization at all; rather it lives by questioning alone. (DD52)

Neither Plato's *Republic* nor Gadamer's interpretation of it constitutes the rationalization for authoritarian rule that Orozco claims.

Orozco finds a "remarkable . . . shift of emphasis" in Gadamer's second essay, "Plato's Educational State," to the need to resist tyranny only because she completely ignores Gadamer's emphasis on the reformist character of Plato's thought in the first. In both essays Gadamer argues that Plato saw a need to reform the traditional Greek education in music (poetry or the works of the "Muses") and gymnastic because that education had been perverted by the sophists into a means of, if not a justification for, pursuing one's self-interest. Evils in cities would not cease, Plato thought, until rulers became philosophical, because philosophy alone would enable them to resist the temptations of wealth and fame. Gadamer himself emphasizes the continuity between the two essays when he begins the second by observing that "the concern here is not even with the right laws for the state but solely with the right education for it, education in citizenship. Ultimately, however, the latter is education in philosophy. This dialogue is a philosophical discussion in which an ideal state is constructed, a utopia which lies far removed from any reality" (DD73). Later Gadamer explicitly states that he "will not repeat the demonstration [provided in the earlier essay] that this state, constructed in words alone, only assumes a political character involving actual power and sovereignty once the discussion comes to the warrior class" (DD83). The warriors embody the tension between the violent drives that lead to tyranny and the gentle philosophical rationality that Plato found in the soul of every human being, the tension that made education necessary. As Gadamer states in his first essay, "It is the goal of paideia to bring about this unification . . . of the philosophical and martial natures in him . . . which keeps the human being from becoming either a tame herd animal (a slave) or a rapacious wolf (a tyrant)." Philosophy enables a man to resist the temptations of power by enabling him "to distinguish the true friend from the false one and what is truly just from flattering appearances. It is philosophy which makes such distinguishing possible, for philosophy is loving the true and resisting the false" (DD56–57).

It is difficult to believe that the man who penned these words was seeking to justify Nazi book burning or concealing his opposition to the popular form of National Socialism.[3] With the (in)famous "myth of the metals," Plato's *Republic* might well have been taken to provide a kind of justification for the eugenic policies of the Third Reich. Gadamer does not deign to mention it. Nor does he suggest that Plato's expulsion of the poets from his "city in speech" (or word, *logos*) should or was intended to be put into practice anywhere. He explicitly argues to the contrary.

Convinced that the meaning of all statements is determined by their historical context, Orozco attends solely to the context—to the scholarship to which Gadamer explicitly responded and the political events and divisions of the times at which he wrote. She does not appear to have bothered to read what he actually argued in his own name. As a result, she emphasizes the political readings of Plato to which Gadamer refers early in both his essays; she does not note the way in which he explicitly distances his own understanding of Plato from them. Likewise, she concludes that because both Gadamer and Alfred Baeumler criticized "the ideal of a harmonious personality and of the 'aesthetic attitude,'" they must have criticized the scholars who advocated such on the same grounds and have drawn the same conclusions from their criticisms. Nothing of the kind follows, either logically or factually.

To support her "opportunistic" reading of Gadamer, Orozco should have attempted to show that Gadamer's reading of Plato changed when the Nazis came into power. That is, she ought to have documented changes from the *Habilitationschrift* Gadamer wrote under the direction of Heidegger in the late 1920s and his essay "Plato and the Poets." Likewise, she should have pointed out the way he modified his understanding of Plato in the *Idea of the Good,* after the Nazis had been defeated. If he made "political concessions" in his work in order to further his career, there should be evidence of such "concessions" or changes. Orozco does not provide it.[4]

Since Gadamer never explicitly mentioned National Socialism in either of the essays he wrote under the regime, one might conclude that the relation between what he wrote and the political context necessarily remains a matter of "interpretation." But are there no canons or standards of interpretation? That would be truly ironic, and perhaps even more devastating to Gadamer than the charge that he collaborated with an immoral regime in order to advance his own scholarly career, since he devoted his major work to articulating just such standards. According to Gadamer, interpretation must begin with an attempt to understand the act, text, or author in its own terms. If no such attempt is made, critics remain confined within their own current understanding, unable to expand their horizon by encompassing or incorporating another. The first step in the case of a literary text is obviously to read what it says. But, if one actually reads what Gadamer contends that Plato advocated—namely, the replacement of traditional "poetic" education by philosophy as the only means of freeing rulers from the temptations of power—one cannot conclude, as Orozco does, that Gadamer was explicating Plato to justify political persecution of intellectuals in Nazi Germany. Gadamer's advocacy for the need for a new education in philosophy in the context of Nazi Germany brings Gadamer closer to his teacher, Heidegger—particularly since Gadamer not only defines philosophy essentially as questioning but also describes the goal of the education as making it possible for someone to "be for others" instead of simply for himself. Yet Gadamer did not ally himself with Heidegger or his politico-educational project when it would have appeared to have been personally and professionally advantageous to do so. In a context in which, Orozco makes clear, it was positively dangerous for an intellectual openly to criticize the regime, Gadamer emphasized the contemporary relevance of Plato's critique of power politics and his advocacy of philosophy as the only way to overcome the attractions of sensual pleasure and fame (considerations to which the leaders of the Nazi party are known not to have been indifferent). Gadamer had obvious practical reasons to mute his criticism of the brutal power politics of the party in power; he had no "practical" reason (beyond the ethical imperatives of friendship and decency) to mute his support.

In a footnote to his essay, Waite suggests that Gadamer may have had a rhetorical reason for remaining silent about the relation between his interpretation of Plato's *Republic* and the political circumstances in which he found himself. (Waite concedes that Orozco's case is purely circumstantial.) Arguments often persuade readers more effectively, Waite observes, if the author leaves them to draw the conclusion from the stated premises on their own.[5] The question, however, is what are the "premises"? Is the "argument" that Gadamer says that Plato recommended the expulsion of the poets and Gadamer thinks that Plato's proposals are both wise and relevant to the present, that the Nazis repressed (which is not even the same as expelling [with honor! cf. *Republic* 398a]) intellectuals, so that we conclude therefore that Gadamer thinks Nazi policy was not merely justifiable, but wise as well? Or, is the argument that, according to Gadamer, Plato "expelled" the poets as part of his argument that the founding of a just regime required that rulers be philosophically educated, that such philosophical education is necessary to free rulers from the temptations of power politics, so that Plato's argument is still relevant to us now, because (implicitly) the heads of the government are obviously neither philosophically educated nor immune to the temptations of power? In that case, the government is and will remain unjust until both magistrates and citizens begin questioning what they now think is good.[6]

The aspect or element of Gadamer's understanding of both Plato in particular and philosophy in general that most distinguished him from his mentor was his insistence on its *ethical* character. (Whereas Heidegger dismissed "ethics" as a subject of the hoary "metaphysical" tradition he was attempting to "destruct," Gadamer entitled the *Habilitationschrift* he wrote under Heidegger's direction *Plato's Dialectical Ethics*.) Philosophical dialogue and textual hermeneutics are essentially ethical, Gadamer argued from the beginning until the end of his career, because they entail respect for the integrity and independence of the other, not only in the initial attempt to understand but also in the peaceful, nonviolent character of the accord or agreement at which the dialogue aims. Orozco's criticism of Gadamer demonstrates, by way of contrast, the unfortunate results of ignoring what an author explicitly says and does in favor of a contextual reconstruction of both his meaning and intent from the postulated effects or results, ex post facto, as it were. She castigates Gadamer for having contributed to the criticism of the classical humanists as well as the sophists, whose teachings have sometimes been associated with liberal politics.[7] But liberal doctrines of right have never countenanced guilt by association or conviction merely on the basis of circumstantial evidence, to say nothing of innuendo, of the kind Orozco employs.

By insisting on reading Gadamer solely in terms of the historical context—academic as well as political—Orozco not merely ignores the explicit contrast Gadamer draws between his own reading of Plato's *Republic,* which he insists is *not* a blueprint for actual reform or action, and that of previous *political* interpreters. Because he was known to associate with members of the Stephen George circle, she also suggests that Gadamer shared their opposition to the Weimar regime. He may well have sympathized with the critics. There were many reasons for Germans to be unhappy with the Weimar government; it was imposed by the allies, and it proved to be weak and ineffective. Being critical of Weimar did not necessarily make someone a Nazi sympathizer.[8]

At the beginning of her essay, Orozco complains that Gadamer rather than Jürgen Habermas was named the "most successful philosopher" in the federal republic because the latter was concerned more with social science than philosophy. The difference between Gadamer and Habermas does not appear to lie in their concern with social science, however. In *Truth and Method* Gadamer presents his own "hermeneutics" or method of interpretation as a critique of and alternative to what he argued were futile attempts to construct a "science" of man on the model of natural science. Moreover, Habermas and Gadamer agree on the nature and utility of interpretation. Habermas not merely concedes but positively urges that the kind of hermeneutical appropriation of the intellectual tradition Gadamer advocates is a necessary and useful component of any social order (and the study of it). But, Habermas contends, such an attempt to preserve the inheritance of the past by adapting it to changing circumstances is inherently conservative. It must, therefore, be supplemented both with technical knowledge of how to control the material foundations and with critical exposure of the cultural myths that develop over time as such.[9] Like his teacher Heidegger, Gadamer argues that such technical approaches tend to transform and thus threaten to destroy what is distinctively human. The difference between Gadamer and Habermas does not lie in the extent of their concern with social science, therefore, but in their respective evaluations of the accuracy and danger (or utility) of technical or technological studies of human affairs. Their respective evaluations of technical knowledge arise, in turn, from their different understandings of the nature of human reason or *logos,* which Gadamer associates primarily with language and Habermas links more to logic. And these different conceptions of reason produce different political inclinations or stands. If Orozco wanted to critique Gadamer's thought in terms of its political effects or implications, like Habermas she could and should have proceeded to do so much more directly.

Gadamer may be criticized for not publicly opposing the rise and rule of National Socialism in Germany in word or deed. If that is the objection Orozco and Waite wish to make, they should say so. The question then would be whether "political correctness" or plain old morality requires a man to become a martyr (like Bonhoeffer). Is it not possible for a person to conclude "prudently" (in the Aristotelian and not the Kantian sense) that it would be better to preserve not merely one's own life and career, but also the lives and livelihood of one's family, friends, and students, by trying to foster change from within, gradually, by means of persuasion rather than force? Such a prudent course of action might require one to remain silent at times or to deliver criticisms indirectly in a veiled manner. In his *Philosophical Apprenticeships,* Gadamer describes his own behavior during the Nazi regime very much in these terms.[10]

WAITE

Gadamer does not appear to be an appropriate focus or even secondary target of Waite's dis-covery of "Radio Nietzsche." In the volumes of Gadamer's *Collected Works,* there is only one piece on Nietzsche, a brief explication of the literary character of *Thus Spoke Zarathustra.* Waite does not even mention it.

Stated in less "figurative" terms than Waite himself employs, the paradox Waite promises to illumine is how Nietzsche, initially embraced by rightwing critics of egalitarian politics, could become the major, indeed virtually the sole, philosophical source of left intellectuals in the late twentieth century. Waite attributes this apparently surprising turn of events to Nietzsche's exo/esoteric form of writing. Although he explicitly called for the emergence of a new race of "supermen" and the end of "herd" or "slave" morality, Nietzsche also gave his readers reason to dismiss such calls for radical inegalitarian political reforms. The "will to power" is only interpretation, Nietzsche declares in *Beyond Good and Evil,* aphorism 22; and in that "Prelude to a Philosophy of the Future," Nietzsche seems to describe himself more as a "free spirit" who seeks to demolish old "idols" or illusions than as a "prophet" (cf. *The Gay Science,* aphorism 1) striving to establish new gods, institutions, or doctrines. Attacking feminists in *Beyond Good and Evil* (aphorism 231), Nietzsche once again claims explicitly that these are merely "my truths."[11] Since the truth as traditionally understood is not the personal possession of any individual—especially when he seeks to communicate it to others by writing—later readers have concluded that Nietzsche cannot be serious. Such statements should not be taken literally; they must be read "figuratively." In the late twentieth century a consensus on the need for such a "figurative" reading has developed, a consensus that extends from left to right, as Max Horkheimer, Theodor Adorno, and Hans Georg Gadamer demonstrate in the conversation broadcast in August 1950 in commemoration of the fiftieth anniversary of Nietzsche's death. (Waite locates Gadamer on the right on the basis of Orozco's article.) In fact, he argues, Nietzsche's texts carry the "radio-active" seeds of Nietzsche's explicit anti-egalitarianism within them. So long as the complex, partly explicit, partly implicit character of Nietzsche's teaching concerning the necessity of an "order of rank" is not merely ignored but explicitly denied, that teaching is insidiously disseminated along with the "new, gentler" Nietzsche promulgated most prominently by Gilles Deleuze.[12] Waite singles Gadamer out to show how far the consensus extends and the extent to which the implicit teaching remains unrecognized. Even a philosopher who agrees with Nietzsche's inegalitarian politics now fails to recognize his own agreement or the character of Nietzsche's texts!

Waite attributes Nietzsche's insidious influence to his use of suppressed premises—in the rhetorical form of argument known as the enthymeme.[13] But it is difficult to see what "premises" Waite thinks Nietzsche suppressed. Nietzsche was perfectly open about his desire to see the emergence of "sovereign individuals" (*Genealogy of Morals* II.2) and the possible utility of modern mass political movements for establishing the right conditions (*Gay Science* I.11). The example of the effect of Nietzschean rhetoric Waite gives is more illuminating. In *What Is Philosophy?* Deleuze and Guattari take Nietzsche' remark that philosophers "must no longer merely permit themselves to accept concepts as gifts . . . but rather first of all *make* them, *create* them, and present them persuasively to others" as their thesis. In adopting a thought of Nietzsche's, Waite implies, they contradict both his and their own words in practice. The saying itself seems to be circular insofar as the persuading of others must render those others nonphilosophers.[14] But that is Waite's point. Apparently seeking to engage others for the sake of educating or even freeing them, the philosopher in fact dominates. Plato is the example par excellence—even though he taught the opposite. Presenting philosophy as contemplation or dialogue, he was actually seeking to forward and support a "social, conceptual, and rhetorical" hierarchy of "spiritual" or "intellectual" leaders (philosopher-kings). His project was rather self-consciously taken up and "incorporated" by Nietzsche, who passed it on

to Deleuze and Guattari without their understanding how their commitment to the "creation" of ever new "incorporeal concepts" served these "premodern, *archaic,* ideological interests and agendas."[15] So long as "individuality" and "originality"—especially imaginative "creation" (as opposed to
mere production) —were valued, Nietzsche recognized, there would continue to be an intellectually or "ideologically" based order of rank. By insisting that there was no "truth" and that everyone could have his or her
own "interpretation," Nietzsche made his thought look radically untraditional and yet at the same time protected and preserved the essentially elitist core.

According to George Bataille, "Nietzsche's position is the only one outside of communism." At the end of the cold war and the apparent "death of
communism," Waite observes in this volume, "Nietzsche and Nietzscheanism have become totalitarian, globally hegemonic" (20). By exposing the
ineradicably intellectualist, and hence elitist, core of Nietzsche's thought,
Waite hopes to reverse the outcome by de-structing the only position outside communism, so leaving the latter dominant and unchallenged.

There are several difficulties with Waite's project, however. First, there is
the presumed method of analysis. Toward the beginning of his essay Waite
claims to be employing a "Straussian" mode of reading "between the lines"
for non-Straussian political ends (see note 5). In *Persecution and the Art of
Writing* Leo Strauss argued that past philosophers did not always state their
own position and arguments straightforwardly in public; from fear of political and religious persecution for their unorthodox views, they have (like
the medieval Jewish philosopher Moses Maimonides) engaged in a kind of
secret writing. But, Strauss warns:

> Reading between the lines is strictly prohibited in all cases where it would be
> less exact than not doing so. Only such reading between the lines as starts
> from an exact consideration of the explicit statements of the author is legiti-
> mate. The context in which a statement occurs, and the literary character of
> the whole work as well as its plan, must be perfectly understood before an in-
> terpretation of the statement can reasonably claim to be adequate or even
> correct.[16]

Waite rests his argument on relatively few statements by Nietzsche, taken
more from letters and the *Nachlass* than from published works. He does not
consider "the literary character of [any] whole work," much less its plan.
The elitist politics and project he claims to find by reading between the lines
can be found very explicitly on the surface.[17]

Waite does not want to determine Nietzsche's intention or meaning so
much as to trace the heretofore unrecognized character of Nietzsche's influence. But in this case his argument appears to be distorted by a political
agenda. By slighting Jacques Derrida and neglecting even to mention Der-

rida's teacher, Michel Foucault, Waite ignores the French intellectuals who
have explicitly tried to purify Nietzsche's thought of its aristocratic elements
and who cannot, therefore, be easily accused of having incorporated and
transmitted them unawares. The reason Waite ignores Foucault and slights
Derrida may be that both declared themselves to be not merely antitotali-
tarian, but anticommunist. Unlike Deleuze and Guattari, who call themselves Marxists, Foucault and Derrida do not share Waite's Althusserian
political commitments. Waite seems to be more interested in building a
Marxist alliance for the ideological class war in which he thinks he is engaged than in exploring what Nietzsche's intention was or his influence is.

What then of the Germans who Waite believes are philosophically superior to the French? The leaders of the Frankfurt School claimed that they
were "deontologizing Marxian critical theory" in opposition to the fundamental ontology of Heidegger. But in the 1950 radio broadcast commemorating the fiftieth anniversary of Nietzsche's death, Max Horkheimer and
Theodor Adorno chose to follow the "Gadamerian doctrine that true philosophy is in essence dialogical. . . . [D]espite minor differences of opinion
about Nietzsche (having to do, [Waite] would argue, with different views of
Heidegger)," there was remarkably little contention. All three easily agreed
that Nietzsche could not be read "literally" in a Russo-American fashion.[18]

According to Waite, both the agreements and the disagreements between
the "rival wings of German philosophy" had their roots in Heidegger.[19] But
Waite has remarkably little to say about Heidegger, either about his powerful influence on twentieth-century interpretations and the consequent dissemination of Nietzsche's thought or about his analysis of the meaning and
effects of modern technology. He does not contrast his own account of Nietzsche's "radio-active" form of writing with Heidegger's claim that Nietzsche's doctrine of the will to power expresses the truth of the technological
age. For Waite, as for Nietzsche, technology simply represents a form of
power. Turning Derrida on his head (or ear), Waite suggests that the radio
succeeds in separating the voice from the body even more than the written
word or typewriter.[20] Rather than disclose the truth, "radio-active" technology perpetuates the traditional belief in the direct communicability of
thought by imperceptibly bringing a universal message into the privacy of
one's own house (and head).

If Waite had paid any attention to Heidegger, he might have discovered
what distinguishes Gadamer from most, if not all, of his contemporaries.
Heavily and explicitly indebted to his teacher, Gadamer shows little interest
in, or influence of, Nietzsche.

In fact, Waite's essay has little to do with Gadamer except at a very general and antagonistic level. Whereas Gadamer argues that philosophy is inherently dialogical and explicitly tries to bring out the meaning of Plato's
text, Waite insists that "philosophy" actually consists in a monologue de-

signed to form the thoughts and deeds of others, by any means available. Perceiving himself to be engaged in ideological class warfare, Waite does not try to understand Nietzsche, Heidegger, Gadamer, Horkheimer, Adorno— or Plato—and so expand his own horizon; he tries to discredit the opposition. He does not analyze or respond to the arguments of others; he merely recasts them in terms of a metaphor he himself admits is stretched. Thus, ironically, it is Waite and not, as he claims, Gadamer who furthers the contemporary dominance of Nietzsche without recognizing that he does so. In the statement from *Ecce Homo* about his being not merely a "destiny" (or disaster) and "dynamite" to which Waite refers, Nietzsche goes on to claim that as a result of his writing "the concept of politics will have merged entirely with a war of spirits [or minds]; all power structures of the old society will have been exploded—all of them are based on lies. There will be wars the like of which have never been seen on earth." In urging his readers to take part in just such "ideological class warfare" Waite fosters Nietzsche's agenda more directly than any of the French or German intellectuals he criticizes. *The* twentieth-century philosopher who opposes such "spiritual" warfare is Hans-Georg Gadamer. Rather than merely criticize (or attack) others from our own vantage point, Gadamer insists, we must first try to see things their way. Rather than impose our interpretation or view, we must engage in a dialogue, the form of thought that Nietzsche said was decadent and democratic, like Socrates, that philosopher of the "rabble."

Gadamer explicitly seeks to mediate. Neither Orozco nor Waite recognizes any center or middle in politics; they see only either/or's. As a result they not only fail to understand the essential character of Gadamer's hermeneutics; their writings also demonstrably lack one of the two primary political virtues—moderation.

NOTES

1. As evidence she quotes Gadamer's own statement (PA79; PL57) that his call to a chair at Leipzig was a consequence of "high politics." She does not explain, as Gadamer does in the following sentence, that the "high politics" consisted of a decision by the Nazis to cease imposing political criteria for academic appointments because they needed the work of the best scientists in the universities to win the war. Gadamer had enrolled earlier in a "rehabilitation" camp in order to keep his position as a *dozent;* he did not exhibit sufficient loyalty to or enthusiasm for the regime to obtain a higher position so long as there were political criteria.

2. As he himself reports in "Heidegger's Later Philosophy," Gadamer was surprised by the "turn" Heidegger's thought had taken in *The Origin of the Work of Art* (which circulated in manuscript form in Germany during the 1930s, well before its official publication in 1954 [PH216; GW6:252]). Gadamer subsequently spent a great deal of time and effort coming to terms with the new direction Heidegger's thought had taken, an effort that culminated in the publication of Gadamer's mas-

terwork, *Truth and Method*. He made his philosophical differences with his mentor explicit in the introduction to the second edition, as well as in the essay "The Heritage of Hegel" (TMxxxvii–xxxviii; GW2:447–48 and RAS56; GW4:477).

3. Cf. Fred Dallmayr, "Hermeneutics and Justice," in *Festivals of Interpretation* (Albany: State University of New York Press, 1990), 95–105, and Catherine H. Zuckert, *Postmodern Platos* (Chicago: University of Chicago Press, 1996), 78–82, for an argument to the contrary. "Gadamer did not explicitly say anything about the relevance of his analysis of Plato's *Republic* to the Nazi regime in which he wrote," I observe. "It is not too difficult, however, to see the implicit critique. If philosophical inquiry constitutes *the* only basis of a true community, the regime then in power in Germany was clearly unjust" (82).

4. In fact, there is a great deal of continuity in Gadamer's thought from beginning to end. In my chapter "Gadamer's Path," in *Postmodern Platos,* 70–103, I have argued that he gradually, but only gradually, indicated the ways in which he came to disagree with his teacher Heidegger.

5. Leo Strauss makes a similar argument about the insidious character of Machiavelli's blasphemous suggestions in *Thoughts on Machiavelli;* Waite claims to be employing Strauss method (against Strauss's political commitments or ends).

6. In his *Philosophical Apprenticeships* Gadamer reports that his piece on Plato and the poets had "been printed under the motto: 'He who philosophizes is not at one with the premises of his time.' This was well camouflaged as a quote from Goethe and thus not quite a heroic act. But it was also not an accommodation" (PA78; PL56).

7. Cf. Eric A. Havelock, *The Liberal Temper in Greek Politics* (New Haven, Conn.: Yale University Press, 1957), and the acerbic critique of the same by Leo Strauss, reprinted in *Liberalism: Ancient and Modern* (New York: Basic Books, 1968), 26–34. Gadamer indicates the source of the association between the sophists and "democratic" (although not, strictly speaking, "liberal") politics when he observes that, as Glaucon makes clear at the beginning of Book II of the *Republic* in his restatement of Thrasymachus's contention that "justice" consists merely in the "advantage of the stronger," "justice" in the form of law (or convention, *nomos*) merely represents the agreement of weak individuals to band together to protect themselves from depredations by the strong. The person who knows (or, like the sophists, can teach someone) how to persuade the many (majority) to enact what he wants as law is, therefore, most powerful. Although Glaucon's argument has often been compared to social contract theory, it is fundamentally different, inasmuch as it does not ground the justice or "right" of the government in the natural rights of each individual party to the contract, but makes law merely a matter of conventional right based effectively on the superior power of the greatest number.

8. One could, for example, also have been a communist.

9. *Knowledge and Human Interests* (Boston: Beacon Press, 1971); "A Review of Gadamer's *Truth and Method,*" in *Zur Logik der Sozialwissenschafter* (Frankfurt am Main: Suhrkamp Verlag, 1970), 251–90, reprinted in Fred R. Dallmayr and Thomas A. McCarthy, ed., *Understanding and Social Inquiry* (Notre Dame, Ind.: University of Notre Dame Press, 1977), 335–63. Likewise, in *The Philosophy of Hans-Georg Gadamer,* Stanley Rosen argues that Gadamer's hermeneutics ultimately fail to preserve the respect for the other, the integrity of individual texts or of the understandings

of their individual authors, that he himself thinks is essential to preserve the ethical character of dialogue by mixing or melding them with contemporary concerns. In *Dialogue and Deconstruction,* Jacques Derrida charges, Gadamer refuses to countenance the possibility of irreconcilable differences.

10. "Certainly it remained difficult to keep the right balance, not to compromise oneself so far that one would be dismissed and yet still to remain recognizable to colleagues and students. That we somehow found the right balance was confirmed for us one day when it was said of us that we had only 'loose sympathy' with the new awakening. . . . I exposed myself a good deal, and when the new National Socialist *Kampf* organization replaced our self-serving union, I was severely slandered. . . . So it was that the objections of the *Dozentenbund* prevented the sought-after title of professor from being bestowed on me. . . . Of course I wanted to save my academic existence in Germany, but without making political concessions that could cost me the trust of my friends in the outer or inner emigration. . . . Finally I found a way. . . . I registered for my 'rehabilitation' voluntarily" (PA76–79).

11. The examples are mine, not Waite's.

12. Cf. *The New Nietzsche,* trans. David Allison (New York: Dell, 1977) for a representative selection of essays and authors arguing for the new, more egalitarian interpretation.

13. Waite refers to Leibniz, but it was Aristotle in *Rhetoric* (1354a) who first defined the enthymeme as a form of argumentation especially suited to popular or political (as opposed to scientific) reasoning. However, in the section entitled "Why I Am a Destiny" in *Ecce Homo* Nietzsche denies that he ever spoke to the "rabble."

14. This is the problem Zarathustra faces in his relations with potential followers: how can a teacher exercise influence without corrupting his students? Gadamer treats the question in the essay on *Zarathustra* that Waite ignores.

15. In *Postmodern Platos,* 10–32, I trace the ambiguous stance Nietzsche took toward Plato throughout his career. Sometimes Nietzsche claims to be overturning Plato; sometimes he suspects that Plato understood everything that Nietzsche himself was arguing.

16. *Persecution and the Art of Writing* (New York: Free Press, 1952), 30.

17. In a letter he wrote to Karl Loewith in 1935 (translated and reprinted in *The Independent Journal of Philosophy* 5/6 [1988]: 183), Strauss explained that he thought Nietzsche wanted "to repeat antiquity . . . at the peak of modernity." Strauss shared Nietzsche's desire; but Strauss had come to believe that the polemical character of Nietzsche's critique of modernity on the basis of probity (a scripturally based virtue) prevented him from realizing his intention. (Strauss explains the reasons Nietzsche's attempt is self-contradictory [and hence necessarily fails] in "Note on the Plan of Nietzsche's *Beyond Good and Evil,*" reprinted in *Studies in Platonic Political Philosophy* [Chicago: University of Chicago Press, 1983], 175–91.) Waite believes that Nietzsche is succeeding surreptitiously, because, in contrast to Strauss, Waite objects to all forms of inequality or "elitism." He does not concern himself with the character of the promised *"Übermensch."*

18. Waite gives a rather inaccurate account of the conversation in which he seems to mistake the polite presentation of different views for agreement. Horkheimer, Adorno, and Gadamer do agree that Nietzsche was a poetic writer. Adorno introduces the problem of the apparently contradictory reception of Nietzsche as a

Nazi, on the one hand, and as a great philosopher, on the other. Gadamer thinks Nietzsche's importance lies (as Heidegger had argued) in his announcement of the onset of European nihilism. Horkheimer criticizes Nietzsche for the absence of dialectic; Gadamer responds that Nietzsche lacks the form, but that his thought is based upon dialectic. Gadamer then emphasizes the psychological depth and influence of Nietzsche's writings. Horkheimer agrees that Nietzsche is a forerunner of Sigmund Freud and the Marquis de Sade. Both he and Adorno fault Nietzsche for his failure to enunciate an effective social critique or program of reform, whereas Gadamer emphasizes the tragic aspect of Nietzsche's teaching concerning the eternal return. He refers, ironically, to the same statement Nietzsche makes in *Ecce Homo* about his being a "destiny," of which Waite makes much. Cf. Max Horkheimer, *Gesammelte Schriften* (Frankfurt am Main: S. Fischer, 1989), vol. 13, 111–20.

19. In his *Introduction to Metaphysics,* trans. Ralph Manheim (New Haven, Conn.: Yale University Press, 1959), Heidegger argued that Germany was caught between the "pincers" of the two technological superpowers, the Soviet Union and the United States.

20. In *Speech and Phenomena,* trans. David Allison (Evanston, Ill.: Northwestern University Press, 1973), 74–87, Derrida argues that the classical belief in the pure, undistorted communicability of ideas is based on the experience of hearing ourselves say what we think and concluding, therefore, that the expression and the thought occur simultaneously, in us as well as in the receiver. He begins *Otobiographies: L'enseignement de Nietzsche et la politique du nom propre* (Paris: Galilee, 1984) (*The Ear of the Other,* ed. Christie V. McDonald [New York: Schocken Books, 1985]) by quoting the section of *Thus Spoke Zarathustra* "On Redemption" in which Zarathustra describes the fragmented, specialized human beings in whom one organ or talent has grown so disproportionately to all others that it almost overwhelms them, e.g., the little man attached to a huge ear, in arguing that Nietzsche *was* implicated in Nazi politics, partly because he could not posthumously control the use of his name or writings (especially by his sister). Authors leave a "trace" that acquires new meaning, a meaning they cannot control (although they try by means of their name—hence the "politics" or attempt to exercise power on subsequent generations of readers).

Chapter 13

The Protection of
the Philosophical Form

A Response to Zuckert

TERESA OROZCO, *translated by Paul Malone*

Although I do not share all the premises of the Gadamerian conception of dialogue, I am convinced that an examination of some of Catherine H. Zuckert's objections to my article can contribute to a better understanding of Gadamer's philosophical interventions under National Socialism. Her commentary gives me the opportunity to clarify some misunderstandings.[1] It is both striking and paradoxical that in Zuckert's polemic, the hermeneutic postulate of openness to the opinions of others and the paradigm of understanding summon up less tolerance and moderation whenever a critical examination of the stock of tradition leads to undesirable results. It should be borne in mind that between truth and method there are various branches of inquiry—and even other theories of interpretation—which, by means of methodical reflection, have rightfully won their place on the field of philosophy and science. These theories grant no validity to the logic: *that cannot be, which may not be.*[2] It might seem plausible that Gadamerian hermeneutics can be applied to their own prehistory with only partial success. The dogmatic authority of tradition and the uncontested continuance of authority exclude any question of their legitimacy. Since the intersection of intellectual traditions with domination and power is fundamental to the act of transmission, we are well advised not to give up critical reflection.

In this short article I refer to my book *Platonische Gewalt*, in which my thesis is supported by considerable evidence and a sentence-by-sentence interpretation. Much of what I formulate here in outline is considered there in its complexity. Since I have concentrated on Gadamer's interpretation of Plato, and have only peripherally treated the details and information that contradict Gadamer's depiction of these years in his autobiographical writings,[3] one should recall the following: in November 1933 Gadamer signed the *Bekenntnis der Professoren an den deutschen Universitäten und Hochschulen zu*

Adolf Hitler und dem nationalsozialistischen Staat (Declaration of the Faith of Professors in the German Universities and Colleges in Adolf Hitler and the National Socialist State);[4] he was a member of the National Socialist Teachers' Union (NSLB);[5] he held lectures in the service of National Socialist foreign propaganda in countries belonging to or occupied by the Axis powers; and he received his chair at Leipzig by means of "high politics" (PL57) and with the assistance of the SS. Representative of Gadamer's interventions during the fascist war is his lecture "*Volk* and History in Herder's Thought," which he delivered in occupied Paris in 1941 before an audience of officers taken as prisoners of war. Here Gadamer offers a *völkisch* interpretation of Herder that he represents as a "purely scientific study" (PL118). This text reappears in 1967 without the *völkisch* passages and with some revisions.[6] The direct and explicit connections to Nazism that Zuckert cannot find in my text are easily found and carry a good deal of weight in my book.[7] The search for explicitly "*völkisch*" thoughts, however, overlooks other forms— as a rule more effective forms, because they take into account the particular logic of philosophy—of philosophical articulation of Nazism.

My work nowhere brings moral charges, nor does it demand an absurd martyrdom or a hidden resistance. My criticism is directed at the one-sided picture Gadamer gives *after 1945* of the relationships at the earlier time. The results of my investigation revise decisively Gadamer's self- image as a "internal emigrant," who of course had to make outward concessions for career reasons, but who remained philosophically and academically at a distance. It is not concerned with exposing Gadamer as a disguised Nazi, but rather with investigating the positions of nationalist conservatism that he then maintained in his philosophical production as well. One of the questions posed by my research was: What does it mean to represent conservative and antidemocratic positions in peacetime under parliamentary democracies, and what does it mean under a dictatorship? What form does the difference take? The interest of my work lay in comprehending the specifics of such forms of intellectual accommodation and in exploring them— not morally, but on the basis of their structural conditions. It was essential to work out how they became possible in the *normality* of the academy and through the medium of interpretation of the classics, without declaring such interpretation irrelevant and void from the outset in view of the cruder and violent forms of the *völkisch* fascist movement.

   The fact that Heidegger appeared as a representative of the *völkisch* movement in party uniform while Gadamer was not a party member is no argument for an opposition to Nazism in the character of the nationalist conservative wing. This is a widespread misreading of the history of fascism, and one that has far-reaching consequences for Zuckert's interpretation of my article. This misreading is based on the acceptance, contrary to fact, that actual existing Nazism consisted only of Hitler and the Nazi Party, in conjunction with a *völkisch* doctrine of crude eugenic and authoritarian concepts. The consequence of this misreading is that any elements that do not fit into this picture are seen as potential loci of resistance. In this view, the conservative elites—with representatives in the economy, the *Bildungsbürgertum,* the churches, the universities, and the armed forces—who determinedly allied themselves with the Nazis are unaccounted for as a driving and supporting power. It is thus hardly astonishing that these positions lay claim to political correctness well into the postwar period.[8] Both the classic and the newer research into fascism prove forcefully that the internal differences between both camps were the very conditions that preserved Nazism as a social formation.[9] They were united in the fight against the Weimar Republic in favor of an authoritarian Führer-state, as is still clearly expressed in the concepts of the conservative resistance.[10] Without a doubt both factions played an active role in the destruction of the foundations of the Weimar Republic.[11] Zuckert's understanding for the criticism of the Weimar Republic, expressed in the argument that it "proved to be weak and ineffective," comes near to justifying its downfall. The fact that this republic was forsaken by large parts of the Wilhelmine middle class does not prove the inevitability of Nazism. Gadamer himself explains subsequently that "interest in the political aspects of Plato" had "nothing at all to do with the Nazis yet"; rather, it arose from "the need to imagine a state according to a model in which there was still a fundamental belief in the state. For there was no such belief in the Weimar Republic."[12] There are many reasons to think that this belief was by no means attached to democracy, but rather to the Wilhelmine authoritarian state. Given this background, it is hardly surprising that with the rise of fascism, the prevalent currents of Plato research participate in the consolidation of National Socialism.[13] Symptomatic of the misreading I have described is the violence and single-mindedness of the debate around the *völkisch* Heidegger, which clearly has the effect of displacing the question of the different forms of collaboration practiced by the remainder of the philosopher's guild.

Zuckert pleads for the recovery of quotations in which Gadamer declares the separation of the political from the scientific. Although it openly contradicts postulates in *Truth and Method,* Gadamer tries to mitigate his teacher Heidegger's entanglement by appealing to the "political incompetence of philosophy."[14] In addition I refer to an interview of 1990, in which he unmistakably stands by his contention that there were also Nazis who pursued "very good science."[15] Gadamer tells us there how it was possible to philosophize undisturbed and scientifically under National Socialism. In fact, the Platonic claim "to lead the leader" released a tremendous philosophical productivity, which had the result of benefiting the consolidation of National Socialism.[16]

My reading does not assume Gadamer to be an opportunist; rather, it documents the astonishing coherence of his position. In the Plato interpretation of 1934, it becomes clear that Gadamer, through the medium of Plato's world of ideas and its hermeneutic renewal, collaborated in consummating the union into which the nationalist conservative middle class (which as "spirit of Potsdam" brought the Reichswehr into National Socialism) entered with the Nazis. I show that in his contribution to the *Kriegseinsatz der Geisteswissenschaften* (mobilization of the humanities) of 1942 the same Prussian group, with the debacle of Stalingrad at hand, loosened this union and strove toward an authoritarian reform of the state. This faction's method of movement is expressed in both texts.[17]

The fact that Gadamer in his lecture "Plato and the Poets" (1934) positively articulates some of the most prominent topoi of the speeches in support of book burning and *Gleichschaltung* (accommodation to National Socialist doctrine), that is, the criticism of liberal humanist education, is by no means the only reason that this text can be read as a justification of Nazism in its incipient phase. The "historical context" is more complex and many-layered than Zuckert assumes. The venue in which this lecture was delivered, namely the Gesellschaft der Freunde des Humanistischen Gymnasiums (Society of Friends of the Classical High School), as well as the self-accommodation of classical philology and the transformation of the humanist canon of Platonic interpretation, stand in the context of fascization, which has left clear traces behind in Gadamer's text. The astonishing effect that the National Socialist present is not directly named, yet is tacitly present, rests on a hermeneutics of allusion: the text is laid out so that in the historical horizon of understanding of the classically educated milieu, it becomes charged with fascist meanings. As a result the perception of the fascist present in the text seems to be achieved by the listener. The records of this course of lectures, which were published regularly in the magazine *Das Humanistische Gymnasium* (The Classical High School),[18] give an impression of this. In the closing commentary to Gadamer's lecture—in accordance with the fascist rhetoric of the *new man*—one reads: "The new man is created for the new state and from nothing. . . . It is the welfare of the entire state that matters. . . . Plato's mythic literature, as much as his dialogic literature, shows true poetic ability, which puts itself in the service of the new idea of man." Zuckert's reproach of "guilt by association" is therefore already untenable, because Gadamer and his audience at the time manufactured these "associations" themselves. The further remarks of the secretary by no means arose by chance; rather, they were guided by connotational elements. The lecture is in its very text shot through with a network of interdiscursive resonances that are no longer accessible to the present-day reader.[19]

I have not maintained, as Zuckert assumes, that Gadamer's interpretation of Plato consists of direct instructions for the persecution of intellectuals. His philosophical *Anschluss* was skillful and unconstrained. I wrote: "Gadamer constructed an interpretive framework for the contemporary situation in Germany that, at the same time, allowed Plato's critique of the poets to be understood in a manner that simultaneously articulated the self-understanding of the present." This projection of the new backwards into the Platonic order showed itself capable of constructing a kind of déjà-vu experience, bestowing a trace of heroic greatness upon the violent National Socialist circumstances through the medium of classical philosophy. What is remarkable here is that such processes as the suppression of enemies of the state, the driving of poets into exile, and the "cleansing" of poetry (i.e., censorship) are placed in charge of the power of the state and not of the hermeneutic dialogue. So it is evident that here the framework of state power forms the *conditio sine qua non* of the dialogue.

Zuckert's argument that in both essays Plato's *Politeia* "does not constitute a blueprint for political reform," and that he backs the philosophical upbringing of the guardians of the state, is philologically a mere half-truth. The theme in the text of 1934 is the "foundation of the state" and "the radical rejection of the existing state,"[20] as well as the philosophical upbringing of youth to become guardians of the state. The defense is directed at the sophistic spirit, which "attacked" and "dissolved" the substance of the state. In 1942 the main idea is that of the "decline of the state under tyranny" and the philosophical upbringing of the guardians with particular consideration given to the state-supporting leaders. Gadamer stresses the seduction of those who govern by their power ("tyrants have no friends"), and the injury to the corporative order of the Platonic state. Both interpretations are transposed into the words of philosophy and thus also into their normative function. The philosophical form is a protection from any crude topical relevance, for the Gadamerian art of allusion lies in the continual working out of the character of the Platonic state as a philosophical model, and to this end it is necessary that Plato's *Politeia* remain a state in thought alone. This exemplary quality is what first sets in motion the hermeneutic effect on the listeners and/or readers. Zuckert pays no heed to the sentence in which this inaccessible model, as "exclusive determination" (*Plato und die Dichter* 14), is assigned an ordering function for the subject of the state: "It is an 'originary image in heaven' for whoever wishes to organize himself and his internal constitution" (ibid.). Contemplating this "originary image in heaven," individuals recognize in themselves the "reality of the state."[21] The frequently appearing motif of "care for the internal state" (*Plato und die Dichter* 29) is addressed to the audience and/or readership. On this model the interior of the civil subject, where morality and religiosity usually have their seat, becomes the place occupied by the state itself. There is no discrepancy between the reality of the state (staatliches Sein)[22] and moral duty (moralisches Sollen). It seems to me a grave matter that Gadamer explicitly refuses as "sophist" any foundation of the authority of the state right (Plato und die Dichter 15) and leaves no room for the acknowledgment of individual basic rights. The establishment of a state in words applies also in 1942: "the educational structure" should further "its citizens' correct belief in the state" (Plato and the Educational State 233). In any case this belief is reduced to the citizen's "joining in the totality of the organization of rule" (Plato and the Educational State 327).

One must visualize how Nazism articulated itself as an "educational state" around 1933 in order to be able to estimate the resonance of the following sentence in the Platonic imaginary: "Although it appears to be a state resting completely on the power of an educational organization, an ahistorical new beginning from nothing through the force of a new habituation, it is in truth a picture, in whose delineation the soul should recognize justice" (Plato und die Dichter 17). The "true state of justice" (Plato und die Dichter 28) has nothing to do, however, with democratic ideas of participation and justice. Gadamer discreetly makes this clear in a footnote, according to which the Platonic state is a state of "masters and servants" and a state for war (Plato und die Dichter note 36; DD54).

Gadamer by no means stands alone in his interpretation of the Platonic paideia. The topos of the education of the guardians forms the kernel of most of the interpretations of Plato at the time. Here the National Socialist discourses of domination, beauty, health, and race found their ideal expression. The successful paideia stands not only for eugenic discourses but also for the development of the internal state that constitutes itself in the mirror of the state order.[23] In opposition to an enlightened educational model, the contemporary elaborations of the Platonic education of the guardians emphasize the manly virtues of military fitness, heroic lifestyle, readiness for death, decisionistic choice, the struggle against the "sophistic" enemy, and the affirmation of the "unwritten law" of the state (Orozco, "Die Platon-Rezeption" 156 ff). Gadamer articulated these individual aspects in his interpretation. The "ethical" component, which Zuckert claims is bound in this text with the anchoring of state domination in the plane of elementary socialization, is the world of the customs and traditions of a community. The "upbringing into a state" (Plato und die Dichter 17) is a process that happens essentially inexpressibly and without a determining and planning subject. "The most important educational effect never reaches the explicit instruction, but rather the 'laws of the state,' particularly the unwritten, the ruling ethic in the state community, in which safe human formation happens in seclusion" (ibid., 14). In this view, those ethical forms that are not prevalent are delegitimated, as for instance those potential elements of solidarity that could support possible resistance against the state. Gadamer's renunciation of the authoritarian command means that he relies on the hidden (and therefore much more powerful) effect of the state. Thereby, however, he comes very near to *völkisch* educational theory, which by no means refers to pure authoritarianism.[24] For instance, Ernst Krieck saw the task of *völkisch* educational theory in the "internal formation of humanity . . . and this upbringing [the *völkisch*] also takes place simply—completely unconsciously and unintentionally at first—in that the state accustoms its people to its legal and political paths, and in that it directs the attitude and consciousness of the new generation according to its norms."[25] One should not, however, be deceived by this proximity. Gadamer's achievement consisted rather of the creation of a sounding board in which *völkisch* educational theory also—but not exclusively—could articulate itself.

In Zuckert's representation of the Platonic *paideia,* its militarization is not in evidence. Gadamer declares the status of guardian to be the "real status of human being" (*Plato und die Dichter* 19).[26] We have here no autonomous individuals who can distinguish the true from the false independently of the state will. The real human is reduced to readiness for war and to subjection under the state. The warrior's self-discipline is not an end in itself: it is necessary to prevent the force of the guardians from turning into power against the domination of the state. The knowledge of the guardian (in accordance with Carl Schmitt) consists of an elementary power of differentiation: "he must be able to distinguish friend from enemy" (ibid., 19). It is in the education of this decisionistic love-and-hate competence that Gadamer in 1934 locates the task of philosophy. In return, any power of differentiation that is based on elementary humanity and that can be mobilized against illegitimate demands of the state has no place, for the decisionistic principle remains in force: "to love the friend just because he is a friend—and not because and as far as he does one good but also, if he does one harm: and to hate the enemy, just because he is the enemy, even if he does one good" (*Plato und die Dichter* 20). That this explanation found resonance is demonstrated by an expert opinion in connection with Gadamer's summons to Leipzig. His text "Plato and the Poets," it is said, provides "a thoroughly original explanation of the Platonic doctrine of the state and gains a completely new relevance through the knowledge that the status of the warrior and guardian in the Platonic state is the status of human being" (Gadamer's personal file in the Leipzig University archive, Doc. 41).

I do not contest the fact that the reception and history of the effect of Gadamer's texts under Nazism attest a plurality of interpretations. A reading, however, that is obligated to the historicity of the interpretation must continue the attempt at reconstruction provided here in its infancy, and make the structure and the interests of the hermeneutic application, in its polyphony, as transparent as possible. The logic of hermeneutic interpretation—and here one must agree with Gadamer—includes an abundance of possibilities. Today, a generation of thinkers, in dialogue with Gadamer not least, have come to some agreement on how to deal with this contingent and unavoidable situation. Philosophers like Paul Ricoeur, Charles Taylor, and Jürgen Habermas strive for theories of interpretation without going back beyond the founding claim of the Enlightenment. This claim was raised by Jürgen Habermas against the disputable postulates of Gadamer's conservative hermeneutics more than twenty years ago. Thereby he referred to Albrecht Wellmer. This criticism is clearly still relevant, given the results of this investigation:

> The enlightenment knew what hermeneutics forgets: That the "dialogue" that we "are" according to Gadamer is also a forced connection and exactly for that reason is no conversation. . . . The universal claim of the hermeneutic attempt [can] only then [be maintained] if one proceeds on the assumption that the context of transmission, as the locus of possible truth and factual communication, is at the same time also the locus of factual untruth and continuing power.[27]

Perhaps the uncomfortable aspect of my research lies in the disclosure of that which Isabelle Kalinowski calls "the decisive pledge," which accrued to the Hitler regime from the combination of the conservative discourse with the National Socialist discourse: "The hatred for the Weimar constitutional state has no doubt found a deeper form of efficacy in Gadamer's commentaries on Plato than in the direct engagement of Heidegger, which perhaps paradoxically proves a greater political naiveté."[28] Zuckert agrees with Gadamer's negative attitude toward the Weimar Republic, but does not want to acknowledge its consequences: the authorization of Nazism, whose astonishing stability was not least the result of a legitimation pursued by many voices in the eternal space of philosophy.

NOTES

1. In the first paragraph of my chapter "The Art of Allusion" I cite a newspaper article. I criticize the statement that Jürgen Habermas is undeserving of the title of philosopher because he has "made too much of a mark in the social sciences and in political debates" (Ross, "Schmuggel: Gadamers Geheimnis," *Frankfurter Allgemeine Zeitung*, vol. 11, no. 2 [Feb. 11, 1995]). Zuckert attributes to me the very opinion criticized by me.

2. An example for this logic is the commentary on my work by Richard Palmer (PHGG588 ff). Without entering into my research, Palmer contents himself with a

series of arguments *ad hominem,* which further contain a series of philological errors—as, for example, his explanation of Gadamer's lecture on Herder (1941).

3. Moreover, if one wishes to use Gadamer's memoirs as an authentic source, it would make sense to demand at least their examination of and their comparison with other sources.

4. The political significance of this document has been described by George Leamann, *Heidegger im Kontext: Gesamtüberblick zum NS–Engagement der Universitätsphilosophen* (Hamburg: Argument-Verlag, 1993), 100, and Thomas Laugstien, *Philosophieverhältnisse im deutschen Faschismus* (Hamburg: Argument-Verlag, 1990), 29 ff.

5. This membership (number 254,387) is substantiated by the files of the former Berlin Document Center. In 1934 Gadamer became a member of the National Socialist People's Welfare Organization (NSV) and in 1938 he joined the German Reich Union for Physical Education (DRL) (Leaman 40).

6. Gadamer published a text in 1967 with the title *Herder und die geschichtliche Welt* (Herder and the historical world). It appears as an epilogue to the edition of J. G. Herder's early writings, *Auch eine Philosophie der Geschichte zur Bildung der Menschheit* (Frankfurt: Suhrkamp, 1967). A comprehensive examination of this text and of the lecture underlying it, "*Volk* and History in Herder's Thought" (Frankfurt: Vittorio Klostermann, 1942), is likewise found in my book. There I reconstruct the official context of this enterprise and analyze the characteristics of National Socialist occupation policy in France, as well as the importance attached to German cultural policy and to the German Institute in Paris.

7. Here it should be mentioned that Gadamer has also shown courage. In 1942, when the Marburg Romanist Werner Krauss was arrested by the Gestapo in their action against the Schulze-Boysen-Harnack resistance group and was condemned to death, an intensive rescue operation was set in motion by Krauss's university colleagues. Among them was Gadamer, who sent a plea for clemency to the Reich court-martial. Cf. Peter Jehle, *Werner Krauss und die Romanistik im NS-Staat* (Hamburg: Argument-Verlag, 1996), 141–50.

8. Habermas attributes the solidarity of the faction of Young Conservatives to their collective convictions: "It is precisely the specifically German offshoots of the lost First World War—which was also lost mentally—who appear as the true guardians of an unbroken national tradition According to what they themselves profess, they had nothing to regret in 1945, for they felt that the movement they had supported in 1933 had let them down. They had seen National Socialism in the light of their own ideas, at least as a variation on what was 'their own'" (Jürgen Habermas, "Carl Schmitt in the Political Intellectual History of the Federal Republic," in *A Berlin Republic: Writings on Germany,* trans. Steven Rendall [Lincoln: University of Nebraska Press, 1997], 116–17).

9. Martin Broszat and Horst Möller, eds., *Das Dritte Reich: Herrschaftsstruktur und Geschichte* (Munich: Beck, 1986). Eberhard Jäckel, *Hitlers Herrschaft* (Stuttgart: Deutsche Verlags-Anstalt, 1986); Martin Broszat and Klaus Schwabe, eds., *Die deutschen Eliten und der Weg in den Zweiten Weltkrieg* (Munich: Beck, 1989); Hans Mommsen, "Zur Verschränkung traditioneller und faschistischer Führungsgruppen in Deutschland beim Übergang von der Bewegung zur Systemphase," in *Der Nationalsozialismus und die deutsche Gesellschaft* (Hamburg: Rowohlt-Verlag, 1991), 39–66.

10. Hans Mommsen, "Gesellschaftsbild und Verfassungspläne des deutschen Widerstands," in *Der Nationalsozialismus und die deutsche Gesellschaft* (Hamburg: Rowohlt-Verlag, 1991), 233–337.

11. "Unlike after the Second World War, after the first World War in Germany the national dreams of greatness and world power were still by no means dreamed out. . . . An especially fateful effect of the humiliation of the Treaty of Versailles was that it prevented the self-critical examination of Wilhelmine imperialist pre-war policies" (Mommsen, "Zur Verschränkung," 36).

12. "The real Nazis, however, had no interest in us at all." Hans-Georg Gadamer in conversation with Dörte von Westernhagen, *Das Argument* 182, 32.4 (July–Aug. 1990): 543–55; here 549.

13. Teresa Orozco, "Die Platon-Rezeption in Deutschland um 1933," in *"Die besten Geister der Nation." Philosophie und Nationalsozialismus,* ed. Ilse Korotin (Vienna: Picus Verlag, 1994), 141–85.

14. Gadamer, "Über die politische Inkompetenz der Philosophie," *Sinn und Form* 45.1: 5–12.

15. Hans-Georg Gadamer in conversation with Dörte von Westernhagen, *Das Argument* 182, 32.4 (July–Aug. 1990), 543–555; here 549.

16. In terms of the society as a whole, this is also substantiated in the new Hitler biography by Ian Kershaw, particularly in the chapter "Dem Führer entgegen arbeiten." *Hitler 1889–1936* (Stuttgart: Deutsche Verlags-Anstalt, 1998), 663–744.

17. The remarks that Zuckert misses with regard to the differences between Gadamer's philosophical texts before 1933 and after 1945 are found in my book (15, 65 ff) and also in my essay in this volume.

18. Fritz Bucherer and Herman Easters, eds., *Das Humanistische Gymnasium* (Berlin and Leipzig: B. G. Teubner, 1934), 100.

19. My attempt to reconstruct these resonances is prompted by the French linguist Michel Pêcheux's concept of interdiscourse and/or cross-discourse. Pêcheux's discourse analysis takes as its task the analysis of the effect of interdiscourse, "which bursts into the organization of what can be said, in the form of the unsaid or the said-elsewhere." Michel Pêcheux, "Über die Rolle des Gedächtnisses als interdiskursives Material: Ein Forschungsprojekt im Rahmen der Diskursanalyse und Archivlektüre," in *Das Subjekt des Diskurses: Beiträge zur sprachlichen Bildung von Subjektivität und Intersubjektivität,* ed. Manfred Geier and Harold Woetzel (Berlin: Argument-Verlag, 1983), 54. The cross-discourse functions "as a kind of axiom of meaning, stabilized in the discursive memory, which seems to make possible evident intradiscursive links." It is a kind of reading "in which the reading subject at the same time is responsible for and is expropriated by the meaning that he deciphers. For the interpretation follows the interdiscursive tracks, which are preconstructed and transversal as such" (54). To this end, discourse analysis describes processes "that expose to the reader those levels of the discourse which are opaque relative to the strategic actions of an information-processing epistemic subject" (54) as presupposed by the cognitivistic variants of discourse analysis. In this sense discourse analysis shares a point of view with Gadamerian hermeneutics, since both oppose the logicistic or cognitivistic theories of meaning. The crucial difference from the hermeneutic position, however, is that concepts like the preconstructed *(préconstruit),* the interdiscourse *(discours transverse),* and indirect or reported dis-

course *(discours rapporté)* have a chance of being decoded. Instead of claiming a "dark" reason as master of the meaning, this form of discourse analysis demands a comprehensive reconstruction of the sociohistoric memory that constitutes and carries each discourse. This reconstruction is not focused at the level of the thread of discourse, at a linear meaning of texts (known in linguistics as intradiscourse), but proceeds from a multilayered and heterogeneous textual corpus. The starting point is thereby furnished by the linguistic sequences "whose interdiscursive material has left behind sociohistoric tracks, constituting the reading process as interpretation" (57).

20. "Only in the context of this founding of the state, and from the motive of a radical rejection of the existing state and its establishment in the words of philosophy, can the critique of poets be understood." *Plato und die Dichter* (Frankfurt am Main: Vittorio Klostermann, 1934), 13.

21. "He who recognizes himself in it certainly does not, indeed, recognize himself as a stateless, isolated being: he recognizes in himself the ground on which the reality of the state is built, however, and in whatever degenerate form the real state may exist" (*Plato und die Dichter* 14).

22. The linguistic difficulty of the usual rendering of German *staatlich* in English as "political" must be considered here in its distorting consequences. The concept of the political does not have to be imagined in conjunction with the attributes of the state, as is generally the case in these texts.

23. As Kurt Hildebrandt, a member of the George circle, sums it up, Plato's state "rests on the human soul, it is a mental construct. For that which we call the total state today, there is no more perfect portrait than Plato's *Politeia.*" Kurt Hildebrandt, *Einleitung zur Platon: Der Staat,* trans. A. Horneffer (Leipzig: Alfred Kröner-Verlag, 1933), 364. Alfred Baeumler believes that Plato encourages artistic and gymnastic upbringing, "not because he considers art to be an educational material," but as "a necessary device for rearing children." By such means a youth would learn "to love and to hate correctly, without first of all being able to indicate the reason." Alfred Baeumler, "Ästhetik," in *Handbuch der Philosophie. Die Grunddisziplinen* (Munich and Berlin: Oldenburg, 1934), 6. Regarding the adoption of Platonic principles in a broad spectrum of National Socialist organizations, the Nazi educational theorist Ernst Krieck writes, "No one, however, has had as profound an understanding of the power of the artistic as Plato, who in this regard can become our teacher yet again. For education in the youth leagues; in the state youth groups; in the army; and in the defense units of the SA, the SS, and the Stahlhelm, artistic education has become a necessity." Ernst Krieck, *Musische Erziehung* (Leipzig: Armanen, 1933), 1.

24. Rolf Nemitz, "Die Erziehung des faschistischen Subjekts," in *Faschismus und Ideologie* (Hamburg: Argument-Verlag, 1980), 141–75.

25. Ernst Krieck, "Erziehungsphilosophie," in *Handbuch der Philosophie,* ed. A. Baeumler and M. Schröter (Munich and Berlin: 1931). See section III, "Mensch und Charakter," pp. 68 and 48.

26. This allotment of status is explicitly contrary to Plato's *Politeia,* in which the guardians constitute a profession between the workmen and the philosopher-kings. More important than the accuracy of this interpretation, however, is the harmony of this reading with the political constellation to which this text speaks, for example,

insofar as the type of the guardian is compatible with the latent militarization of society and the appearance of the SS and SA.

27. Albrecht Wellmer, quoted in Jürgen Habermas, "Der Universalitätsan-
pruch der Hermeneutik," in *Zur Logik der Sozialwissenschaften* (Frankfurt: Suhrkamp,
1985), 361.

28. Isabelle Kalinowsky, "Les ambiguités de Gadamer," *Liber: Revue internationale
des livres* 30 (Mar. 1997): 14.

Chapter 14

Salutations

A Response to Zuckert

GEOFF WAITE

There's the old panegyric, the festive convention where the one to be lauded finally gets his public praise. . . . Being born was being born into the praxis of politics.
GADAMER, "Praise of Theory"

Ave, imperator, morituri te salutant!
Cited in Suetonius, *De vita Caesarum*

Debaxo de mi manto, al rey mato.
CERVANTES, *Don Quixote*

Si campu t'allampu. Si moru ti pirdugnu.
Sicilian saying

"SI QUID NOVISTI RECTIUS ISTIS"

With her promotion of "mediation," "dialogue," and "moderation," Catherine H. Zuckert is to be saluted for her triumphant response to the essays of Orozco and Waite, a response that could be used as a textbook case for careful study, not necessarily for its specific object of analysis (needless to say), but for its overall and well-nigh seamless hermeneutic approach and rhetorical technique. Any momentary appearance to the contrary, this concession is ultimately *not* meant ironically. Certainly Zuckert's response has the virtue of exemplifying the temper of our times. This is to say that it not only could be read with profit by anyone interested in grasping the hegemonic *theory (theoría)* of the "discursive practice"[1] of the "postmodern," "postindustrial," "postcommunist" present, and likely some years ahead (as de Gaulle used to say, "the future lasts a long time"), but it also could be emulated in practical wisdom and *(nota bene)* prudence *(phrónēsis)* by anyone in the reserve labor army seeking gainful employment or institutional mobility in today's academy, whether in the social or human sciences—even, or especially, in its currently depressed job market. (As a parenthetical aside, we might note that the attempt to produce "discursive practices" that are an alternative to business as usual could be expected to have a rather different significance for, say, a tenured professor at a financially solvent academic institution than for, say, a younger scholar who had been effectively black-balled from the same profession for trying to challenge aspects of its busi-ness as usual. In other words—for let us not be reduced to vulgar Marxist rhetoric or even to simple political economy—in each case the Haitian proverb takes on rather different meaning: "Do not insult the mother alli-gator until after you have crossed the river.")

Before proceeding any further in this salute, however, Waite also em-phatically stresses that there would be something quite unseemly in any *en-tretien préliminaire* (Lacan) between Zuckert and Waite (Orozco will respond in her own way) in a festschrift saluting Hans-Georg Gadamer and his cen-tury. Any interest in this *entretien* must be minimal compared to Gadamer's influence as one of "his century's" leading philosophers—*the* leading phi-losopher, in the opinion of many serious people. And this influence is a remarkable achievement, one might add, for someone who entered into extended or profound dialogue with neither Freud nor Marx nor their lega-cies, and hence with neither the unconscious nor with the political econ-omy and capitalism, nor with anything more than one limited aspect of Spinozism—arguably a related lacuna.[2] Nor did Gadamer really heed the advice given to all professional philosophers by Bachelard: *"Se mettre à l'école des sciences"* (to go to school with the sciences).[3] And Gadamer did not engage so-called mass or popular culture (where the ancient philosophical problems are often more vital and effectual than in academic institutions) or problematize the Eurocentric and phallogocentric structures and ideol-ogy of classical and modern philosophy. One can't do everything and many continue to expand what they think of as philosophical hermeneutics into areas unoccupied by Gadamer, if not always with his approval. Be all this as it may, "Gadamer" will outlive Gadamer, and certainly "us." So readers may be reminded, when reading the Zuckert-Waite logomachy, of Samuel John-son's retort when asked to compare the talents of two of his own contem-poraries: "Sir, there is no settling the point of precedency between a louse and a flea."[4] Or, as the unseemly folk wisdom put it around where Waite was growing up, "It takes a big flea to run with a big dog."

As for an appropriate solution to this problem of unseemliness—that is, the inappropriateness on this occasion of any *entretien préliminaire* be-tween Zuckert and Waite—the latter is of the following mind. With regard perhaps to any celebration, critique, or criticism of Gadamer, but in any case with regard to the internecine exchange between Zuckert and Waite, the latter two are especially well advised to heed the Horatian dictum and say, each to the other, "Si quid novisti rectius istis, / Candidus imperti; si non, his utere necum" *(Epist.* 1:6, 67); which for our purposes might be loosely rendered "If you know something that is more correct than the mat-ter here under dispute, then tell me frankly; if not, then stick with me to this matter only." No matter how this matter be defined, the current *entretien préliminaire* can be interesting *only* insofar as it extends to larger issues, including, most notably here, those addressed by Gadamer himself, but also including ones that even he does not open up—and this imperative, too, is in full accord with what Waite imagines part of Gadamer's own recommendation might be in such situations, *at least in theory*. Adapting Plato, Aristotle, Cervantes, Luther, Althusser, and Gadamer himself we might then say: *Amicus Gadamer, sed magis amica Veritas.*[5] The question here, however, appears to be whether we should say instead (or in addition): *Adversarius Gadamer, sed magis amica Veritas.*

Before proceeding along these lines, however, we could note that a reader (assuming the existence of someone at all interested in the Zuckert-Waite *entretien préliminaire*) might remark that there is an unfair quantitative imbalance built into the structure of this festschrift: Waite (like Orozco) has been given two chances to speak, Zuckert only one. (As for Gadamer himself, the general template of how he enters into dialogue with critics may be found in his responses to the essays on his work in The Library of Living Philosophers volume, and it is not overly difficult to extrapolate from his responses there to what he might have said and not said about this festschrift.)[6] So we will not discover, at least not here, what Zuckert's response is to the response of Waite (or Orozco)—nor for that matter, and more mercifully, Waite's (or Orozco's) response to that hypothetical second Zuckertian response, and so on *ad infinitum et absurdum*. But this would not really be a fair objection to the structure of this anthology insofar as Waite (for one) accepts Zuckert's response as triumphant, and to be saluted as such. This is not to mention the impression Zuckert gives, at the conclusion of her (first and here only) response, "On the Politics of Gadamerian Hermeneutics," that, in this one case at least, there is no point in further discussion or dialogue, that these have been effectively terminated—notwithstanding her prior commitment to "dialogue" and to "moderation." (Zuckert's ethical ideology *in nuce* is that of many a conquering civilization or system throughout history, which is only currently parliamentary-democratic, free-market capitalism. "I respect differences, but only, of course, in so far as that which differs also respects, just as I do, the said differences. . . . Become like me and I will respect your difference.")[7] This paradox to one side for now, however, Waite much prefers to salute Zuckert's victory and to analyze how it is hermeneutically and rhetorically achieved, in the aforementioned attempt to address issues less restricted than the merely intestine. Compare the Platonic Socrates: "'that is what we said, was it not?' 'Yes.' 'But that is only half the story. Let us look at it more fully'" (*Republic* 601b–c). *Only* in that spirit (and any appearance to the contrary again aside) let us continue— and continue to engage as dispassionately (and, yes, as *objectively*) as possible, "the politics of Gadamerian hermeneutics."

TU QUOQUE!

"Incapable of having a conversation" seems to me to be more the accusation one makes against someone who doesn't want to follow his thoughts than a deficiency actually possessed by the other.
    GADAMER, "The Incapacity to Converse"

It is perhaps symbolic that Plato initiated his Dialogues with the murder of Socrates. In subsequent works Socrates assumes various guises, yet even as he does so, we are reminded that he has already been killed. Plato obsessively recounts that Socrates dared to commit suicide to prove the immortality of the law. . . . What Plato (Socrates) proposed was not the idea that reason resides immanently in the world or self but the idea that only those propositions that pass through the dialogue can be acknowledged as rational. Those who reject the dialogue are considered irrational, no matter how profound or how vigorously argued their truth.
    KARATANI, *Architecture as Metaphor*

Zuckert's response is particularly successful in conveying to her readers a sense of surprise, indignation even, about a situation that the naive reader of philosophy might well have thought to be a simple *donnée:* Gadamer (like any philosopher or anyone else) is opposed to certain philosophical and political positions; and proponents of these or other positions are, in turn, opposed to Gadamer. Concomitantly, Zuckert is successful in downplaying any reservations about Gadamer's position that she herself might have (though some might be inferred even in her brief response here, and more extensive ones have been published elsewhere) and in embracing the aforementioned principle, which she basically attributes to Gadamer and which she conclusively calls "one of the two primary political virtues—moderation." By not explicitly *constating* what the second primary political virtue might be, she leaves the reader to assume that it has been integrated into her response.[8] In this (what might be called "art of allusion"), Zuckert would appear to follow the time-honored principle that it is generally more effective to *perform* basic virtues than it is (only) to give them names. Presumably we are to infer that Zuckert's *entire response* is informed by that *unstated* virtue in addition to moderation—not the least reason why her response is exemplary. In any event, this is her response's culmination:

Gadamer explicitly seeks to mediate. Neither Orozco nor Waite recognizes any center or middle in politics; they see only either/or's. As a result they not only fail to understand the essential character of Gadamer's hermeneutics; their writings also demonstrably lack one of the two primary political virtues—moderation.

Now, any question of the failure of Orozco's or of Waite's specific understanding of Gadamer aside, their falling short of (a) philosophy, the general theoretical and practical issue here under dispute would appear to be as follows. What if *ex hypothesi* someone (if Zuckert is right, it would obviously have to be someone other than Orozco and Waite) *has* succeeded in understanding the essential character of another's work—and yet does not *like* what she or he sees, and has *reasons* not to like it? What, then, is to be done? At particular issue here would be the precise nature of the "fusion of horizons," "mediation," "dialogue," or "moderation" being promoted by Gadamer and *mutatis mutandis* by his Zuckert.[9] The question "What is to be done?" (and, it is necessary to add, *not* done) could now take two primary, at least preliminary, tacks.

1. One could attempt to argue that the post-Platonic Gadamerian "moderation" in question has certain *internal* inconsistencies *and/or* that it allows only some *kinds* of dialogue, on its *own* terms, but refuses *others*. This first, possibly double, tack has long existed in the reception history of Gadamer's work, not to mention Plato's, and more about that later. But the more immediate problem, of course, is that Gadamer and his (non)interlocutors have then all ended up engaging in a more or less sophisticated form of *tu quoque* (thou, too!) argument that always eventually leads to an impasse: not to the aporia *(a-poros)* that the Greeks saw as the *beginning* of dialogue and philosophical wisdom *(philo-sophia)*, but to a simple *dead* end and point of *termination* —in the colloquial senses of the words.[10] The one side is accused by the other of failing to participate in a dialogue that the other claims is a dialogue in name only—and so on. And thus it is that we all find ourselves singing a skewed version of an old ditty: "You say 'dialogue,' I say '*dialógos*' (but read, perhaps, 'monologue')—let's call the whole thing off." But the whole thing is precisely *not* called off, and the vaudeville act drones on disguised as philosophy. So it appears that this first tack is at best necessary but at worst wholly insufficient. Because (demonstrably) little or nothing has ever been achieved by attempting to point out inherent contradictions (let alone ideological interference) either in Gadamer's (and perhaps Plato's) *theory* of dialogue or (a rather different thing) in his *use* of it, and because (demonstrably) there is little or nothing to be achieved in logic by *tu quoque* arguments, another tack becomes possible, necessary even.

2. One can shift exclusive emphasis away from logic, including the dialogic, and attempt to show that the philosophical system here in dispute—philosophical hermeneutics and its obsessive affirmation of "dialogue" (which tends to be chanted as a conclusive mantra at the end of all encounters with both friends and enemies)—can best be understood as part of the long tradition of *quasi*-logical, *quasi*-dialogic Western (and not only Western) philosophy. This tradition can be given various names, say, "the art of allusion," "exo/esotericism," or some more common cognate (e.g., the "holy" or "noble lie," the "double rhetoric").[11] On this second tack, apparent contradiction—both *within* the theoretical description of dialogue and

between this theory and its applicative practice—is understood as being, in essence, not contradictory at all, but rather as *precisely* apparent: namely, as "paradox" *(para-doxa)* and as "paranoia" in the strict philosophical and etymological sense *(para-nous)*. Which is to say that any exoteric contradiction (communism exceptionally) in the system is now understood as an epiphenomenal manifestation of an unstated *tertium quid* ("God" or "Capital," traditionally), as part of a parallel or supplemental *"para*-system" that is necessarily (systematically or intentionally) concealed from logical and dialogical purview. To be sure, taking this second basic tack, making this hypothesis, we can *still* not assume that we can enter into a dialogue with the dominant philosophical and rhetorical system of "mediation" and "moderation." And, inversely, neither can that bourgeois system enter into dialogue with its new (communist) opponent. Indeed, according to this argumentative tack, both sides can *never* enter into *such* dialogue—not only because exo/esotericism would *per definitionem* refuse to expose itself fully to view but also, more generally, because there is no such thing as a metalanguage, hence no metadialogue, that covers all empirical or theoretical cases.[12] What each side still can and must do, instead, is stake out its own philosophical, rhetorical, and political position, and let the chips fall where they may. Yet the problem persists that to say this amounts to ceding to the problem—as ancient as it always appears new—of relativism and to a view of philosophy as an antinomic *Kampfplatz* (Kant or Carl Schmitt) or *différend* and "phrase in dispute" (Lyotard) without the possibility of dialogue between the warring parties.

   The argument thus far can be summed up in five points and one question. 1) The question of whether or not Orozco or Waite have themselves failed or succeeded "to understand the essential character of Gadamer's hermeneutics" may be a *related* question but in any case is a *different* question from whether or not "their writings also demonstrably lack one of the two primary political virtues—moderation." These are distinct questions because the essential characters of both Gadamer's hermeneutics and Zuckert's version of it are—arguably—*also* lacking in precisely this one virtue (if not the second virtue or some other unspecified virtue as well). 2) This *tu quoque* argument gets none of us anywhere beyond where we all already are, which is in a state of relativism and Mafia-like combat without appeal to a subtending metadiscourse. 3) This perceived lack of at least one primary virtue can be interpreted not as an inherent failing of the philosophical system under dispute but as being due to its concealed exo/esoteric design. 4) Nonetheless, both of Zuckert's questions (i.e., "the essential character of Gadamer's hermeneutics" and the nature and number of the "primary political virtues") persist independently of the ability of an Orozco or a Waite (or a Zuckert) to identify and understand them—or to construct a set of questions that would provide an alternative to this dead end. 5) Zuckert is to be saluted for having constructed such a triumphant response to Orozco and Waite that makes this search—not merely to locate exo/esotericism but also for alternatives—appear not merely undesirable but simply impossible. Finally, one question now opened up by this festschrift is what about Gadamer himself. Is he, and thus philosophical hermeneutics, to be similarly saluted?

PHRASE IN DISPUTE:
"THE PERHAPS EVEN MORE DEVASTATING CHARGE"

At one crucial juncture in her response to Orozco and Waite, Zuckert writes:

> Since Gadamer *never explicitly mentioned* National Socialism in either of the essays he wrote under the regime, one might conclude that the relation between what he wrote and the political context necessarily remains a matter of "interpretation." But are there no canons or standards of interpretation? That would be truly ironic, and *perhaps even more devastating* to Gadamer than the charge that he collaborated with an immoral regime in order to advance his own scholarly career, since he devoted his major work to articulating just such standards. [emphases added]

This is a remarkable statement because effective on several levels. It will be necessary to return to Gadamer's relationship to "National Socialism" in a moment, but first note that the argument Zuckert is contesting suggests that there is a standard and canon of mentioning *without explicitly* mentioning. This is what "allusion" in the phrase "art of allusion" means, and what the virgule in "exo/esotericism" also indicates (as does the concept "Radio Nietzsche" or "Nietzsche's corps/e").[13] Of course, one *might* conclude from this "art of allusion" (or its cognates) that a text's relation to the context in which it appears is therefore "a matter of 'interpretation'"; obviously, if it is *all* "a matter of 'interpretation,'" one can indeed conclude anything about anything—a particularly vexing problem if there is no metadiscursive system to which all sides can appeal for adjudication of their disputes. But this is *not necessarily* or *only* what the canon and standard of interpretation called, say, "the art of allusion" concludes. That there *are* canons and standards of interpretation goes without saying; this is something we know from, and as, the history of philosophy. And, of course, Gadamer has articulated one standard of interpretation and is part of one canon of interpretation. But, as already intimated, the problems here are these: 1) *rival* standards and canons eventually come into collision with one another; 2) there is, according to relativism and historicism, no metacanon or metastandard to adjudicate between them; and 3) at least one other standard and canon attacks relativism and historicism on the grounds that something like a metastandard does exist and it certainly has existed. For example, Straussians—at least *exoterically*—mount their attack on this basis. Readers of this festschrift will likely also know that, from a very different side than the Straussian, Derrida (a Heideggerian on the "left") has attacked Gadamer (one on the "right") for not being *sufficiently* relativist.[14] And also well known is the argument that Strauss's attack against Nietzsche and relativism (and hence, *mutatis mutandis,* perhaps also against Heidegger and Gadamer) was merely exoteric, concealing Strauss's own deeper, esoteric commitment to a form of Nietzschean relativism.[15] Finally two other things are well known: that the charge of relativism and historicism was first leveled against Gadamer by what arguably remains the most significant (if not even definitive) response to *Wahrheit und Methode* (Truth and method)—that of Leo Strauss in private correspondence with Gadamer; and that Gadamer, as Strauss immediately pointed out, was simply *silent* about this charge, particularly with regard to being a *relativist.*[16] This is obviously not to say that Gadamer never wrote subsequently about his position on relativism, attempting to defend himself against the charge, because he did. Gadamer has defended himself on both fronts of attack (that of Strauss and that of Derrida) on several other occasions (if only, ultimately, by continuing to chant that mantra of "dialogue" and "fusion of horizons"); but the fact remains that *neither* Straussians (classical politico-philosophical rationalists or liberals) *nor* Derrideans (poststructuralists) have been fully satisfied with this response, to say the least. Obviously, Gadamer has not been successful in this regard to everyone's satisfaction, and so relativism remains a sticky and thorny point for philosophical hermeneutics. But not only for it: it is one of the constitutive problems of the entire secular modern era, if not also *mutatis mutandis* of the preceding or subsequent millennia.

In one view, relativism and historicism (and pluralism) conclude that relativism and historicism are true, hence the only truth. But what they cannot then account for is the fact that since, according to their own argument, they themselves have come into existence historically, there was a position that was nonrelativist and nonhistoricist that preceded them, and since everything is here argued to be historical, hence fated not only to be born but to die, historicism and relativism, having been born at a specific historical moment, will also die, and be replaced again by, say, the nonrelativist and nonhistoricist.[17] Actually, however, these teleological terms are simplistic and misleading, even in historical terms, insofar as in each period there is not only overlap *between* relativist and nonrelativist arguments, but also even *within* all arguments, whether they present themselves as relativist or as nonrelativist. The basic question remains, however: To which canon do *we* adhere, and which do *we* choose to combat, or are we forced to combat? ("The truth is that one cannot always choose the form of war one wants.")[18] Let us be clear: appeal to moderation and dialogue is part of the *problem,* not the solution, *if* that appeal is precisely what is being challenged. In a sense, viewed historically, no matter which position one adapts, it *is* all "a matter of 'interpretation,'" even if at least one canon and standard holds that it is *not* all "a matter of 'interpretation.'" But obviously no amount of dialogue can in principle or in fact convince the other side in lieu of mutual acknowledgment of a metastandard. To repeat, clearly Gadamer has not been successful in convincing everyone (apparently he has not even convinced the Zuckert whose own standard of interpretation is to begin, if not also end, with positivist or empiricist appeal to "what an author actually wrote"—but more about that later) that his standard and canon are cogent and applicable to all situations. And so we remain locked within an overall situation in which his standard and canon are indeed, quite precisely, "a matter of 'interpretation.'"

Returning, however, to another part of Zuckert's statement, even if Gadamer has not convinced everyone that his standards are internally coherent and appropriate, this can hardly be a "devastating charge" to Gadamer specifically. It would hold true of everyone in the history of philosophy to date, assuming that no one can appeal to a metadiscourse able to adjudicate between contesting opinions. Nor would this fact either *be* "more devastating" or be "*perhaps* more devastating" than the "charge" that Gadamer "collaborated with an immoral regime in order to advance his own scholarly career." Gadamer himself has admitted (though not quite in so many words) that he collaborated with arguably the most immoral regime in human history. (Though we need not argue in absolute or quantitative terms. Any immoral regime will do nicely, and which "regime" is not in some sense immoral, not least capitalism? Questions like this prompt Waite with the communist philosopher and self-described Platonist Alain Badiou to define "thought" *sensu stricto* as "nothing other than the desire to finish with the exorbitant excess of the State.") [19] Gadamer has also implied (as Zuckert will also note) that his motivations for this collaboration were opportunist in that they included not only the preservation of his own life and that of his "family, students, and friends," but (as Zuckert ventriloquizes him) also the salvation of philosophy (both as institution and as philosophical hermeneutics) in for him profoundly antiphilosophical times. With regard to opportunism more generally, Gadamer turned an interesting phrase in his 1988 response to the attacks on Heidegger in Victor Farías's book (French from the Spanish in 1987; German from the French in 1989): "Yet he was no mere opportunist" *(Er war doch kein bloßer Opportunist).* [20] Which is not to say, however, that either Heidegger or *mutatis mutandis* Gadamer were not opportunists—only that they were not *mere* opportunists.[21] Moreover, Heidegger was arguably far less an opportunist or collaborator than Gadamer, if Heidegger was indeed a true believer in what Gadamer calls Heidegger's "political illusion."[22] True believers are *sensu stricto* neither opportunists nor collaborators. And, by his own admission, Gadamer was *both* (at least to some degree, which still needs to be specified).

But the point so far is that neither Gadamer's acts of collaboration and opportunism nor their admission has proven "devastating" to him. Nor were Heidegger's acts ultimately devastating to Gadamer's greatest teacher, who did lose his academic teaching position after the war, but who has also become incomparably more influential than his at times quite critical student, who did not. Certainly the charge of collaboration *can* be devastating. Some collaborators are tried and executed or incarcerated; some are beaten to death by outraged compatriots before they can stand before the victor's trial. But this is not what happened to these two philosophers. Quite to the contrary: sooner or later they were both quite lavishly rewarded. Let us leave Heidegger aside to return to Zuckert's argument: Gadamer is not, and apparently cannot be, devastated either by the charge that he has not developed universally binding, or even internally coherent, standards of interpretation, or by the charge that he collaborated with an immoral regime, or that he practiced (or practices) the art of allusion or exo/esotericism.

If by "devastation" one means, at least in part, physical death or some form of psychological death (trauma), or even simply loss of influence, prestige, and honor, those people who have been really devastated include those from early 1934 on who were (legally) incarcerated and murdered by the "immoral regime" (which had its own *kind* of morality and laws) with which many others alongside Gadamer collaborated. One can even say that Hitler himself and all the true believers and collaborators tried at Nuremberg after the war were devastated in this sense; as were their victims, including Jews, communists, and many others both inside and outside Germany, in the *Großdeutsches Reich* and its imperialist and capitalist war. But *Gadamer* was not, is not, and apparently *cannot* be devastated in this sense, either.

Furthermore, Gadamer cannot be devastated for the *reasons* of his collaboration and opportunism, which (as he himself says, and as Zuckert reminds us) were precisely to save himself and his friends and family, to save his academic career, and to save philosophy itself—*one version* of philosophy, it should go without saying. This philosophy survived the Third Reich to live on in postwar divided Germany and now in once-again unified Germany, where it has as many friends as it does abroad. Not only has this philosophy not been devastated, and apparently cannot be, but it has survived both by *means* of collaboration with Hitlerian Germany, obviously, and subsequently it has survived the *admission* that it was collaboratory and opportunistic. Other questions doubtless remain as to whether this version of philosophy has been devastating to some people (who, say, cannot find academic employment because they attack it), or whether it can and should be devastated by others. But in any case, Zuckert is to be saluted for having opened up this can of worms, too, and for her agility in wriggling out of it by so successfully not taking her own clear stand in the matter beyond appealing to the virtue of moderation (which, according only to ineffective *tu quoque* argument, she does not herself practice).

The (hermeneutic or, better, transferential) question remains as to what Zuckert's *own* position in all this "aporia" might be, both as objective political scientist and as prescriber of political virtues. Surely part of the success of her approach depends on keeping the precise nature of this position (her "site of enunciation") as concealed, implicit, and allusive as possible. What, then (for her or for others), would constitute the *most* "devastating charge"—against Gadamer or anyone? In her response to Orozco and Waite, Zuckert appears to take Gadamer's position *grosso modo* by defending and promoting "moderation" on both objective and prescriptive grounds, as we have begun to see. In her book *Postmodern Platos: Nietzsche, Heidegger, Gadamer, Strauss, Derrida* (1996), however, one may find a related but at the same time rather different position. Her chapter on Gadamer concludes with this remark: "Gadamer is fundamentally a liberal. Arguing that history has no necessary direction and that it may even be reversed, both Strauss and Derrida raise questions about the character of human freedom as well."[23]

Interrupting the slyly vacuous Zuckert briefly, one might note that if it is true that Gadamer is "*fundamentally* a liberal," his foundation, or at least his conceptual edifice and hermeneutic practice, seems to be rather different from other kinds of liberalism, including that of Strauss; and it is perhaps not too much to infer that Zuckert herself would define herself as some sort of liberal, and certainly she presents herself as an advocate of moderation and dialogue. Be this as it may, Zuckert is correct to imply that the position of Waite, in its immoderation, is that of neither a liberal nor a humanist insofar as humanism is defined as practicing the virtue of moderation, in her sense, or rather what Lenin might call the "illusion of moderation," and insofar as Waite would attack any merely formal democracy in which de facto powerless individual subjects "possess" theoretical, de jure rights that "thousands of obstacles" (Lenin) prohibit them from ever putting into practice.[24] As Spinoza showed in his *Political Treatise,* rights can have meaning only when they are coextensive with actual power; and when rights are coextensive with power, then the individual (the Cartesian *imperium in imperio*) cannot form the basis for analysis or practice insofar as isolated ("liberal-humanist") individuals in fact never have more than a little actual power. As succinctly put by folk wisdom, "dui sunnu li putenti: Cu' havi assai e cu' nun havi nenti" (the powerful are two: those with much and those with nothing). Only what Spinoza called the *multitudo* can be the true bearer of reason against the destructive passions of individual subjects and small groups of individual subjects. It is "natural" (to paraphrase both Lenin and Spinoza) for a liberal to speak of "moderation," "dialogue," or "democracy" *in general;* but then the question always is: *On behalf of what interest, indeed of what class?*

But it seems that we must abandon *that* position to understand Zuckert's or Gadamer's, at least as the latter is represented by Zuckert.

Now, whether one might agree or disagree with Zuckert's depiction in her book either of Gadamer as "fundamentally a liberal" or with her ensuing analysis of Strauss and Derrida, including their different critiques of teleology and human freedom, one recognizes that the voice speaking in the just-cited statement from her book is that of a (dare one say, *relatively?*) neutral observer, whose observations, as such, are presumably open to dispute, acceptance, or dialogue. This political-scientific voice does not necessarily endorse or reject Gadamer, nor anyone else, though obviously one might well assume that the spirit of this neutral voice does not preclude taking sides with a version of Gadamerian dialogue and moderation (though, of course, whether such neutrality is compatible with Gadamer's notion of the constitutive role of prejudgment and prejudice in all hermeneutic acts may pose an insuperable problem here), even in response to the different (prima facie opposed) criticisms of Gadamer by Strauss and by Derrida. The reader might infer the existence of this Gadamerian Zuckert from the aforementioned conclusion to her response to Orozco and Waite—a conclusion immediately prefaced by the emphatic statement that "*The* twentieth-century philosopher who opposes such 'spiritual' warfare [*sc.* that of Nietzsche and *mutatis mutandis* Waite] is Hans-Georg Gadamer." And we recall that Orozco and Waite are being charged with two things: 1) that they have understood neither Gadamer's supreme import in our century nor "the essential character of Gadamer's hermeneutics," incapable or unwilling as they are to attend to what Gadamer "actually says"; and 2) that this essential character lies in the principle of moderation, in opposition to all "either/or's," and that we all *should* or *must* adapt this principle. However, in her book *Postmodern Platos,* having proceeded to discuss both Strauss and Derrida (and much else besides), Zuckert concludes her entire argument by an apparent embrace not of Gadamer (nor of Derrida) but of Strauss. Here are her book's final sentences:

> By challenging his readers to reread the history of philosophy in terms of a *strict disjunction* between reason and revelation, Strauss asks them to study that history in a most untraditional way. All his own readings of individual philosophers, including preeminently his reading of Plato, have proven to be extremely controversial. That is, they invite debate and rebuttal. But if the purpose of the contemporary return to Plato is to show that philosophy has a future, he may have succeeded in fulfilling that purpose by demonstrating the need for an untraditional reading of the tradition better than anyone else.[25]

So, although Gadamer is "*the* twentieth-century philosopher" of "moderation," Strauss may have done something else: namely, "to show that philosophy has a future . . . by demonstrating the need for an untraditional reading of the tradition *better than anyone else.*" In other words, Zuckert appears, eclectically, to be *both* Gadamerian *and* Straussian, to one extent or another. And the interesting problem here is that—arguably—these two positions are simply incompatible and incompossible. At least they appear to be such from the point of view of at least one of the two positions, namely, of Strauss, whose charge against Gadamer for being a relativist, as we noted, was never adequately responded to by Gadamer to Straussian satisfaction, quite simply because Gadamer, in this view, *has* no response inasmuch as he simply *is* a relativist—any imagined Gadamerian protestation notwithstanding. Besides, there are times when moderation (or mediation) may be decidedly undesirable—this is ultimately our question posed. If Gadamer was not a relativist yet did practice esotericism in some form, then what was he? Insofar as Zuckert rejects the "art of allusion" hypothesis it is opaque how her position (that is, positions) on Gadamer's position on relativism could even desire to be. To paraphrase Schopenhauer against Hegel (we'll not go there now), Zuckert's best opacity is the best available lucidity.

In sum, Zuckert's own position in all this thus appears to be twofold. 1) Unlike Zuckert's Gadamer, who "explicitly seeks to mediate," "neither Orozco nor Waite recognizes any center or middle in politics; they see only either/or's." And this, for Zuckert, is both objectively true and lamentable. By contrast, for her, Gadamer's position against "either/or" positions is both objectively true and laudable. And yet 2) Strauss is also right to suggest that there is, and should be, at least one very basic and primary "strict disjunction" (i.e., "between reason and revelation" or "Athens and Jerusalem"): in other words, a very strict "either/or" position that—ultimately—can not and should not be mediated (although Strauss, in one of his moods, certainly did mediate between them in some respects). In yet other words, it is by taking sides with these two—themselves incompatible —positions that Zuckert can triumph over any opponent who is in search of alternatives.[26] In this, Strauss himself might say that Zuckert is Gadamerian, not Straussian, due to her own brand of eclecticism and relativism—her appeal to him at the end of her book notwithstanding. For Zuckert appears here to follow one of Gadamer's dictums, given in response to another collection of essays on or about him, which is at once historicist and relativist: "Can one create a solidarity which rests solely upon communal interests? In light of what humanity is and has become, it seems to me more sensible for us to take the advice that Aristotle is said to have given Alexander the Great: 'To be a Greek to the Greeks, a Persian to the Persians.'"[27] Or, in Zuckert's case, "When writing in a festschrift on Gadamer, do like Gadamer; when writing a book appealing to Straussians, do like Strauss." Or, if you prefer, "When in Rome, do like a Roman; or, when in Syracuse, do like a Syracusian." What can one do but salute such a powerful and mobile *thēoría,* such a *phrónēsis?* That is the question.

WHAT ANYONE "ACTUALLY SAYS"

The scenario here is of a philosophy presenting itself, like all idealist philosophies, as being "without any exterior" (Althusser)—as a theoretical system which if it even ac- knowledges the external world does so only for the purpose of completely absorbing and dominating it by claiming the truth of everything past, present and future in advance.

LECOURT, *Les piètres penseurs*

Before entering into more details of Zuckert's response (i.e., the *entretien préliminaire* with Waite), one general comment about her technique of read- ing may be helpful. A particularly intriguing feature of Zuckert's technique is her remarkably firm commitment to what she repeatedly calls reading what an author, in her words, *"actually said"* (or "wrote," or "argued") about a given topic. So while Orozco is explicitly charged with not reading what one author, Gadamer, "actually argued," Waite is implicitly charged with not trying to understand, analyze, or respond to what any author "actually wrote." In each case, what an author "actually said" remains the bedrock (though one might also suspect, Procrustean bed) on which Zuckert builds the edifice of her triumphant argument, her "will to architecture" (Kara- tani) *qua* moderation. Defeated in advance by Zuckert's ploy would be the objection that her appeal to the "actually said" in defense of Gadamer jibes ill with: 1) Gadamer's (Heideggerian) opposition to positivism and empiri- cism (and, for related but different reasons, to the Husserlian *epoché*), let alone a basic principle of some history of science, which is that its concepts are not just lying around to be picked up and applied to facts but instead have to be produced; 2) Gadamer's insistence that we approach the "actual" through an elaborate matrix (alluded to by Orozco as *one* part of his argu- ment) of prejudgments or prejudices *(Vorurteile, Vorverständnisse, Vorgreiflich- keiten);* and 3) what a Marxist might simply call "ideology." To paraphrase Nelson Goodman, we "always come ancient to our work"—but then to para- phrase Kafka, we all "knew that already," so Zuckert's position here is pre- sumably much more complex.

Be this as it may, Waite's "horizon" now suitably "expanded" by Zuckert's triumph, and since he had thought all along (wrongly, it turns out) that he was not just out to "discredit the opposition" but was attempting to "analyze or respond to the arguments of others," and since he refuses to engage in the *tu quoque* and must here abandon discussion of the exo/esoteric, Waite has no recourse but return to look at the reasons for Zuckert's victory more fully. Surely the key must lie in, or somewhere in close proximity to, atten- tiveness to the specifically Zuckertian principle of attending to what any au- thor "actually said," purportedly free of any ideological prejudice, contam- ination, or agenda, including what we find Zuckert, claiming to read what Waite "actually wrote," calls "ideological class *warfare*" and what Waite, following one Althusserian definition of philosophy, would actually call "class *struggle* in the field of theory" or "class *struggle* in the specific element of theory." (From the Marxist perspective, Zuckert's phrase succeeds in conflating two things. For Marxism, all warfare is struggle, but not all struggle is warfare. "Struggle" is a primary concept of the "left," "warfare" of the "right," as was most cogently articulated by Carl Schmitt.) [28]

"GADAMER AND NAZISM"

When the legend becomes fact, print the legend.
  The Man Who Shot Liberty Valence (John Ford, 1962)

These preliminaries behind us, here is the first sample on the plate of what Zuckert herself "actually writes" that Orozco and Waite "actually write."

> Teresa Orozco accuses Gadamer of having written "Plato and the Poets" to justify Nazi suppression of liberal humanist education and "Plato's Educational State" to support national conservative efforts to reform the regime. Geoffrey Waite repeats her accusation in "Radio Nietzsche." Whereas most twentieth-century readers of Nietzsche have unintentionally fostered his elitist politics by adopting a perspectivist reading, Waite charges, Orozco shows that Gadamer did so intentionally. In my view, there is little evidence to support either charge.

Leaving to one side what Orozco actually wrote, for her to repeat if she wishes, we are here condemned to remain with Waite. But perhaps some of us can take slight hope in the fact that the statement that "there is little evidence" (also with regard to what we will soon hear Zuckert calling the question of whether it is possible to "cite any statement, vote, or action by which Gadamer explicitly supported National Socialism") does not actually say that there is "*no* evidence" or even that there is not "*big* evidence." But before we become too hopeful, let us first turn to Zuckert's second mention of Waite in her response, since this provides the evidence for her just-cited statement that "Geoffrey Waite repeats her [Orozco's] accusation in 'Radio Nietzsche.'"

> In a footnote to his essay, Waite suggests that Gadamer may have had a rhetorical reason for remaining silent about the relation between his interpretation of Plato's *Republic* and the political circumstances in which he found himself. (Waite concedes that Orozco's case is *purely* circumstantial.) [emphasis added]

Now here is part of what Waite "actually wrote" in his footnote (emphasis again added):

> "Orozco has made *a good* circumstantial case . . ."

So it is that, for Zuckert, "a good circumstantial case" becomes "*purely* circumstantial." What that Waite does indeed "concede," however, as the same footnote continues, is that there is a partial problem with "the art of allusion" as defined by Orozco, and that Zuckert herself is implicated in it.[29] Because of this very implication the reader may wish to consult that footnote in full, a footnote to which Zuckert evidently and "presumably"—to use one of her own key terms, as we will see—has no response (much as Gadamer "presumably" had no response to Strauss's charge of radical historicism and relativism).

Does Waite "actually write" anything to indicate that he "repeats" Orozco's specific accusations about why Gadamer wrote what he did in the Third Reich, namely, "to justify Nazi suppression of liberal humanist education and . . . to support national conservative efforts to reform the regime"? On the face of it, the important bone of contention (with Orozco and Waite gnarling noisily on one side, Zuckert silently on the other) is a methodological principle (i.e., not "truth," necessarily, but in any case "method"): Was (and is) Gadamer some form of *esoteric* writer? There is evidence for this that *is* circumstantial (and, on the strong self-definition of esotericism, evidence here can be circumstantial only); whether this is good or bad evidence, it exists, and it is not purely circumstantial. One cannot ask this question (cf. "the piety of thinking," ostensibly for Heidegger and for Gadamer) if one does not acknowledge even the existence of the great tradition of exo/esoteric thought leading from Plato to the post-Platonists, who most notably include, in Zuckert's view, Nietzsche, Heidegger, Gadamer, Strauss, and Derrida. Obviously space does not permit a full discussion of this tradition here, nor is such discussion required to get at its basic structure.[30] But Zuckert has successfully occluded access to precisely this question. Why?

Although Zuckert does not appeal to what Waite "actually said" about the charge that "Gadamer was a Nazi" (to put it in the vernacular), if for no other reason than Waite does not "actually say" this, Zuckert successfully links Waite to Orozco here, nonetheless. Specifically, Zuckert writes, "Orozco does not (and presumably cannot) cite any statement, vote, or action by which Gadamer explicitly supported National Socialism." One might ask what "presumably" means here. If Orozco could cite such evidence, then she would have? Or, that such evidence for explicit support does not exist and/or never existed, quite simply because Gadamer did not in fact "support National Socialism" by "any statement, vote, or action"? Again leaving Orozco's response to this problem aside (both that in her book, to which Zuckert does not allude, and in her current response to this specific charge), and because he is linked to this position, Waite will respond with six major, interrelated theses.

1) Whether or not Gadamer "was a Nazi," is not the central issue. (The same goes for Heidegger, incidentally.) By his own not quite explicit ad-

mission, or at least by strong implication, Gadamer was a *collaborator* with Nazism, albeit a *critical* one. In other words, philosophical hermeneutics was prepared to collaborate with National Socialism, and then, *after* the fact, so to speak, attempted to criticize it from within. 2) *Pace* Zuckert, however, the historical record shows that Gadamer *did in fact explicitly support National Socialism by his statements, votes, and actions* (no matter how critically in the end). 3) This support is so explicit that no recourse to exo/esoteric hypothesis or analysis is required to see it at this level, in addition to the fact that Zuckert refuses to engage in serious discussion of exo/esotericism. 4) Dialogue from Waite's position with Gadamer and with philosophical hermeneutics about this issue is both *impossible* and *undesirable*—and this from *both* sides of the dispute insofar as it is not a dialogue in the first instance, but a *struggle.* 5) Waite (for one) thinks that Gadamer's collaboration and explicit support were and remain *wrong,* but for reasons that are complex and will need to be identified and elaborated below. 6) At larger issue, for both sides of the confrontation, would be not National Socialism but rather: a) *fascism qua a form of relativism;* and b) the specific relationship of both fascism and relativism to *capitalism.*[31] (Space dictates giving relatively short shrift to the last thesis here.)

In other words, Waite does not align himself with *all* of Orozco's argument and project. He *does,* however, align himself strongly not only with her right to be heard (which does not appear to be a given to at least some of the Gadamer industry; this festschrift is a *major* exception because of its willingness to let Orozco speak), but also, and more important, with the *methodology* Orozco is attempting to develop to analyze Gadamer and the history of philosophy generally (even though, again, Waite does not agree fully with her specific theorization and application of this methodology to the issue of National Socialism). In any case, however, let us be clear about one thing: It is Zuckert (even more than Orozco and certainly more than Waite) who has most explicitly broached the question of "Gadamer and Nazism." So we have no choice but to take it seriously in this *entretien.*

"Was Gadamer a Nazi?" Well, the answer to this question, as is appropriate in the relativist system, is precisely "a matter of 'interpretation,'" or, more simply put, of definition. If, for example, formal membership in the Nazi Party is one (partial or sole) definition, then the answer is both no and yes. "But that is only half the story. Let us look at it more fully," as we heard Socrates saying—beginning with the "actually said," or rather done.

Gadamer was not a member of the NSDAP (National Socialist German Workers Party), he was a member of the NSLB (National Socialist Teachers Union). Founded in 1927, the NSLB was officially classified by the NSDAP as its "connected organization" *(angeschlossener Verband).*[32] Membership in both the NSDAP and the NSLB was voluntary, and the party leadership of both were quite aware that opportunism was a common reason for application; they commonly turned down petitions on the grounds that a petitioner was not "politically reliable." (Over the course of the eleven-year history of the Thousand Year Reich, this situation changed, and membership in all party organizations became increasingly difficult.) [33] There is no record of any professor being forced to join either organization, though obviously there was indirect pressure insofar as membership could, and often did, help one's career, and certainly did nothing to hinder it. Partly because prospective members had to petition to join, membership was understood both officially and publicly as an attempt, at the very least, to accommodate oneself to the regime. On the other hand, some professors had successful careers in the Third Reich without being members of any National Socialist organization. It was possible to leave the NSLB without penalty, which some did; and it was of course also possible to be asked to leave or to be expelled (at least one such philosopher died in a concentration camp).[34] Reasons for expulsion were not limited to direct political opposition (overactive identification with Catholicism was one criterion, for example).

Membership in the NSLB was by charter open and limited to "jeder unbescholtene Lehrer und sonstige Erzieher, der das 18. Lebensjahr vollendet hat und arischer Abstammung [ist]" (every respectable teacher and other educator who has completed the eighteenth year of his life and is of Aryan decent).[35] In other words, the basic criterion was racialist and racist. By his own free choice (but not subsequent admission after the war), Gadamer was a member of NSLB in "Fachschaft 1: Lehrer an Hochschulen" (Professional Association 1: Teachers at Universities). Too, Gadamer had previously been a supporter or adherent (Anhänger) of the ultra-right-wing, and racist, German National People's Party (DNVP).[36] Hans-Georg Gadamer's NSLB card number was 254–387.[37]

Gadamer joined the NSLB on August 1, 1933, as did at least two other philosophers who later became famous.[38] (In March the first concentration camp had been built at Dachau near Munich, initially for communist and socialist political prisoners, as was reported in the press.) For the philosophical cadre, August 1933 was an early date to join. Gadamer's teacher and mentor Heidegger waited until December 1, 1933, though, unlike Gadamer, he was additionally to join the NSDAP (publicly on May 1 or 3, 1933, though having committed himself in secret several years earlier). But most philosophers waited until 1934 to join either organization.[39] The other two philosophers joining the NSLB on the same date as Gadamer were Hugo Fischer and Arnold Gehlen. Fischer left the NSLB two years later to the day (August 1, 1935) and eventually emigrated over Norway to England; after the war he returned to take a professorship at Munich. Like Heidegger, Gehlen joined the NSDAP, and, like Gadamer and Heidegger, remained

very prolific and influential after 1945 (and sometimes embattled).⁴⁰ Gadamer, like Gehlen and Heidegger, remained in the NSLB until the Allies dis-
banded it at the same time as the NSDAP.

In response, then, to one part of Zuckert's statement, if membership in
a political party can be construed as its "explicit support," and surely this is
one plausible definition, then Gadamer's membership in the explicitly racist NSLB, officially affiliated with the NSDAP, certainly can qualify as at least
one "action by which Gadamer explicitly supported National Socialism." To
be sure, to say this is not yet to say anything about what this support *means,*
either for Gadamer or for philosophical hermeneutics, nor even whether
this support can be deemed a good thing or a bad thing ethically or morally.
So far we remain exclusively at the level of what Zuckert likes to call the
"actual."

Turning to another part of Zuckert's statement—the matter of voting—
one can note that in November 1933, Gadamer joined other philosophers
who were members of the NSLB, some of whom were also members of the
NSDAP, to sign the "Bekenntnis der Professoren an den deutschen Universitäten und Hochschullen zu Adolf Hitler und dem nationalsozialistischen
Staat" (Declaration of faith of professors in the German universities and
colleges in Adolf Hitler and the National Socialist state).⁴¹ This declaration
explicitly supported a single list of NSDAP candidates *(Einheitsliste)* for the
immediately upcoming elections to Parliament *(Reichstag),* as well as Germany's definitive withdrawal from the League of Nations and all its inter-
nationally binding principles. This declaration was signed on the eve of the
plebiscite on November 12, 1933, which granted carte blanche to, and established the legality of, each and every decision made by Adolf Hitler.
Again *pace* Zuckert, Gadamer thus voted to disallow any one else from voting in Germany except for NSDAP candidates. In this way of voting, too,
Gadamer explicitly supported and legitimated Hitler's one-man rule and its
decisionistic legality.⁴²

In further response to Zuckert's request to know about any "statement,
vote, or action by which Gadamer explicitly supported National Socialism,"
at least one case is freely admitted by Gadamer himself. Gadamer was one
of a small handful of philosophers allowed to travel abroad during the Third
Reich, including during World War II: he gave lectures in Florence (January
1940), Paris (May 1941), Prague (June 1943), and Lisbon (March–April
1944). The other philosophers given this relatively rare privilege and sign
of trust included fellow members of the NSLB, some of whom were also in
the NSDAP, but also some who were in neither organization.⁴³ Of these
trips, Gadamer has stated: "I did not fail to recognize that one was thereby
being misused for foreign propaganda," adding, "for which often someone
politically innocent [*ein politisch Unbescholtener*—that word again] was precisely the right man" (PL118). Although Gadamer does not explicitly say

that he himself was either this "one" or this "someone" and "man," to participate with full recognition in an activity is, in effect, to perform an explicit
action in its support—no matter what one's motivations or subsequent actions may be. Again, however, we are not talking yet about motivations or
ethics. So far we are talking of the Zuckertian "actual" only.

Gadamer is also on record as having said in 1990, "whoever went into the
Party [NSDAP], in order to keep his position or to gain one, and then as a
teacher of philosophy practiced reasonable philosophy, is ten times prefer-
able to me than, say, people like [Oskar] Becher or [Hans] Freyer, who were
not in the Party but who talked like the Nazis."[44] Ten times can be quite a
lot (more than zero but less than, say, a thousand); but is then a *collaborator*
× times worse than a "true believer"? This is an old question and, as they
say, the jury is still out on it. But why Gadamer's quantitative distinction in
the first place? Is vociferous "symbolic" support of NSDAP any better or
worse (and how many times?), in principle or effect, than actual support of
the racist DNVP or actual membership in the officially affiliated and also
racist NSLB or other forms of collaboration with the NSDAP? As Gadamer
himself states, some of the most heinous and vocal advocates of National Socialist principles were not members of the NSDAP, of which he was not a
member; nor, presumably, as he does *not* suggest, of the NSLB, of which he
was a member.

The equally, if not more, important issue, however, is whether Gadamer's
teaching—*qua* his statements and actions, including the preservation and
development of philosophical hermeneutics during the Third Reich—
qualifies as what he calls "reasonable philosophy." Teaching (and only "after all else is said and done") is what matters most in Gadamer's oral/aural
tradition, in which "it is impossible for what is written not to be disclosed.
That is the reason why I have never written anything about these things, and
why there is not and will not be any written work by Plato. . . . As soon as you
have read and reread this letter, burn it" (Plato, Second Letter 314b–c).
But this, too, in his own terms *and* in Zuckert's, is "a matter of 'interpretation,'" as we will see. Though apparently this cannot be a matter for "dialogue" with Gadamer himself (or with Zuckert), but only a matter of contestation. But before addressing this pedagogic question ("teaching as
resistance") at the appropriate time later, a brief excursus is necessary for
historical and theoretical perspective.

An appropriate epitaph (by Thomas Laugstien) has been given to the attempt of all German philosophers in "'inner emigration': during the Third
Reich to preserve 'authentic philosophy'": "It reproduced itself in the consciousness that, in the philosophical sphere, one was permitted to do what
one wanted. But what one wanted above all was what one was permitted to
do."[45] But it should also be stressed that the same can be said for the situation of philosophers (and others) living under all forms of capitalism, two

of which are explicitly fascist and National Socialist. In any case, the question of whether the political or apolitical pedagogic form of the "reasonable" or "authentic" Gadamerian philosophy can be specified as "collaboration," and/or as "resistance," and/or as the attempt somehow to "redirect" National Socialism—all this is *also* "a matter of 'interpretation.'" In just this regard, a basic political question facing Gadamer's readers might be reformulated. Can the proper name "Gadamer" be substituted for "Shostakovich" and the terms "philosophical hermeneutics" or *"Truth and Method"* be substituted for "late music" or "string quartets" in the following remark? "A celebration of Shostakovich as a closet heroic dissident is not only factually false, it even occludes the true greatness of his late music. Even to a listener with minimal sensitivity, it is clear that his (deservedly famous) string quartets are not heroic statements defying the totalitarian regime, but a desperate commentary on Shostakovich's own cowardice and opportunism."[46] All this was another matter Hans-Georg Gadamer may have wished to sort out, as they used to say, between himself and his Maker, but for no one else. Otherwise stated, his activities before, during, and after the Third Reich were free decisions insofar as decisions can ever be free—decisions "grounded" ultimately only on the bottomless abyss of freedom. In that sense, any search for the "reasons" behind his decisions is doomed from the start. In any event, it remains we who must sort these things out, and not just between ourselves and Gadamer, but also among ourselves and within each one of us.

In conclusion to his reply to a would-be—only somewhat aggressive—interlocutor in the Library of Living Philosophers volume, Gadamer writes:

> I thank the author for her intensive dedication to the problems she takes up. But I would like to add the request that one should first presume that one did not understand the other properly when one believes that one can find contradictions everywhere in the opinion of the other.[47]

The soundness of this advice aside (which seems to follow one basic Straussian heuristic, though not necessarily the Zuckertian principle of the "actually said"), and aside also the way the qualifiers "first" and "properly" beg important hermeneutic questions, we can at least note that this response is at once *descriptive,* if one assumes that the critic in question has in fact done what Gadamer says she has done, and *prescriptive,* insofar as it tells that critic what to do. "Properly," posits as its precondition the distinction between "proper" and "improper"—a distinction that relativism cannot draw. (This may mean, of course, that Gadamer, in this one case at least, was not a relativist; but it may also mean that he was an exo/esotericist.) This simultaneously constative and performative response establishes what the limits of any dialogue for Gadamer have been, are, and will be. It produces a hermeneutic circle, or tautology, in which no alternative, exterior position is possible, confirming the insight that "not every discourse is a relation with exteriority."[48]

And in his reply to another would-be—and much more aggressive—critic writing in the same Library of Living Philosophers volume, Gadamer tells her, in effect, that she should not have analyzed one of his texts *(Philosophical Apprenticeships)*, which she analyzes from a feminist perspective that emphasizes the way Gadamer and philosophical hermeneutics refer to women, as well as to the way both might relate to "Nazism." Gadamer recommends that this critic should have analyzed two other texts instead: his autobiographical sketch in the Library of Living Philosophers volume, and his essay "Die politische Inkompetenz der Philosophie" (The political incompetence of philosophy). Gadamer goes on to indicate how the latter text should, indeed must, be "actually read." "In the essay 'Über die politische Inkompetenz der Philosophie,'" Gadamer states, "I illustrated with Plato and Heidegger what I myself think about the relation between philosophy and politics. With modesty, I lay claim to the same incompetence."[49] In other words, we should accept an author's word about a subject when that author proclaims that he (in this case) is incompetent about that subject and we should not attempt to analyze it ourselves—the subject here being the Gadamerian relation between philosophy and politics. Now if, as Zuckert writes in "On the Politics of Gadamerian Hermeneutics, "philosophical dialogue and textual hermeneutics are essentially ethical," as "Gadamer argued from the beginning until the end of his career, because they entail respect for the integrity and independence of the other, not only in the initial attempt to understand but also in the peaceful, nonviolent character of the accord or agreement at which the dialogue aims," and if the ethical has to do with the political (as the naive reader may have thought, and as not a few philosophers have argued over the centuries), then to declare oneself "incompetent" in the political is simultaneously to declare oneself incompetent in the ethical (as many have also thought and argued). For example, from a neo-Spinozist, neo-communist perspective, not only is it the case "that the relationship between philosophy and politics is such that each implies the other," but also that "the dilemma which would lead us to distinguish between 'speculative' philosophy, on the one hand, and philosophy 'applied' to politics, on the other, is not simply meaningless, it is the principle obstacle to achieving wisdom."[50] If this is true, the very basis of Gadamerian philosophical hermeneutics—notably, its self-admitted "incompetence" in politics, and its entailed, ostensible respect for the other and nonviolence—would all be undermined radically. But, again, so far this is only potentially a truly "devastating charge" against Gadamer and his entire philosophical position.

But one thing should be crystal clear to anyone attempting to enter into a dialogue, and in that sense an ethical or political encounter, with Gadamer concerning his relationship to "Nazism" (or to "the question of woman," evidently). She or he will continue to encounter an adamant: *No pasaran!* (They will not pass!).[51] It may boggle the mind, therefore, that a few naive, benighted critics persist in assuming that Gadamer would enter into dialogue on the specific matter of "Nazism." (Not to mention the fact that so many Gadamerian philosophers, theologians, and literary theorists, as well as perhaps more practically inclined souls, persist in developing Gadamer's self-described "incompetence" apropos "the relationship between philosophy and politics" into many political and ethical applications of philosophical hermeneutics, including health or hospice care.) At the very least it is exceedingly problematic to "dialogue" with Gadamer himself in this quixotic endeavor. Gadamer simply does not want to talk, or cannot talk (whether for reasons that are psychoanalytic and/or consciously exo/esoteric), beyond a *very* circumscribed point about his relationship to National Socialism. Apologies to Quixote and the quixotic aside, what then is the point in continuing to bang one's head against this theoretically and practically closed door? (Again parenthetically, this situation may well be even less amusing to Orozco than it is to Waite.) Wittgenstein once remarked that "A person is *trapped* when the door is unlocked and opens inwards, and he or she does not arrive at the idea to *pull,* rather than to push against it."[52] But *can* we still think to push here, and can we do so effectively?

With regard to ethics specifically, as Zuckert correctly notes, even the most cursory reader of the self-described politically "incompetent" Gadamer's extensive œuvre will encounter an extensive, lifelong preoccupation with the subject—in terms of both interpreting the history of philosophy from at least Plato on, and the application of this preoccupation to current topics, including his aforementioned way of responding to critics who attempt to penetrate into his *Horizontverschmelzung* from some imagined exterior. What, then, about the *ethics* of "the politics of Gadamerian hermeneutics"?

In terms of an ethics that is nonprescriptive, and as such more properly described as "ethology,"[53] Gadamer in his (part collaborative, part critical) relationship to "Nazism" was simply refusing "to cede to his desire," understood as the only cogent ethical imperative.[54] And there is not a damn thing anyone can do about this fact, including hopelessly attempting to enter into dialogue with it. Which is not to say, however, that Gadamer's position cannot, should not, be combated. In Marx's terms, this is the very definition of "criticism" when confronting an objectionable "content." "Criticism dealing with this content is criticism in hand-to-hand combat, and in such a fight the point is not whether the opponent is a noble, equal, interesting opponent, the point is to strike him."[55] But the problem, here, is this: whether or not Gadamer is "noble" or "equal" is hardly at issue; philosophical hermeneutics remains obviously "interesting"—but interesting also in the sense that it is so elusive (cf. *inter-esse,* "between being") that it cannot be easily "struck" (whether one would want to or not).

As paraphrased by no less an authority than Zuckert, in her response to Orozco and Waite, "Gadamer had obvious practical reasons to mute his criticism of the brutal power politics of the party in power; he had no 'practical' reason (beyond the ethical imperatives of friendship and decency) to mute his support." Much is at stake in the parenthetical remark. But in any case Gadamer refuses to, cannot, and arguably *should* not, practice friendship and moderation with those who are his enemies. Like Kant's categorical imperative and Spinoza's attempt to elicit the rational core of ethics from Jewish-Christian Scripture, the Christian injunction "Love your neighbor as thyself" is radically problematized, not merely by who "thyself" often in fact is (psychologically, one is often one's own worst enemy), but also by the fact that this option is simply unavailable to oneself if it transpires, as it often does in history, that the same neighbor is about to kill you (excepting the case of consistent pacifists) or *has killed you* (in all cases).

So it is, then, to leap backward and forward in the argument, that Zuckert and Gadamer demand dialogue and moderation but 1) refuse it in some cases, and 2) encounter those who refuse dialogue and moderation, at least on Gadamerian terms. All of which, however, only disproves that dialogue and moderation are universal principles in fact, and only suggests that, perhaps, they should be—but not necessarily in our current world. Again, we reach only the level of the *tu quoque* and an "aporia"—not as the beginning of complex inquiry but as its simple termination.

Gadamer's theory of the relationship between ethics and *friendship,*[56] and *mutatis mutandis* of the relationship between philosophy and politics (disingenuous disclaimer of "incompetence" aside), seems to run aground or adrift on his collaboration-cum-resistance with what has been, and what announced itself from its inception to be, what is arguably—alongside fascism—the *most* successful, *least* friendly and philosophico-political regime in human history (as Zuckert affirms). But that regime (Waite would argue) is not merely what we call "The Third Reich," or "Nazi Germany." For it is also that regime's subtending "discursive practice" (at once philosophical, political, ethical, cultural, and psychological, as well as economic) that is *capitalism.* Which assertion, however, certainly does not, or should not, entail that the historically longest sustained attempt to oppose capitalism, namely a more or less Stalinist socialism in one country (the former Soviet Union and its satellites), was itself either fully friendly or fully anticapitalist. Focusing here only on the former point, to say that millions of inmates of the Gulag were the victims of a system that differed from Nazi Germany and the millions of its inmates and that in the former their incarceration was *sensu stricto* illegal and in the latter legal—this is a pathetically weak argument to make either to all those inmates and corpses (and who, in both systems, included communists and Jews, among many others) or to history itself. For all of them, the distinction between incarceration *de facto et de jure* (the case of Nazism) and *de facto sed non de jure* (the case of Stalinism) is existentially moot, no matter how important it may be structurally.[57] It is important to acknowledge this fact not least if one is attempting to find alternatives to capitalism's long, overdetermined arc extending from its inception, through all its modes, to the present.

"ALTHUSSERIAN POLITICAL COMMITMENTS"

In turn, however, this is not to say that all distinctions in this terrible matter (i.e., that fascism and National Socialism are forms of capitalism; and that to date communism has not been fully anticapitalist and has been willing to murder many people) are *wholly* insignificant. Since Waite's "political commitments," as Zuckert puts it, are "Althusserian," in some sense, and since, in her view, these are what have prevented him from understanding Gadamer, and much else besides, Waite is required to say something in this regard. Althusser has been used to justify absolute quietism in the face of pressing political exigencies; on the other hand, he has done the opposite; and he continues to inspire urban and rural guerrilla fighters in the "third world" as well as cyberpunk hackers everywhere. Neither last nor least, Althusserians in blood-drenched former Yugoslavia found themselves, in friendship with Lacanians, being attacked and ultimately defeated by the two dominant parties who shared little else in common but this very antipathy: "Heideggerians among the opposition and Frankfurt school Marxists among the 'official' Party circles."[58] And for "Heideggerians" read here also: Gadamerians.

Implying that Waite's "political commitments" are not only "Althusserian" but Nietzschean (*pace* Waite himself, according to Zuckert, and in opposition to her own Nietzsche, one may assume),[59] Zuckert herself (fighting for the moment alongside her Gadamer) offers the following description-cum-prescription: "rather than merely criticize (or attack) others from our own vantage point, Gadamer insists, we must first try to see things their way." Rudely interrupting Zuckert again, one might ask what should we do after we have tried to see things in the other's way, and we discover that the other either will not enter into dialogue with us and/or is irrevocably committed to combating our position? If we assume what should not necessarily be assumed (this is one of the things that readers of the *entretien préliminaire* must decide for themselves), namely that Waite (and Orozco) has made an attempt to see beyond his own vantage point (though clearly not nearly to the satisfaction of Zuckert), it is at moments such as these that Waite recalls the recommendation once given by Gramsci, *anno* 1917 (a few years before landing in the Italian Fascist prison system, in which he was eventually to die):

> When debating with an opponent, try to put yourself in his shoes: you will understand him better, and may end by recognizing that there is some truth in what he says, and perhaps a lot. For some time I myself followed this sage advice. But my adversaries' shoes got so filthy that I was forced to conclude it's better to be unfair than risk fainting from the stink they give off.[60]

At this point, quite unseemly insults aside, however, Waite stresses that he does not really know what he would have done in circumstances the same as faced by Gadamer in the Third Reich. (He can at best know what he is doing now, in the United States of America, or rather in transnational capitalism.) Zuckert does not tell us what *she* (thinks she) would have done back then, either, though someone reading her response to Orozco and Waite, and her own (at least partial) defense of Gadamer, may surmise that she implies that she might well have done what Gadamer did (*were* she permitted by the regime, of course), or at least that, today, she finds his behavior legitimate and defensible insofar as he was defending his own life and that of his family and friends ("the ethical imperatives of friendship and decency").

Not speaking for Orozco (never to mention Zuckert), Waite would say that *none* of us can know what we would have done before, during, or immediately after the events that propelled Hitler into power in 1933–34. If, however, in those years Waite was what he is now (namely, a member of a Communist Party [CPUSA], albeit with certain tendencies officially rejected by that party—including not only Althusserianism, but Trotskyism, Gramscianism, and Maoism, and writing about topics anathema to the party, including Nietzsche, Heidegger, Strauss, and Gadamer), then Waite does know exactly what would have happened to him: incarceration on May 1, 1933, or thereafter. But, to repeat, he does not know for certain if he would have also been a communist (or whatever) in those years. Since Waite's current form of internationalist identity ("cosmopolitan rootlessness" in the National Socialist and fascist terminology, *"nicht unbescholten"* in that of the NSLB) is neither Jewish, Romani, nor any racial type or sexual orientation proscribed or punished by the NSDAP and NSLB, he would not have been arrested at that time for that reason—unlike what would have happened, undoubtedly, for one or more reasons (taking not arbitrary examples) to Strauss, Rosen, Derrida, and Trotsky. But not have happened, for that reason, to Heidegger or to Gadamer.

Nor does Waite know what he would have done in the Stalinist Union of Soviet Socialist Republics (USSR) or its satellites, say, the German Democratic Republic (GDR). His current adherence to a quasi-Stalinist party leads him to think that were he a communist in the latter regime he might have been a collaborator of the Stasi type. On the other hand, his equal allegiance to the Althusserian critique of Stalinism and to aspects of Trotskyism (etc.)—in addition to any residual trace of humanist scruples—would have disallowed that very collaboration. But Waite, again, does not know any of this—neither generally nor as an Althusserian.

As a member of the Stalinist French Communist Party (PCF), and hence also a collaborator with the Stalinist Soviet Union, Althusser tried to reform the party from within, combating Stalinism.[61] But is this not exactly—or more or less—the same thing that Gadamer was doing within the NSLB as official affiliate of the NSDAP and in Nazi Germany generally? And does not Waite here have a double standard: affirming Althusser and attacking Gadamer, to adopt Zuckert's way of thinking? Here the answer is more complex on both accounts: yes *and* no. But first we must stress that the penalties for criticizing a party (in Althusser's case) and a party *and* a regime (in Gadamer's case) are not strictly comparable in terms of risk. In Gadamer's case the risk, if we believe him, was physical removal from his teaching position, danger to family and friends, and possible incarceration and even death. In Althusser's case the comparable risk was "merely" expulsion from the PCF—not physical death. To be precise, however, this would have been, for Althusser, a kind of philosophical, political, and psychological death. And, in the event, the latter "death" Althusser in fact suffered, though for overdetermined reasons. (He was irrevocably expelled from his party when he killed his wife, and fellow communist, Hélène Rytman.) Too, Althusser developed his strongest alternative to Stalinism, even most Marxism, mainly in private, esoterically if one will. His "aleatory materialism" was designed to complement, at the level of textual production (based on principles derived not only from Spinoza but from Nietzsche, *inter alia*), the technique of reading the "symptomatic silences" not only of texts, notably Marx's *Capital,* but also, as in the case of the USSR and the PCF, political movements, as well as, and most especially, of capitalism itself.[62] But, yes, Althusser did all this, including his public attacks against the PCF, from *within* his party; and it *remained* Stalinist despite his efforts—largely, if not even wholly, quixotic—to transform it radically "from within." But, once again, to accept *one* kind of collaboration is not to defend *all* kinds. And this includes defending, as Althusser notably did not, collaboration with capitalism *tout court,* including its fascist or National Socialist variants.

But the specific question in this festschrift being asked by Waite (and by Orozco, albeit in a rather different way that Waite does not fully share but shares generally) is about Gadamer's silences, including those of his supporters and insufficiently savvy readers. Gadamer demonstrably (in his responses in the Library of Living Philosophers volume, for example) tries to reduce his more vigorous attackers to silence, and (unwittingly or not) Zuckert appears to be collaborating with him in this effort—victoriously.

Yet if Zuckert's own performance of "moderation" contradicts her own affirmative constatation of "moderation," this is not to be imagined as some
sort of more or less nefarious "error" or "fault," or so Waite would say.
Rather, such performance, in general, is one of the more successful ways of
reproducing the dominant "discursive practice" not only of philosophy and
politics but also of liberal-democratic and pluralistic capitalism generally.
And were Waite to suggest a clear parallelism or isomorphism between
Zuckert's institutional opportunism (now a Gadamerian, now a Straussian,
yet always also "objective" and "moderate") and Gadamer's admitted philosophico-political opportunism combined with self-described political incompetence, Waite is convinced that Zuckert would find all the appropriate counterarguments, and that they would be convincing. Not to Waite, of
course, but to the dominant "discursive practice," since Zuckert (like Gadamer or Strauss, and even Derrida) is successfully reproducing precisely that
order. This fact (or, if you prefer, hypothesis) in mind, we begin to turn at
last to the question of Gadamerian "pedagogical resistance."

"IF THAT IS THE OBJECTION . . . , THEY SHOULD SAY SO"

Zuckert writes:

> Gadamer may be criticized for not publicly opposing the rise and rule of Na-
> tional Socialism in Germany in word or deed. *If that is the objection Orozco and
> Waite wish to make, they should say so.* The question then would be whether "po-
> litical correctness" or plain old morality requires a man [or woman, we should
> add] to become a martyr (like Eric Bonhoeffer). Is it not possible for a person
> to conclude "prudently" (in the Aristotelian and not the Kantian sense) that
> it would be better to preserve not merely one's life and career, but also the
> lives and livelihood of one's family, friends and students, by trying to foster
> change from within, gradually, by means of persuasion rather than force?
> Such a prudent course of action might require one to remain silent at times
> or to deliver criticisms indirectly in a veiled manner. In his *Philosophical Ap-
> prenticeships,* Gadamer describes his own behavior during the Nazi regime very
> much in these terms. [emphasis added]

Ipse dixit appeal to Gadamer aside,[63] as well as Gadamer's own disclaimers
about *Philosophical Apprenticeships,* Zuckert is quite correct to demand, prescriptively, clarity about "the objection Orozco and Waite wish to make" and
that they "should say so." Leaving Orozco's response to her, of course, Waite
says the following. His objection to Gadamer in this regard (keeping in
mind the aforementioned caveats about not knowing apodeictically what he
himself would have done) is *this:* The *only* acceptable ethical position with
regard to National Socialism—before, during, and after 1933—was not accommodation and collaboration, no matter how critical from within it. *The
only acceptable ethical position was resistance at the risk of being killed.*

Resistance does not necessarily lead to martyrdom, if one is not apprehended, or, in other situations, if one does not take it upon oneself (unlike
Socrates or Jesus, who did). Being apprehended in Nazi Germany (or Stalinist Russia) was more dangerous than, say, in Fascist Italy or Spain, or in occupied France and elsewhere in Europe—where, however, it was *sufficiently*
dangerous. *And* resistance in Nazi Germany was similarly more dangerous
than in Stalinist Soviet Union or its satellites—though it was certainly
dangerous enough there, too. Resistance against capitalism can be similarly
dangerous today, particularly in "third-world" countries, but even *hic et
nunc.* This is a very old and universal problem: "Cu' dici la virità va 'mpisu"
(speaking the truth will get you hanged). We will return to Gadamer's position on martyrdom, but with all due respect to Zuckert's reference to the
"martyrdom" of Eric Bonhoeffer (with whom Gadamer apparently associated), this is perhaps the *worst* example of resistance for her to mention in
this context, common currency though it is.

In addition to other reasons why he is a very bad example,[64] Bonhoeffer
is best known today for the quotation that appears on T-shirts available in
"alternative shops" in different versions, one of which begins: "They came
for the communists [more commonly replaced by 'socialists'], *and I did
nothing;* they came for the trade unionists, *and I did nothing;* they came for
the Jehovah's Witnesses, *and I did nothing;* they came for the homosexuals,
and I did nothing," and so forth. This series concludes with Bonhoeffer's own
quite fitting epitaph: "Then they came for me, *and there was no one left to protect me.*" And so Bonhoeffer was murdered, but hardly as a legitimate "martyr": by his own final admission, he was murdered as much for his (initial)
collaboration as for his (too tardy) resistance. Too, returning to Zuckert and
Gadamer, and to repeat, there are many *forms* of death: there is physical
death, as absolute physiological "limit condition" (at least for the atheists
among us); but this is *not* (for some of us), the *worst* form of death, which
might be psychological death (trauma), ethical and moral death (the secular version of Hell, no doubt), and so on. *True philosophy, however else it is
defined, is a matter of life and/or of death.* Ethically, in philosophy as in politics,
death (in *all* its forms) often has been and remains the *only* risk worth taking—both in those National Socialist circumstances and in these capitalist
times. "Homo liber de nulla re minus, quam de morte cogitat, & ejus sapi-
entia non mortis, sed vitæ meditatio est" (The free man thinks of nothing
less than of death, and his wisdom is a meditation not on death, but on life)
(Spinoza, *Ethica,* IVP67).

To summarize and to speak even more bluntly, Waite's requested "objection" to Gadamer's relationship to "the rise and rule of National Socialism
in Germany" is that Gadamer did not *risk death* and, if required, did not *die.*
And, yes, this might well have meant taking both family and friends *and* all
of philosophical hermeneutics, at least as we know it from Gadamer, with

him to the grave. Moreover, to legitimate not risking death, and not dying, in those National Socialist circumstances, on the grounds of what Zuckert calls "trying to foster change from within"—all this amounts to a *massive* "incompetence" (at the time, and not just retroactively) to judge the essence of this particular system, which was *per definitionem* unchangeable from within (beginning, one might say, no later than the vote for the *Einheitsliste*). Once instaurated, such movements can only be crushed from *without*—as the fascists and National Socialists themselves openly declared, and as capitalism (and *not* all Marxism) knows in its heart of hearts. What is even more, to justify collaboration with such systems—even in tandem with "internal resistance" or "inner emigration" to them—on the grounds of "saving philosophy" demands that we know everything we can—from within *and* without—about this philosophy of collaboration-cum-resistance. Although it is clear that the history of mathematics and the natural sciences is *in no way* compromised by the fact that a genius like Frege was a rabid anti-Semite, it is equally clear (if one accepts the position of Gadamer, and so many others in the Diltheyan tradition) that the human sciences represent a different and more complex case. As Nietzsche liked to say (with the pre-Socratics and Socrates in mind, as well as himself), there is a sense in which philosophy is nothing, ultimately, but the confession of its philosopher. (And what else does Heideggerian *Dasein* ultimately entail?) Otherwise the life and thought of Socrates (and Jesus . . . or Gramsci) would be without ultimate meaning. And so it is at least *questionable* (or *fragwürdig*, "questionworthy") to suggest, *ex hypothesi,* that any philosophical system may be rejected if one rejects the life of its philosopher. At the very least, philosophy itself has the responsibility to keep this terrible question open. To put the resulting new question (and it is not "rhetorical") again most bluntly and terribly: Ought such a philosophy, philosophical hermeneutics and its ancestry to ancient Greece, live and not rather die? In light of this question— and it most assuredly cannot be answered here—the issues now swirling around "the politics of Gadamerian hermeneutics" may remind us of a *bon mot* from the pen of the Canadian economist and humorist Stephen Butler Leacock (1869–1944): "My friend the professor of Greek tells me that he truly believes that the classics have made him what he is. This is a very grave statement, if well founded."[65] And make no mistake: Gadamer is among the greatest professors of Greek—arguably even the last of the greats, given the seemingly irreversible global state of things.

Unseemly witticisms again to one side, however, it is *immediately* necessary to add that Waite's "objection" is made on extremely tenuous grounds, *if* indeed on any ultimate *grounds* at all, insofar as Waite has no certain way of knowing if this, his objection or consequent course of action, are, in fact, what he himself would have made or done at that time. In that sense his objection has *no* prescriptive force. In Lacanian terms, to repeat, Gadamer took the ethical position of "following his desire" with regard to National Socialist essentialism, and has apparently made his peace with that position, as have most Gadamerians, whether they be "in the know" or "out of the know" apropos of what that position "actually was," in "statement, vote, or action."

And so it also is that Waite simply refuses to accept Zuckert's premise (itself part collaboratory, part resisting) that "Gadamer may be criticized for not publicly opposing the rise and rule of National Socialism in Germany in word or deed." To which Waite emphatically responds: *No,* Gadamer may *not* be criticized on *these* grounds. "Criticism" in this case is surely irrelevant; what *may* be demanded, however, is *opposition.*

Quite apart from the fact that Gadamer himself not only did not "oppose" the "rise and rule of National Socialism in Germany in word or deed," but instead, as one significant part of his response (his "dialogue" with National Socialism, as it were), explicitly embraced it, the fact is that no one can ethically "criticize" the past actions of another unless he or she knows what she or he would have done in similar circumstances, and this one simply cannot know, at least not apodeictically for times past. One can sometimes know, often with great difficulty, what one is doing in the present. And Zuckert is silent, in her response in this *entretien préliminaire,* about her own "criticism" of Gadamer in this matter. She is silent about what (she thinks) she might have done. Whatever she herself may think, however, her argument can be read to suggest that she thinks she may have done *grosso modo* what Gadamer did inasmuch as, for Zuckert,

> *The* twentieth-century philosopher who opposes such "spiritual" warfare [*sc.* of the type "fostered" by Waite] is Hans-Georg Gadamer. Rather than merely criticize (or attack) others from our own vantage point, Gadamer insists, we must first try to see things their way. Rather than impose our interpretation or view, we must engage in a dialogue, the form of thought Nietzsche said was decadent and democratic, like Socrates, that philosopher of the "rabble."

But let us not overlook one thing: Socrates was physically killed for his troubles, and Gadamer was neither physically killed nor otherwise "devastated." And if neither Waite nor Zuckert can know what they themselves would have done in Hitler's Germany, then they can at least attempt to know, or they can refuse to know, what Gadamer did; they can deem this knowledge relevant, or irrelevant, to understanding his philosophy; and, on this basis, they can accept or reject the "reasonable philosophy" that Gadamer saved for its current posterity, its afterlife, its corps/es.

For his own part, Gadamer has spoken eloquently about death, to the extent that one can speak eloquently about what has been defined *a priori* as incomprehensible and unspeakable.[66] Gadamer writes that "the incomprehensibility of death is the highest triumph of life *[Die Unbegreiflichkeit des Todes ist der höchste Triumph des Lebens].*"⁶⁷ And, "To thoughtful thought *[dem nachdenkenden Gedanken]* it must mean something as incompressible as it is illuminating that the true overcoming of death can lie in nothing other than in the resurrection from the dead—for the believer the greatest certainty, for the others something incomprehensible, but which is not more incomprehensible than is death itself."⁶⁸ What this articulation of death with incomprehension or incomprehensibility leaves unasked, however, as does the patent attempt to forge a dialogue between believers and nonbelievers around this articulation, is what happens when the death at stake is not merely physical death, but psychological and ethical, and when one has contributed (with whatever motivation) to the various kinds of death of others who are thereby simply unavailable for dialogue. For teachers, this context includes one's students.⁶⁹

ON "PEDAGOGICAL RESISTANCE" AND "CHANGE FROM WITHIN"

But it is high time for us look more closely at what Zuckert depicts as Gadamer's attempt "to foster change from within, gradually, by means of persuasion rather than force." This assumes, of course, that Nazi society could be changed by persuasion, not force—a mechanism that Goebbels anticipated and built into his propaganda machine.⁷⁰ To repeat, only *massive* politico-philosophical *Unbescholtenheit* or "incompetence" could ever have thought that National Socialism (or fascism and capitalism) were radically alterable in this way. But this point aside, there are only two main examples given by Gadamer himself for how he attempted to "foster change from within," and with what results. "Presumably" if there were others we would know about them.

What Gadamer "actually wrote" in *Philosophical Apprenticeships* (which he has chided one reader for even having read, let alone attempting to interpret critically):⁷¹

Just how in solidarity one was ["one"—German *man*—appears to refer to oppositional philosophers and their interpellated listeners in seminars] may be shown by the following anecdote, which I forgot and which was related to me later by its originator *[Urheber].* I gave a Plato lecture. In the discussion a soldier, who found himself on leave, asked what Plato would have said if a criminal tyrant were to stand as the leader *[Führer]* of a state. I answered: Obviously *[Selbstverständlich]* he would have approved of the murder of the tyrant.—There was no repercussion [or consequence: *Es erfolgte keine Weiterung*]. (PL116)

When did the soldier relate this story to jog Gadamer's memory: during the Third Reich or after the war (if the soldier survived with Gadamer)? What repercussion or consequence, *exactly,* did not result? Does this mean that neither Gadamer nor the student was punished? But then why not? Was it because the remark never left the classroom or because it did and the regime didn't care? In any case, Hitler was not murdered (notwithstanding the late failed attempt by a former member of the George circle with which Gadamer had been associated, namely, the true believer, then collaborator, and finally "martyr," Stauffenberg). Hitler committed suicide. Gadamer's remark here is a *Leerstelle,* a structured textual gap or "art of allusion" that can be differently interpreted. But so can the reference to Plato, which is, after all, a merely hypothetical interpretation of what Plato himself would have said and, as paraphrased in indirect discourse by Gadamer long after the war, does not necessarily establish what he himself—given his overall interpretation both of "the relation between philosophy and politics" either in Plato or in Gadamer's own self-proclaimed "incompetence" to know what this relation is—held to be true. If Gadamer's implication is that he was inciting his auditors to attempt to murder Hitler, based on a claim about what Plato would have thought and commanded, then how responsible is this innuendo pedagogically, politically, ethically, philosophically? Might this suggestion, this displacement unto others, not be irresponsible, cowardly, and unethical *in the extreme?* Such questions are no more or less open to interpretation than is the anecdote itself. The latter does not speak of resistance *any more* than it speaks of collaboration. Rather, it simply *states,* leaving it up to the auditor (or reader) to decide what its author means, and what to *do* about criminal tyrants—if anything at all. And, at the end of the day, in *this* case, "there was *no* repercussion," *no* "consequence."

So, with regard to repercussions and consequences, we need to turn to the second of the two main anecdotes illustrating Gadamer's simultaneous "pedagogical resistance" to National Socialism and his collaboration with it.

> Once there was a dangerous repercussion *[Weiterung].* In a seminar I had used an example in logic: All donkeys are brown. Great laughter—and a female student enthusiastically told a girlfriend. The letter was read by her parents. A denunciation followed. The poor girl had to go into factory work. I was ordered before the clever and well-meaning rector, who allowed himself to be satisfied with the acknowledgment that I had indeed used an example in logic. (PL116)

"Presumably," as we say, "brown" could be taken to refer to the "brown shirts" (the Sturmabteilung or SA), whereas, say, "black" would refer to the Schutzstaffel or SS. And "pink," in the concentration camp semiotic system, would have designated homosexuals, "yellow" the Jews, "green" the Jehovah's Witnesses, "red" the communists, and so forth. This time, however, the repercussions of Gadamer's actions were indeed dangerous to *someone* ("the poor girl"), though once again not ultimately to *him.* (Sometimes mere logic does

have its advantages, hermeneutical and other critiques of logic notwithstanding.) And we do not learn the further fate of this student (according
to Zuckert, Gadamer acted to save his students), who was immediately reas-
signed from university to factory work, or what the kind, conditions, and lo-
cation of that work were (many died in work camps)—perhaps simply because Gadamer did not or does not know. Once again, we have a *Leerstelle* or
"art of allusion": the student and the rector were equally correct to have different (or the same) interpretations of Gadamer's example from logic—
philosophically and/or politically. Gadamer's example, and his recounting,
allow both possibilities without being required to take a stand in either case,
or rather to take a stand in both cases. He can imply that he meant one
thing but not the other depending on who the interlocutor is, depending
on who wields the power to decide what is (the) truth. This is part of what
is meant by such concepts as "collaboration and/or resistance," "ethico-
political responsibility and/or irresponsibility"—*in fine,* this is what is meant
by it's all "a matter of 'interpretation'" and by relativism. Furthermore, however, this anecdote also appears to be a splendid example of the practical
ethics of philosophical hermeneutics and its politics, its *phrónēsis* or "art of
allusion." What Gadamer certainly does admit is that this practical reason is
potentially dangerous or devastating for someone—but to date it has not
been dangerous or devastating to him. Dangerous and devastating it was
only to someone else who might listen with his (or, more precisely in this
case, her) Gadamerian "inner ear," purportedly. Gadamer (who in 1946 was
to find himself a university rector, having been appointed such by the Allies,
including the Soviets—one of the last major nominally communist regimes
on the planet) today gives no clear sign that he regrets or takes responsibility for the fate of the young woman student, nor in his system need he do
so. *Logisch,* as the Germans like to say. It is simply a "category mistake" to
insist that Gadamer or philosophical hermeneutics take such responsibility. That's just the Hell of it. While there exist several logical refutations of
relativism, it has proven itself to be quite impervious to them, especially
when it conceals its esoteric first principle. In a different discourse: *La lucha
continua!*

EPITAPH ON MARTYRDOM

*He [Socrates]—despite all the preparations and political justifications that Critias
offers for himself—refuses flight from prison to avoid execution. The Platonic question thus asked through Socrates was this. How is it possible that a man can so de-
tach himself from everything in his environment, that he comport himself so differently, when our own comportment, as we generally see, consists precisely in
conforming ourselves to the natural and social conditions of the life in which we
stand? That a man goes so far out of bounds as Socrates, and, unaffected by what*

everyone does and by what everyone says, holds fast to the Idea of what is Right?
What must this Idea be? It must be obvious, visible and incontestable, for him who
lives accordingly and thus unwaveringly makes his decision.

GADAMER, "Amicus Plato"

"Whoever philosophizes will not be in agreement with the conceptions of the times."
As a quotation from Goethe it was indeed well masked, as it was in continuity with
Goethe's characterization of the Platonic writings. But if one does not want to make
a martyr of oneself or voluntarily choose emigration, such a motto can nevertheless
convey a certain emphasis to the understanding reader in a time of enforced confor-
mity, and affirmation of one's identity.

HANS-GEORG GADAMER, Reflections on my Philosophical Journey

Pairing these two epigraphs from Gadamer (even without our previous discussion of "Gadamer and Nazism" in mind) may raise uncanny questions.
Do Gadamer and philosophical hermeneutics more or less tacitly concede
that they can only always fail to understand or interpret (never mind live up
to, meaning die for) the seminal Socratic definition of philosophy and its
one ultimate test? Does what Gadamer ultimately meant by his obsessive recurrence to *phrónēsis* amount to nothing more or less than this abject falling
short of philosophy? Perhaps this is why Gadamer (said that he) turned in
the one direction away from Socrates and the pre-Socratics ahead to Plato
and Aristotle, and in the other direction away from Nietzsche and Heidegger through Dilthey back to Plato. The uncanny sensation lingers as it does
at all Janus-faced portals. According to our two epigraphs read together,
Gadamer and philosophical hermeneutics could never have understood or
interpreted the Platonic Socrates who defined himself in terms of his willingness to be a martyr for his greatest Idea, his Idea of Right. Any full understanding or interpretation of this Socrates is simply impossible if Gadamer himself was unwilling—even in theory let alone in practice—*either* to
"make a martyr" of himself *"or"* to "voluntarily choose emigration." This is
an uncanny "or" (inasmuch as Socrates precisely rejected the option of emigration, in favor of martyrdom), its meaning obscure. But what should remain plain as day is that there is nothing whatsoever uncanny in Gadamer's
decision to live for whatever reason and cause (including theoretically endless interpretations of Aristotle's relationship to Plato). This decision can be
ultimately no more or less uncanny than any of our own decisions. Instead,
what lingers so uncannily in the Gadamer Industry is the unanalyzed aura
around what Gadamer in our second epigraph (mediated by reference to
the quintessential mediator, Goethe) states is *his own* "masking." Due to this
lack of clarity, what will remain at the end of the day is the question mark
after just how far Gadamer's own canniness extended. If Waite has his way,
this question mark will always adhere to philosophical hermeneutics as to
all other philosophy (if only as one flea the dog can't quite scratch).

But let us not get too personal. If, as Gadamer suggests in his essay "Amicus Plato magis amica veritas" (1968), the Socratic refusal to avoid death is the very ground and inception of the philosophical and ethical project, and if the philosopher (nearly *per definitionem*) is willing to die for what is Right, even for the Idea of the Right, then in what sense was Hans-Georg Gadamer a philosopher? According to this definition, he could not have been a philosopher (at best a great historian of hermeneutics)—unless we have misunderstood all along what Gadamer really thought philosophy and the Idea of Right to be. If Gadamer were to return this question to us, by saying that the point of philosophical hermeneutics is not (only) what Gadamer thinks but (also) what we think, he would seem justified. For what about us, what do we think philosophy and the Right are, and do we act accordingly? But there would persist the huge problem with this imagined response by Gadamer. If it is informed by unacknowledged esotericism, philosophical hermeneutics may be more of the problem than the solution to even formulating ultimate questions, let alone helping us answer them.

Actually, the official English translation of Gadamer's now famous quotation from Goethe, as recited in "Reflections on my Philosophical Journey," is typically inaccurate and misleading (whether the fault here be Gadamer's or his acolyte translator's is unclear). As cited by Gadamer in his original 1934 text, *Plato und die Dichter* (Plato and the poets), the quotation could sooner be translated: "Whoever philosophizes is not one with the modes of the conception of his times or with his preceding ones" *(Wer philosophiert, ist mit den Vorstellungsarten seiner Vor- und Mitwelt uneins).*[72] At strict issue therefore is not (contemporary) *conceptions* but rather (transhistorical) *types* or *modes* of conception. And these include, in Plato's case just to begin, exo/esoteric transmission. In any event, Gadamer's (new) remark emphatically rejects martyrdom as an option, at least for himself; and apparently this issue is simply *closed* to what Gadamer means and practices as "open dialogue," Zuckert as "moderation."

In our contemporary or "postcontemporary" world, however, such so-called ethical appeals to "dialogue," "moderation," and their cognates are simply redundant insofar as they are always already part and parcel of precisely that hegemonic ideology and discourse of parliamentary-democratic, free-market capitalism which they (wittingly or unwittingly) reproduce. In this conjuncture, these appeals certainly can have nothing important or even interesting to do with philosophy, and are at most the quintessentially bourgeois "commonsense" or *sensus communis,* which for communists (to paraphrase Gramsci) can never be "*good* sense." In properly political-ontological terms, "infinite alterity is quite simply *what there is*" and the "commonsense discourse" of "toleration" (like that of all relativism or historicism) possesses "neither force nor truth," not least because "we need . . . to make explicit the axioms of thought that *decide* such an orientation."[73]

The big problem occurs whenever these axioms are unwritten, even unsaid, or otherwise esoterically concealed. In any case, if we are indeed to take seriously the specifically political in the question informing what Zuckert calls "the politics of Gadamerian hermeneutics," which obviously includes the politics of Gadamer's repercussions, that question must be radically reformulated: Who among us is in some sense or part *not* fascist?

In *one* sense, then, Zuckert is quite right to infer (though she cannot cite anything "actually said" on this score) that Waite doesn't accept dialogue (or the dialectic, for that matter) and moderation as *the* basis of philosophy and of criticism, or as "one of the *two* primary political virtues." This is not to say that dialogue and moderation are not virtues or should not be practiced, in some sense.[74] The problem remains that *true* dialogue and moderation have long been co-opted not only by exo/esotericism but also by capitalism, in its various political modes, just as it has co-opted virtually everything else. Communism, or other alternative practices to capitalism, must thus be leery of prophets crying "dialogue, dialogue, dialogue!" (or "peace, peace, peace!") when there precisely *is* no dialogue (or peace). And, what is more, there *should be none*—if and when the only dialogue (or peace) is the one controlled and manipulated by transnational capitalist hegemony (Gramsci's "non-coercive coercion"), when the discrepancy between the hyperrich and hyperpoor grows by the nanosecond, and when all of us (meaning by "all of us," *all of us*) run the risk of collaborating with it and of ignoring or concealing this simple fact.

"Gripped as we are by the vortex of this war-time, our information one-sided, without distance from the mighty transformations which have already occurred or are beginning to occur, and without a sense of the future that is formation,"[75] Freud opened his 1915 "Thoughts for the Times on War and Death" as one might today open a reflection on the struggle against capitalist hegemony.[76] And Freud concluded his remarks on "our attitude towards death" with these words:

> We remember the old saying: *si vis pacem, para bellum*. If you want to obtain [*erhalten*] peace, prepare for war. It would be timely thus to paraphrase it: *Si vis vitam, para mortem*. If you want to endure [*aushalten*] life, be prepared for death.[77]

"Thus: for *your* death," Jean Laplanche adds, echoing Heidegger.[78] Yet, he continues,

> In the unconscious, death would be always the death of the other, a destruction or a loss we provoke, and we would accede to some intuition of our own mortality only through and ambivalent identification with a loved person whose death we simultaneously fear and desire. . . . So that, more modestly perhaps in relation to the temptations of the heroic formulation, "If you want life, prepare for death" might be translated as "If you want life, prepare for the

death of the other." If a certain ethic in relation to death might be evolved
from the Freudian attitude, it would be in the sense of a distrust concerning
every form of enthusiasm, be it that of *amor fati,* and of a lucidity that does not
hide the irreducible meshing of my death with that of the other.[79]

So it is, in conclusion and Waite's own voice, that I salute Zuckert and
(her) Gadamer and their discursive practice as triumphant, as currently far
more successful than the one I present or represent. God knows, as one
used to say, Zuckertian and Gadamerian moderation serves well the unconscious God that is Capital. *"Le mort,"* as Marx wrote in *Capital, "saisit le vif!"*[80]
And today capitalism remains nothing if not Death Triumphant. Yet I salute,
as I began, with the salute of the gladiators: "Those [or we: *te salutamus—*
another variant] who are about to die salute you!" Some among us will take
far more solace than others in the fact that among the first required to ut-
ter this salute (until one very fine day in 73 B.C.E.) was a person named
Spartacus, "the most splendid bloke the entire history of antiquity has to
show for itself"[81]—among the many immoderate blokes with whom Hans-
Georg Gadamer and his repercussions have not tried to enter into dialogue.
Or is this just strategic, more or less eloquent, silence?

NOTES

I would like to thank Bruce Krajewski for his *true* Gadamerian *generositas.*

1. Following Foucault's most succinct definition, "Discursive practices are not
purely and simply ways of producing discourse. They are embodied in technical processes, in institutions, in patterns for general behavior, in forms for transmission and
diffusion, and in pedagogical forms which, at once, impose and maintain them."
Michel Foucault, "History of Systems of Thought" [1970–71], *Language, Counter-
Memory, Practice: Selected Essays and Interviews,* ed. Donald F. Bouchard, trans. Donald F. Bouchard and Sherry Simon (Ithaca, NY: Cornell University Press, 1977),
199–204; here 200. In terms more familiar to some, a discursive practice is at once
theōría and *phrónēsis.* But then note the necessity on our occasion to violate Strauss's
great (public) dictum. "In practical matters there is a right of the first occupant:
what is established must be respected. In theoretical matters this cannot be. Differently stated: The rule of practice is 'let sleeping dogs lie,' do not disturb the established. In theoretical matters the rule is 'do not let sleeping dogs lie.'" Leo Strauss,
On Plato's Symposium [Chicago, fall semester 1959], ed. Seth Benardete (Chicago:
University of Chicago Press, 2001), 1. An authentically critical memorial of Gadamer requires that *phrónēsis* be treated exactly like *theōría.* Prod all the dogs and dare
the consequences. (Memorialized communists should be so lucky.)
2. I am thinking here specifically of the work of Balibar and Negri on the imbri-
cation of philosophy and politics in Spinoza, but also more generally of what today
is called "the new Spinoza." See Étienne Balibar, "Spinoza, the Anti-Orwell: The Fear
of the Masses" [1982], in *Masses, Classes, Ideas: Studies on Politics and Philosophy Before*

and After Marx, trans. James Swenson (New York: Routledge, 1994), 3–37, and *Spinoza and Politics* [1985], trans. Peter Snowdon (London: Verso, 1998); Antonio Negri, *The Savage Anomaly: The Power of Spinoza's Metaphysics and Politics* [1981], trans. Michael Hardt (Minneapolis: University of Minnesota Press, 1991); and all the essays (of generally but not exclusively post-Althusserian inspiration) in Warren Montag and Ted Stolze, eds., *The New Spinoza* (Minneapolis: University of Minnesota Press, 1997).

3. Cited in Dominique Lecourt, *Marxism and Epistemology: Bachelard, Canguilhem and Foucault* [1969–72], trans. Ben Brewster (London: NLB, 1975), 34. Whatever Gadamer does discuss he illuminates. But, of course, as he is the first to acknowledge, he does not illuminate it fully, and to illuminate one thing is necessarily to obscure another. And there is much that Gadamer does not discuss, and hence does not illuminate and so obscures in another way. But all this is true *grosso modo* of any philosopher. More specifically, as put by Stanley Rosen: "At his best, namely, in presenting his textual analyses, Gadamer demonstrates that the gift of understanding is indeed superior to method, and even, thanks to his own *phrónēsis* or *prudentia,* to an internally incoherent theoretical foundation. When Gadamer is illuminating about Plato, Dilthey, or Heidegger, it is because the doctrine of *Horizontverschmelzung* is erroneous, just as its philological equivalent, the relativity of historical perspectives, is erroneous. Both fall short of the ontological complexity of history, which is intelligible despite its multiplicity of perspectives." Rosen, *Hermeneutics as Politics* (New York: Oxford University Press, 1987), 165. For the further development of this argument, see Rosen, "Horizontverschmelzung," in PHGG207–18.

4. Cited from Betty Ramsey, ed., *The Little Book of Famous Insults* (Mount Vernon, NY: Peter Pauper, 1964), 49.

5. Compare "Amicus Plato, sed magis amica veritas" (I am a friend of Plato, but a greater friend of truth) (Cervantes, *Don Quixote,* pt. 2, ch. 48); and "Amicus Plato, amicus Socrates, sed præhonoranda veritas" (I am a friend of Plato, and a friend of Socrates, but still higher to be honored is the truth) (Luther, "De servo arbitrio," 1). This phrase had passed (via Aristotle's *Nicomachean Ethics*) to Cervantes and to Luther (and to Nietzsche's *Zarathustra*) from the Platonic Socrates himself: "ὑμει μέντοι, ἄν ἐμοὶ πείθησθε, σμιχρὸν φροντίσαντες Σωχράτους, πης δὲ ἀληθείας πού μαλλον" (But you, when you follow me, concern yourselves far less about Socrates, and much more about the truth) (*Phaedo* 91c). Another explicit adherent to this principle was the communist Louis Althusser. See "Portrait du philosophe matérialiste" [1982], in *Écrits philosophiques et politiques, Tome I,* ed. François Matheron (Paris: Stock/IMEC, 1994), 581–82; here 582. Gadamer's eponymous essay on what we can now call the *"amicus sed principle"* is one of his many reconstructions of Aristotle's responses to Plato. Because "the authentic Platonic philosophy [was] never fixed in writing" it must be reconstructed "not only qua Plato's dialogic form but also through his student Aristotle's written interpretations." Hans-Georg Gadamer, "Amicus Plato magis amica veritas" [1968] (GW 6: 71–89; here 74). But what Gadamer does not address are the consequences for his own truth, his own discourse. For a powerful, albeit brief and indirect, critique of Gadamer's definition of the political in *Die Idee des Guten zwischen Plato und Aristoteles* (1978), see Reiner Schürmann, *Heidegger on Being and Acting: From Principles to Anarchy* [1982], trans. Christine-Marie Gros and the author (Bloomington: Indiana University Press, 1987), 328, n. 30. Fi-

nally, in this vein, we should note that when Nietzsche chose a title for the compilation of his earliest university lectures it was "Plato amicus sed—." Friedrich Nietzsche, "Einführung in das Studium der platonischen Dialog" [Basel winter semester 1871–72], in *Kritische Gesamtausgabe, Werke*, ed. Giorgio Colli and Mazzino Montinari (Berlin: Walter de Gruyter, 1967 ff), 2/4: 1–188; here 1. Hereby elided is reference to (the) truth.

6. Too, as pleased as Waite imagines Gadamer might have been at receiving a festschrift in his honor, Waite also imagines a certain unease on Gadamer's part, given the ancient (not to mention psychoanalytic) tradition that to honor a living person is also in effect to produce that person's epitaph. Furthermore, presented with any essay containing uncritical celebrations of his work, Gadamer (still in Waite's imagination) would find himself in the position of the fourth-century B.C.E. Athenian general and statesman Phocion, who, upon hearing the applause of the crowd he was addressing, famously is said to have muttered to one side, "What asininity could I have uttered that they applaud me *thus?*" (In his case, however, Phocion was later sentenced, like Socrates, to die by hemlock and was buried outside Athenian walls). Gadamer has earned a certain right not to suffer fools gladly, be they adversaries *or* friends. Finally, whatever one might think of it theoretically or practically, what Gadamer intends by "dialogue" is a very specific, rigorously argued philosophical principle that has little or nothing to do with the touchy-feely, New Age "Let's dialogue!"—even though the latter can, and sometimes does, appeal to Gadamer for philosophical legitimation. For an apposite (if necessarily schematic) depiction of the tension in Gadamer's writing and personal demeanor between boldness and modesty, combativeness and the desire to please "all possible audiences," as well as a fair- but tough-minded analysis of his "detached opportunism," see George Steiner, "But Is That Enough? Hans-Georg Gadamer and the 'Summons to Astonishment,'" *Times Literary Supplement* (January 12, 2001): 11–12; here 12. Gadamer's "opportunism" may not have been as "detached" as Steiner makes it out to be, however. (He sure was wrong about Heidegger in that regard.)

7. Alan Badiou, *Ethics: An Essay on the Understanding of Evil* [1998], trans. Peter Hallward (London: Verso, 2001), 24–25. For more on the theoretical and practical consequence of this *Denk- und Berufsverbot*, see Slavoj Žižek, *Did Somebody Say Totalitarianism? Five Interventions in the (Mis)use of a Notion* (London: Verso, 2001) and *Welcome to the Desert of the Real! Five Essays on September 11 and Related Dates* (London: Verso, 2002).

8. Of course, the history of philosophy provides many versions of what this second virtue *(virtus)* might be. In the case of Gadamer, for example, a Machiavellian cynic might define it, in part, as the willingness to practice also a certain degree of immoderation when the case demands, as occurred during the Third Reich with which Gadamer, by his own admission, voluntarily collaborated, at least initially—but let us all strive not to be just cynical Machiavellians.

9. It is important to add that most of the following argument applies equally well to what remains today of the Frankfurt School's "critical theory" (e.g., Jürgen Habermas and Axel Honneth) and to its current "debate" with Anglo-Saxon "Left Rawlsianism." For a useful short critique of their unacknowledged common ground, see Alessandro Ferrara, "Left Rawlsianism and Social Philosophy," *Radical Philosophy* 91 (Sept./Oct. 1998): 30–32—even though the author ultimately falls into the same

pitfall of uncritically affirming the priority of "dialogue." The same is true of Ferrara's more extended analyses in *Reflective Authenticity: Rethinking the Project of Modernity* (London: Routledge, 1998).

10. *Aporía* is intimately related to the dialectic *(dialektiké)* and therefore also to the (Platonic) Socrates' technique of interlocutory dialogue *(diálogos)* (*Meno*, 80d; *Sophist*, 244a; *Theaetetus*, 210b–c). For Aristotle, this entire process both defines the philosophical project proper and is its heaviest burden and responsibility (*Metaphysics*, 996a). By contrast, as it is commonly used in much contemporary deconstructive discourse (e.g., de Man and his uncritical followers—unlike Jacques Derrida, who has written explicitly on some of the term's complexity in *Aporias: Crossing Aesthetics* [1993], trans. Thomas Dutoit [Stanford, Calif.: Stanford University Press, 1993]), "aporia" today widely means simply "insurmountable impasse." And so it is that the (ancient Greek) *terminus a quo* or birth of philosophy has become philosophy's (postmodern) *terminus ad quem* or death. If there be any "epistemological break" in history, this is it.

11. That Gadamer is aware of the *problem* of esotericism should go without saying (see, e.g., Hans-Georg Gadamer, "Dialektik und Sophistik im siebenten Platonischen Brief" [1964]; GW6:90–115). The question however, remains: did Gadamer also *use* esotericism?

12. The Lacanian thesis that "there is no metalanguage" is shared by both Derridean poststructuralism and Gadamerian hermeneutics, albeit, in Lacan's own case, "in a way that is completely incompatible with post-structuralism, as well as hermeneutics." Slavoj Žižek, *The Sublime Object of Ideology* (London: Verso, 1989), 153.

13. One might say that one of the most basic impulsions of Waite's engagement with Nietzsche and Nietzscheanism is derived from a single remark by Trotsky: "How can a corpse be entrusted with deciding whether Marxism is a living force? No, I categorically refuse to participate in that kind of endeavor." Leon Trotsky, "The Future of *Partisan Review:* A Letter to Dwight MacDonald" [1938; first published 1950], in *Leon Trotsky on Literature and Art*, ed. Paul N. Siegel (New York: Pathfinder, 1970), 101–3; here 103.

14. See DDe here, esp. 52–54, and Lawrence K. Schmidt, "Introduction: Between Certainty and Relativism" (SR1–19, esp. 12–13). Incidentally, the reason Waite normally puts the terms "right" and "left" in scare quotes is in the attempt (failed it appears) to preclude a Zuckert from removing them to assert, say, that "Waite locates Gadamer on the right on the basis of Orozco's article [but also her book]." The scare quotes are intended by Waite to indicate that in certain cases, like the case of Nietzsche, the "right" and the "left" are part of an unacknowledged consensus in important respects, hence that there is no distinction between them, hence no real left, though perhaps therefore a real right. ("Vulgar Marxists," in this view, are not merely economistic reductivists but also include those who ignore even the existence of the right's exo/esotericism.) One could add to this reason for the scare quotes that to be "left" or "right" in philosophy is not *necessarily* to be "right" or "left" elsewhere, say, in politics.

15. See the hostile account of Shadia B. Drury, *The Political Ideas of Leo Strauss* (New York: St. Martin's, 1988), but also the sympathetic account of Lawrence Lampert, *Leo Strauss and Nietzsche* (Chicago: University of Chicago Press, 1996).

16. Leo Strauss and Hans-Georg Gadamer, "Correspondence Concerning *Wahr-*

heit und Methode," *The Independent Journal of Philosophy* 2 (1978): 5–12; here 11. For an early (at the time fairly judicious) overview of Gadamer's position on relativism, see Richard J. Bernstein, *Beyond Objectivism and Relativism: Science, Hermeneutics, and Praxis* (Oxford: Basil Blackwell, 1983). Oddly uncritical by comparison two decades later on the same topic is John McDowell, "Gadamer and Davidson on Understanding and Relativism," in *Gadamer's Century: Essays in Honor of Hans-Georg Gadamer,* ed. Jeff Malpas, Ulrich Arnswald, and Jens Kertscher (Cambridge, Mass.: MIT Press, 2002), 173–93, as well as Bernstein's recent essay, "The Constellation of Hermeneutics, Critical Theory and Deconstruction," in *The Cambridge Companion to Gadamer,* 267–82. Already in 1983 Bernstein was wrong (read also: uncritically Gadamerian) to describe the contretemps between Strauss and Gadamer as their "friendly quarrel" (Bernstein, *Beyond Objectivism,* 153). Obviously enough, this is how Gadamer himself preferred to present the matter whenever he addressed it, but there was a very keen and hostile edge to Strauss's intervention, one which Gadamer tried very hard to blunt, and with enormous success. Similarly, in response to the old suspicion that Aristotelian *phrónēsis* was essentially elitist, Gadamer "softens this elitist aura," as Bernstein put it, "by blending his discussion of *phrónēsis* with his analysis of a type of dialogue and conversation that presupposes mutual respect, recognition, and understanding" (165). But to soften anything (let alone elitism) is hardly to eliminate it, and the question would remain as to why Gadamer did so, to what ideological ends.

17. See, for example, Strauss, "What Is Political Philosophy? [1955], in *What Is Political Philosophy? and Other Studies* (Chicago: University of Chicago Press, 1959), 9–55.

18. *Selections from the Prison Notebooks of Antonio Gramsci,* ed. and trans. Quintin Hoare and Geoffrey Nowell Smith (New York: International, 1971), 234.

19. Badiou, *L'être et l'événement* (Paris: Seuil, 1988), 312.

20. Gadamer, "Oberflächlichkeit und Unkenntnis: Zur Veröffentlichung von Victor Farías," in *Antwort: Martin Heidegger im Gespräch,* ed. Günther Neske and Emil Kettering (Pfullingen: Neske, 1988), 152–55; here 153. See, further, Victor Farías, *Heidegger und der Nationalsozialismus,* trans. (from the Spanish and French) Klaus Laermann, introduction by Jürgen Habermas (Frankfurt am Main: S. Fischer, 1987). It was of course the publication of Farías's book that launched the most recent, ongoing version of *l'affaire Heidegger.* Because Gadamer has been subsequently implicated, it is important to say something about this affair and his reaction. The main title of Gadamer's indignant response in *Antwort: Martin Heidegger im Gespräch* translates as "superficiality and ignorance," which would likely be his retort to attempts to embroil him in the same controversy. In any event, Gadamer joined in the outright rejection of Farías that cut across the ideological spectrum, forming a united front of Gadamerians, Derridians, and Levinasians, among others. Two claims made by this consensus are noteworthy. 1) Farías's work was nothing more than an opportunist *succès de scandale.* Arguing guilt by association, when not based on factual errors, it contributed "nothing new" to what had long been "common knowledge" about Heidegger's "brief" political involvement in National Socialism. 2) Farías's work lacked any conceptual merit, and thus was unable to articulate the political to the philosophical in any convincing way. In particular, Heidegger's masterpiece, *Being and Time,* remains wholly unsullied by the (merely alleged) political

revelations. (Even Levinas was of the latter opinion in *Antwort: Martin Heidegger im Gespräch*, though he was particularly distressed by Heidegger's actions in the 1930s. Gosh, isn't it odd? Just when you don't give a damn about the other, the other gives a damn about you.) Now, the problem with claim number one is that, despite the errors, there *were* new facts in Farías and in Ott, indicating that Heidegger's political involvement was not nearly so brief or innocuous as he claimed. Furthermore, the old facts about Heidegger's activities in the Third Reich were no longer available in print to the general public in the 1980s. (This may have been due to pressures from Heideggerians on publishers, researchers, librarians, and archivists.) The problem with claim number two may be more serious. "Even" *Being and Time* is hardly as politically innocent as is commonly asserted. Leo Strauss, for one, certainly did not read it this way when it was published in 1927. Today, defenders of that position must settle accounts with Johannes Fritsche's meticulous semantic analyses of sections 72 to 77 of *Being and Time*. See Johannes Fritsche, "On Brinks and Bridges in Heidegger," *Graduate Faculty Philosophy Journal* 18, no. 1 (1995): 111–86, and *Historical Destiny and National Socialism in Heidegger's* Being and Time (Berkeley: University of California Press, 1999). One may reject Fritsche's more strident formulations of his thesis, for example that "Heidegger's notion of historicality is identical with the notions of history and politics as developed by the revolutionary rightists and as exemplified here in regard to Hitler's and Scheler's works" (*Historical Destiny*, 135–36). Nevertheless, Fritsche's exceptionally close readings require thoughtful *philosophical* response (as Farías and even Ott may not), not least from Gadamerians. The Gadamer Industry is still a long, long way from what is at long last demanded of the Heidegger Industry and its "ways" of publication and translation, namely, "an independent account." Dieter Thöma, "The Name on the Edge of Language: A Complication in Heidegger's Theory of Language and its Consequences," in *A Companion to Heidegger's* Introduction to Metaphysics, ed. Richard Polt and Gregory Fried (New Haven, Conn.: Yale University Press, 2001), 103–22; here 105.

   21. Compare also this remark: "Where Heidegger's startlingly nihilistic thinking places no barrier in his way toward Nazism and may even encourage him, Gadamer's thinking most certainly places a barrier in his way. Everything in Gadamer's thinking points him away from Nazism, not in the direction of mass popular democracy certainly, but surely in the direction of the well-integrated political community. If Gadamer did have a flirt with Nazism, it can only be accounted for in terms of the career ambitions of a young German academic." Robert R. Sullivan, *Political Hermeneutics: The Early Thinking of Hans-Georg Gadamer* (University Park: Pennsylvania State University Press, 1989), 180–81. Of course, the contradiction in this judicious-sounding remark is that if someone "flirts" with something, then it cannot be—logically or psychoanalytically—that "everything" in that person points away from that object of flirtation; too, "career ambitions" cannot be so neatly severed from "thinking" if it is to more than a merely academic pursuit, and if "the well-integrated political community" in question is to *exclude* "mass popular democracy." Similarly, what evidence is there, exactly, that the Gadamer who, in Sullivan's words, "wrote in an Aesopian political language similar to Bakhtin . . . until the collapse of the German state in 1945" (p. 187), did not *persist* in writing in such a language *after* 1945? This question is aside from the notorious problem haunting current

Bakhtin studies: what *were* Bakhtin's political commitments, and were they really as "democratic" as many readers imagine?

22. Gadamer, "Oberflächlichkeit und Unkenntnis," 153.

23. Catherine H. Zuckert, *Postmodern Platos: Nietzsche, Heidegger, Gadamer, Strauss, Derrida* (Chicago: University of Chicago Press, 1996), 103.

24. See Lenin, *The Proletarian Revolution and the Renegade Kautsky* [1918], *Collected Works,* various translators (Moscow: Progress, 1972), 28: 227–326; here 235.

25. Zuckert, *Postmodern Platos,* 276.

26. Contrast Zuckert's own position with a thesis from the recent history of science: "There is no idea, however ancient and absurd that is not capable of improving our knowledge. The whole history of thought is absorbed into science and is used for improving every single theory. Nor is political interference rejected. It may be needed to overcome the chauvinism of science that resists alternatives to the status quo." Paul Feyerabend, *Against Method: Outline of an Anarchist Theory of Knowledge* [1975] (Verso: London, 1978), 47.

27. Gadamer, "Reply to Karl-Otto Apel" (PHGG94–97; here 97).

28. For a recent discussion of this distinction and its import, see Žižek, "Multiculturalism, Or, the Cultural Logic of Multinational Capitalism," *New Left Review* 225 (Sept./Oct. 1997): 28–51; esp. the conclusion.

29. If Waite can be forgiven his momentary lapse, in the footnote alluded to, into humanism (with regard to the question of his "sadness" concerning the Gadamer case), we can continue with the structural problem at hand. Undoubtedly Waite could and certainly should have been more clear: Orozco's suggestion that Gadamer's writings in the Third Reich constituted an "art of allusion" would, Waite believes, have been strengthened by more attentiveness to the long tradition of philosophy in which Gadamer was arguably working, and by more consideration both of how Gadamer and this tradition strive to implement this "art" rhetorically (the illocutionary level) and also of how this implementation is successful (the perlocutionary level). By distinct contrast, the use-value of Zuckert's discussion of "postmodern Platos" is almost obviated by her failure to take adequate stock of this tradition. In other words, generally and specifically, Orozco's argument would be strengthened by attentiveness to the Straussian technique of reading, which is not the Strauss Zuckert appears to know. In short, Waite is in basic solidarity with Orozco's attempt to develop a methodology adequate to grasp the exo/esoteric tradition, though he thinks it could be elaborated; he is not in solidarity with Zuckert's apparent lack of interest in this entire problematic. Certainly, Zuckert nowhere follows Strauss's great dictum, articulated with regard to Plato but also more generally binding, that "One cannot separate the understanding of Plato's teaching from the understanding of the form in which it is presented. One must pay as much attention to the How as to the What. At any rate to begin with one must even pay greater attention to the 'form' than to the 'substance,' since the meaning of the 'substance' depends on the 'form.'" Strauss, *The City and Man* (Chicago: University of Chicago Press, 1964), 52.

30. For a preliminary attempt to identify, analyze, and criticize Heidegger's version exo/esotericism, near its public inception, see Geoff Waite, "On Esotericism: Heidegger and/or Cassirer at Davos," *Political Theory* 26, no. 5 (Oct. 1998): 603–51.

31. On the fascists' self-definition as "relativists" (explicitly opposed to National Socialist racist essentialism), see Waite, *Nietzsche's Corps/e: Aesthetics, Politics, Prophecy, or, The Spectacular Technoculture of Everyday Life* (Durham, N.C.: Duke University Press, 1996), 211–12; on the link of both to what he calls "the fascoid" and "the fascoid liberal," see 71–76. For his part, Waite adheres to what Zižek, developing a point argued by Badiou, calls "Lenin's premise—which today, in our era of postmodern relativism, is more pertinent that ever," namely, "that universal truth and partisanship, the gesture of taking sides, are not only not mutually exclusive, but condition each other: the *universal* truth of a concrete situation can be articulated only from a thoroughly *partisan* position; truth is, by definition, one-sided." Zižek, "Afterword: Lenin's Choice," 177. (To be sure, the undergirding thesis here is little more than a plausible interpretation of Heraclitus's fragment B 41 [Diels-Kranz] when we include its site of enunciation: "Listening to the Logos, and not to me, it is wise to agree that all things are one.") Yes, this position is *mutatis mutandis*—that is, *formally*—similar to the position against relativism in adamant favor of "standpoints," as taken by Heidegger in the Third Reich. See, especially, Heidegger, *Logik als die Frage nach dem Wesen der Sprache* [Freiburg winter semester 1934], ed. Wilhelm Hallwachs, in *Gesamtausgabe* (Frankfurt am Main: Vittorio Klostermann, 1998), 38: 79–80. On the other hand, as is clear from public lectures delivered by Heidegger in 1934 (first published only in 2000), he understood the content of National Socialism—indeed its very "essence"—to be the reproduction and preservation of (pro-Nietzschean and anticommunist) "order of rank" *(Rangordnung)*. Heidegger, "25. Jahre nach unserem Abirturium" [May 26–27, 1934] and "Die deutsche Universität" [August 15–16, 1934], both in *Reden und andere Zeugnisse eines Lebensweges, 1910–1976*, ed. Hermann Heidegger, in *Gesamtausgabe* (Frankfurt am Main: Vittorio Klostermann, 2000), 16: 279–84 (here 282) and 285–307 (here 304), respectively. It would have been interesting to know what Gadamer's own position in 1934 on this problem was in detail, since he cannot not have had one. If the following remark is true of political theory it is *mutatis mutandis* true of all theory. "The theoretician of the political must be a political theoretician. A treatise about the political can only be . . . a political treatise, determined by enmity and exposing itself to enmity." Heinrich Meier, *Carl Schmitt & Leo Strauss: The Hidden Dialogue* [1988], trans. J. Harvey Lomax (Chicago: University of Chicago Press, 1995), 4.

32. Fully two-thirds (66 percent) of German philosophy professors were members of the combined NSDAP, NSLB, and NSDDB (National Socialist Lecturers Union). Breaking down the Thousand Year Reich into three periods (1933–37, consolidation of power; 1933–42, stabilization; and 1943–45, collapse), it has been noted that between May 1933 and May 1937 new membership in the NSDAP was practically closed. Anyone joining after May 1937 had had to petition several years earlier; anyone joining between January 1933 and May 1, 1933, had to have undergone two years of trial membership in order to be admitted (otherwise one's political commitment was held suspect). See George Leaman, *Heidegger im Kontext: Gesamtüberblick zum NS-Engagement der Universitätsphilosophen*, trans. Rainer Alisch and Thomas Laugstien (Hamburg: Argument, 1993), 17–27; on Gadamer specifically, see 40–41. Other useful historical surveys of the situation and activities of German philosophers during the Third Reich include: the anthology *Deutsche Philosophen 1933*, ed. Wolfgang Fritz Haug (Hamburg: Argument, 1989), esp. Haug's introduc-

tory essay, "Philosophie im Deutschen Faschismus," 5–28; Thomas Laugstien, *Philosophieverhältnisse im deutschen Faschismus* (Hamburg: Argument, 1990); Martha Zapata Galindo, *Triumph des Willens zur Macht: Zur Nietzsche-Rezeption im NS-Staat* (Hamburg: Argument, 1995); and, building on, or complementary to, these studies, Orozco, *Platonische Gewalt: Gadamers politische Hermeneutik der NS-Zeit* (Hamburg: Argument, 1995), But particularly important—because it properly shifts attention from exclusive focus on the relationship between German philosophers and National Socialism toward their relationship to the itself more philosophically oriented (Italian) *fascism*—is Bernhard H. F. Taureck, *Nietzsche und der Faschismus* (Hamburg: Junius, 1989).

33. See Leaman, *Heidegger im Kontext,* 20–22.

34. Johannes Maria Verweyen, a professor of medieval philosophy at Bonn, joined the NSLB in June 1933. He had fought on the front in World War I, had publicly supported the German Socialist Party (SPD) (though was not a party member), and had remained a Freemason and a Catholic. After he was expelled from the NSLB in 1935, largely for the latter reason, his response was to give a public speech against Nazi racist ideology in Dresden. After several warnings and restrictions, he was arrested by the Gestapo in 1941. First interred in Sachsenhausen, Verweyen died in Bergen-Belsen shortly before the liberation, in March 1945.

35. Leaman, *Heidegger im Kontext,* 105 n. 1. *Unbescholten,* translated here as "respectable," also signifies several senses of "guiltless" and "innocent." In German legal discourse, *unbescholten sein* is "to be free of any prior conviction"; in sexual discourse, *ein unbescholtenes Mädchen* is "a chaste or pure girl." (Though of course the NSLB charter referred to masculine teachers and educators only.) Thus one might say that the Nazis and their affiliates combined legal with sexual terminology to arrive at what in such charters was meant primarily and specifically as *racial* innocence, purity, or "respectability." Presently we will hear Gadamer retroactively describing himself in the Third Reich as "ein politisch Unbescholtener."

36. Leaman, *Heidegger im Kontext,* 40. The DNVP had been instrumental in bringing Hitler into legal power on January 30, 1933. Indeed, initially the NSDAP and the DNVP held power jointly, until the latter was deemed redundant, dissolved, and absorbed into the NSDAP in the spring of 1933. In the words of Leaman, "The DNVP was a conservative, anti-communist, and anti-parliamentarian oriented party, which had many objectives in common with the Nazis: the revocation of the Treaty of Versailles, the rejection of the Weimar Constitution, and the founding of authoritarian central rule. It was a militant National Socialist organization, which just like the Nazis was convinced that Germany had only lost the first world war because liberals, socialists, and Jews had 'ambushed' the Imperial regime and its army . . . ; it supported the building of concentration camps for domestic opponents of the regime and the laws against the German Jews" (*Heidegger im Kontext,* 18).

37. Ibid., 40

38. Ibid., 40, 105.

39. Ibid., 105.

40. In 1938 Gadamer, who tells only part of this story himself in *Philosophische Lehrjahre* (Philosophical apprenticeships) and elsewhere, became visiting professor at Leipzig, replacing Gehlen (who became section head of the Amt Rosenberg, and was later chair of the German Philosophical Society). With Gehlen's approval, in

1939 Gadamer became full professor in Leipzig, and in 1940 director of the Philosophy Institute. Gadamer had already held several teaching posts in the Third Reich: at Marburg (1933–34); as visiting professor in 1934–35 at Kiel (replacing Richard Kroner, who had been transferred to Frankfurt for being "non-Aryan" but allowed to become emeritus, and who later emigrated to England in 1938, teaching at Oxford in 1939–40 before further emigrating in 1940 to the United States, where he taught at Union Theological Seminary); and again at Marburg in 1935–36 (now replacing Erich Frank, another student of Heidegger's, who was forced to retire in 1935, and who emigrated in 1939 to the United States, where he taught at Bryn Mawr College and the University of Pennsylvania). Gadamer received National Socialist political education in Weichselmünde in the fall of 1935; and he was promoted to professor in Marburg in 1937. Thus Gadamer's career movement during the period falls into two basic categories: 1) either he replaced a *persona non grata* with the National Socialist regime (sometimes, he says, in consultation with the man replaced); or 2) he filled in for a professor who was higher in academic rank (sometimes a party member) and momentarily otherwise occupied (who most certainly approved). Note that in general regard to Gadamer's activities during the Third Reich one should take the currently most authoritative biography with a very large grain of salt. Jean Grondin's *Hans-Georg Gadamer—eine Biographie* (Tübingen: J. C. B. Mohr [Paul Siebeck], 1999) tells us little important that Gadamer had not already said about these years, and rather less than the facts themselves state or suggest. (On some of Grondin's more strictly philosophical deficiencies, see Hans Albert, "Der Naturalismus und das Problem des Verstehens," in *Hermeneutik und Naturalismus,* ed. Bernulf Kanitschneider and Franz Josef Wetz [Tübingen: J. C. B. Mohr (Paul Siebeck), 1999], 3–20, esp. 17–20.) The two most recent presentations in English of Gadamer's activities during the Third Reich follow Grondin and/or Gadamer without the slightest critical distance. See Robert J. Dostal, "Gadamer: The Man and His Work," in *The Cambridge Companion to Gadamer,* 13–35, and Lawrence Schmidt, "Hans-Georg Gadamer: A Biographical Sketch," in *Gadamer's Century,* 1–13. Symptomatic of the abysmal level of serious analysis of Gadamer's *phrónēsis* during one of the gravest periods of world history is the way that Teresa Orozco's work is treated in those two anthologies. In the MIT volume, her work is mentioned only once in noncommittal passing, precisely where commitment is required (see Schmidt, "Hans-Georg Gadamer," 6). Even worse on this score is the Cambridge anthology, in which it is said of Orozco that "she cannot look past Plato's critique of democracy in the *Republic* and has no ear for Plato's irony" (Dostal, "Gadamer," 33, n. 12). (Dostal's criticisms of Orozco's reading of Gadamer's work on Herder are to be taken seriously, however. See 34, n. 13.) This remark is uncritically embraced in the only other mention of Orozco in the same volume, also a footnote. See Catherine H. Zuckert, "Hermeneutics in Practice: Gadamer on Ancient Philosophy," *The Cambridge Companion to Gadamer,* 201–24, n. 3. The remark is idiotic (in the Greek sense of "private," needless to say) for two reasons. 1) Whether or not one agrees with it, there is a long-established and well-reasoned tradition of being unable to look past Plato's critique of democracy. (Imagine Dostal having said this to Karl Popper's face, just for starters.) 2) Whether or not one agrees with Orozco, as soon as the problem of esotericism enters the game, all bets about irony are off. Not incidentally it seems, Gadamer himself is a source of the conflation of irony and esotericism. See his now infamous footnote in *Truth and Method* on the only exception to the concept of "Vor-griff der Vollkommenheit" (GW1 : 300, n. 224).

41. For the complete list of signatories from the philosophy profession, see Lea-man, *Heidegger im Kontext,* 100.

42. Hugo Ott has argued that Heidegger's signature on this declaration, com-bined with his speech on its behalf (Gadamer did not go this far), was *"the worst* pub-licly expressed aberration of the philosopher." *Heidegger: Unterwegs zu seiner Biogra-phie* (Frankfurt am Main: Campus, 1988), 196; emphasis added.

43. In addition to Gadamer, other professors granted the much-desired and difficult-to-obtain privilege of foreign travel included Hans Freyer (who was not officially in either the NSDAP or the NSLB, but, as Gadamer also notes, was an avid supporter of the regime), Nicolai Hartmann (a member of neither organization), Hans Heyse (a member of both organizations), and Erich Rothacker (also in both organizations). Gadamer was also granted the privilege of publishing during the Third Reich: between 1934 and 1944 he published two books and some eleven articles.

44. Gadamer, as cited in the interview "' . . . die wirklichen Nazis hatten doch überhaupt kein Interesse an uns': Hans-Georg Gadamer im Gespräch mit Dörte von Westernhagen," *Das Argument* 182 (July–Aug. 1990): 543–55; here 551.

45. Laugstien, *Philosophieverhältnisse im deutschen Faschismus,* 186.

46. Žižek, *Did Somebody Say Totalitarianism?* 125. It should go without saying that for now this question must remain unanswered (hard enough to pose it).

47. Gadamer, "Reply to Herta Nagl-Docekal" (PHGG205–6; here 206).

48. Emmanuel Levinas, *Totality and Infinity: An Essay on Exteriority* [1961], trans. Alphonso Lingis (Pittsburgh, Penn.: Duquesne University Press, 1969), 70. But also consider the popular adage, "Cunsigghia siminari, ma tu nun siminari" (rec-ommend sowing but don't you sow); or, more germanely translated, "recommend dialogue, but don't enter into real dialogue, and thus sow your monologue surrep-titiously." Which in turn follows another adage (the thought is at least as "old" as Sun Tsu and at least as "new" as Nietzsche and Heidegger): "Cui nun sapi finciri nun sapi vinciri" (he who doesn't know how to feign, doesn't know how to win). Finally, note that when Zuckert attributes to Waite the "[insistence] that 'philosophy' consists in a monologue designed to form the thoughts and deeds of others, by any means available," he should modestly decline the attribution of this position to himself and *a fortiori* decline any claim of having invented it—out of deference to Plato, just for starters.

49. Gadamer, "Reply to Robin May Schott" (PHGG508).

50. Balibar, *Spinoza and Politics,* 4.

51. Compare Paul Celan, "Schibboleth" [1954], in *Von Schwelle zu Schwelle* (Stutt-gart: Deutsche Verlags-Anstalt, 1955), 55–56. Originally the shibboleth of French soldiers at Verdun in World War I, *No pasaran!* was adapted as battle cry in the Span-ish Civil War by the Spanish Communist leader Dolores Ibarruri (La Pasionaria) and subsequently by the Republicans and the International Brigade (see further Peter Horst Neumann, *Zur Lyrik Paul Celans* [Göttingen: Vandenhoeck & Ruprecht, 1968], 59). Gadamer does not mention this line in his commentaries on Celan.

52. Ludwig Wittgenstein, *Culture and Value,* ed. G. H. von Wright in collabora-tion with Heikki Nyman, trans. Peter Winch (Oxford: Basil Blackwell, 1980), 42.

53. See Gilles Deleuze, *Spinoza: Practical Philosophy* [1970], trans. Robert Hurley (San Francisco: City Lights, 1988), 125.

54. See *The Seminar of Jacques Lacan, Book VII: The Ethics of Psychoanalysis 1959–1960* [1986], trans. Dennis Porter (New York: W. W. Norton, 1993), 311–25.

55. Karl Marx, "Contribution to the Critique of Hegel's Philosophy of Law: Introduction" [1844], in Karl Marx and Frederick Engels, *Collected Works,* various translators (New York: International, 1976), 3: 175–87; here 178.

56. See Gadamer, "Wertethik und praktische Philosophie" [1982] (GW4: 203–15).

57. As Žižek has correctly noted in related regard, "precisely as Marxists, we should have no fear in acknowledging that the purges under Stalin were in a way more 'irrational' than Fascist violence: paradoxically, this very excess is an unmistakable sign that Stalinism, in contrast to Fascism, was the case of a perverted authentic revolution." Žižek, *Did Somebody Say Totalitarianism?* 127–28.

58. Žižek, *Tarrying with the Negative: Kant, Hegel, and the Critique of Ideology* (Durham, N.C.: Duke University Press, 1993), 228.

59. Althusser's relationship to Nietzsche is very complex, as is being revealed by the publication of his *œuvre posthume,* and is part of his version of exo/esotericism (see note 62). Much needs to be said about this, on another occasion; suffice it here to say that this relationship should not be trivialized by ad hominem and self-serving anecdotes, as occurs in Derrida, "Text Read at Louis Althusser's Funeral" [1990], trans. Robert Harvey, in *The Althusserian Legacy,* ed. E. Ann Kaplan and Michael Sprinker (London: Verso, 1993), 241–45; here 244.

60. From an article by Gramsci in *La Città Futura,* 1917; as cited in Giuseppe Fiori, *Antonio Gramsci: Life of a Revolutionary* [1965], trans. Tom Nairn (London: NLB, 1970), 107.

61. For one of many of Althusser's published criticisms of Stalinism, much the most succinct, see his introduction, "Unfinished History," in Dominique Lecourt, *Proletarian Science? The Case of Lysenko* [1976], trans. Ben Brewster (London: NLB, 1977), 7–16.

62. See, for example, Althusser, "Le courant souterrain du matérialisme de la rencontre" [1982], in *Écrits philosophiques et politiques, Tome I,* 539–79, and *Sur la philosophie* (Paris: Gallimard, 1994). When one is aware of Althusser's "esoteric" commitment to the aleatory, however, all his published "exoteric" work takes on new meaning, since "aleatory" indications infuse it everywhere.

63. According to Gadamer, "The stubborn clinging to prejudices or even the blind appeal to authority is nothing but the laziness to think. Nobody who thinks for himself will deceive himself about this" ("Reply to David Detmer" [PHGG287]).

64. As even his friend and biographer Eberhard Bethge acknowledged, not the least reason for Bonhoeffer's delay in resisting National Socialism was what Bethge calls the "theoretical anti-Judaism" that so deeply informed his thought (cited and discussed in Saul Friedländer, *Nazi Germany and the Jews,* vol. 1: *The Years of Persecution, 1933–1939* [New York: Harper Collins, 1997], 45–46).

65. Cited from *The Little Book of Famous Insults,* 51.

66. Compare also Gillian Rose's remark that "if the nothingness of death is presented in Heidegger as the 'possibility of impossibility,' and in Levinas as 'the impossibility of possibility,' and in Blanchot as two deaths, one possible, one impos-

sible, then all three accounts attribute a pseudo-Kantian hermeneutic circle to the nothingness of death: where nothing as possible or as impossible becomes the condition of all possible experience—experience which is therefore nugatory." Gillian Rose, *Mourning Becomes the Law: Philosophy and Representation* (Cambridge: Cambridge University Press, 1996), 133.

67. Gadamer, "Der Tod als Frage" [1975] (GW4:161–72; here 172).

68. Gadamer, "Die Erfahrung des Todes" [1983] (GW4:288–94; here 294).

69. See, for instance, Alfred Hitchcock's most explicitly "Nietzschean" film, *Rope* (1948). And most of the history of Western philosophy is haunted by the question of the precise nature of the relationship of Socrates to Alcibiades—was the "tyrant" exo/esoterically *following* and/or *betraying* his teacher? Was he not, in either case, a corps/e—like all of Nietzsche's own corps/es centuries later?

70. As the master of propaganda, Goebbels, memorably put it in March 1933, the strong state does not need overt propaganda, which indeed is a sign of weakness: "The best propaganda is not that which is always openly revealing itself; the best propaganda is that which as it were works invisibly, penetrates the whole of life without the public having any knowledge at all of the propagandistic initiative." Cited in Julian Petley, *Capital and Culture: German Cinema 1933–45* (London: BFI, 1979), 101. Note that Zuckert, in her response to Orozco and Waite, tends to reduce the historical phenomenon of Nazism to "brutal power politics" (to which Gadamer was quite obviously opposed, and certainly did not explicitly support)—a reduction that effectively conceals the complexity and success of National Socialist and fascist "hegemony," or what Gramsci also called "non-coercive coercion," and which enabled at least fascism to survive its defeat in war, within other forms of capitalism.

71. See, again, Gadamer, "Reply to Robin May Schott" (PHGG508).

72. Gadamer, *Plato und die Dichter* [1934] (GW5:187–211; here 187). This monograph is of course one of Orozco's main exhibits, both in her essay in this anthology and in her book, *Platonische Gewalt*.

73. Badiou, *Ethics*, 25, 20, 21.

74. Is there a solution or an alternative to relativism? Is there any beyond the reversion to essentialism, fundamentalism, or totalitarianism? It helps to begin by reformulating the *question* in Althusserian terms. Referring to the apparent disjunction between the fact and the effect of Spinoza's ruthlessly deductive *more geometrico*, Althusser asks, "How then could dogmatism not only result in the exaltation of freedom but also 'produce' it?" ("The Only Materialist Tradition, Part I: Spinoza" [ca. 1985], in *The New Spinoza*, 3–19; here 4). The suggestion here would be that true philosophy (like the best science and mathematics) does not, and should not, *begin* and *end* with more or less vapid appeals to "dialogue" that conceal class and other interests, and thus are not genuine dialogues at all; rather, true philosophy begins dogmatically—but it is a dogmatism that is not, *in principle*, exo/esoterically disguised as "dialogue," and only in order to prepare for more genuine, maximally free and accessible dialogues. For a very preliminary attempt to distinguish Marxist and communist "relativism," "constructivism," and "exo/esotericism" from other types, see Waite, "On Esotericism."

75. Sigmund Freud, "Zeitgemäßes über Krieg und Tod" [1915], in *Gesammelte Werke* [1946], ed. Anna Freud et al. (Frankfurt am Main: S. Fischer, 1981), 10: 323–55; here 324.

76. Note, in this context, the tightly linked trajectory formed in communist discourse: from Gramsci's vision from his fascist prison cell in 1930 that "the crisis consists precisely in the fact that the old is dying and the new cannot be born" (*Selections from the Prison Notebooks,* 276); through Althusser's 1977 thesis, describing and appropriating Gramsci's Machiavelli, that what is necessary is not to "think the *accomplished fact* . . . but rather . . . *the fact to be accomplished* . . . and under extraordinary circumstances, since these are *the conditions of the absence of any political form appropriate to the production of this result*" (Althusser, "Machiavelli's Solitude" [1977], trans. Ben Brewster, *Economy and Society* 17, no. 4 [Nov. 1988]: 468–79; here 472–73); and, finally, to Antonio Negri's depiction of "the scandal of pretending to enact a revolution in the absence of all its conditions and the provocation of always telling a revolutionary truth that is unacceptable to the given conditions" ("Notes on the Evolution of the Last Althusser," trans. Olga Vasile, in *Postmodern Materialism and the Future of Marxist Theory: Essays in the Althusserian Tradition,* ed. Antonio Callari and David F. Ruccio [Hanover, N.H.: Wesleyan University Press, 1996], 51–68; here 54).

77. Freud, "Zeitgemäßes über Krieg und Tod," 355.

78. Jean Laplanche, *Life and Death in Psychoanalysis* [1970], trans. Jeffrey Mehlman (Baltimore, Md.: Johns Hopkins University Press, 1976), 6.

79. Ibid.

80. Marx, *Capital: A Critique of Political Economy,* preface to the first German edition [1867], ed. Frederick Engels, trans. Samuel Moore and Edward Aveling (New York: International, 1967), 1: 7–11; here 9. Marx concludes this preface by citing Dante (*Inferno* 5: 17): "Segui il tuo corso, e lascia dir le genti" (Go your way, and let people talk).

81. "In the evening for relaxation Appian's *Roman Civil Wars* in the original Greek. Very valuable book. . . . Spartacus emerges as the most splendid bloke *[der famoseste Kerl]* the entire history of antiquity has to show for itself. Great general (no Garibaldi), noble character, true representative of the ancient proletariat." Marx to Engels, February 27, 1861, in *Karl Marx, Friedrich Engels: Der Briefwechsel,* ed. D. Rjazanov (Munich: Deutscher Taschenbuch Verlag, 1983), 3: 14–16; here 15. (Alas, Garibaldi succeeded where Spartacus had not, to invade and conquer Sicily.)

CONTRIBUTORS

Ronald Beiner is Professor of Political Science at the University of Toronto. He is the author of *Philosophy in a Time of Lost Spirit: Essays on Contemporary Theory* (University of Toronto Press, 1997) and *Liberalism, Nationalism, Citizenship: Essays on the Problem of Political Community* (University of British Columbia Press, 2003).

Andrew Bowie is Professor of German and Director of the Humanities and Arts Research Centre at Royal Holloway, University of London. He is the author of *From Romanticism to Critical Theory: The Philosophy of German Literary Theory* (Routledge, 1997). He is also editor and translator of *Hermeneutics and Criticism* by Friedrich Schleiermacher (Cambridge University Press, 1999).

Gerald L. Bruns is the William P. and Hazel B. White Professor of English at Notre Dame University. He is the author of *Hermeneutics Ancient and Modern* (Yale University Press, 1992) and *Tragic Thoughts at the End of Philosophy* (Northwestern University Press, 1999).

Hans-Georg Gadamer was Emeritus Professor of Philosophy at the University of Heidelberg. He died in March 2002. Gadamer is widely recognized as the leading exponent of philosophical hermeneutics. His best-known book is *Truth and Method* (German edition, 1960).

Jürgen Habermas is Emeritus Professor of Philosophy at the University of Frankfurt. He was awarded the Friedenspreis des Deutschen Buchhandels 2001. He has published numerous books, including *The Liberating Power of Symbols: Philosophical Essays* (MIT Press, 2001).

Michael Kelly is the former Managing Editor of the *Journal of Philosophy,* is currently Executive Director of the American Philosophical Association. He is the editor of the *Encyclopedia of Aesthetics* (Oxford University Press, 1998), and author of *Iconoclasm in Aesthetics* (Cambridge University Press, 2003).

Bruce Krajewski is Chair of the Department of Literature and Philosophy at Georgia Southern University. He is author of *Traveling with Hermes: Hermeneutics and Rhetoric* (University of Massachusetts Press, 1992) and, together with Richard Heinemann, editor and translator of *Gadamer on Celan* (SUNY Press, 1997), which won the MLA's Scaglione Prize for translation.

Paul Malone is Assistant Professor of Germanic and Slavic Studies at the University of Waterloo. He is editor of *Germano-Slavica: A Canadian Journal of Germanic and Slavic Comparative and Interdisciplinary Studies.*

Donald G. Marshall is Professor of English at the University of Illinois, Chicago. He is the translator (together with Joel Weinsheimer) of Hans-Georg Gadamer's *Truth and Method.* He has published *Literature as Philosophy, Philosophy as Literature* (Iowa University Press, 1987) and *Contemporary Critical Theory: A Selective Bibliography* (Modern Language Association Publications, 1993).

Teresa Orozco teaches political theory at the University of Frankfurt am Main. She is the author of *Platonische Gewalt: Gadamers politische Hermeneutik der NS-Zeit* (2d ed., Argument, 2002).

Richard Palmer is Emeritus Professor of Philosophy and Religion at MacMurray College. He is the author of *Hermeneutics* (Northwestern University Press, 1969) and editor and translator of *Gadamer in Conversation* (Yale University Press, 2001). He is working on a translation of the *Gadamer Lesebuch* (Mohr Siebeck, 1997).

Richard Rorty teaches at Stanford University. He is the author of *Philosophy and the Mirror of Nature* (Princeton University Press, 1980) and *Philosophy and Social Hope* (Penguin, 2000).

Charles Taylor is Emeritus Professor of Philosophy at McGill University. His books include *Sources of the Self* (Harvard University Press, 1992), *Philosophical Arguments* (Harvard University Press, 1995), and *Varieties of Religion Today: William James Revisited* (Harvard University Press, 2002).

Geoff Waite is Associate Professor of German Studies at Cornell University. He is the author of *Nietzsche's Corps/e: Aesthetics, Politics, Prophecy, Or, the Spectacular Technoculture of Everyday Life* (Duke University Press, 1996).

Georgia Warnke is Professor of Philosophy at the University of California, Riverside. She is the author of *Gadamer: Hermeneutics, Tradition and Reason* (Stanford University Press, 1987) and *Legitimate Differences: Interpretation in the Abortion Controversy and Other Public Debates* (University of California Press, 1999).

Joel Weinsheimer is Professor of English at the University of Minnesota. He is (together with Donald G. Marshall) translator of Hans-Georg Gadamer's *Truth and Method.* He is Series Editor of the Yale Series in Hermeneutics and, as part of that series, editor and translator of Jean Grondin's *Hans-Georg Gadamer: An Intellectual Biography.* His numerous publications include *The Humanities in Dispute: A Dialogue in Letters* (Purdue University Press, 1998).

Catherine Zuckert is Nancy Reeves Dreux Professor of Political Science at Notre Dame University. She is the author of *Postmodern Platos: Nietzsche, Heidegger, Gadamer, Strauss, Derrida* (University of Chicago Press, 1996).

INDEX

Abraham, 33
acknowledgment, 129
Adorno, Theodor, 18, 67, 78, 192–95, 237, 240
aesthetic consciousness, 103, 110–13
aesthetics, 49, 103, 105, 106, 108–16, 160
Albert, Hans, 67, 174, 176
aletheia, 106
Alexander the Great, 268
alterity, 93, 137
Althusser, Louis, 178, 182, 189, 196, 198, 258, 269, 280, 282
analytic philosophy, 22
Apel, Karl-Otto, 18, 74–76, 78, 213
application, 89–90, 251
arche, 36
Aristophanes, 218
Aristotle, 29, 34–35, 47, 87–88, 91, 115, 117, 130, 133, 172, 224, 258, 268, 290
Armstrong, Edwin H., 183
art, 6, 63, 66, 69–70, 74, 76–77, 103–08, 110–14, 116, 161, 191, 218
Artuad, Antonin, 186
Augustine, Saint, 152
Ayer, A. J., 26

Bachelard, Gaston, 257
Badiou, Alain, 264
Baeumler, Alfred, 219, 233
Balibar, Etienne, 179
Bataille, Georges, 186, 191, 196, 238
Baudelaire, Charles, 184

beautiful, analysis of the, 116
beauty, 115, 160–61
Becher, Oskar, 275
Beethoven, Ludwig von, 58, 160
Beiner, Ronald, 158–59, 164
being, 48
Benn, Gottfried, 191–95
Bergman, Gustav, 26
Bergson, Henri, 22
Berkeley, George, 25–26
Bernasconi, Robert, 37
Bernstein, Richard, 18
Berve, Helmut, 214
Bettleheim, Bruno, 86
Bible, 184
Bildung (education), 108
Blake, William, 29
Blanchot, Maurice, ix, 44, 135–40
Bohr, Niels, 24–25
Bonhoeffer, Dietrich, 125, 236, 283–84
Booth, Wayne, 130
Brandes, Georg, 189
Brandom, Robert, 24, 28
Brecht, Bertolt, 219
breeding, 186
Brown v. Board of Education, 96–97
Bruns, Gerald, x, 138
Buddha, 182
Butler, Judith, 133

capitalism, 169, 176, 196, 199, 264–65, 275, 279–85, 287, 291–93

Caputo, John, 124–25
care, 31
Carnap, Rudolf, 22
Celan, Paul, 141–43
Cervantes, Miguel de, 256, 258
Christ, Jesus, 124, 284–85
Christianity, 185
Cioran, E. M., ix
circle, 171, 173, 177, 276
class struggle, 190
classic, 16, 17
Cliburn, Van, 160
cogito, 34
Cohen, Leonard, 198
common sense, 109, 291
communism, 191, 193, 196, 238, 261, 281,
    284, 288–89, 292
community, 127. *See also* common sense
consciousness, 36, 40, 46, 73, 93–94,
    113–14, 164–65, 178, 184, 193, 195
consensus, 78, 131, 133, 191
Constitution, 89
conversation. *See* dialogue
Curie, Marie, 183
Curie, Pierre, 183

Dalton, John, 22, 24, 29
Darwin, Erasmus, 185
Davidson, Donald, 28, 64, 71, 128
death, 183, 286–87, 292–93
Deleuze, Gilles, 180–81, 189, 194, 196, 198–
    99, 237
deliberation, 88
democracy, 77, 198, 266
Derrida, Jacques, x, 28, 124, 134–35, 145–
    46, 148–53, 158, 169–71, 180, 194, 196–
    97, 238–39, 263, 266–67, 281, 283
Descartes, Rene, 36, 65, 68
Deussen, Paul, 177
dialogue, 38–39, 44, 46, 65, 91–92, 126,
    129–32, 135, 137–43, 150–52, 154, 160,
    169–71, 173, 175–76, 180, 192, 194,
    196, 212, 216, 232, 234, 239–40, 244,
    248, 251, 256–61, 263–64, 266–67,
    277–79, 286–87, 291–93; and conver-
    sation, 29, 95, 123–24, 127, 137–40,
    143, 159
Dilthey, Wilhelm, 60, 131, 169–71, 290
Dionysus, 190
due process, 89

Edison, Thomas, 184
effect in history *(wirkungsgeschichtliches
    Bewusstsein)*, 59–60, 62, 69, 112, 117,
    170
ego, 37
eminent text, 17
encryption, 172–73
Enlightenment, 56–57, 59, 64, 68, 70–71,
    125, 146, 191, 219–20, 251
environment, 8
episteme, 34
esotericism, 152–53, 158–59, 170–73, 175–
    76, 179, 181, 183–84, 195, 197–98, 220,
    236, 260–63, 265, 268–69, 271–72, 278,
    291–92
ethics, 49
Euclidean geometry, 2
Europe, 1, 4
experience, 35, 40, 60, 93, 103, 109–14, 130.
    See also openness

face, 32, 40–41, 45, 49
Farías, Victor, 264
Faust, 187
Fichte, Johann Gottlieb, 68–69, 71
finitude, 32–33, 46–47. *See also* reason
Fischer, Hugo, 273
Foerster, Friedrich Wilhelm, 219
Ford, John, 270
Foucault, Michel, 239
Frank, Manfred, 57, 64–67, 69, 70, 74
Frankfurt School, 192, 194, 239
Fraser, 24
Frederick the Great, 222
Frege, 26, 285
Freud, Sigmund, 24, 67, 186, 190, 257,
    292–93
Freyer, Hans, 222, 275
Fricke, Gerhard, 214
Friedländer, Paul, 217
friendship, 279–80
fusion: of cultures, 3; of horizons, 29, 46, 62,
    71, 125, 129, 149–50, 159, 160, 164, 215,
    230, 260, 263, 278. *See also* horizon

Gadamer, Hans-Georg, x, 8, 17. *See also* Na-
    tional Socialism
Galileo, 29
Gass, William, 84
Gast, Peter, 188

Gehlen, Arnold, 18, 273–74
Gelassenheit, 39
generosity, 101
George, Stefan, 235
Gibbon, Edward, 125
globalization, 3
God, 16
Goebbels, 219, 287
Goethe, Johann W., 290–91
Gompertz, Heinrich, 217
Gramsci, Antonio, 280, 285, 291
Grivel, Charles, 182
Grondin, Jean, 17, 19, 171–73, 213
Guattari, Felix, 180–81, 189, 237
Gundolf, Friedrich, 219

Habermas, Jürgen, 27–28, 34, 49, 56, 67,
    76–77, 99–100, 130, 212, 235–36, 251
habitation, 31
Hamann, Johann Georg, 67
Harder, Richard, 214
Hartmann, Nicolai, 15, 215
Haydn, Franz Joseph, 58
Hegel, Georg., 3–4, 16, 23, 28, 36, 40, 59,
    62, 65–66, 71, 131, 163, 179, 222, 268
Hegel Prize, 19
Heidegger, Martin, ix, 16–19, 23, 26, 28–
    29, 35, 39, 43, 48, 55, 65–67, 69–70, 76,
    106, 112, 127, 135, 140, 145–50, 152,
    158, 165, 169–71, 174–76, 185, 188,
    192–93, 212, 214, 224, 229–30, 233–34,
    239–40, 245–46, 251, 264–65, 271, 273,
    274, 277, 281, 290, 292; *Being and Time,*
    15, 31, 32, 42
Heidelberg, 214
Heinse, Wilhelm, 59
Henning, Ritter, 212
Henrich, Dieter, 18, 66–68
Herder, Johann Gottfried, 245
hermeneutics, philosophical: of facticity, 31;
    of suspicion, 152
Hildebrandt, Kurt, 214, 217
Hitler, Adolf, 214, 246, 265, 274, 281, 286,
    288
Hobbes, Thomas, 23–24, 36, 222–23
Hofmannsthal, Hugo von, 139
Hölderlin, Friedrich, 29, 170, 193
Holocaust, 37
Homer, 3, 33, 128, 218
Horace, 257

horizon, concept of, 46, 88, 90–91, 97, 125,
    129, 146, 148, 195, 221, 233. *See also* fu-
    sion, of horizons
Horkheimer, Max, 192–95, 237, 240
hostage, 41
human sciences, 5, 16, 18
humanistic tradition, 219–20, 235
Hume, David, 57
Hutchins, Robert M., 123

iconography, 7
idealism, 25–26
identity, 35
ideology, 177–78, 221, 238, 260, 269, 291
imagination, 28
imitation, 218
incompetence, 277–78
intentional, 96
interpretation, 64, 165, 170–71, 173–74,
    215, 217, 224, 235, 238, 250–51, 262,
    264, 270, 272, 275–76, 288–89, 293

Jacobi, Friedrich Heinrich, 67–68
Jaeger, Werner, 216–17
James, Henry, 82, 86, 101
Jaspers, Karl, 18, 191, 194, 214
Jefferson, Thomas, 124
Johnson, Samuel, 257
judgment, 87, 108–09, 115–16, 267
jurisprudence, 4
justice, 38, 49, 161, 249

Kafka, Franz, 219, 269
Kalinowski, Isabelle, 251
Kant, Immanuel, 17, 28, 34, 36, 56–58, 61,
    63–64, 68–70, 93, 103, 108–11, 114–16,
    131, 189, 261, 279
Karatani, Kojin, 196, 259
Kaufmann, Walter, 191, 194
Kimmerle, Heinz, 63
Kittler, Friedrich, 187–88
Kleist, Heinrich von, 127, 182
knowledge, 2, 34, 47, 57, 97, 105, 114–15
Kraftwerk, 169
Kraus, Karl, 133
Krieck, Ernst, 250
Krüger, Felix, 214
Krüger, Gerhard, 19
Kuhn, Helmuth, 18
Kuhn, Thomas, 28

Lacan, Jacques, 182–83, 196, 257
Lacoue-Labarthe, Philippe, 190
Lamentations, 38
language, 190
Laplanche, Jean, 292
Laugstien, Thomas, 275
law, 82
Leacock, Stephen B., 285
Lecourt, 269
legal interpretation, 163
Leibniz, Gottfried Wilhelm, 169
Leipzig, 214, 229, 245, 250
Lenin, Vladimir, 266
Lessing, Theodor, 17
Levinas, Emmanuel, 30, 32
lie(s), 103, 104, 109, 111, 260
Lifton, Robert J., 86
listening, 41
literary criticism, 82, 90, 95, 196
Litt, Theodor, 215
Lledó, Emilio, 213
Locke, John, 26, 114
logic, 288–89
Löwith, Karl, 17–19, 214
Lucretius, 29
Lukács, Georg, 192
Luther, Martin, 258
Lyotard, Jean-François, 261

Machiavelli, Nicolo, 222
Maimonides, Moses, 238
Mann, Thomas, 219
Marx, Karl, 180, 189, 196, 257, 282
Marxism, 192, 282
mass culture, 184, 192–93
McDowell, John, 56
meaning, 42–43
measuring, 5–7
Mendeleev, 22
metaphysics, 173, 176, 181
method, 125, 143, 213, 244, 271
Michelfelder, Diane, 135
Milbank, John, 129
Milton, John, 29
Misgeld, Dieter, 131–33
misinterpretation, 86
model (Vorbild), 6
moderation, 169, 240, 256, 258–61, 266–67, 279, 291, 293
monologue, 195, 239, 260
Mozart, Wolfgang Amadeus, 58

multiculturalism, 193
music, 58–59, 61, 66–67, 74, 76, 160, 177, 186, 190, 232, 276

Nabokov, Vladimir, 84–85
National Socialism, 192, 212–24, 229–34, 244, 246–51, 262, 270–81, 283–84, 290
natural sciences, 55–56, 59–61, 76, 285
Nehamas, Alexander, 82–87, 91, 98, 101
negation, 178
neighbor, 31
Neo-Kantianism, 15, 216–17
Nietzsche, Friedrich, 2, 26, 29, 67, 76, 145–52, 158, 169–70, 172–73, 176–83, 184–99, 229, 236–40, 263, 267, 270–71, 282, 285–86, 290; *Beyond Good and Evil*, 197, 237; *Birth of Tragedy*, 187; *Ecce Homo*, 188, 189, 240; *The Gay Science*, 190; *Thus Spoke Zarathustra*, 171, 178, 183, 198, 236; *The Wanderer and His Shadow*, 188
nominalism, 22–23
Novalis, 57, 61, 64, 67–68, 71–74, 78
NS Teachers Union, 174, 245, 272, 274–75, 281–87
NS Workers Party, 272, 274–75, 281–82
Nussbaum, Martha, 82–87, 126

Oakeshott, Michael, 123
Occident, 1
Odysseus, 33, 41
Olivier, Laurence, 160
ontology, 32, 162, 171, 175, 192, 212
openness, 34, 38, 107, 130, 134, 213, 244; in interpretation, 8
order of rank (*Rangordnung*), 179, 198
Orozco, Teresa, x
Ossietzsky, Carl von, 219
Othello, 160
Otherness, 164–65. *See* alterity

Palmer, Richard, 135
Pangle, Thomas, 153
Paul, Saint, 124
Peirce, Charles, 26
Peperzak, Adrian, 38
perception, 106
performance, 160
persecution, 37
persuasion, 213, 236
Philosophische Rundschau, 18

phronesis, 34, 35, 49, 256, 268, 290. *See also* practical knowledge; prudence
piloting, 132
Pindar, 218
Plato, 2–3, 5, 7, 22–23, 25–26, 36, 44, 47–49, 57, 72, 105, 107, 110–11, 114–15, 117, 128, 140, 145–46, 148–50, 152, 161, 170–72, 180–81, 215–24, 230–35, 237, 239–40, 244, 246–51, 258–60, 267, 271, 275, 277–78, 287–88, 290–91; *Phaedrus,* 160; *Republic,* 47, 104, 124, 215
Platonism, 45, 164
play, 115–16
Plessy v. Ferguson, 96–99, 100
poetic language, 61
poetry, 6, 7, 231
polis, 224
politics, 171, 174, 180, 189, 214, 216–17, 230–31, 233, 235–36, 238, 240, 245–46, 259, 264, 276–78, 280, 283–84, 289, 291–92
Pope, Alexander, 25
Popper, Karl, 18
positivism, 56
Posner, Richard, 82–83, 86–87, 91, 101
postmodernism, 145–46, 154, 158, 165, 179, 181, 187, 256
Pound, Ezra, ix
power, 127, 131, 137, 232, 251
practical knowledge, 90–91, 98. See also *phronesis;* prudence
prejudice, 32, 59–60, 92, 93, 95, 97, 99–101, 125, 131, 174, 213, 267, 269
Priestley, Joseph, 25
prolepsis, 175–76
prophets, 44
proximity, 36
prudence, 173, 236, 256, 283. See also *phronesis;* practical knowledge
psychoanalysis, 178, 196
Putnam, Hilary, 28, 73, 75

quantity, 5
quarrel of ancients and moderns, 172
Quine, Willard Von Orman, 23, 128
Quixote, 278

Ranke, Leopold von, 131
reason, 171, 180, 236. *See also* finitude
recognition, 108, 136
Rée, Jonathan, 24

Reik, Theodor, 190
relativism, 71–72, 74, 153, 262–63, 268, 271, 276
Remarque, Erich Maria, 219
representation, 57–58
responsibility, 36, 39, 41, 48
rhetoric, 170, 177, 194, 237, 256–57
Ricoeur, Paul, 152, 251
Rilke, Rainer Maria, 141
Rohde, Erwin, 187
romanticism, 56–62, 64, 66–69, 73–74, 76
Rorty, Richard, 18, 55–56, 65, 70–73, 75–78, 193–94, 213
Rosen, Stanley, 149, 152–53, 281
Ross, Jan, 223
Rothacker, Erich, 214
rules, 64
Rytman, Hélène, 282

Sameness, 165, 175
Sartre, Jean-Paul, 33
Schadenwaldt, Wolfgang, 214
Schelling, Friedrich Wilhelm Joseph von, 17, 57, 61, 67
Schlegel, Friedrich von, 57, 61–62, 67, 72–75
Schleiermacher, F, 57, 61–65, 67, 69, 73–75, 172, 216
Schmitt, Carl, 175, 222–23, 250, 261, 270
Schopenhauer, 190, 268
science, 1–4, 23–24, 26, 58, 109
self-consciousness, 67–68, 76
self-knowledge, 109
self-understanding, 115
sensus communis, 108–09. *See also* common sense
Shelley, Percy Bysshe, 185
Shostakovich, Dmitri, 276
slavery, 178
socialism, 197
Socrates, 2, 29, 129, 140–41, 149, 180–81, 218–19, 240, 258–59, 284–86, 289
solidarity, 48, 141
Spaemann, Robert, 18
Spartacus, 293
Spengler, Oswald, 1, 17
Spinoza, Baruch, 185, 188–89, 257, 266, 279, 282, 284
Spranger, Eduard, 214–15, 222
Stalinism, 280, 282
Stauffenberg, 288

Stenzel, Julius, 217
Stevens, Wallace, 139
Strauss, David Friedrich, 183
Strauss, Leo, 145–50, 152–53, 158, 169,
    171–73, 238, 263, 266–68, 271, 281, 283
Suetonius, 256

Talmud, 37
taste, 108, 111, 114
Taylor, Charles, 251
Taylorism, 185, 193
techne, 34, 63
technology, 183, 185–87, 191, 239
theory, 47, 181, 189, 268, 270
Theunissen, Michael, 18, 28
time, 15
tolerance, 132
tradition, 16, 39, 41, 43–44, 46–47, 60, 62,
    71, 89, 92, 165, 213, 244, 267
translation, 181, 195
Trotsky, Leon, 281
truth, 23, 35, 40, 57, 59–61, 69–70, 72–77,
    92, 98–99, 103–10, 112–15, 117, 129,
    137, 140–41, 147–48, 161–62, 231, 244,
    259, 263, 269, 291; correspondence the-
    ory of, 161
Truth and Method, 15, 18, 57, 61–62, 64, 104,
    108, 112, 115–16, 125, 130, 134, 160,
    164, 169–70, 172, 212–13, 224, 230, 235,
    246, 263, 276
Tucholsky, Kurt, 219
Tugendhat, Ernst, 18
Tyler, Stephen, 129
typewriter, 188

understanding, 9–10, 17, 24, 27, 30, 32, 39,
    41, 44, 59, 64, 71, 73, 75, 86, 88–89, 91–
    95, 97–101, 107–08, 110, 112, 116–17,
    123, 125–26, 129–32, 142, 145–46, 151,
    159, 164–65, 171, 173, 213, 269

Vattimo, Gianni, 28–29, 213
violence, 138, 140
Virgil, 25
Virmond, Wolfgang, 62
virtue, 261, 266, 292
voice, 184, 190, 194–95, 267

Wagner, Richard, 183, 185–86, 190
Waite, Geoff, x
Walcott, Derek, 128–29
Weber, Max, 216
Weimar Republic, 17
Weiss, Allen S., 183–84
Wellmer, Albrecht, 251
Wilamowitz-Moellendorff, Ulrich von, 217
Wilde, Oscar, 137
will, 177
will to power, 150, 170, 184
Wittgenstein, Ludwig, 18, 176, 182, 192,
    278
Wolin, Richard, ix

Zuckert, Catherine, 145–49, 153–54
Zweig, Arnold, 219
Zweig, Stefan, 219

Compositor:	G&S Typesetters, Inc.
Text:	10/12 Baskerville
Display:	Baskerville
Printer and binder:	Edwards Brothers, Inc.